The Arrogant and the Weird

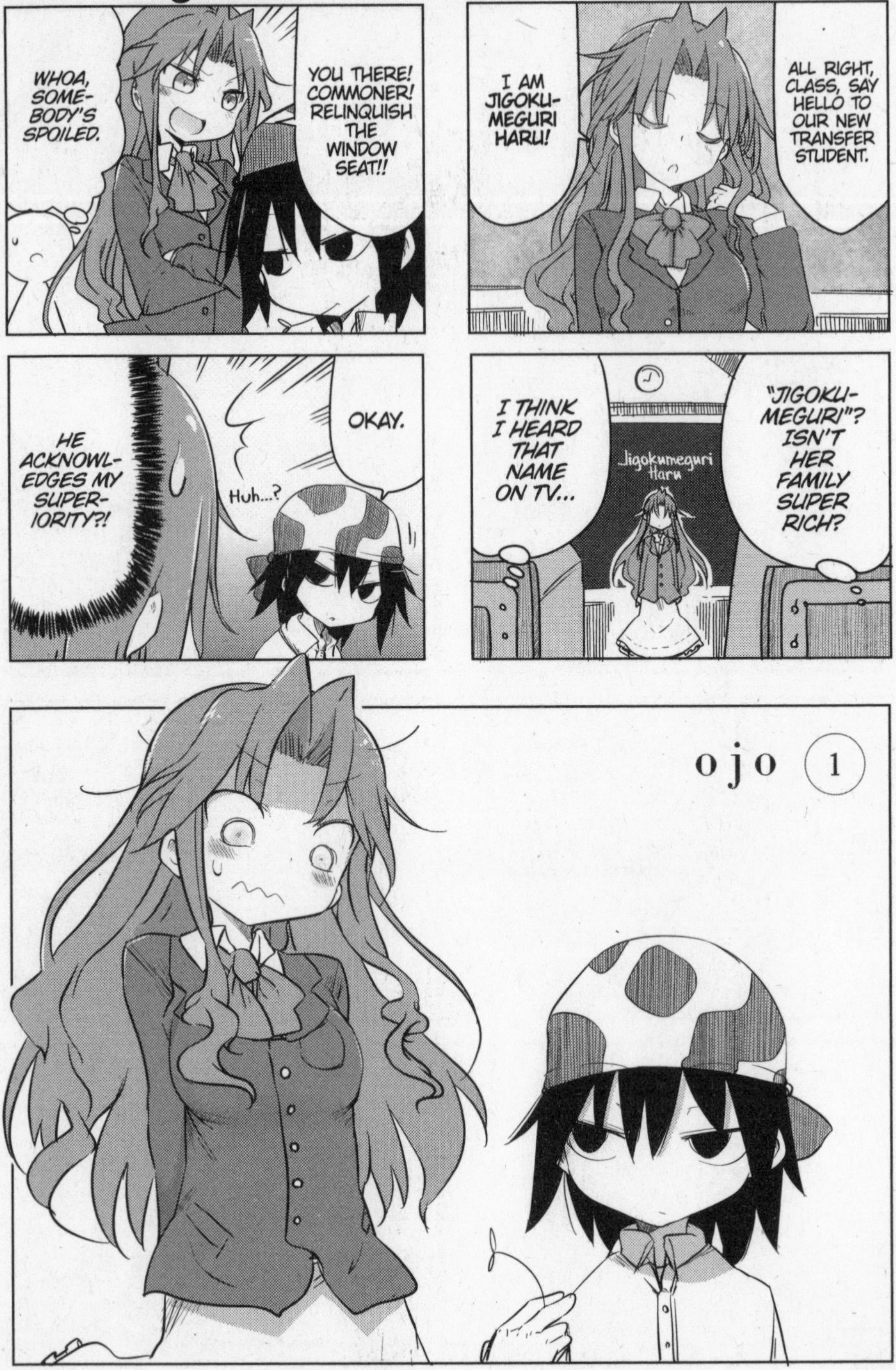
ALL RIGHT, CLASS, SAY HELLO TO OUR NEW TRANSFER STUDENT.
I AM JIGOKU-MEGURI HARU!
YOU THERE! COMMONER! RELINQUISH THE WINDOW SEAT!!
WHOA, SOMEBODY'S SPOILED.
"JIGOKU-MEGURI"? ISN'T HER FAMILY SUPER RICH?
Jigokumeguri Haru
I THINK I HEARD THAT NAME ON TV...
OKAY.
Huh...?
HE ACKNOWLEDGES MY SUPERIORITY?!
ojo 1

Two Weirdos

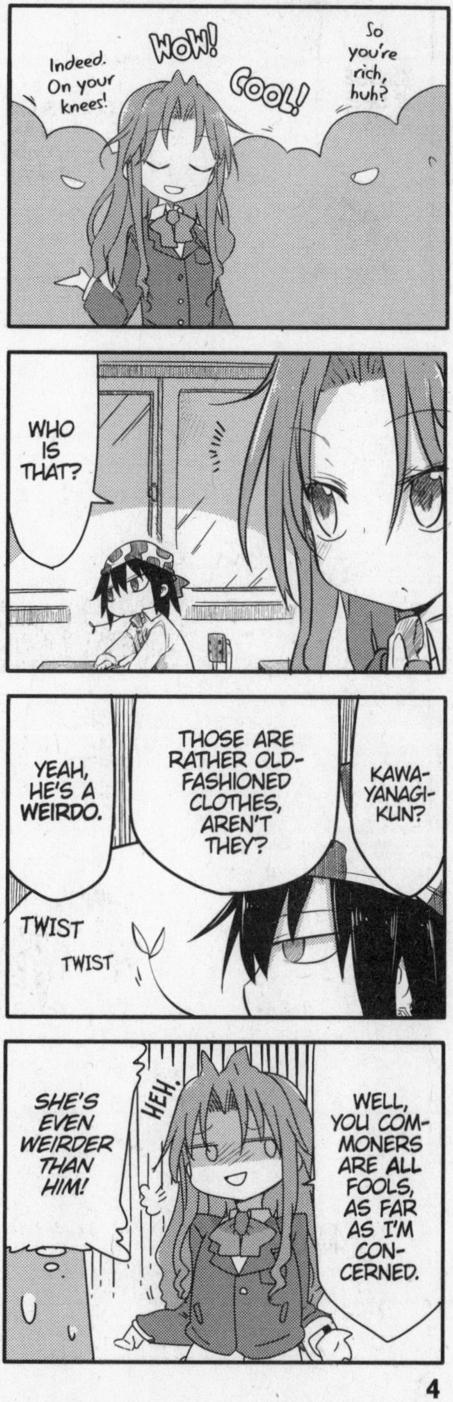

So you're rich, huh?
COOL!
WOW!
Indeed. On your knees!
WHO IS THAT?
KAWA-YANAGI-KUN?
THOSE ARE RATHER OLD-FASHIONED CLOTHES, AREN'T THEY?
YEAH, HE'S A WEIRDO.
TWIST
TWIST
WELL, YOU COMMONERS ARE ALL FOOLS, AS FAR AS I'M CONCERNED.
HEH.
SHE'S EVEN WEIRDER THAN HIM!

The Outcasts

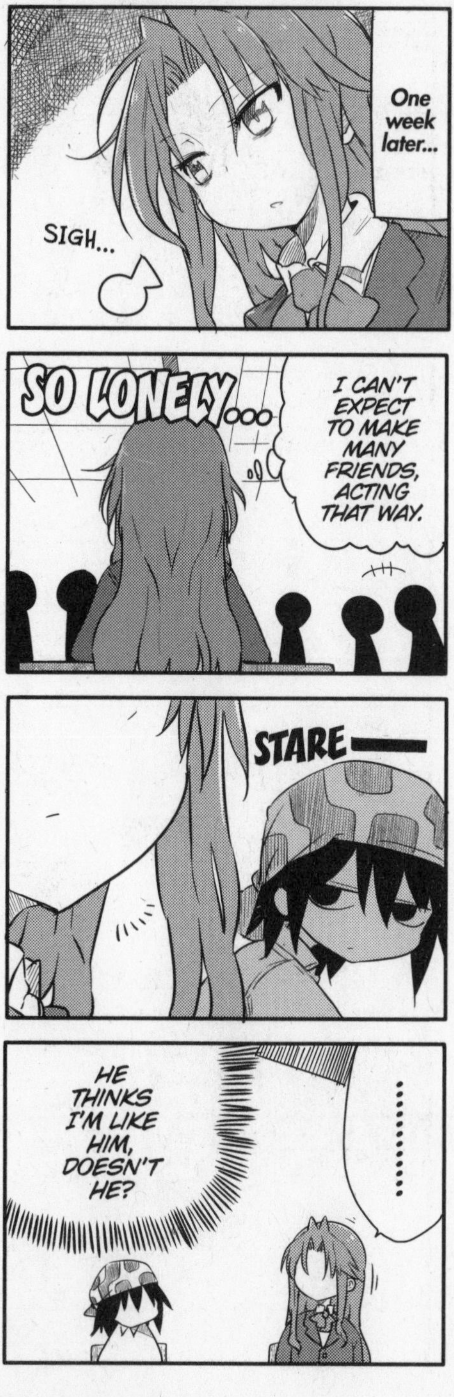

One week later...
SIGH...
I CAN'T EXPECT TO MAKE MANY FRIENDS, ACTING THAT WAY.
SO LONELY...
STARE—
....
HE THINKS I'M LIKE HIM, DOESN'T HE?

Misleading

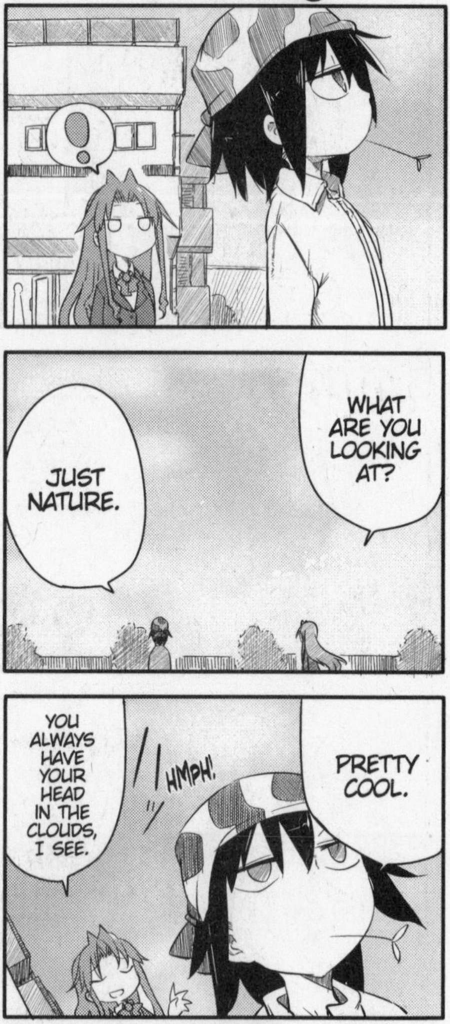
!
WHAT ARE YOU LOOKING AT?
JUST NATURE.
PRETTY COOL.
HMPH!
YOU ALWAYS HAVE YOUR HEAD IN THE CLOUDS, I SEE.
MORE LIKE IN A WEB, ACTUALLY.
I'M AFRAID I DON'T FOLLOW.

Way of Life

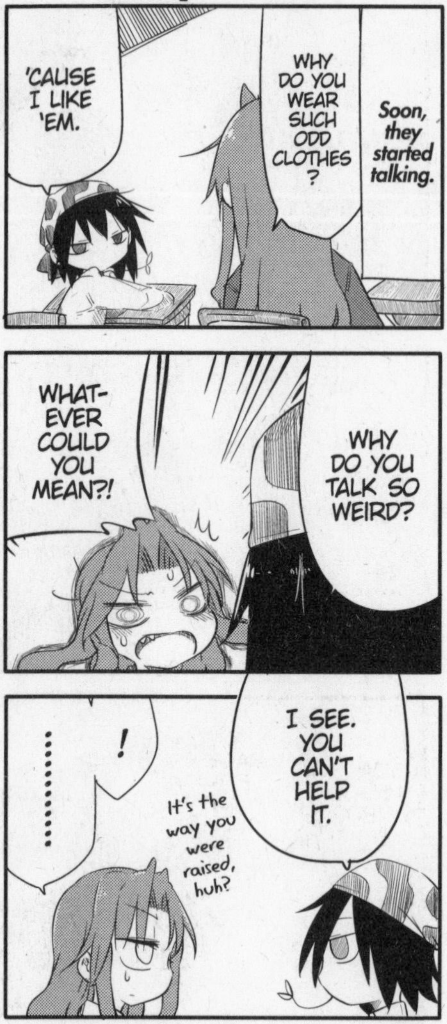
Soon, they started talking.
WHY DO YOU WEAR SUCH ODD CLOTHES?
'CAUSE I LIKE 'EM.
WHY DO YOU TALK SO WEIRD?
WHATEVER COULD YOU MEAN?!
I SEE. YOU CAN'T HELP IT.
It's the way you were raised, huh?
......!
INDEED. BUT YOU HAVE NO SUCH EXCUSE FOR YOUR BEHAVIOR.
Fix your fashion.
NOPE.

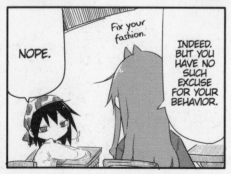

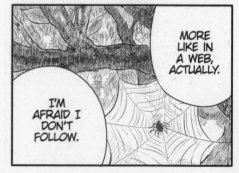

Lack of Understanding

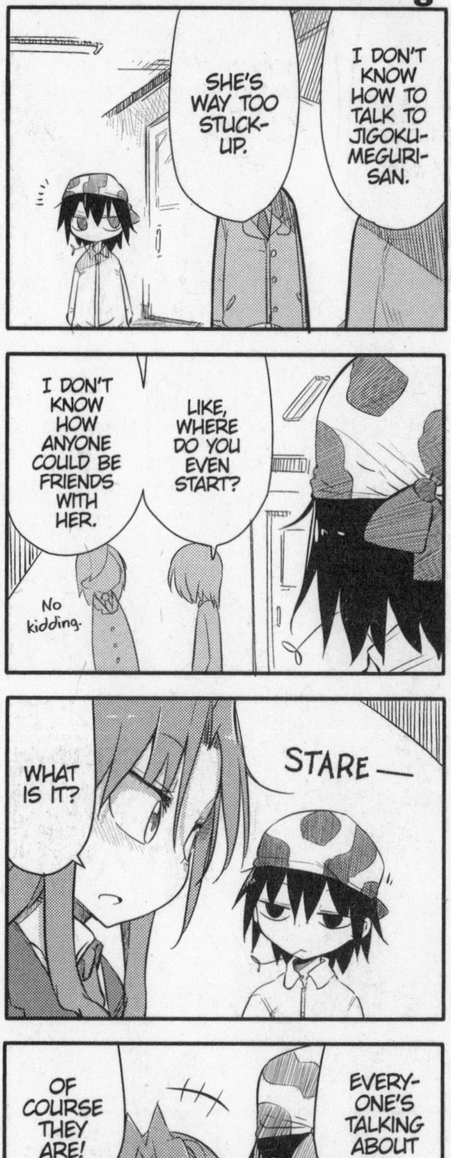
I DON'T KNOW HOW TO TALK TO JIGOKU-MEGURI-SAN.
SHE'S WAY TOO STUCK-UP.
LIKE, WHERE DO YOU EVEN START?
I DON'T KNOW HOW ANYONE COULD BE FRIENDS WITH HER.
No kidding.
STARE—
WHAT IS IT?
EVERY-ONE'S TALKING ABOUT YOU.
OF COURSE THEY ARE!
HEH!

Just Stopping by the Cafeteria

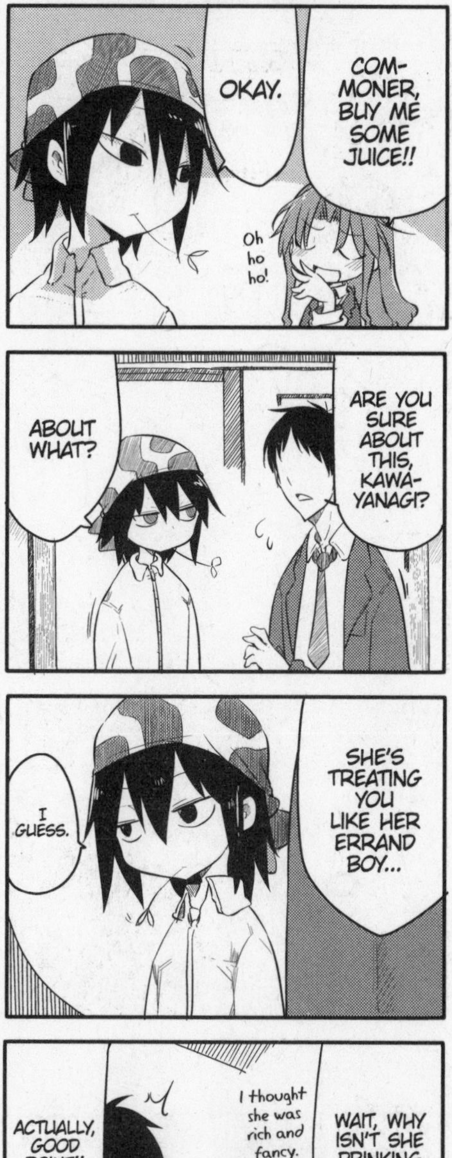
COMMONER, BUY ME SOME JUICE!!
OKAY.
Oh ho ho!
ARE YOU SURE ABOUT THIS, KAWAYANAGI?
ABOUT WHAT?
SHE'S TREATING YOU LIKE HER ERRAND BOY...
I GUESS.
WAIT, WHY ISN'T SHE DRINKING TEA?
I thought she was rich and fancy.
ACTUALLY, GOOD POINT!!
She's full of surprises!

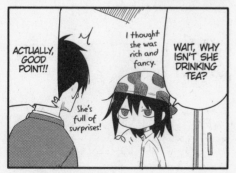

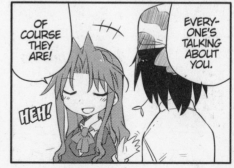

Zero Resistance

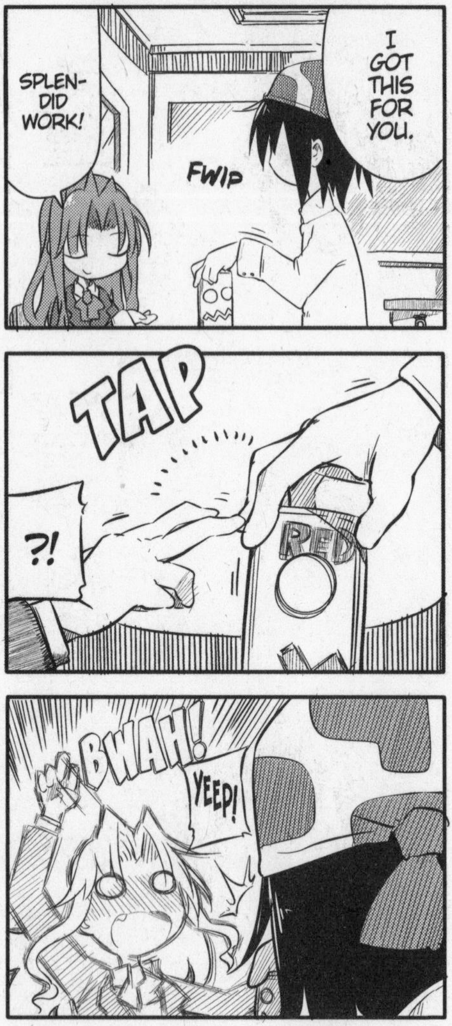
I GOT THIS FOR YOU.
SPLENDID WORK!
FWIP
TAP
?!
RED
BWAH!
YEEP!
WHAT'S WRONG?
NOTHING YOU NEED CONCERN YOURSELF WITH!!
HUFF! HUFF!

Impossible to Understand

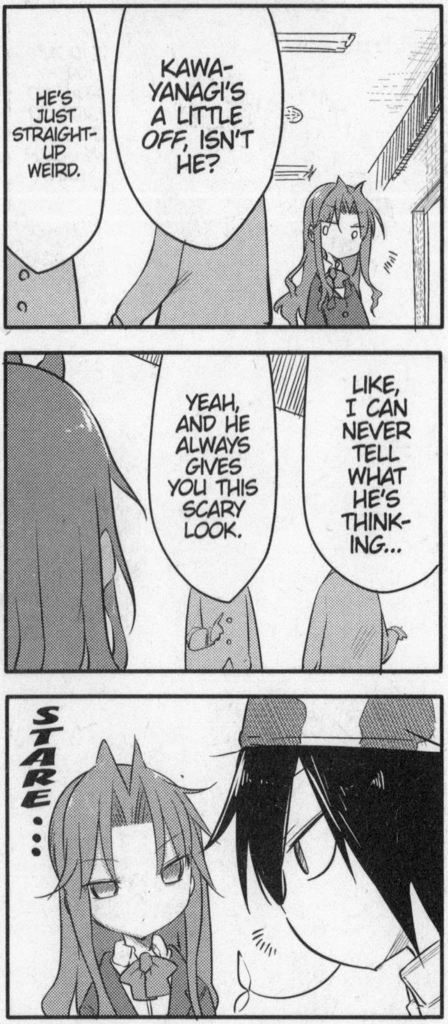
KAWA-YANAGI'S A LITTLE *OFF*, ISN'T HE?
HE'S JUST STRAIGHT-UP WEIRD.
LIKE, I CAN NEVER TELL WHAT HE'S THINKING...
YEAH, AND HE ALWAYS GIVES YOU THIS SCARY LOOK.
STARE...
STOP STARING AT PEOPLE.
?

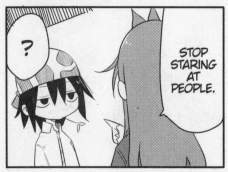

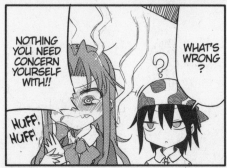

Good Friends

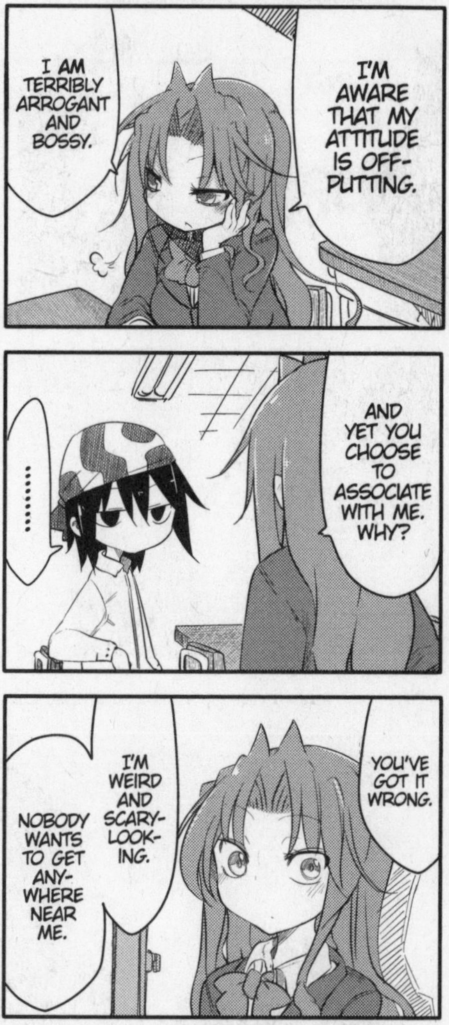

I'M AWARE THAT MY ATTITUDE IS OFF-PUTTING.
I AM TERRIBLY ARROGANT AND BOSSY.
AND YET YOU CHOOSE TO ASSOCIATE WITH ME. WHY?
......
YOU'VE GOT IT WRONG.
I'M WEIRD AND SCARY-LOOKING.
NOBODY WANTS TO GET ANYWHERE NEAR ME.
BUT ALL YOU THINK ABOUT IS YOURSELF, SO YOU DON'T CARE ABOUT ANY OF THAT.
WELL, EXCUSE ME!

Haru

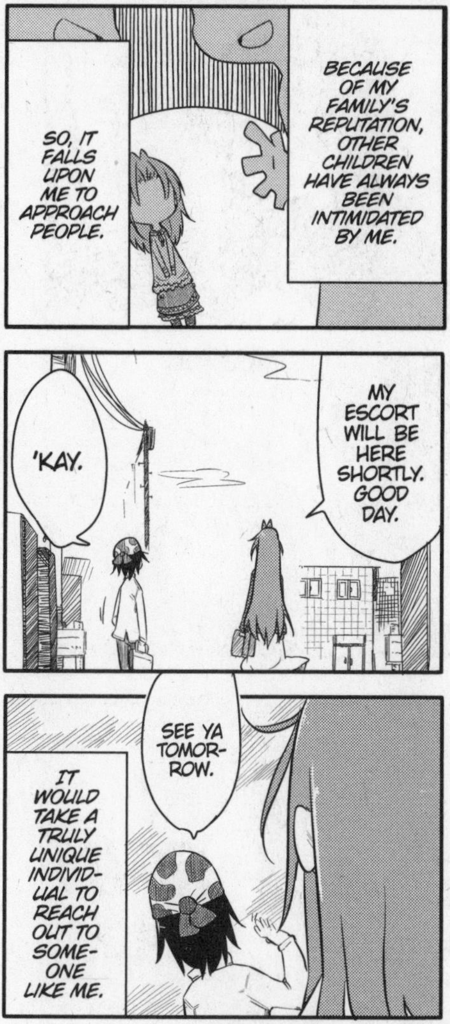

BECAUSE OF MY FAMILY'S REPUTATION, OTHER CHILDREN HAVE ALWAYS BEEN INTIMIDATED BY ME.
SO, IT FALLS UPON ME TO APPROACH PEOPLE.
MY ESCORT WILL BE HERE SHORTLY. GOOD DAY.
'KAY.
SEE YA TOMORROW.
IT WOULD TAKE A TRULY UNIQUE INDIVIDUAL TO REACH OUT TO SOMEONE LIKE ME.
BUT IF THEY DID, THEN I...
YES...
I'LL LOOK FORWARD TO IT.

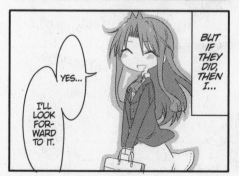

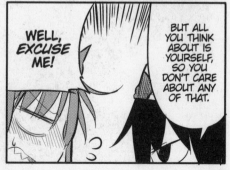

Borrowed Authority

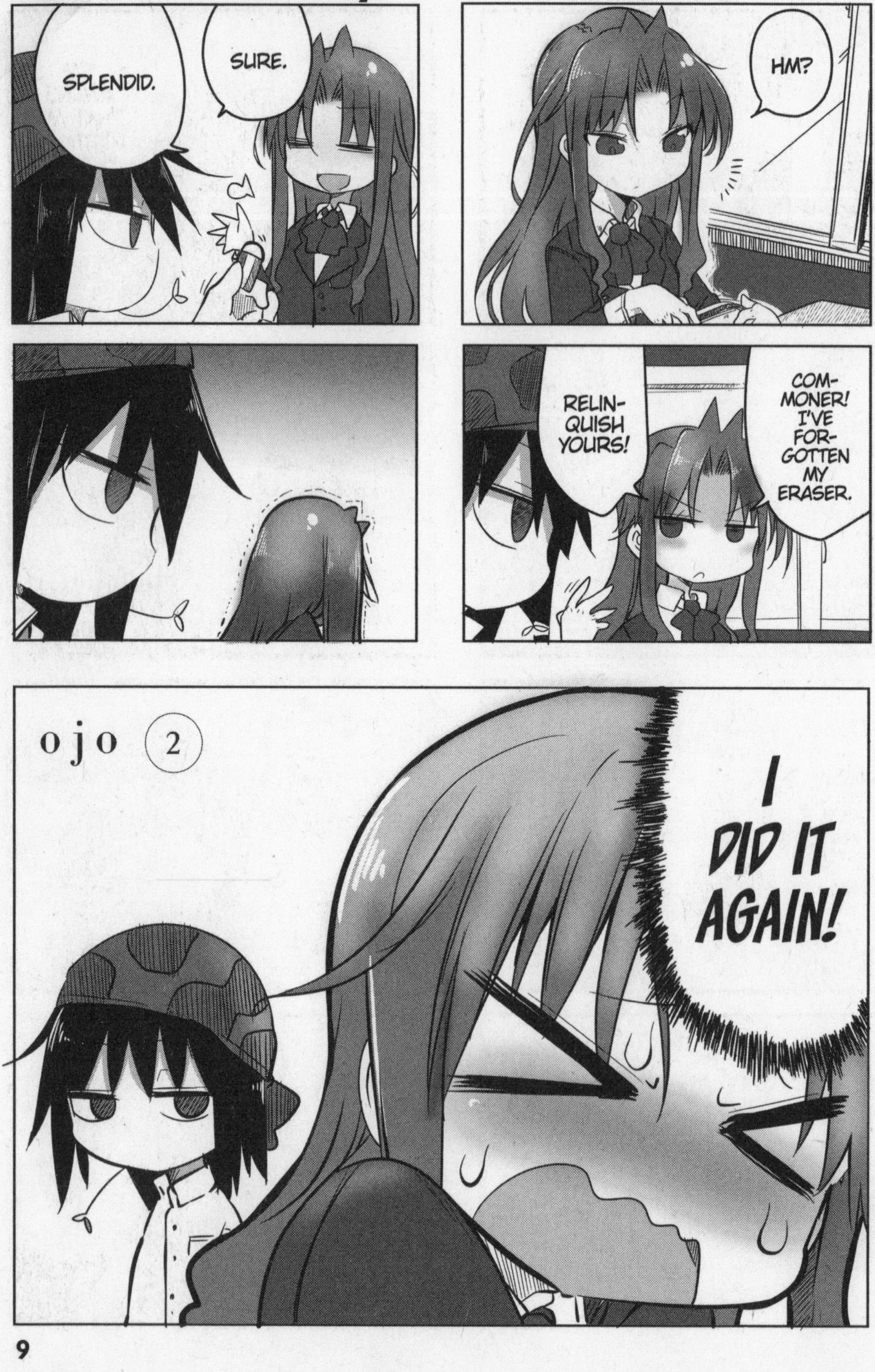
HM?
SURE.
SPLENDID.
COM-MONER! I'VE FOR-GOTTEN MY ERASER.
RELIN-QUISH YOURS!
I DID IT AGAIN!
ojo 2

Force of Habit

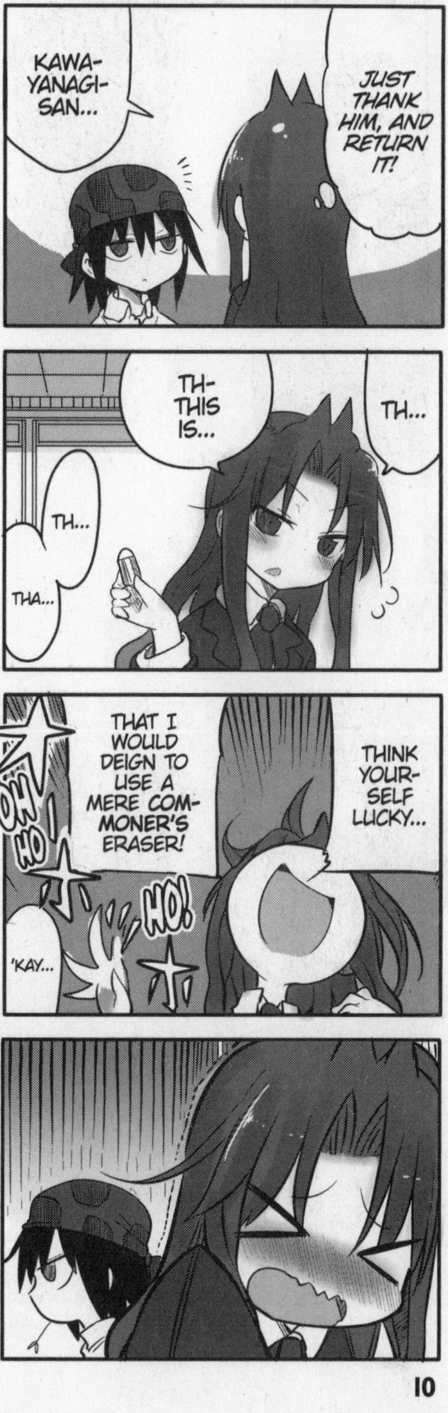
JUST THANK HIM, AND RETURN IT!
KAWA-YANAGI-SAN...
TH...
TH- THIS IS...
TH...
THA...
THINK YOUR-SELF LUCKY...
THAT I WOULD DEIGN TO USE A MERE COM-MONER'S ERASER!
OH HO
HO!
'KAY...

Spot On

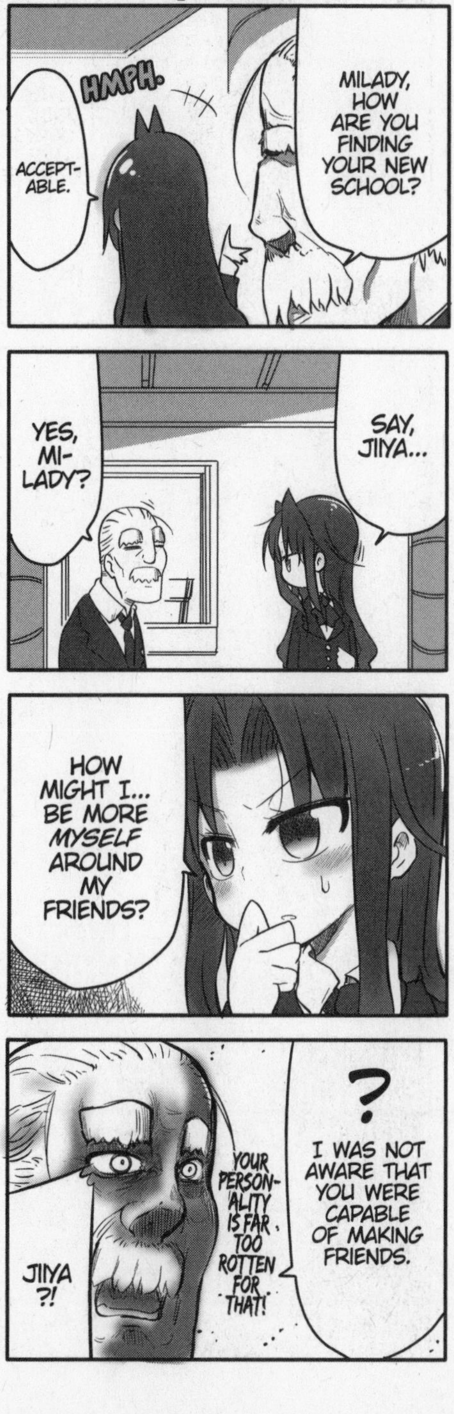
MILADY, HOW ARE YOU FINDING YOUR NEW SCHOOL?
HMPH.
ACCEPT-ABLE.
SAY, JIIYA...
YES, MI-LADY?
HOW MIGHT I... BE MORE *MYSELF* AROUND MY FRIENDS?
?
I WAS NOT AWARE THAT YOU WERE CAPABLE OF MAKING FRIENDS.
YOUR PERSON-ALITY IS FAR TOO ROTTEN FOR THAT!
JIIYA ?!

No Boyfriends Either

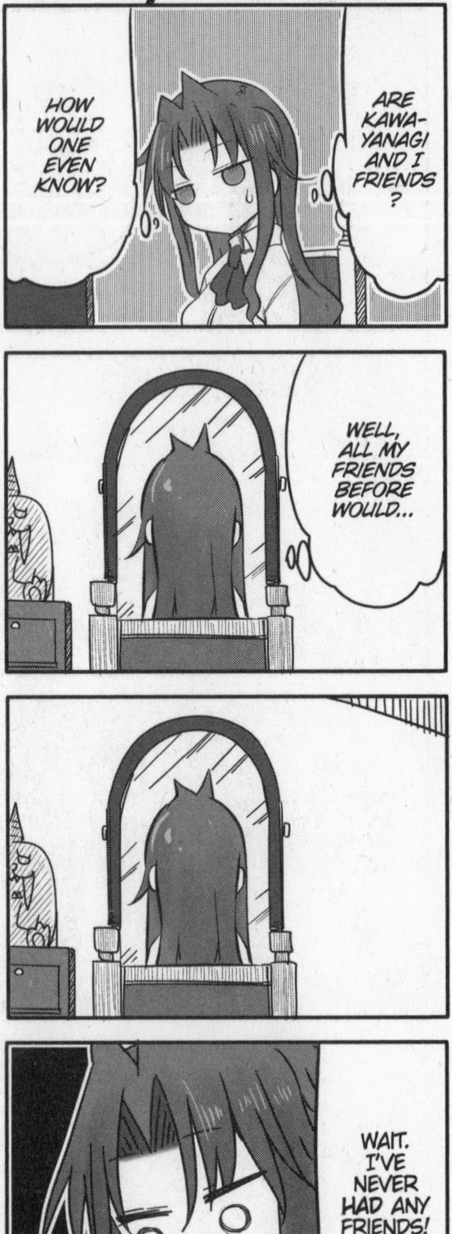
ARE KAWA-YANAGI AND I FRIENDS?
HOW WOULD ONE EVEN KNOW?
WELL, ALL MY FRIENDS BEFORE WOULD...
WAIT. I'VE NEVER HAD ANY FRIENDS!

A Childish Problem

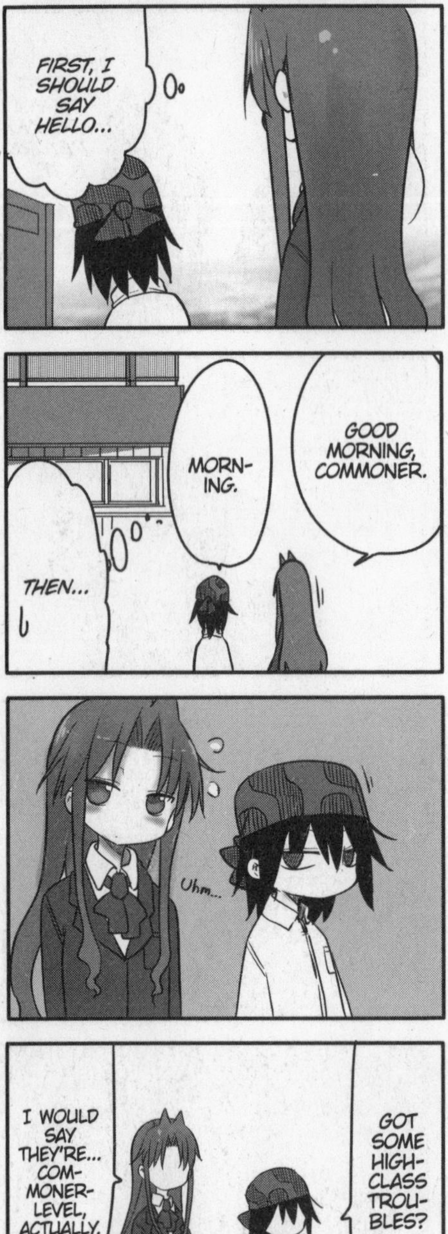
FIRST, I SHOULD SAY HELLO...
GOOD MORNING, COMMONER.
MORN-ING.
THEN...
Uhm...
GOT SOME HIGH-CLASS TROU-BLES?
I WOULD SAY THEY'RE... COM-MONER-LEVEL, ACTUALLY.

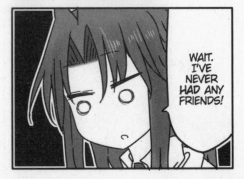

Just Following Orders

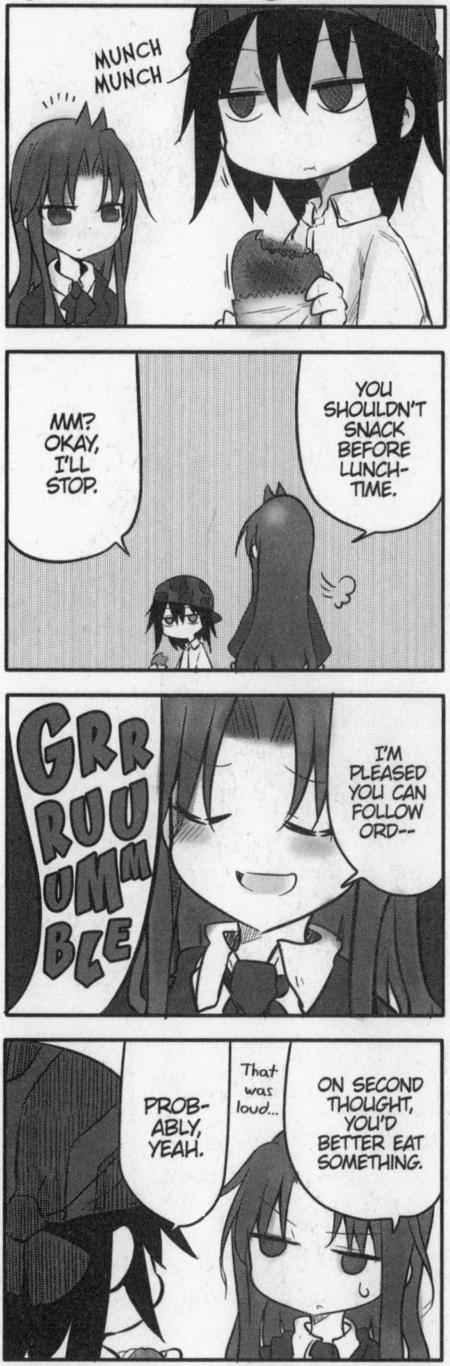
MUNCH MUNCH
YOU SHOULDN'T SNACK BEFORE LUNCH-TIME.
MM? OKAY, I'LL STOP.
I'M PLEASED YOU CAN FOLLOW ORD--
GRRRUUUMMBLE
ON SECOND THOUGHT, YOU'D BETTER EAT SOMETHING.
That was loud...
PROB-ABLY, YEAH.

Eyes Do the Talking

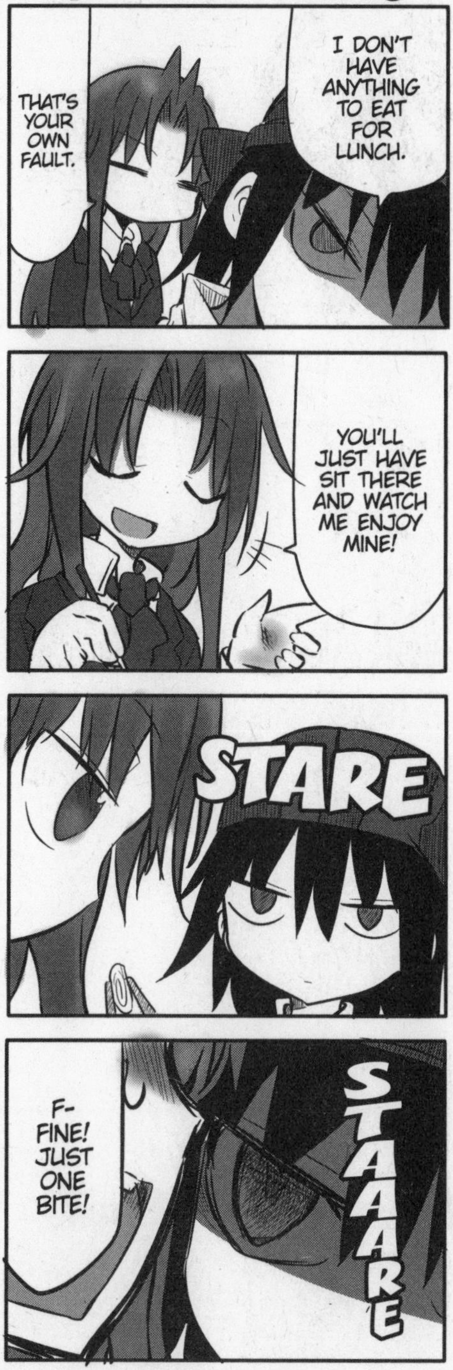
I DON'T HAVE ANYTHING TO EAT FOR LUNCH.
THAT'S YOUR OWN FAULT.
YOU'LL JUST HAVE SIT THERE AND WATCH ME ENJOY MINE!
STARE
STAAAARE
F-FINE! JUST ONE BITE!

170 and 140

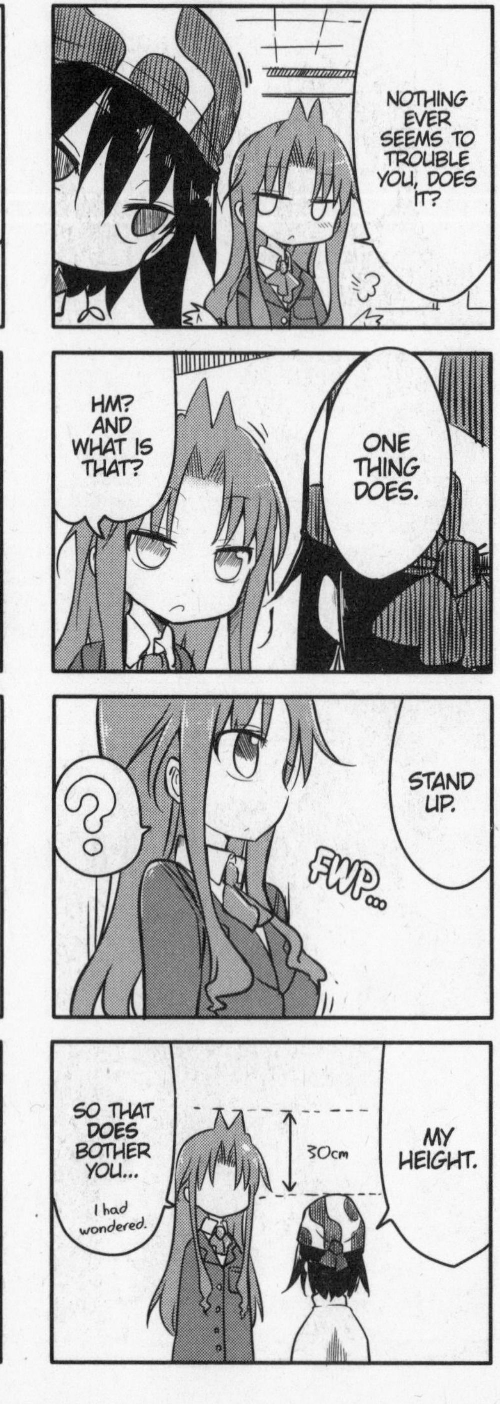

NOTHING EVER SEEMS TO TROUBLE YOU, DOES IT?
ONE THING DOES.
HM? AND WHAT IS THAT?
STAND UP.
FWP...
?
MY HEIGHT.
30cm
SO THAT DOES BOTHER YOU...
I had wondered.

A Helping Hand

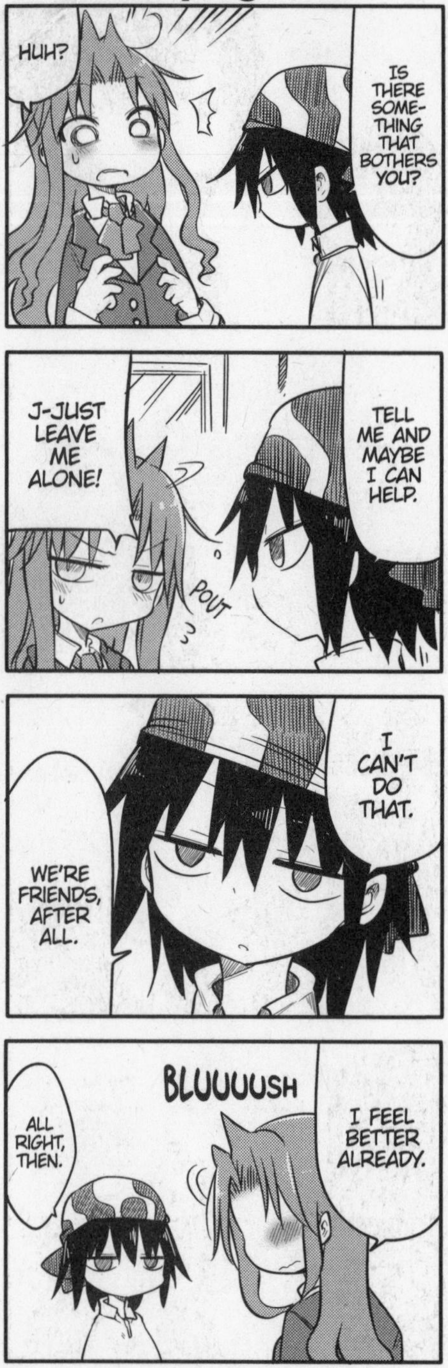

IS THERE SOME-THING THAT BOTHERS YOU?
HUH?
TELL ME AND MAYBE I CAN HELP.
J-JUST LEAVE ME ALONE!
POUT
I CAN'T DO THAT.
WE'RE FRIENDS, AFTER ALL.
I FEEL BETTER ALREADY.
BLUUUUSH
ALL RIGHT, THEN.

Arrogance Is Part of It

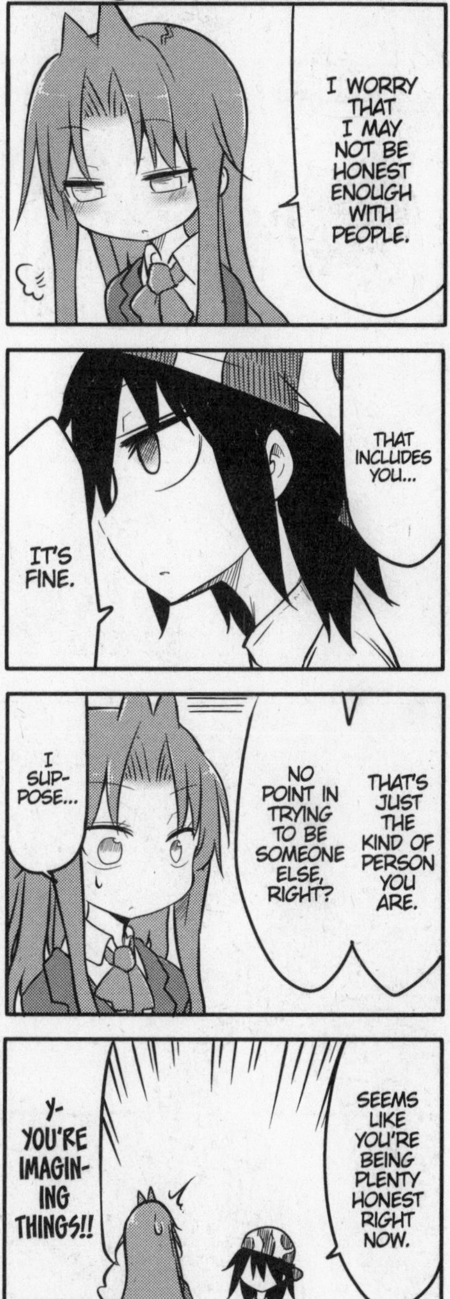
I WORRY THAT I MAY NOT BE HONEST ENOUGH WITH PEOPLE.
THAT INCLUDES YOU...
IT'S FINE.
THAT'S JUST THE KIND OF PERSON YOU ARE.
NO POINT IN TRYING TO BE SOMEONE ELSE, RIGHT?
I SUPPOSE...
SEEMS LIKE YOU'RE BEING PLENTY HONEST RIGHT NOW.
Y-YOU'RE IMAGINING THINGS!!

Simple but Accurate

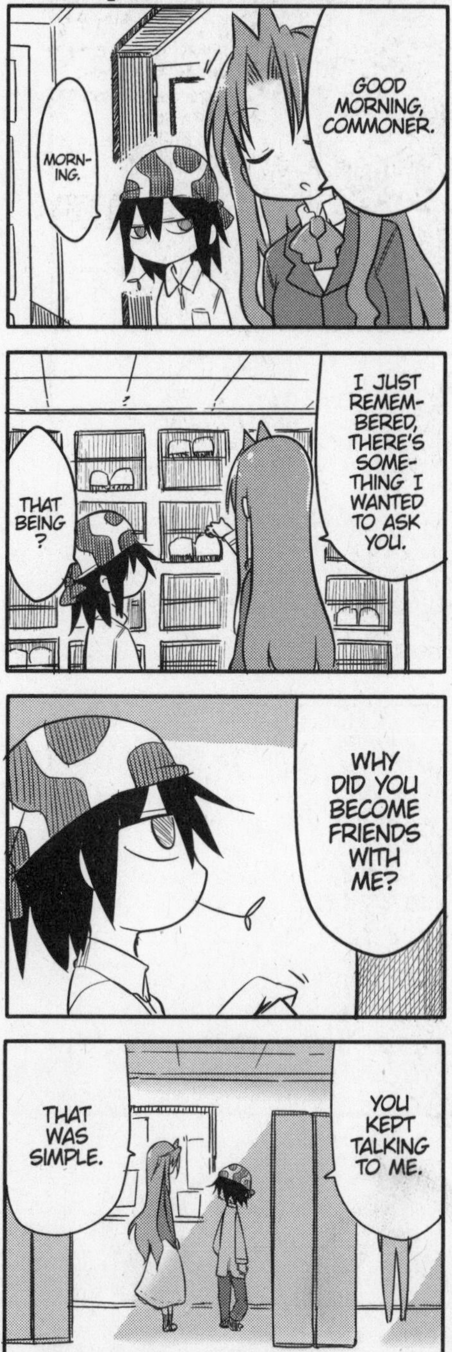
GOOD MORNING, COMMONER.
MORN-ING.
I JUST REMEM-BERED, THERE'S SOME-THING I WANTED TO ASK YOU.
THAT BEING?
WHY DID YOU BECOME FRIENDS WITH ME?
YOU KEPT TALKING TO ME.
THAT WAS SIMPLE.

Transportation

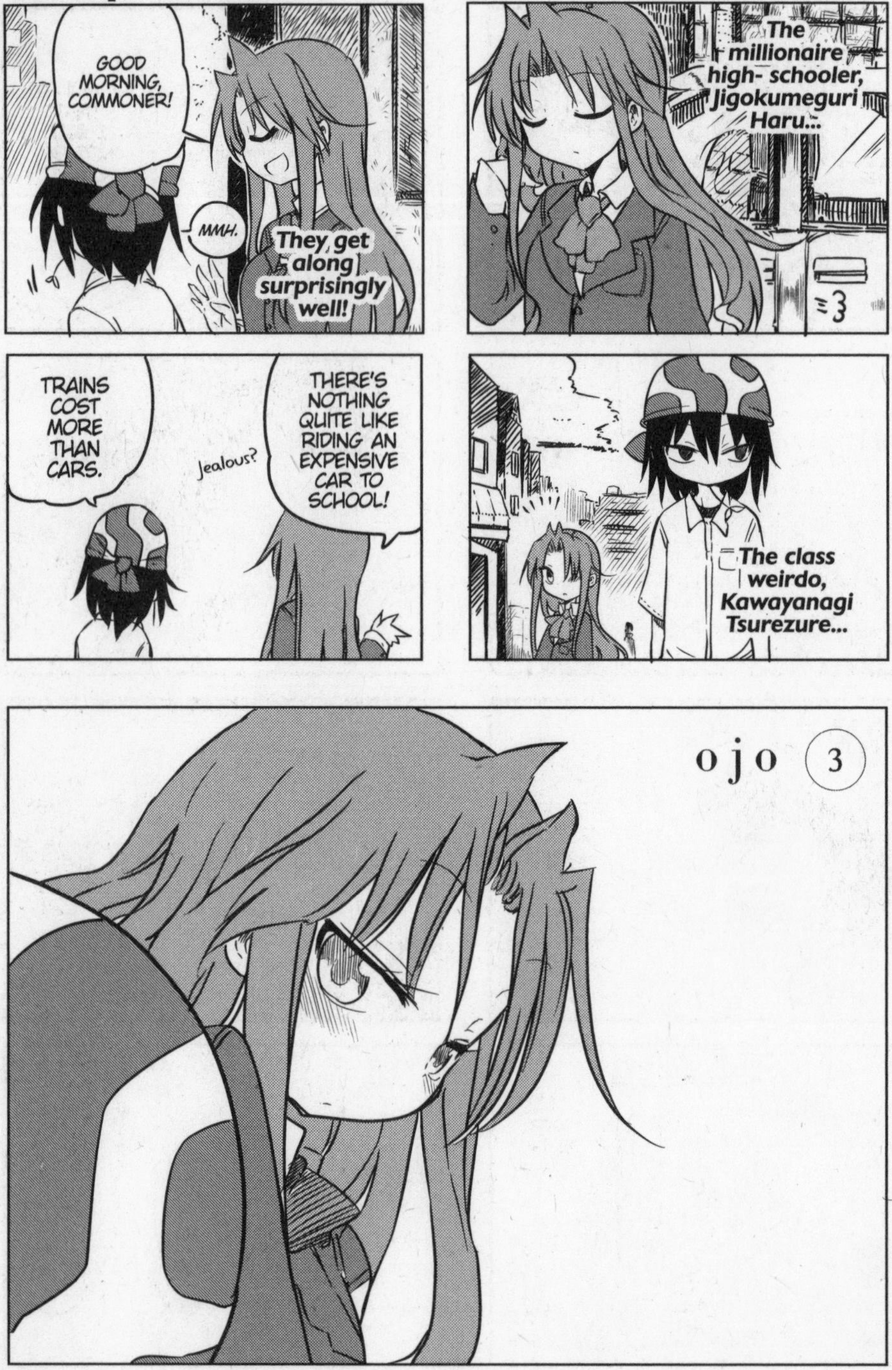
The millionaire high-schooler, Jigokumeguri Haru...
GOOD MORNING, COMMONER!
MMH.
They get along surprisingly well!
The class weirdo, Kawayanagi Tsurezure...
THERE'S NOTHING QUITE LIKE RIDING AN EXPENSIVE CAR TO SCHOOL!
Jealous?
TRAINS COST MORE THAN CARS.
ojo 3

Curious

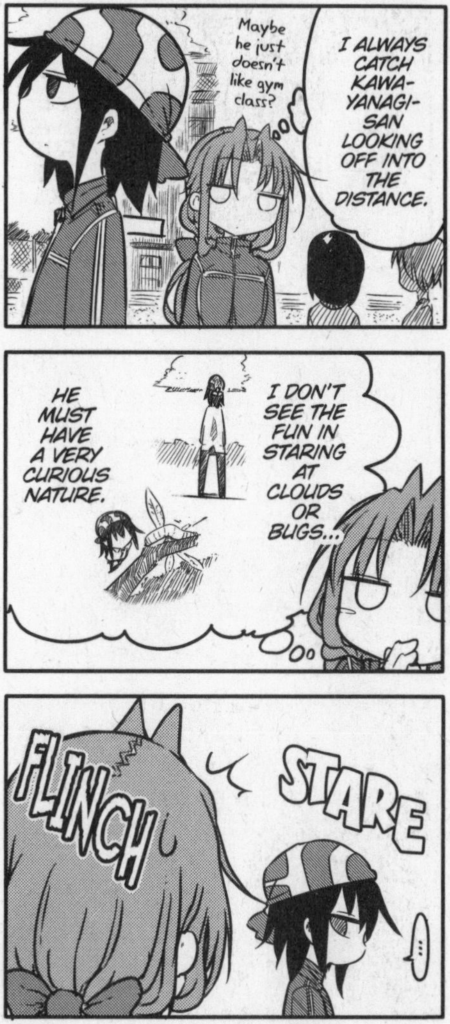
I ALWAYS CATCH KAWA-YANAGI-SAN LOOKING OFF INTO THE DISTANCE.
Maybe he just doesn't like gym class?
I DON'T SEE THE FUN IN STARING AT CLOUDS OR BUGS...
HE MUST HAVE A VERY CURIOUS NATURE.
STARE
FLINCH
...
WH-WHAT ARE YOU LOOKING AT?!
YOU LOOKED AT ME FIRST.

Surprisingly Plain

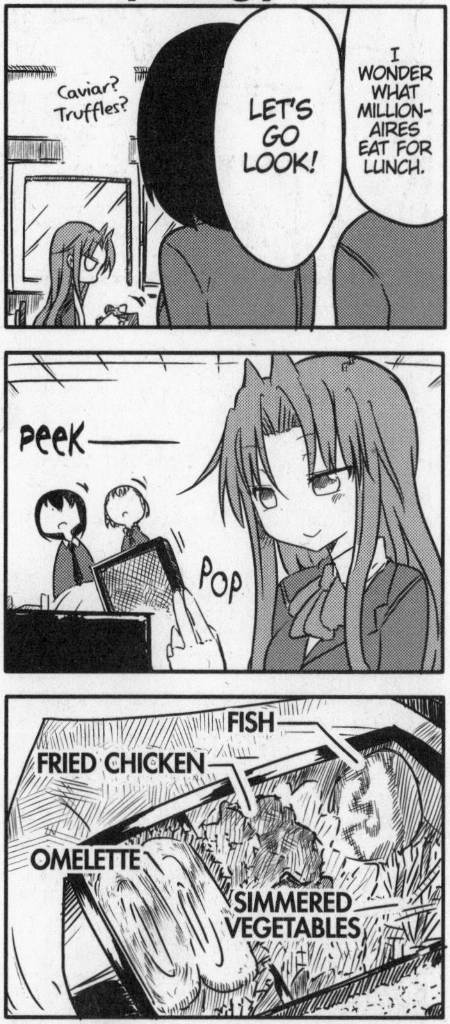
I WONDER WHAT MILLION-AIRES EAT FOR LUNCH.
LET'S GO LOOK!
Caviar? Truffles?
POP
PEEK—
FISH
FRIED CHICKEN
SIMMERED VEGETABLES
OMELETTE
IT'S JUST A NORMAL BENTO.
BUT IT'S MADE WITH THE HIGHEST QUALITY INGREDI-ENTS!

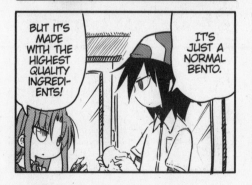

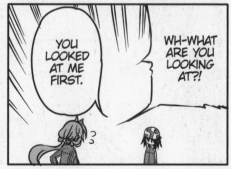

Reason

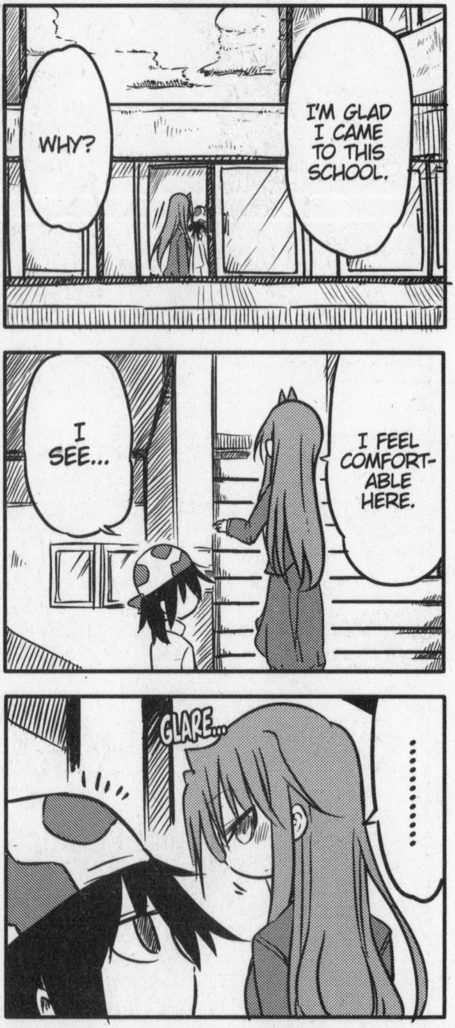
I'M GLAD I CAME TO THIS SCHOOL.
WHY?
I FEEL COMFORTABLE HERE.
I SEE...
....
GLARE...
DON'T LET IT GO TO YOUR HEAD!!
?
OKAY.

Reason 2

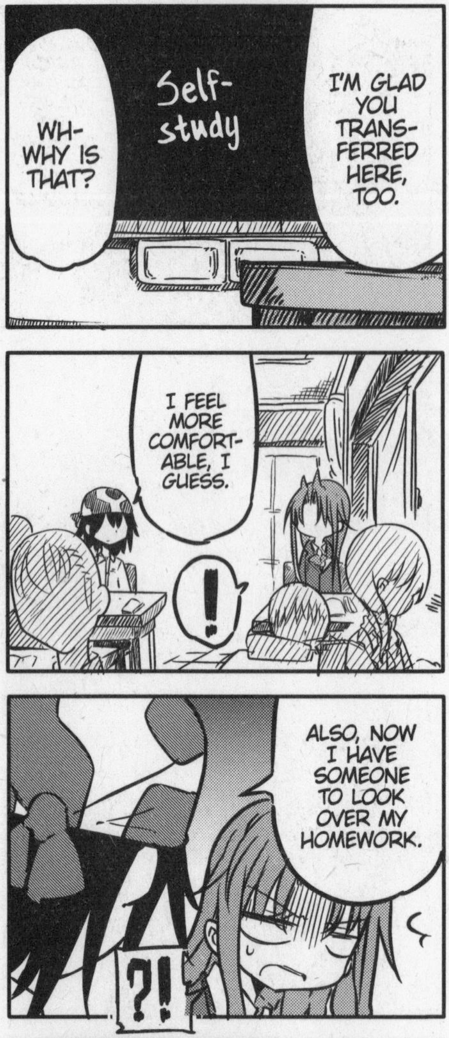
I'M GLAD YOU TRANSFERRED HERE, TOO.
Self-study
WH- WHY IS THAT?
I FEEL MORE COMFORTABLE, I GUESS.
!
ALSO, NOW I HAVE SOMEONE TO LOOK OVER MY HOMEWORK.
?!
AND SOMEONE WHO WILL GIVE ME FOOD DURING LUNCH...
THAT'S QUITE ENOUGH!

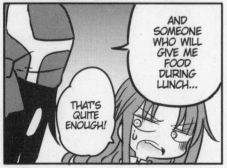

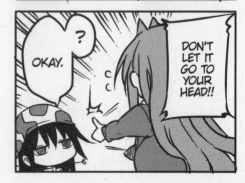

Doubt

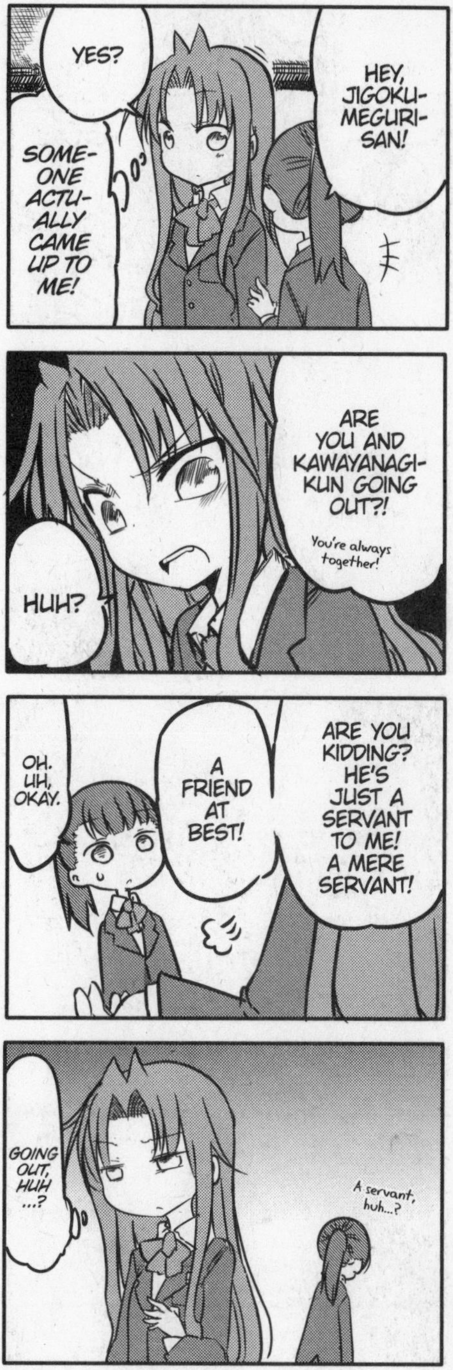
HEY, JIGOKU-MEGURI-SAN!
YES?
SOME-ONE ACTU-ALLY CAME UP TO ME!
ARE YOU AND KAWAYANAGI-KUN GOING OUT?!
You're always together!
HUH?
ARE YOU KIDDING? HE'S JUST A SERVANT TO ME! A MERE SERVANT!
A FRIEND AT BEST!
OH. UH, OKAY.
A servant, huh...?
GOING OUT, HUH ...?

The Silence of Kawayanagi

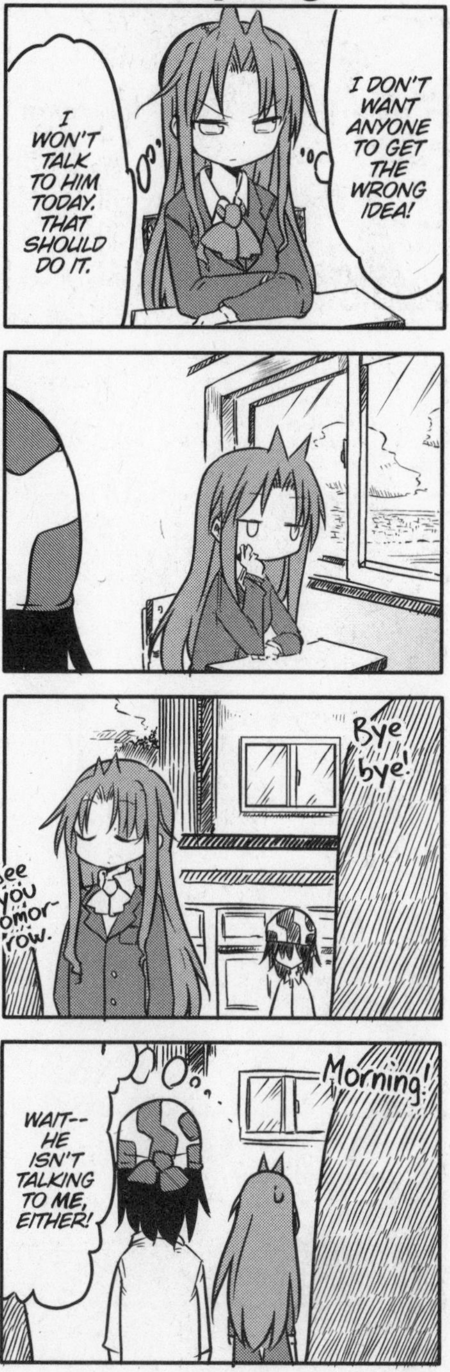
I DON'T WANT ANYONE TO GET THE WRONG IDEA!
I WON'T TALK TO HIM TODAY. THAT SHOULD DO IT.
Bye bye!
See you tomor-row.
Morning!
WAIT-- HE ISN'T TALKING TO ME, EITHER!

Shouted at for No Reason

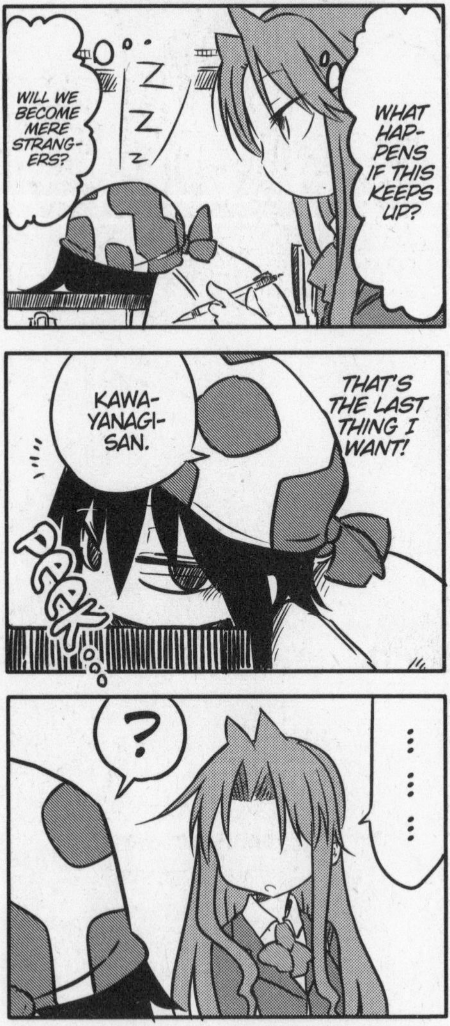
WHAT HAP-PENS IF THIS KEEPS UP?
WILL WE BECOME MERE STRANGERS?
Z Z z
THAT'S THE LAST THING I WANT!
KAWA-YANAGI-SAN.
PEEK...
......
?
DON'T YOU DARE START WITH ME!!
POINT
OKAY.

His Expression

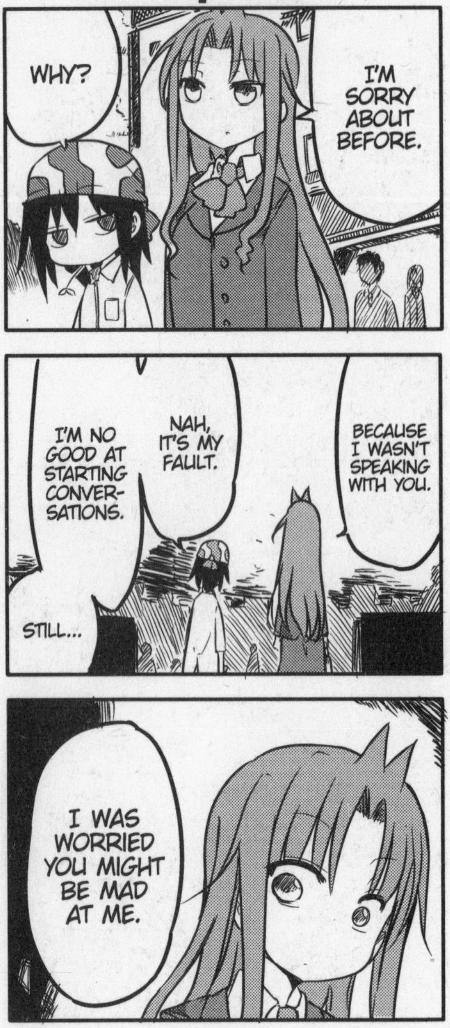
I'M SORRY ABOUT BEFORE.
WHY?
BECAUSE I WASN'T SPEAKING WITH YOU.
NAH, IT'S MY FAULT.
I'M NO GOOD AT STARTING CONVER-SATIONS.
STILL...
I WAS WORRIED YOU MIGHT BE MAD AT ME.
...HEH HEH...
WHY ARE YOU LAUGH-ING?
SO THAT'S WHAT HE THOUGHT...

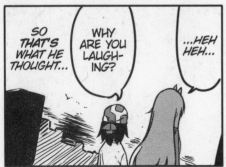

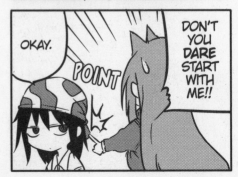

As Long as You're Here

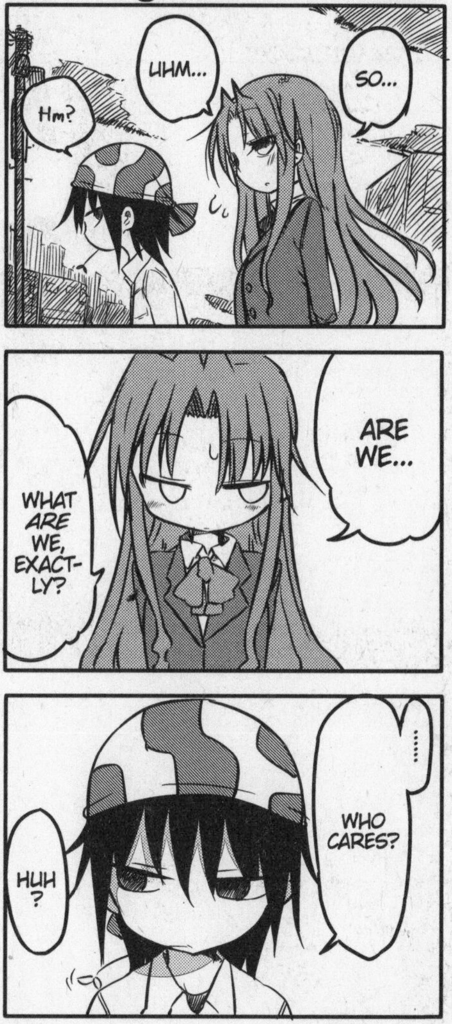
SO...
UHM...
Hm?
ARE WE...
WHAT ARE WE, EXACTLY?
......
WHO CARES?
HUH?
CALL IT WHATEVER...
IT DOESN'T MATTER.
IT'S FINE, RIGHT?

Realization

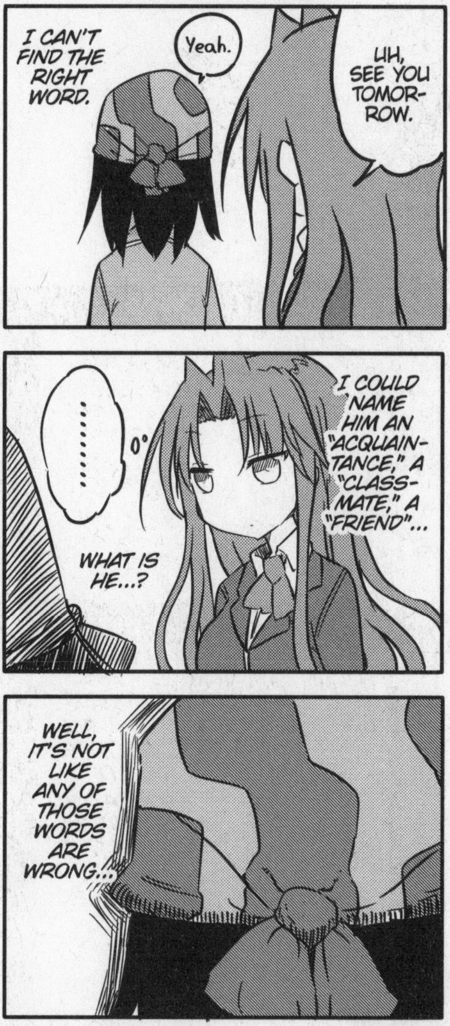
UH, SEE YOU TOMORROW.
Yeah.
I CAN'T FIND THE RIGHT WORD.
I COULD NAME HIM AN "ACQUAINTANCE," A "CLASSMATE," A "FRIEND"...
....
WHAT IS HE...?
WELL, IT'S NOT LIKE ANY OF THOSE WORDS ARE WRONG...
BUT NONE OF THEM SEEM TO FIT.
SIIIGH!
?

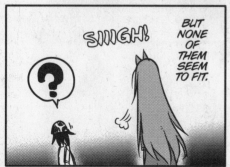

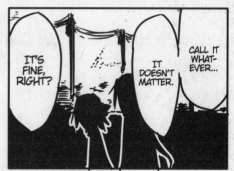

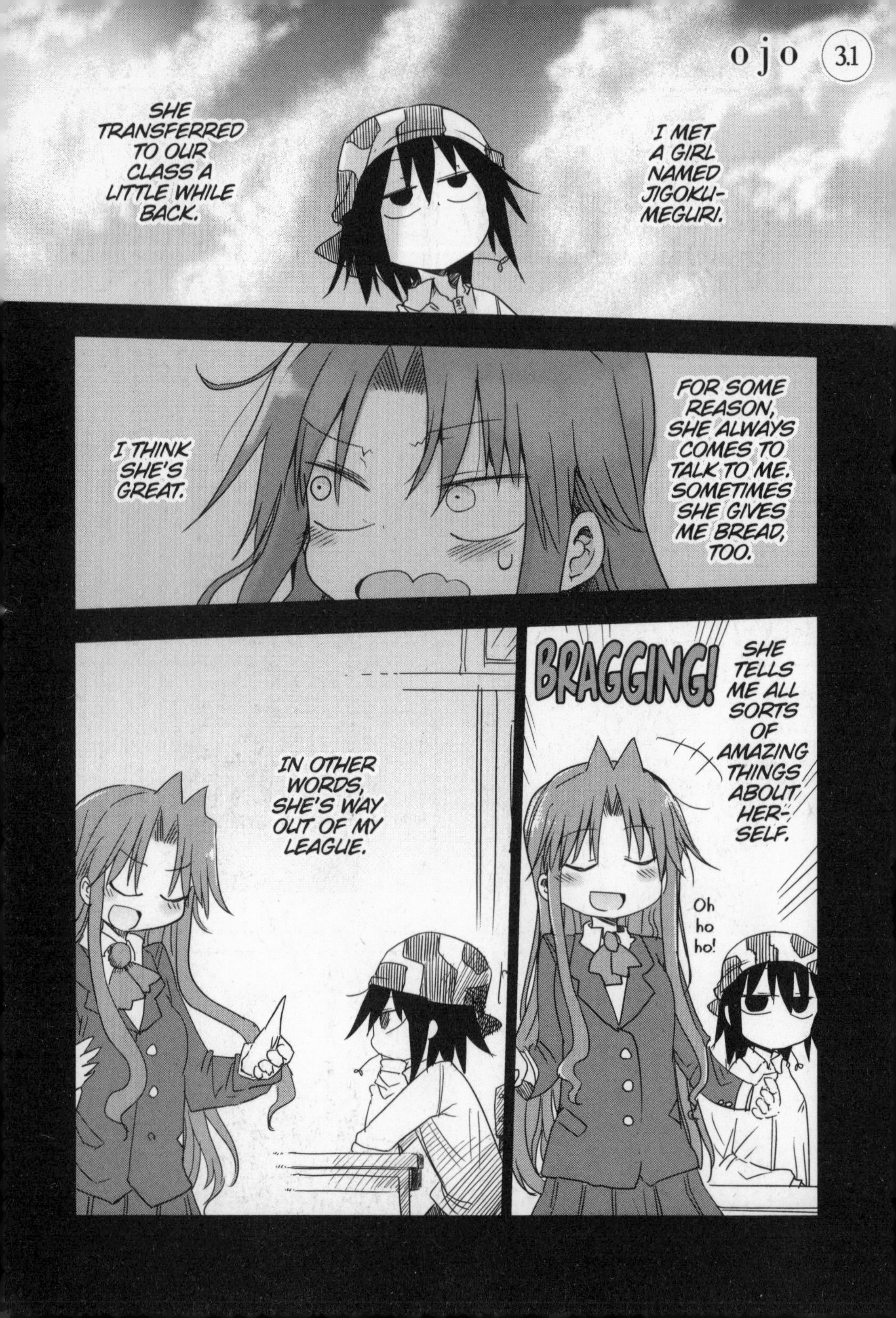
ojo 3.1
I MET A GIRL NAMED JIGOKU-MEGURI.
SHE TRANSFERRED TO OUR CLASS A LITTLE WHILE BACK.
FOR SOME REASON, SHE ALWAYS COMES TO TALK TO ME. SOMETIMES SHE GIVES ME BREAD, TOO.
I THINK SHE'S GREAT.
BRAGGING!
SHE TELLS ME ALL SORTS OF AMAZING THINGS ABOUT HER-SELF.
Oh ho ho!
IN OTHER WORDS, SHE'S WAY OUT OF MY LEAGUE.

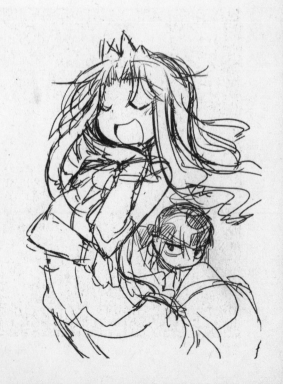

Someone on Her Mind

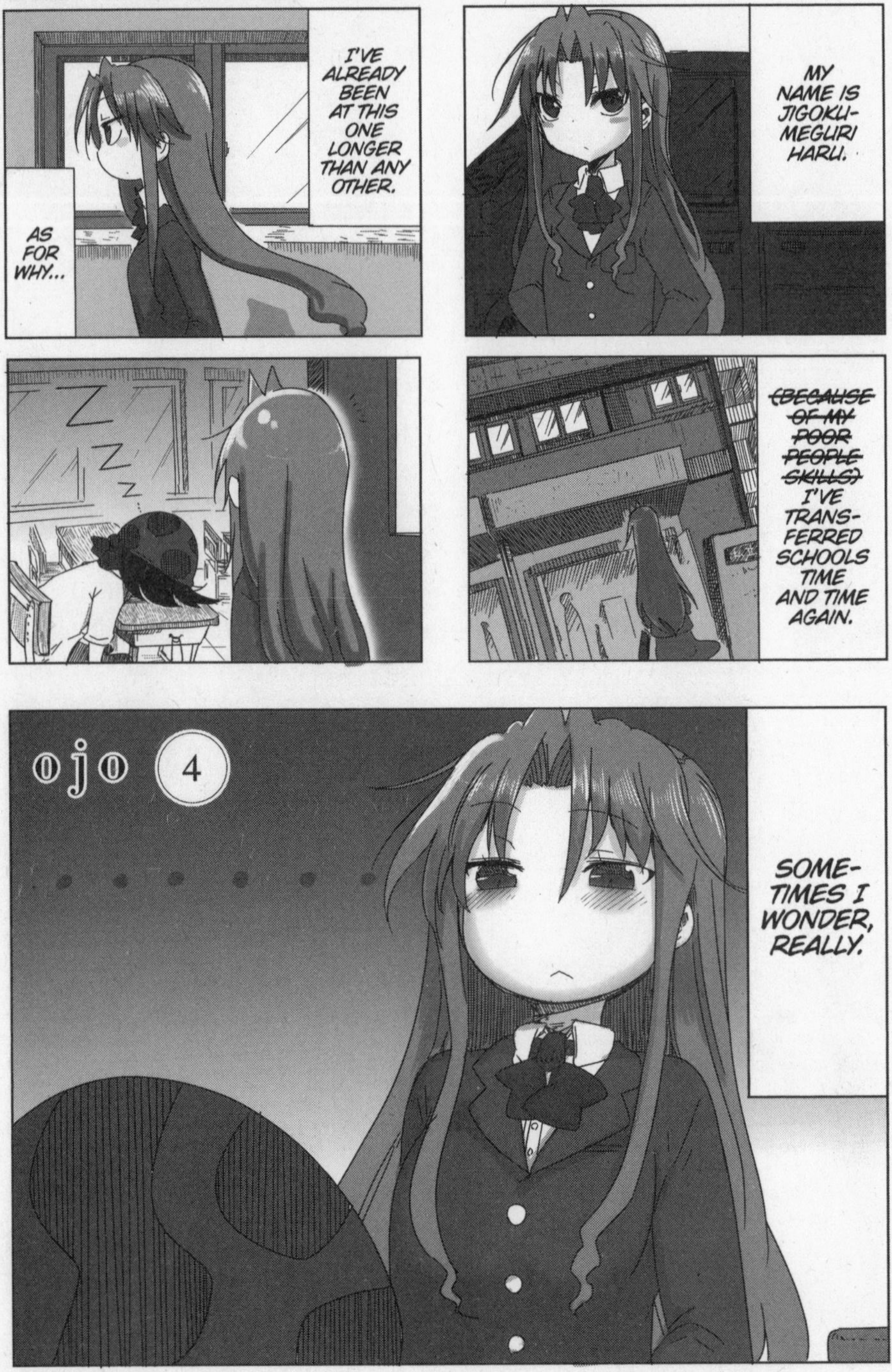
MY NAME IS JIGOKU-MEGURI HARU.
I'VE ALREADY BEEN AT THIS ONE LONGER THAN ANY OTHER.
AS FOR WHY...
~~(BECAUSE OF MY POOR PEOPLE SKILLS)~~ I'VE TRANS-FERRED SCHOOLS TIME AND TIME AGAIN.
SOME-TIMES I WONDER, REALLY.
ojo 4
.....

Blacked Out, and It Was Morning

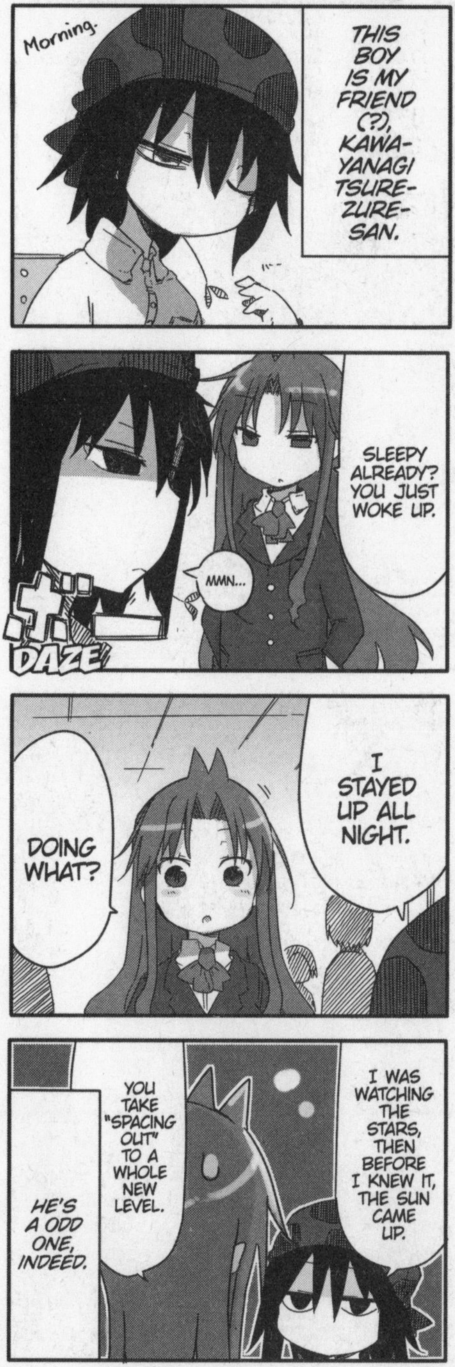
THIS BOY IS MY FRIEND (?), KAWAYANAGI TSURE-ZURE-SAN.
Morning.
SLEEPY ALREADY? YOU JUST WOKE UP.
MMN...
DAZE
I STAYED UP ALL NIGHT.
DOING WHAT?
I WAS WATCHING THE STARS, THEN BEFORE I KNEW IT, THE SUN CAME UP.
YOU TAKE "SPACING OUT" TO A WHOLE NEW LEVEL.
HE'S A ODD ONE, INDEED.

Helping the Economy

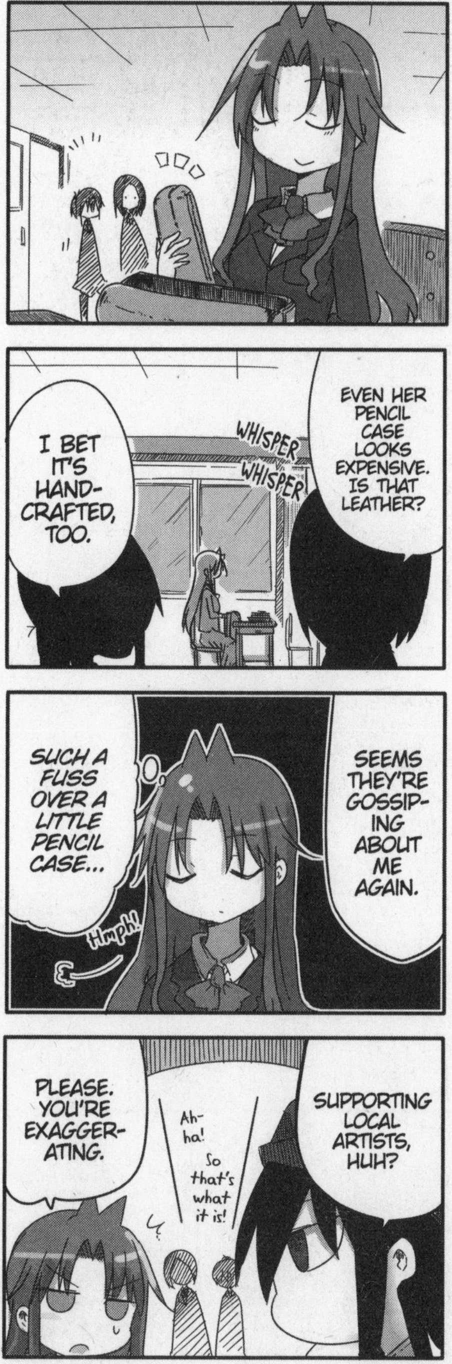
EVEN HER PENCIL CASE LOOKS EXPENSIVE. IS THAT LEATHER?
WHISPER WHISPER
I BET IT'S HAND-CRAFTED, TOO.
SEEMS THEY'RE GOSSIP-ING ABOUT ME AGAIN.
SUCH A FUSS OVER A LITTLE PENCIL CASE...
Hmph!
SUPPORTING LOCAL ARTISTS, HUH?
Ah-ha!
So that's what it is!
PLEASE. YOU'RE EXAGGER-ATING.

Mistaken Trust

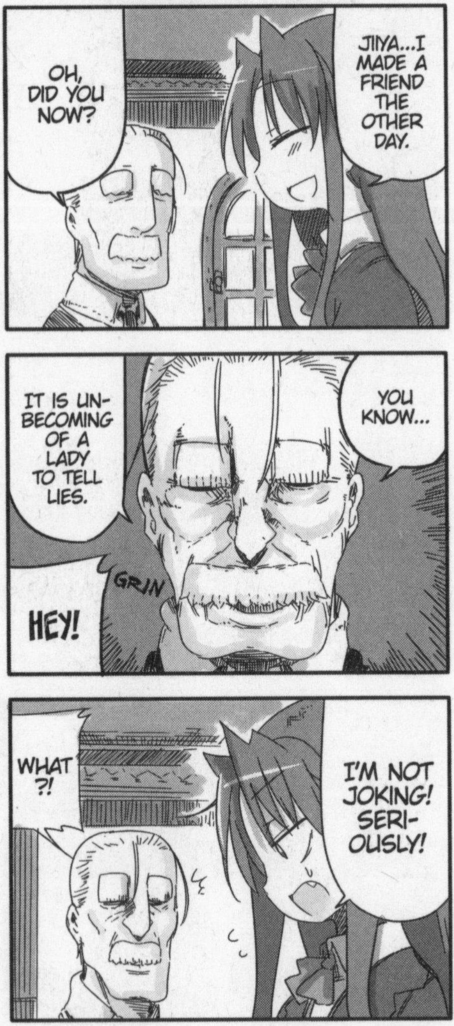
JIIYA...I MADE A FRIEND THE OTHER DAY.
OH, DID YOU NOW?
YOU KNOW...
IT IS UN-BECOMING OF A LADY TO TELL LIES.
GRIN
HEY!
I'M NOT JOKING! SERI-OUSLY!
WHAT?!
HOW MUCH ARE YOU PAYING THEM?!
WHAT KIND OF MONSTER DO YOU TAKE ME FOR?!

Birds of a Feather

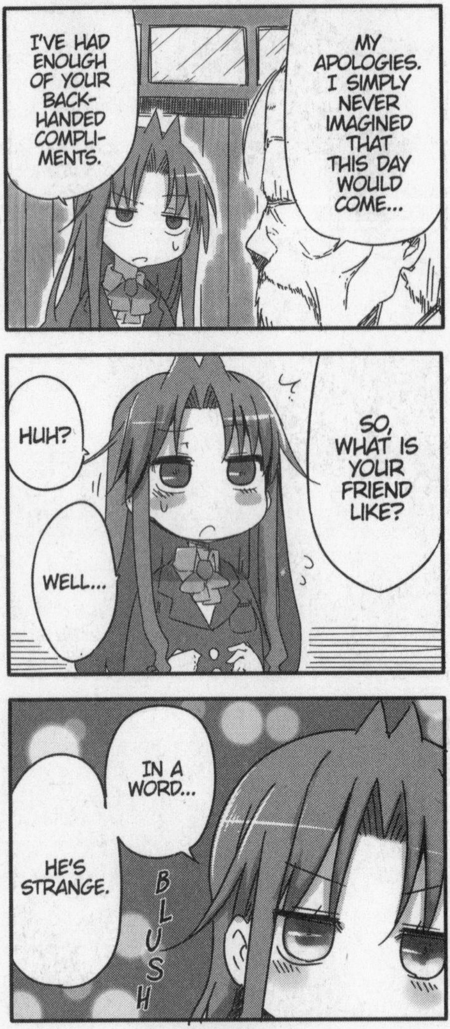
MY APOLOGIES. I SIMPLY NEVER IMAGINED THAT THIS DAY WOULD COME...
I'VE HAD ENOUGH OF YOUR BACK-HANDED COMPLI-MENTS.
SO, WHAT IS YOUR FRIEND LIKE?
HUH?
WELL...
IN A WORD...
HE'S STRANGE.
BLUSH
THEN YOU HAVE ONE THING IN COMMON... UH, I MEAN, CONGRATU-LATIONS.
NOW YOU'RE JUST ANTAGO-NIZING ME.

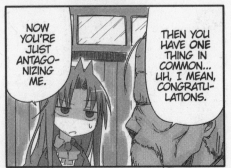

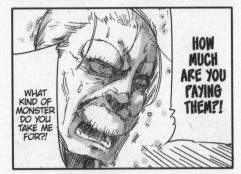

The Usual Routine

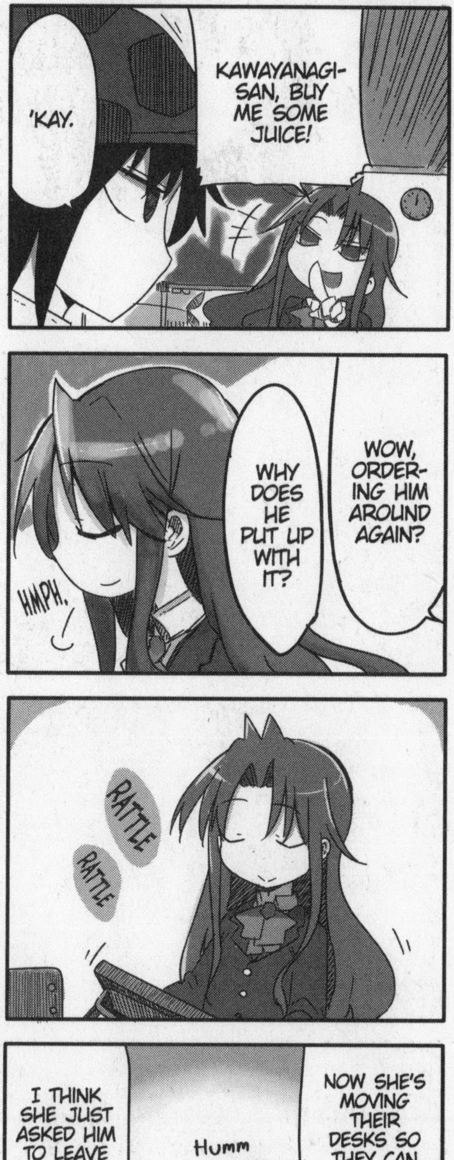
KAWAYANAGI-SAN, BUY ME SOME JUICE!
'KAY.
WOW, ORDERING HIM AROUND AGAIN?
WHY DOES HE PUT UP WITH IT?
HMPH.
RATTLE
RATTLE
NOW SHE'S MOVING THEIR DESKS SO THEY CAN EAT LUNCH TOGETHER!
I THINK SHE JUST ASKED HIM TO LEAVE SO HE WOULDN'T SEE HER DO IT...
Humm humm!

First Encounter with Gel

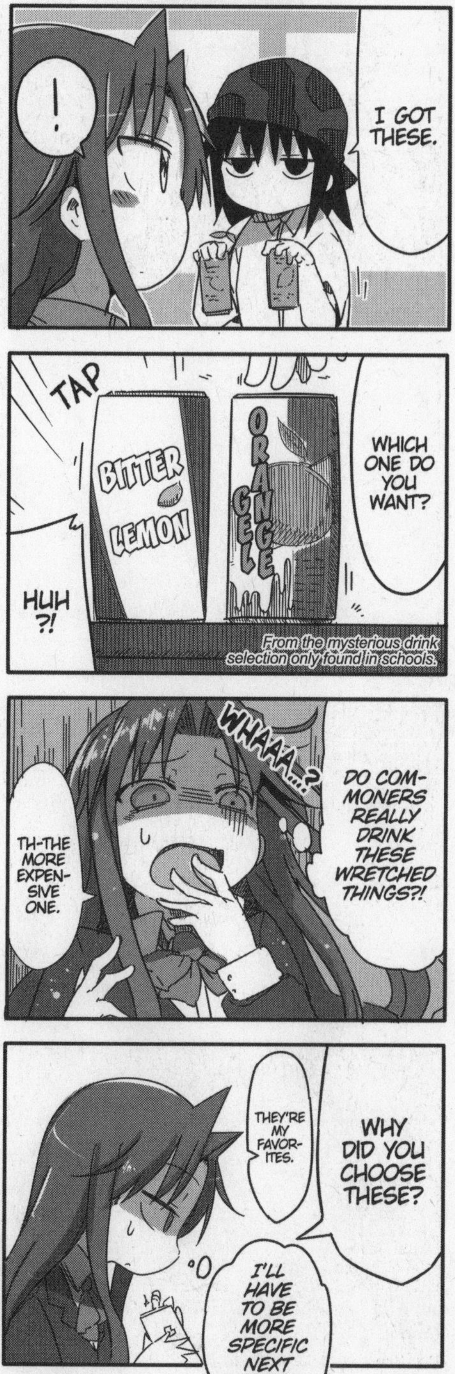
I GOT THESE.
!
WHICH ONE DO YOU WANT?
ORANGE GEL
BITTER LEMON
TAP
HUH ?!
From the mysterious drink selection only found in schools.
DO COMMONERS REALLY DRINK THESE WRETCHED THINGS?!
WHAAA...?
TH-THE MORE EXPENSIVE ONE.
WHY DID YOU CHOOSE THESE?
THEY'RE MY FAVORITES.
I'LL HAVE TO BE MORE SPECIFIC NEXT TIME.

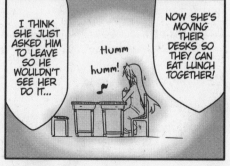

Doubtful Nobility

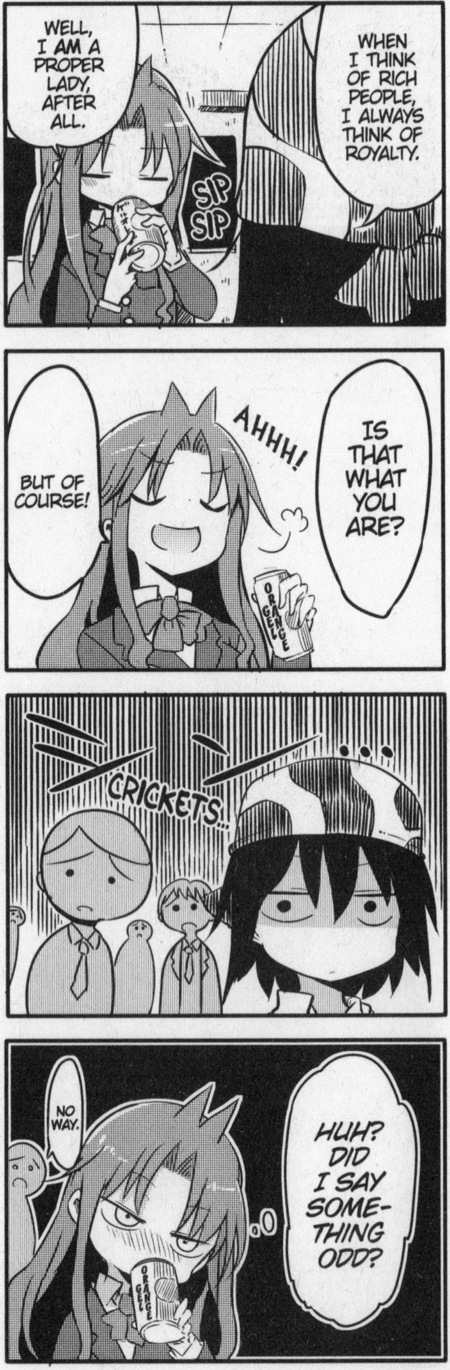
WHEN I THINK OF RICH PEOPLE, I ALWAYS THINK OF ROYALTY.
WELL, I AM A PROPER LADY, AFTER ALL.
SIP SIP
IS THAT WHAT YOU ARE?
AHHHH!
BUT OF COURSE!
ORANGE GEL
CRICKETS...
...
HUH? DID I SAY SOME-THING ODD?
NO WAY.
ORANGE GEL

Turns Out She Likes Dogs

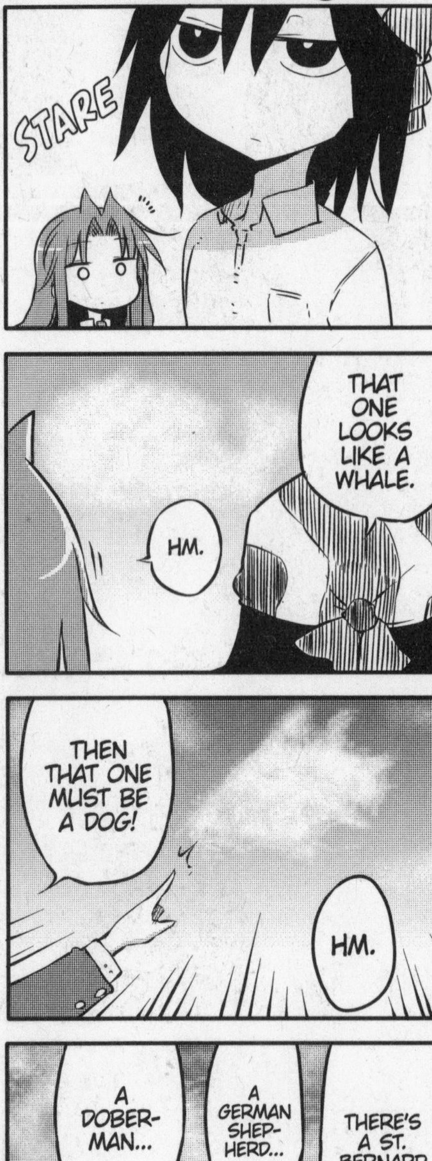
STARE
THAT ONE LOOKS LIKE A WHALE.
HM.
THEN THAT ONE MUST BE A DOG!
HM.
THERE'S A ST. BERNARD CLOUD...
A GERMAN SHEP-HERD...
A DOBER-MAN...
THEY'RE ALL DOGS, HUH?

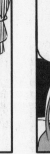

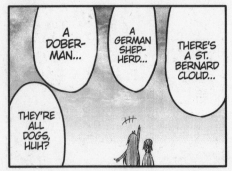

Pity

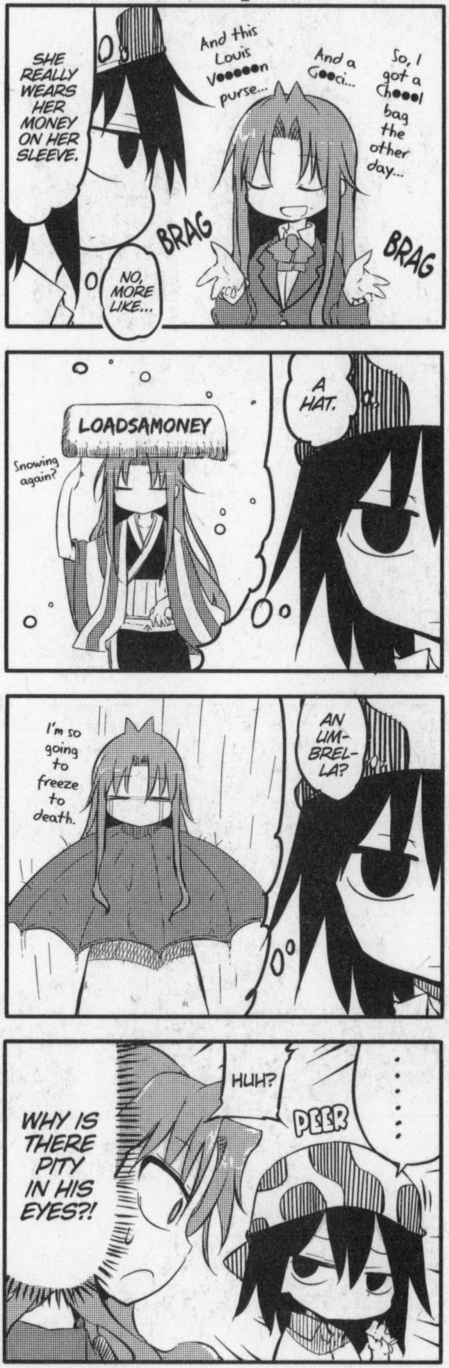
So, I got a Chooool bag the other day...
And a Goooci...
And this Louis Voooooon purse...
BRAG
BRAG
SHE REALLY WEARS HER MONEY ON HER SLEEVE.
NO, MORE LIKE...
A HAT.
LOADSAMONEY
Snowing again?
AN UM-BREL-LA?
I'm so going to freeze to death.
......
PEER
HUH?
WHY IS THERE PITY IN HIS EYES?!

Viva la Gel

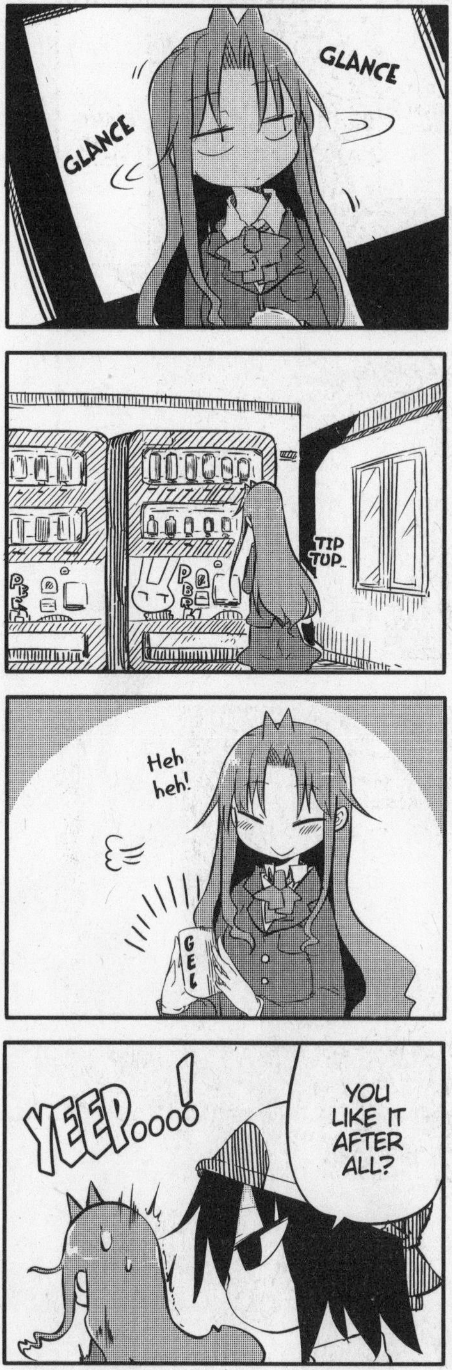
GLANCE
GLANCE
TIP TUP...
Heh heh!
GEL
YOU LIKE IT AFTER ALL?
YEEPoooo!

It's an Inherent Right

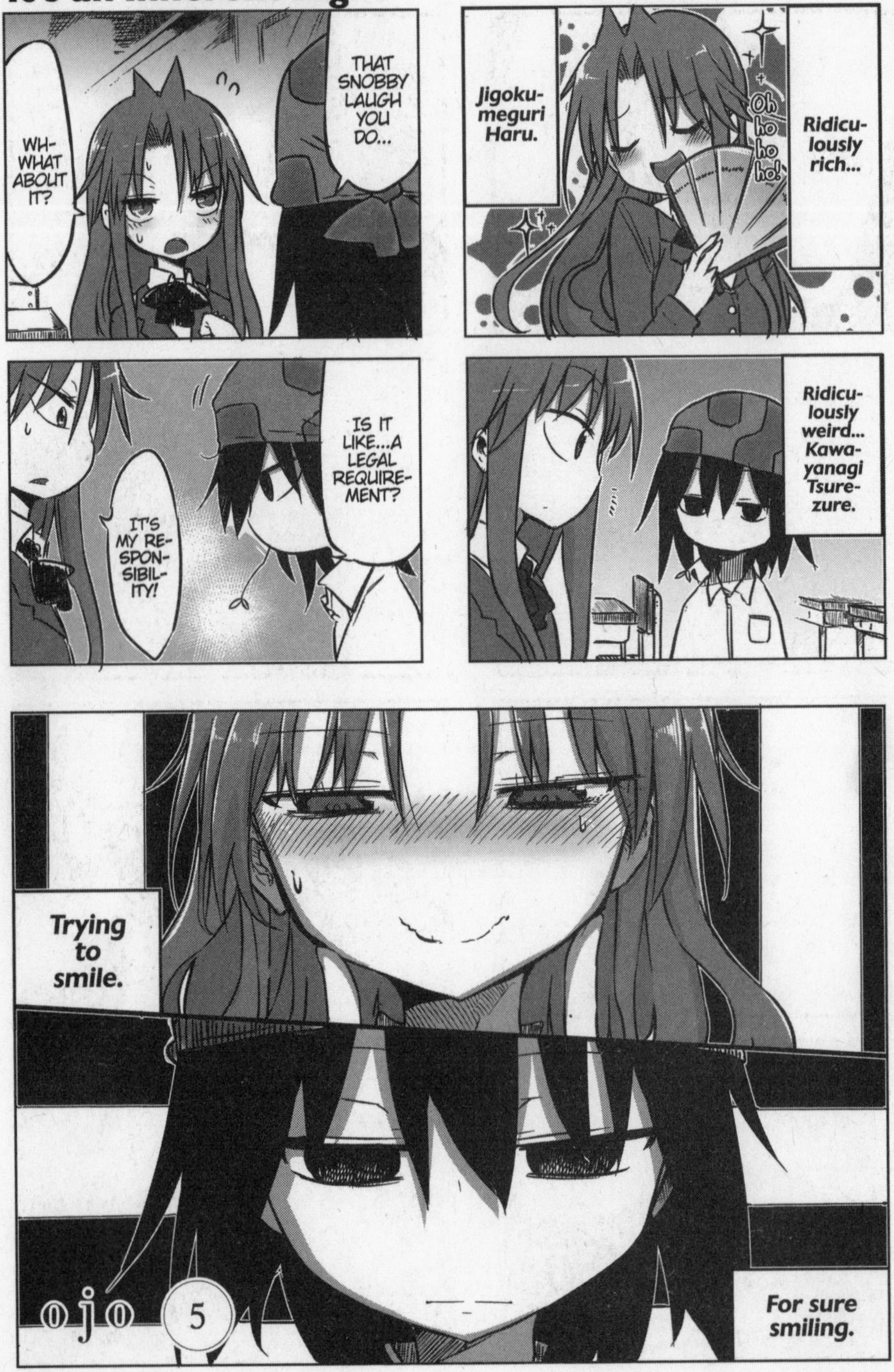
Ridiculously rich...
Oh ho ho ho!
Jigokumeguri Haru.
THAT SNOBBY LAUGH YOU DO...
WH-WHAT ABOUT IT?
Ridiculously weird... Kawayanagi Tsurezure.
IS IT LIKE...A LEGAL REQUIREMENT?
IT'S MY RESPONSIBILITY!
Trying to smile.
For sure smiling.
ojo 5

Someone from the Crowd

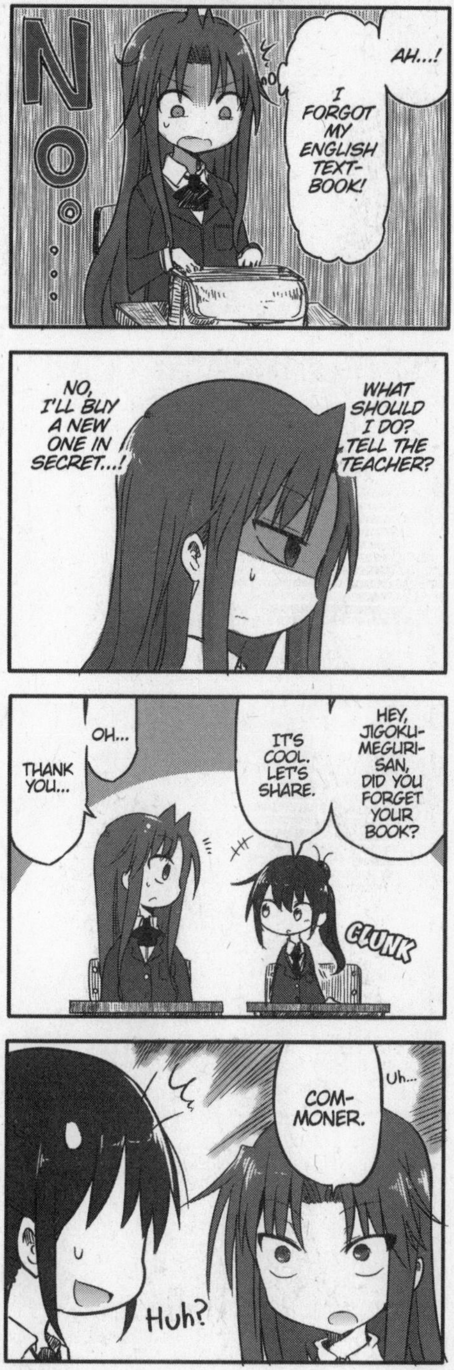
AH...!
I FORGOT MY ENGLISH TEXT-BOOK!
NO...
WHAT SHOULD I DO? TELL THE TEACHER?
NO, I'LL BUY A NEW ONE IN SECRET...!
HEY, JIGOKU-MEGURI-SAN, DID YOU FORGET YOUR BOOK?
CLUNK
IT'S COOL. LET'S SHARE.
OH...
THANK YOU...
Uh...
COM-MONER.
Huh?

But This Is Just How I Smile

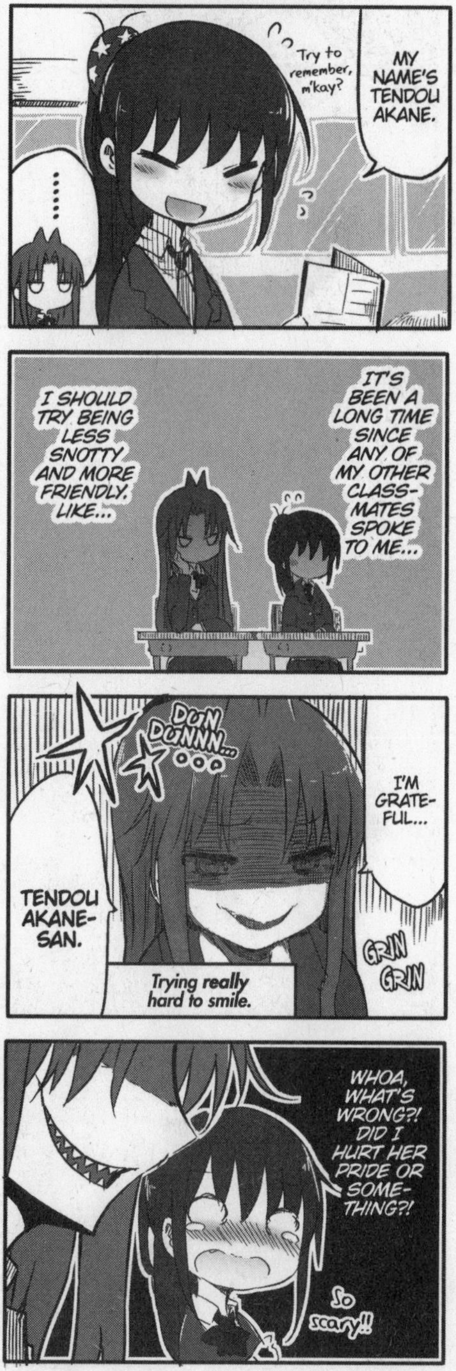
MY NAME'S TENDOU AKANE.
Try to remember, m'kay?
......
IT'S BEEN A LONG TIME SINCE ANY OF MY OTHER CLASS-MATES SPOKE TO ME...
I SHOULD TRY BEING LESS SNOTTY AND MORE FRIENDLY. LIKE...
I'M GRATE-FUL...
DUN DUNNN...
TENDOU AKANE-SAN.
GRIN GRIN
Trying really hard to smile.
WHOA, WHAT'S WRONG?! DID I HURT HER PRIDE OR SOME-THING?!
So scary!!

Sometimes She Does

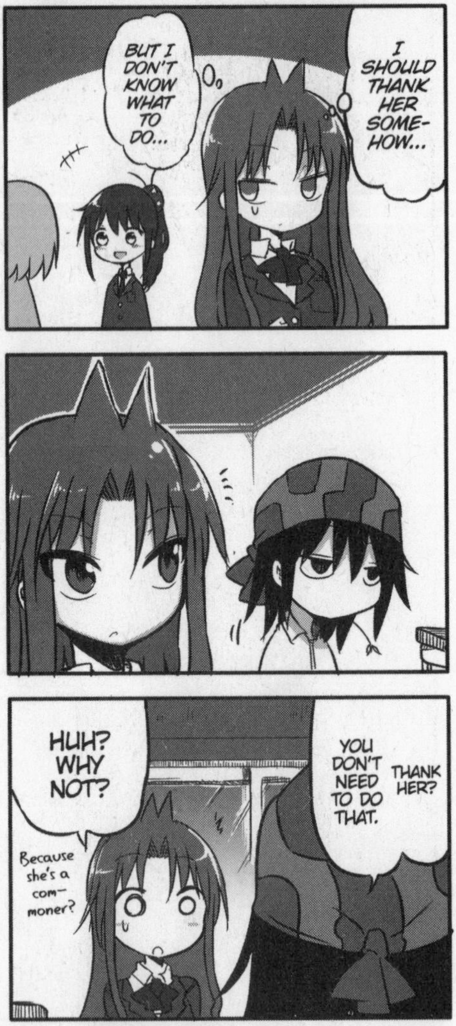
I SHOULD THANK HER SOME-HOW...
BUT I DON'T KNOW WHAT TO DO...
THANK HER?
YOU DON'T NEED TO DO THAT.
HUH? WHY NOT?
Because she's a com-moner?
YOU NEVER THANK ME (NOT THAT I'M ASKING YOU TO).
WHAT?!

Changing Vectors

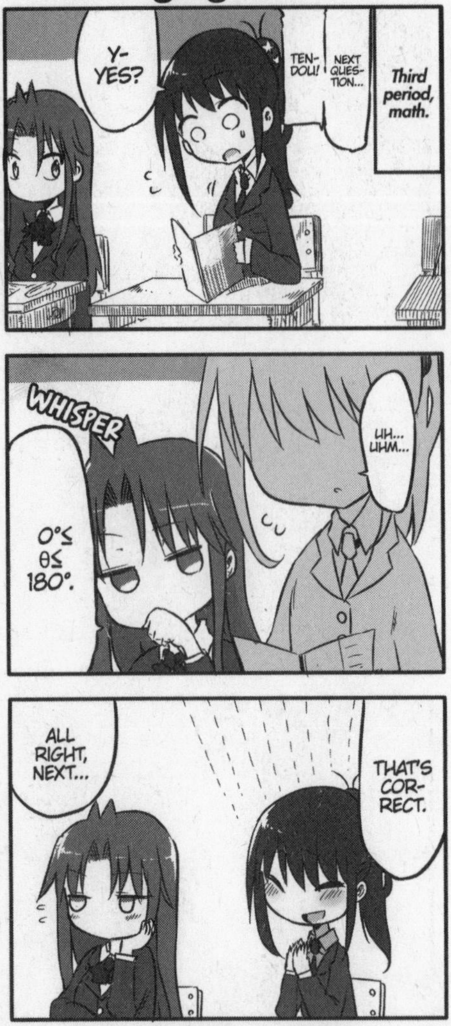
Third period, math.
NEXT QUES-TION...
TEN-DOU!
Y-YES?
UH... UHM...
WHISPER
0°≤ θ≤ 180°.
THAT'S COR-RECT.
ALL RIGHT, NEXT...
KAWA-YANAGI!
KAWA-YANA-GI?
HELLOOOO?

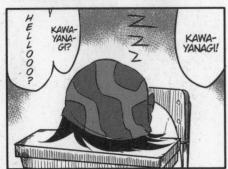

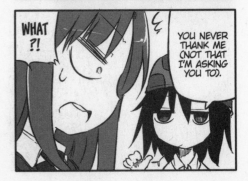

Doesn't Know the Word Or the Feeling

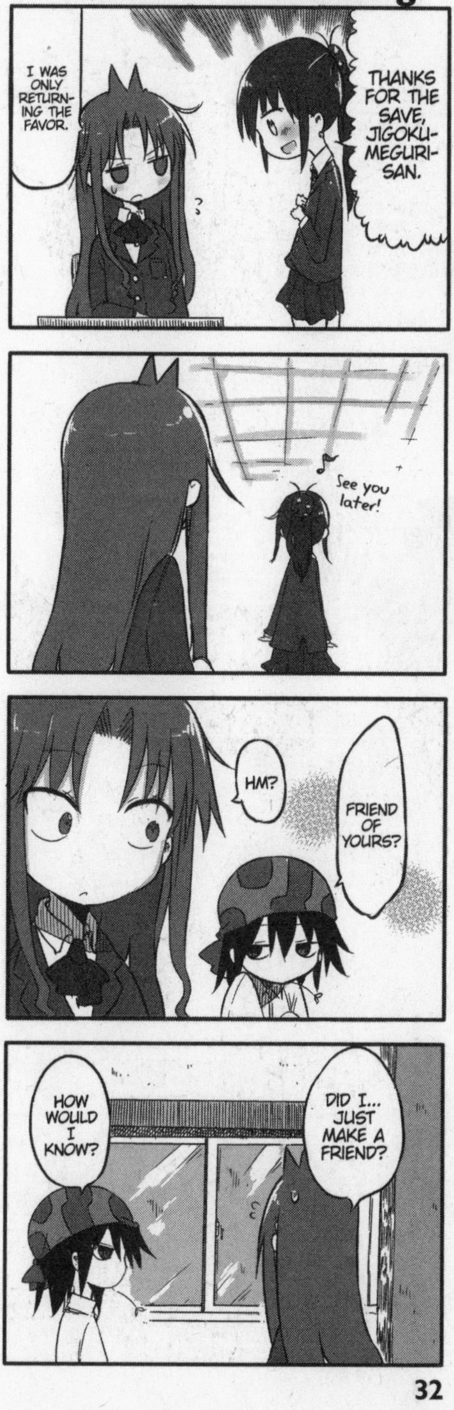
THANKS FOR THE SAVE, JIGOKU-MEGURI-SAN.
I WAS ONLY RETURNING THE FAVOR.
See you later!
FRIEND OF YOURS?
HM?
DID I... JUST MAKE A FRIEND?
HOW WOULD I KNOW?

"Friends"

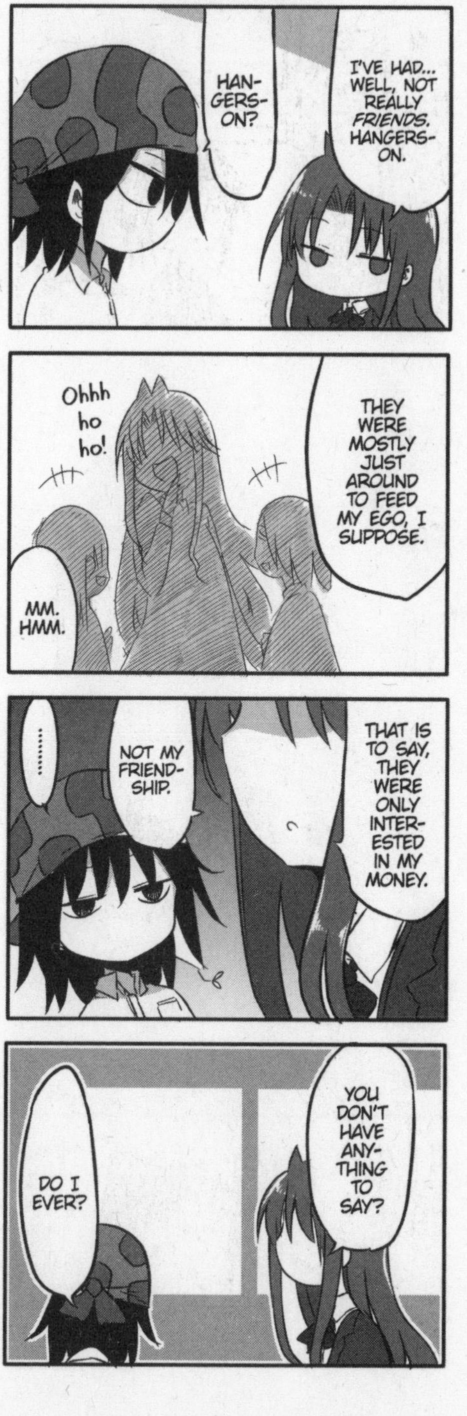
I'VE HAD... WELL, NOT REALLY FRIENDS. HANGERS-ON.
HANGERS-ON?
THEY WERE MOSTLY JUST AROUND TO FEED MY EGO, I SUPPOSE.
Ohhh ho ho!
MM. HMM.
THAT IS TO SAY, THEY WERE ONLY INTERESTED IN MY MONEY.
NOT MY FRIENDSHIP.
......
YOU DON'T HAVE ANYTHING TO SAY?
DO I EVER?

Re-take

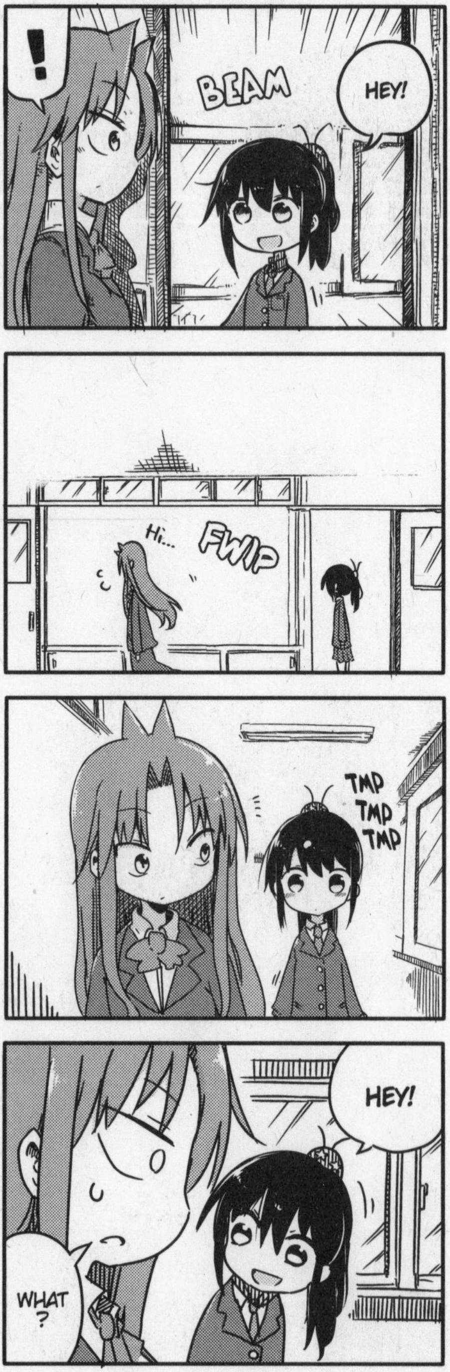
HEY!
BEAM
!
FWIP
Hi...
TMP TMP TMP
HEY!
WHAT?

Talking About a Crush?

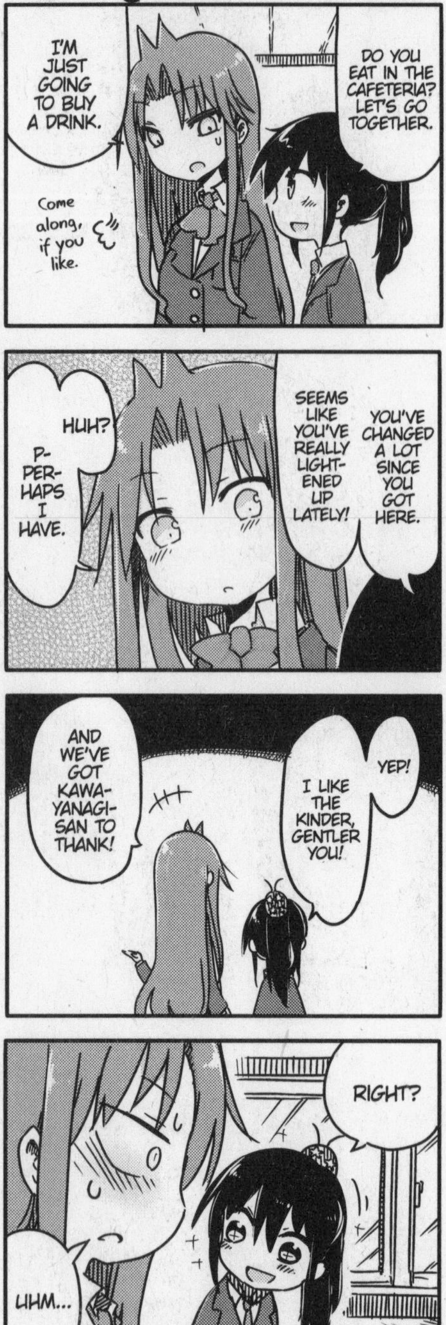
DO YOU EAT IN THE CAFETERIA? LET'S GO TOGETHER.
I'M JUST GOING TO BUY A DRINK.
Come along, if you like.
YOU'VE CHANGED A LOT SINCE YOU GOT HERE.
SEEMS LIKE YOU'VE REALLY LIGHT-ENED UP LATELY!
HUH?
P-PER-HAPS I HAVE.
YEP!
I LIKE THE KINDER, GENTLER YOU!
AND WE'VE GOT KAWA-YANAGI-SAN TO THANK!
RIGHT?
UHM...

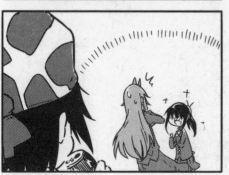

Everything She's Got

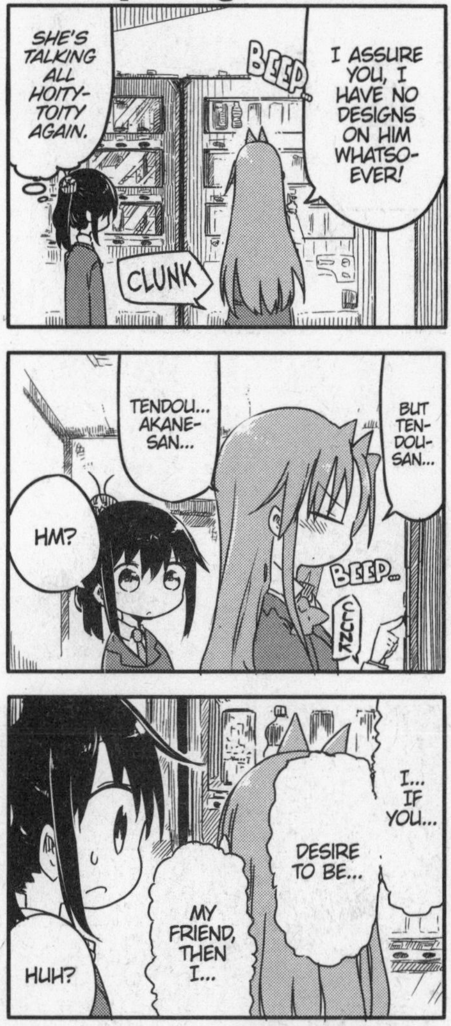
I ASSURE YOU, I HAVE NO DESIGNS ON HIM WHATSO-EVER!
BEEP
SHE'S TALKING ALL HOITY-TOITY AGAIN.
CLUNK
BUT TEN-DOU-SAN...
TENDOU... AKANE-SAN...
HM?
BEEP...
CLUNK
I... IF YOU...
DESIRE TO BE...
MY FRIEND, THEN I...
HUH?
YEAH, OF COURSE.
I'D LOVE TO BE FRIENDS.

Things Given and Things Received

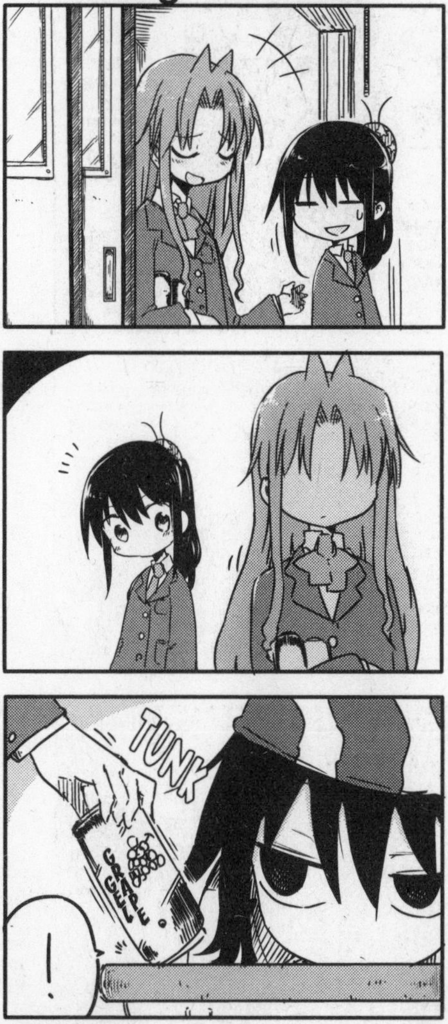
TUNK
GRAPE GEL
!

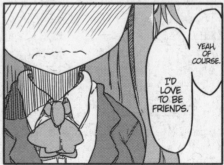

Sort of Alike and Sort of Not

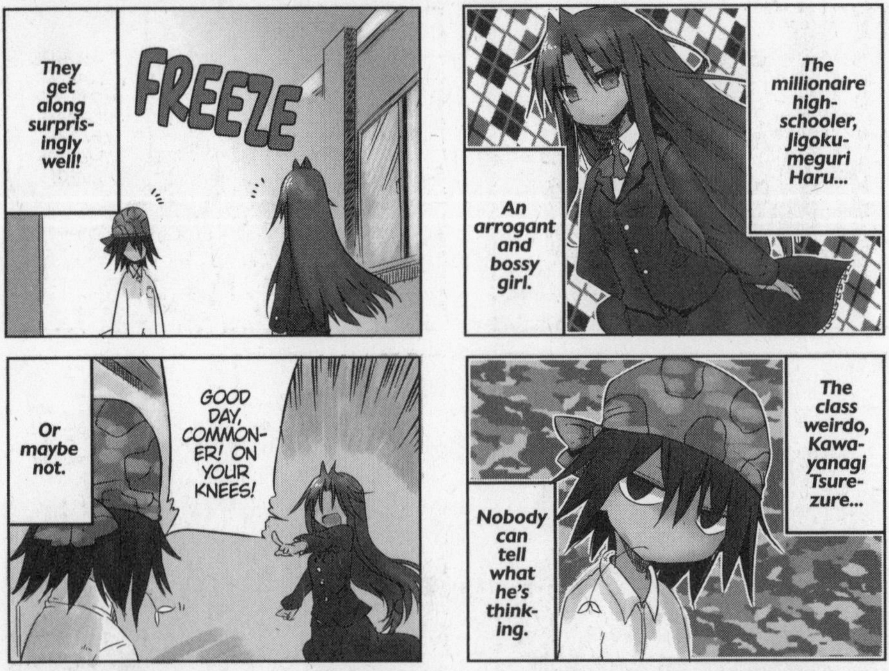
The millionaire high-schooler, Jigokumeguri Haru...
An arrogant and bossy girl.
The class weirdo, Kawayanagi Tsurezure...
Nobody can tell what he's thinking.
FREEZE
They get along surprisingly well!
GOOD DAY, COMMONER! ON YOUR KNEES!
Or maybe not.

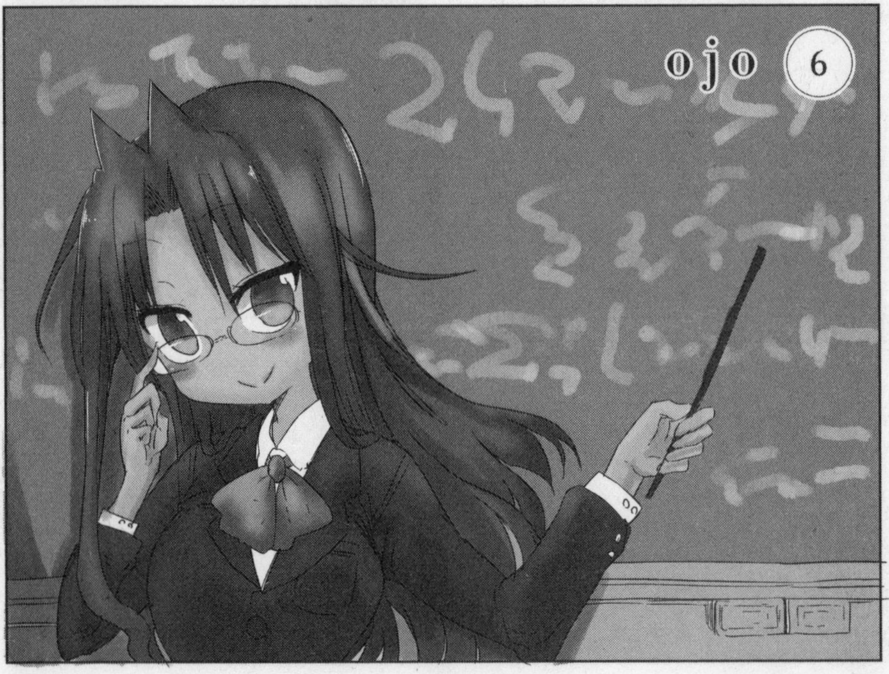
ojo 6

Suddenly Senpai

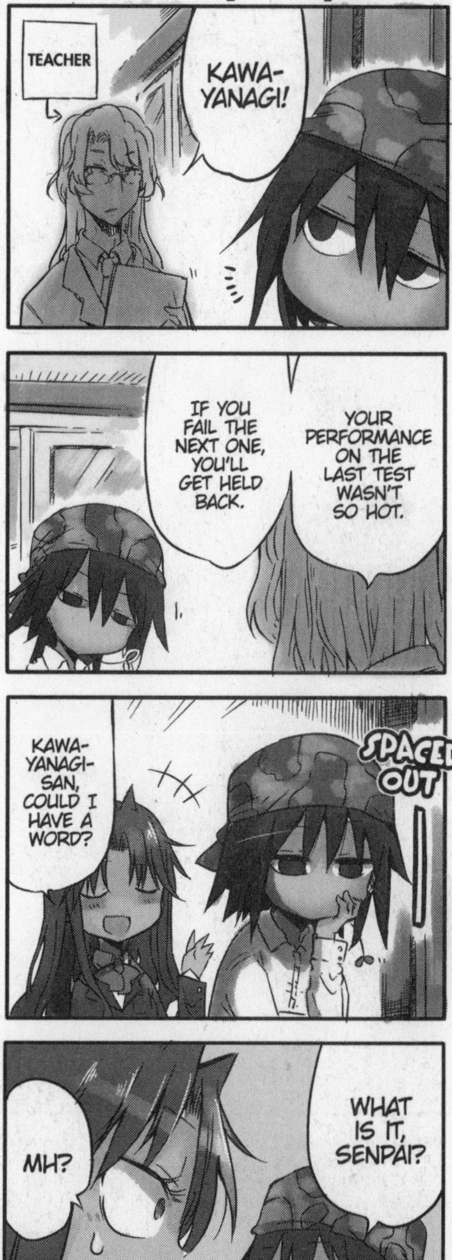
KAWA-YANAGI!
TEACHER
YOUR PERFORMANCE ON THE LAST TEST WASN'T SO HOT.
IF YOU FAIL THE NEXT ONE, YOU'LL GET HELD BACK.
SPACED OUT
KAWA-YANAGI-SAN, COULD I HAVE A WORD?
WHAT IS IT, SENPAI?
MH?

Suddenly Senpai 2

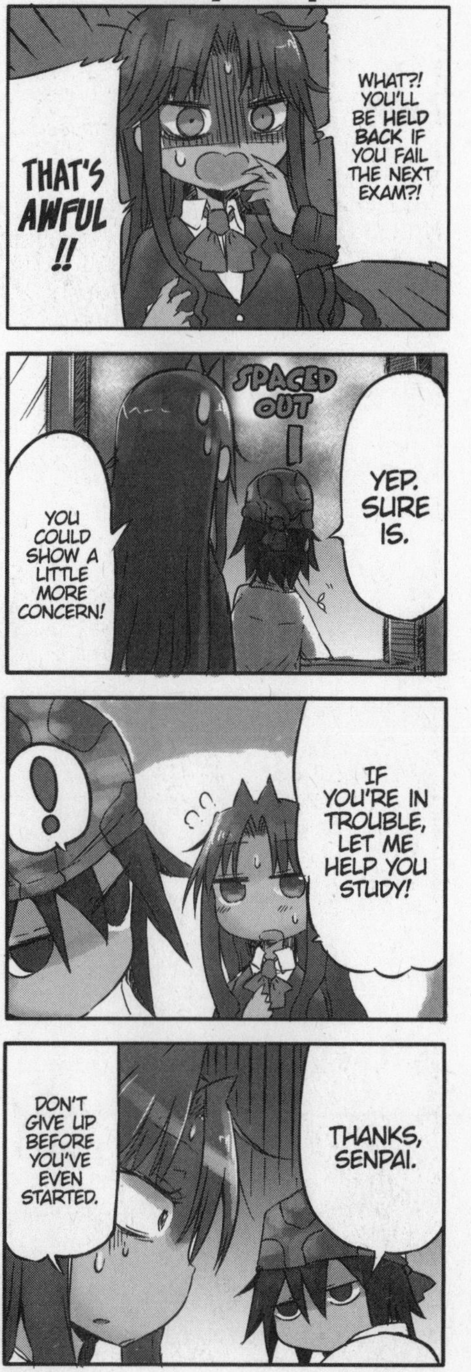
WHAT?! YOU'LL BE HELD BACK IF YOU FAIL THE NEXT EXAM?!
THAT'S AWFUL!!
YEP. SURE IS.
SPACED OUT
YOU COULD SHOW A LITTLE MORE CONCERN!
IF YOU'RE IN TROUBLE, LET ME HELP YOU STUDY!
!
THANKS, SENPAI.
DON'T GIVE UP BEFORE YOU'VE EVEN STARTED.

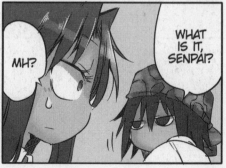

Taking a Direct Approach

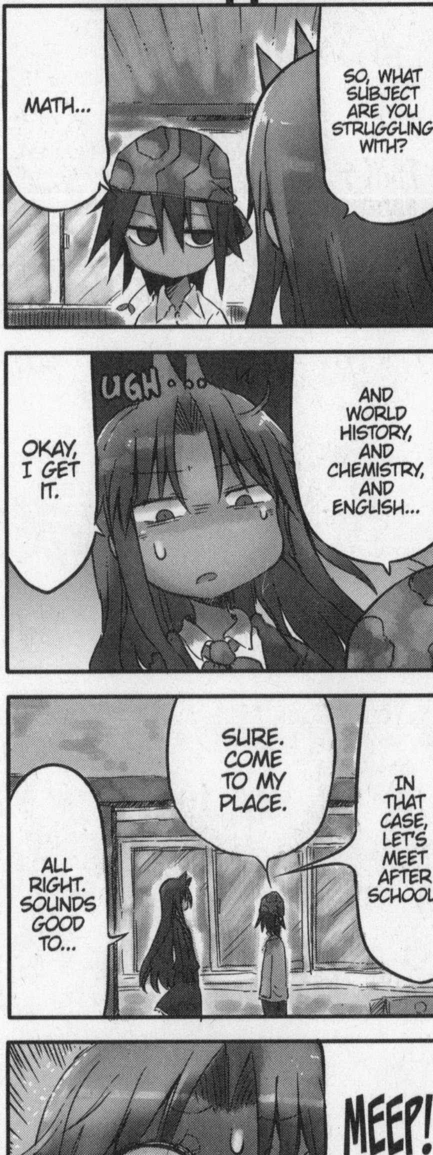
SO, WHAT SUBJECT ARE YOU STRUGGLING WITH?
MATH...
AND WORLD HISTORY, AND CHEMISTRY, AND ENGLISH...
UGH...
OKAY, I GET IT.
IN THAT CASE, LET'S MEET AFTER SCHOOL.
SURE. COME TO MY PLACE.
ALL RIGHT. SOUNDS GOOD TO...
MEEP!

A Wealth of Experience?

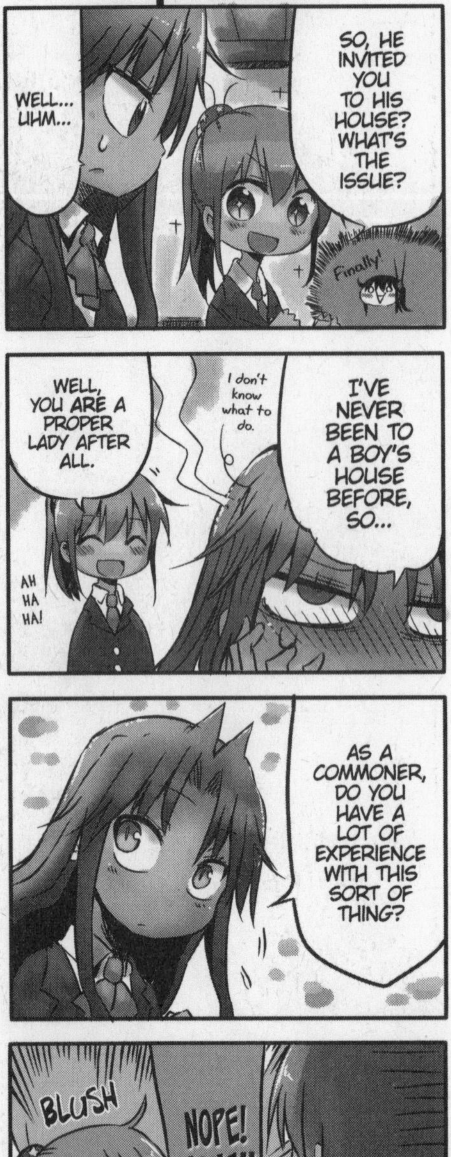
SO, HE INVITED YOU TO HIS HOUSE? WHAT'S THE ISSUE?
WELL... UHM...
Finally!
I'VE NEVER BEEN TO A BOY'S HOUSE BEFORE, SO...
I don't know what to do.
WELL, YOU ARE A PROPER LADY AFTER ALL.
AH HA HA!
AS A COMMONER, DO YOU HAVE A LOT OF EXPERIENCE WITH THIS SORT OF THING?
NOPE! NONE!!
BLUSH

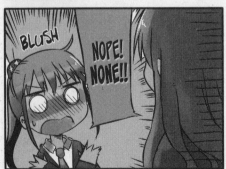

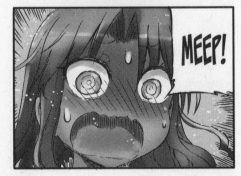

Unnecessary Outburst

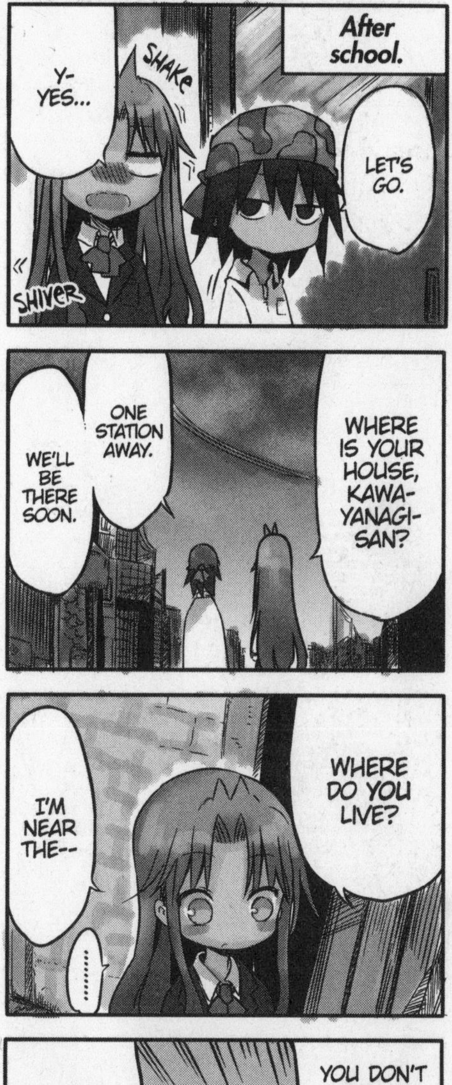
After school.
SHAKE
LET'S GO.
Y-YES...
SHIVER
WHERE IS YOUR HOUSE, KAWA-YANAGI-SAN?
ONE STATION AWAY.
WE'LL BE THERE SOON.
WHERE DO YOU LIVE?
I'M NEAR THE--
......
YOU DON'T NEED TO COME OVER TO MY PLACE!!
WHAT-EVER.

Standard

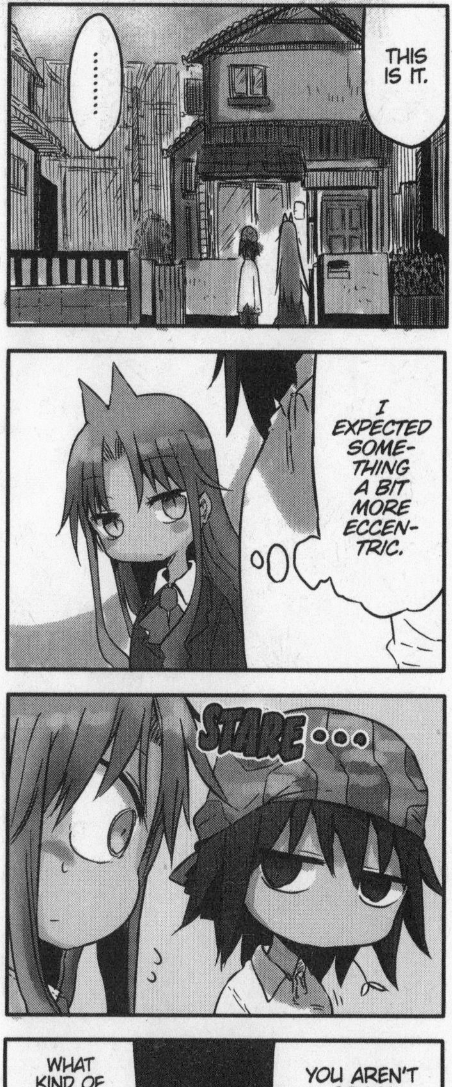
THIS IS IT.
......
I EXPECTED SOME-THING A BIT MORE ECCEN-TRIC.
STARE...
YOU AREN'T GONNA SAY "THIS IS WHERE YOU LIVE? IT LOOKS LIKE A DOGHOUSE!"
WHAT KIND OF MONSTER DO YOU TAKE ME FOR?

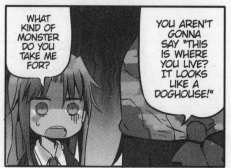

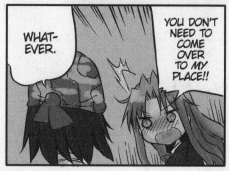

Imagination Running Wild

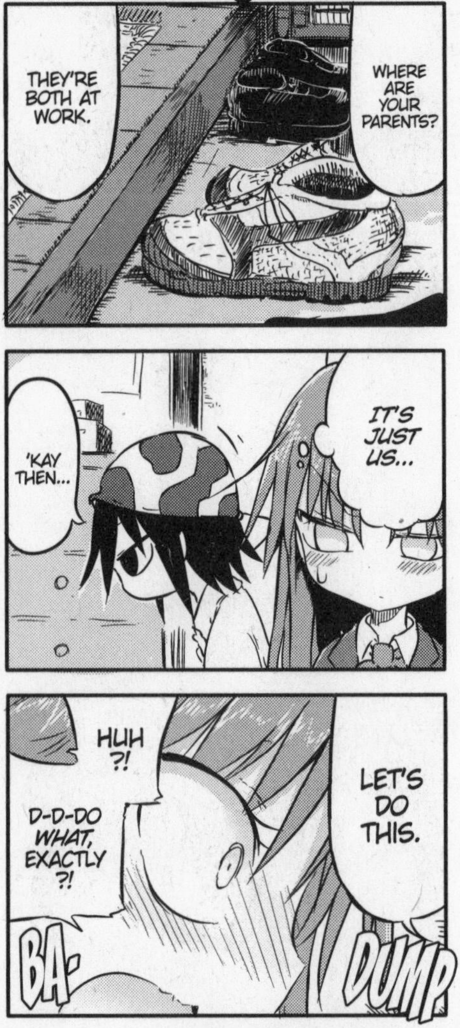
WHERE ARE YOUR PARENTS?
THEY'RE BOTH AT WORK.
IT'S JUST US...
'KAY THEN...
LET'S DO THIS.
HUH ?!
D-D-DO WHAT, EXACTLY ?!
BA-
DUMP
HM?
OH. RIGHT.
WORLD HISTORY

Difficult Problem

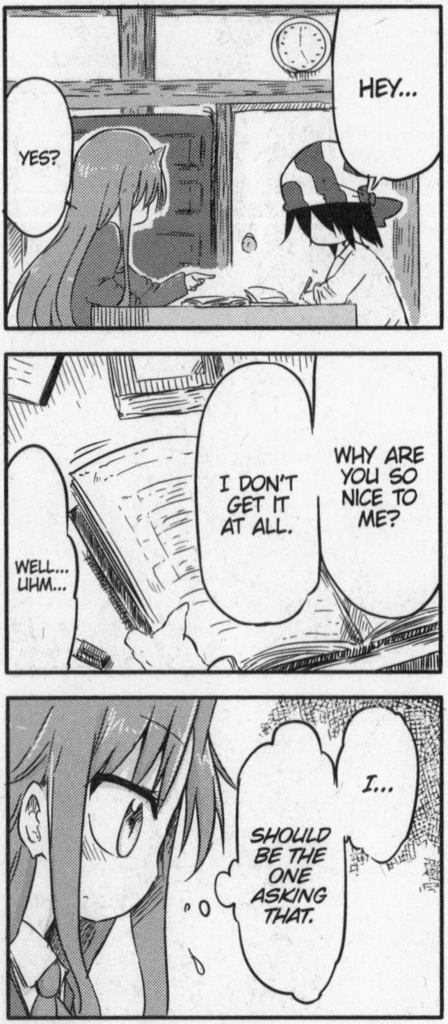
HEY...
YES?
WHY ARE YOU SO NICE TO ME?
I DON'T GET IT AT ALL.
WELL... UHM...
I...
SHOULD BE THE ONE ASKING THAT.
THE WEALTHY HAVE A DUTY TO SUPPORT THE LESS FORTUNATE.
I SEE.

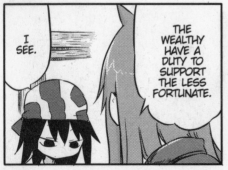

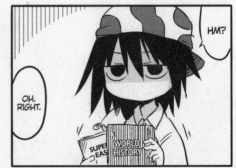

Uneventful

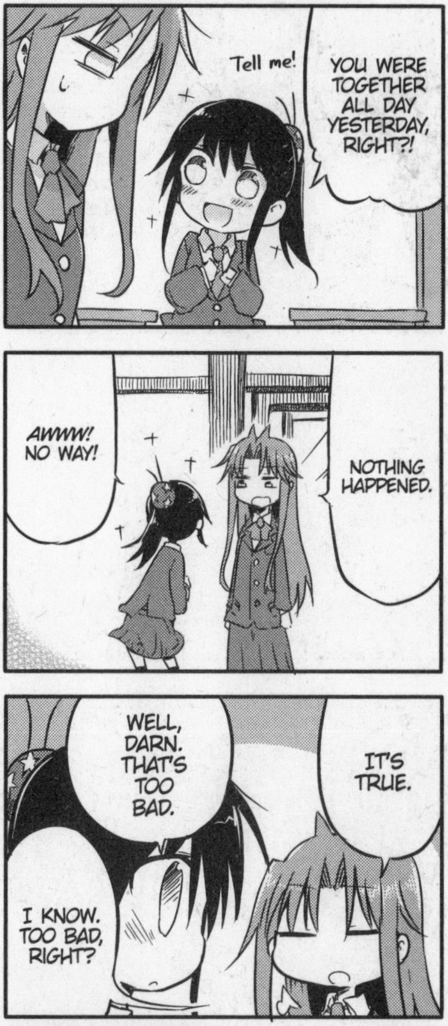

YOU WERE TOGETHER ALL DAY YESTERDAY, RIGHT?!
Tell me!
NOTHING HAPPENED.
AWWW! NO WAY!
IT'S TRUE.
WELL, DARN. THAT'S TOO BAD.
I KNOW. TOO BAD, RIGHT?
AH.

Eventful

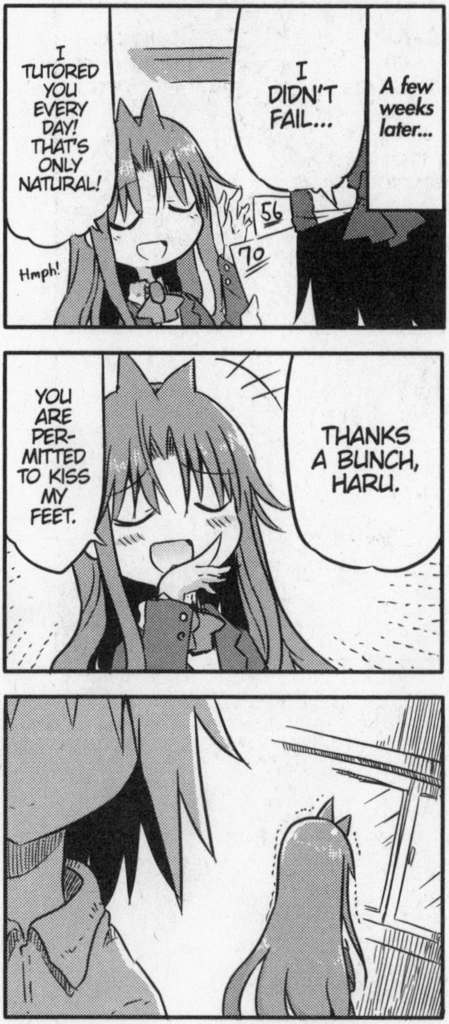

A few weeks later...
I DIDN'T FAIL...
56
70
I TUTORED YOU EVERY DAY! THAT'S ONLY NATURAL!
Hmph!
THANKS A BUNCH, HARU.
YOU ARE PERMITTED TO KISS MY FEET.
HE SAID MY NAME.
MY FIRST NAME...
MY FIRST NAME!!

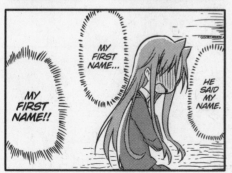

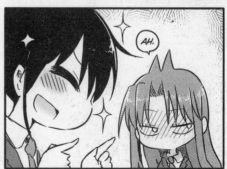

Perspective

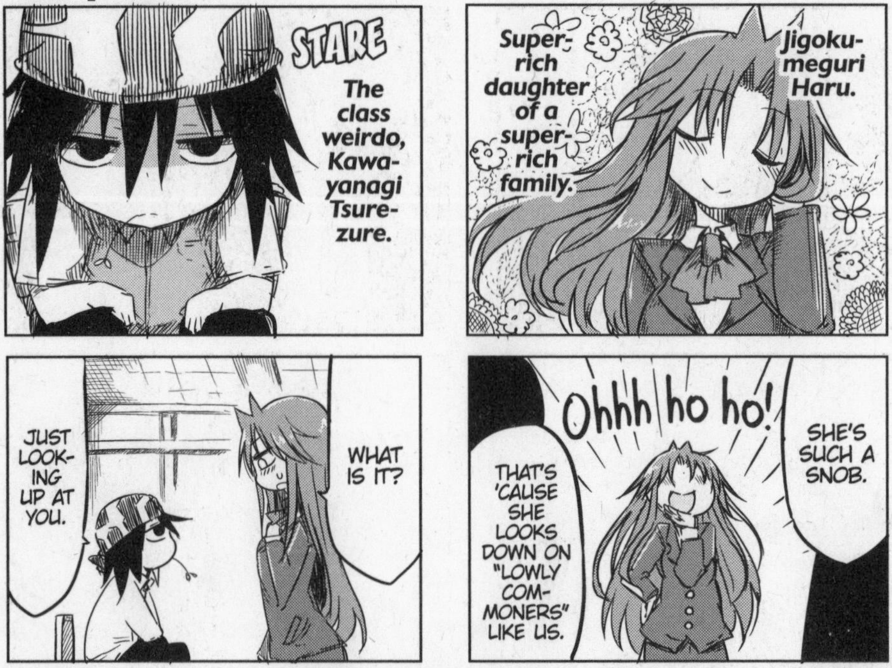
Jigoku-meguri Haru.
Super-rich daughter of a super-rich family.
STARE
The class weirdo, Kawa-yanagi Tsure-zure.
SHE'S SUCH A SNOB.
Ohhh ho ho!
THAT'S 'CAUSE SHE LOOKS DOWN ON "LOWLY COM-MONERS" LIKE US.
WHAT IS IT?
JUST LOOKING UP AT YOU.

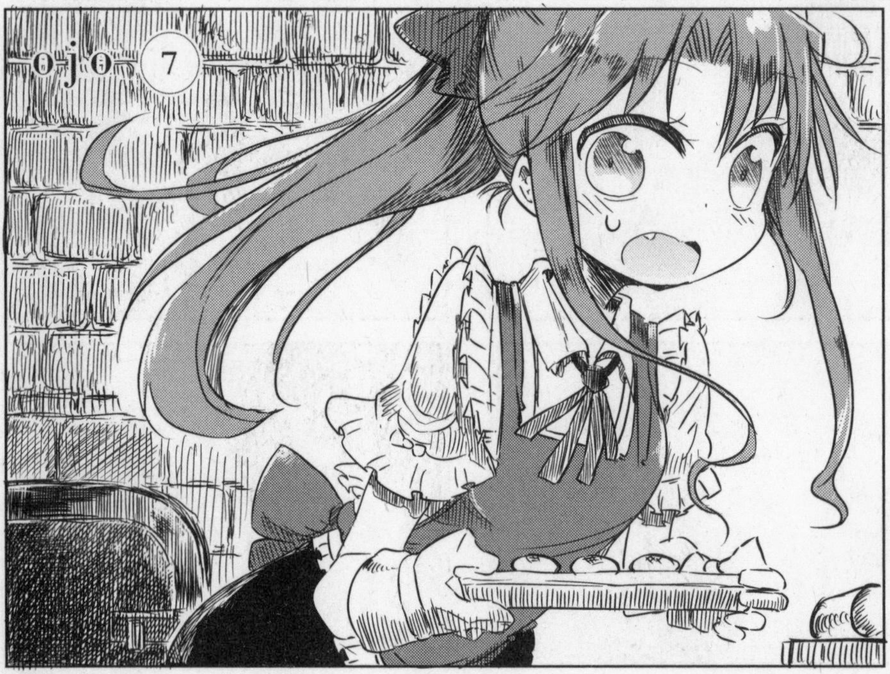
ojo 7

Usually Just Orders Food

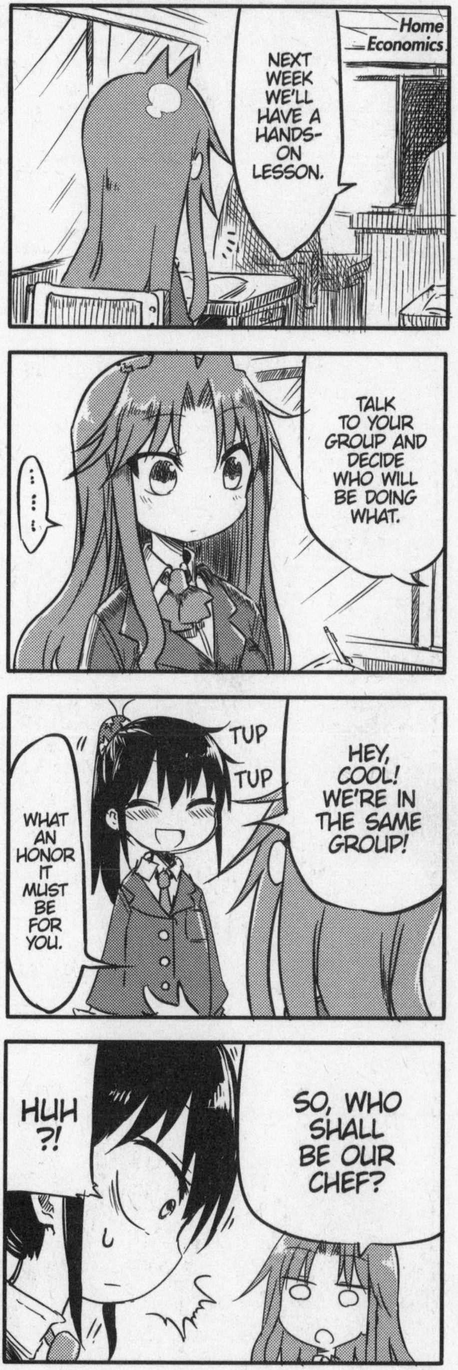
Home Economics
NEXT WEEK WE'LL HAVE A HANDS-ON LESSON.
TALK TO YOUR GROUP AND DECIDE WHO WILL BE DOING WHAT.
......?
HEY, COOL! WE'RE IN THE SAME GROUP!
TUP TUP
WHAT AN HONOR IT MUST BE FOR YOU.
SO, WHO SHALL BE OUR CHEF?
HUH ?!

His Usual Role

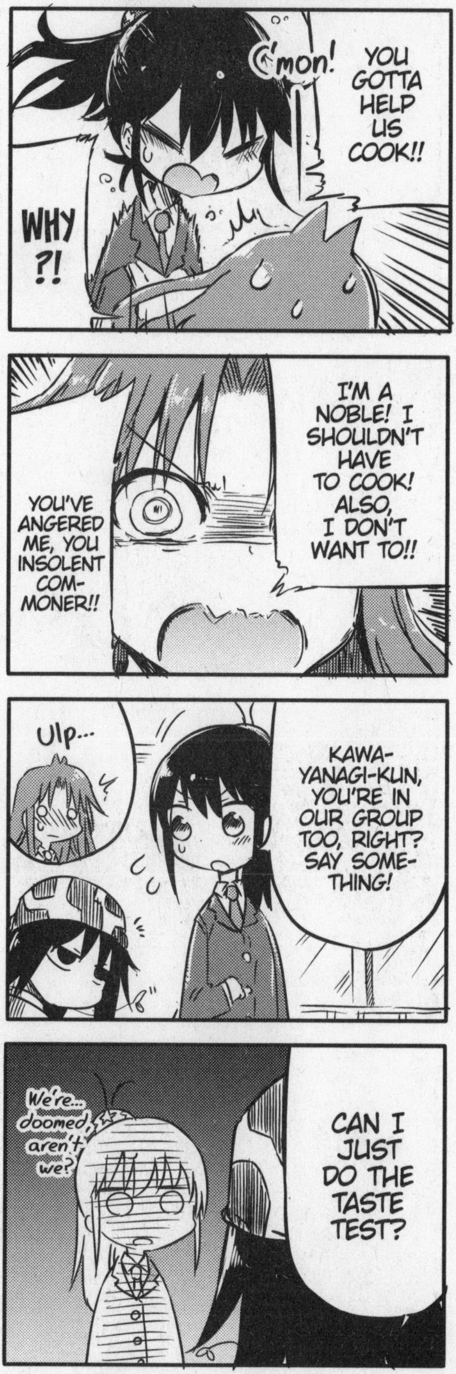
YOU GOTTA HELP US COOK!!
C'mon!
WHY ?!
I'M A NOBLE! I SHOULDN'T HAVE TO COOK! ALSO, I DON'T WANT TO!!
YOU'VE ANGERED ME, YOU INSOLENT COM-MONER!!
KAWA-YANAGI-KUN, YOU'RE IN OUR GROUP TOO, RIGHT? SAY SOME-THING!
Ulp...
CAN I JUST DO THE TASTE TEST?
We're... doomed, aren't we?

Easy to Handle, Once You Get the Hang of Her

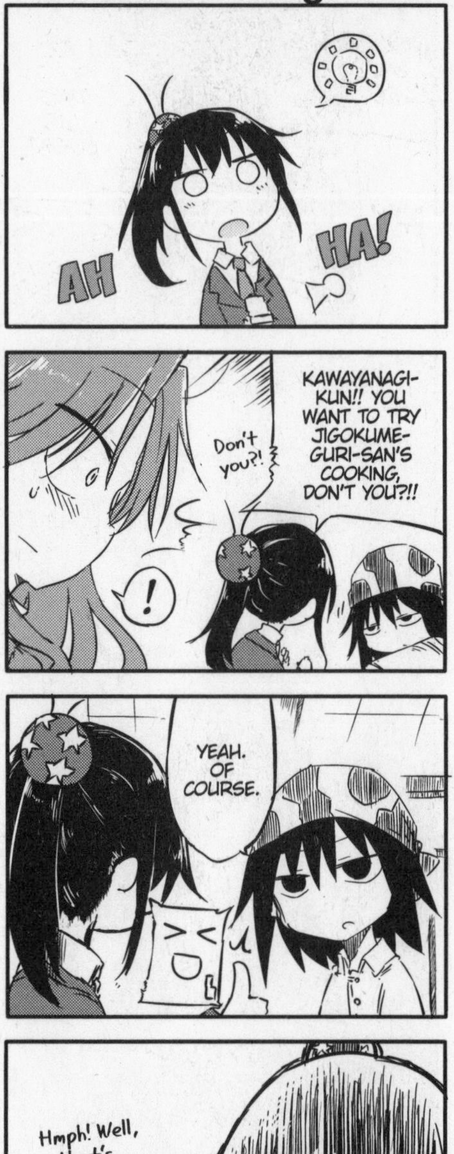
AH HA!
KAWAYANAGI-KUN!! YOU WANT TO TRY JIGOKUME-GURI-SAN'S COOKING, DON'T YOU?!!
Don't you?!
!
YEAH. OF COURSE.
Hmph! Well, that's... That's...

Never Allowed in the Kitchen Again

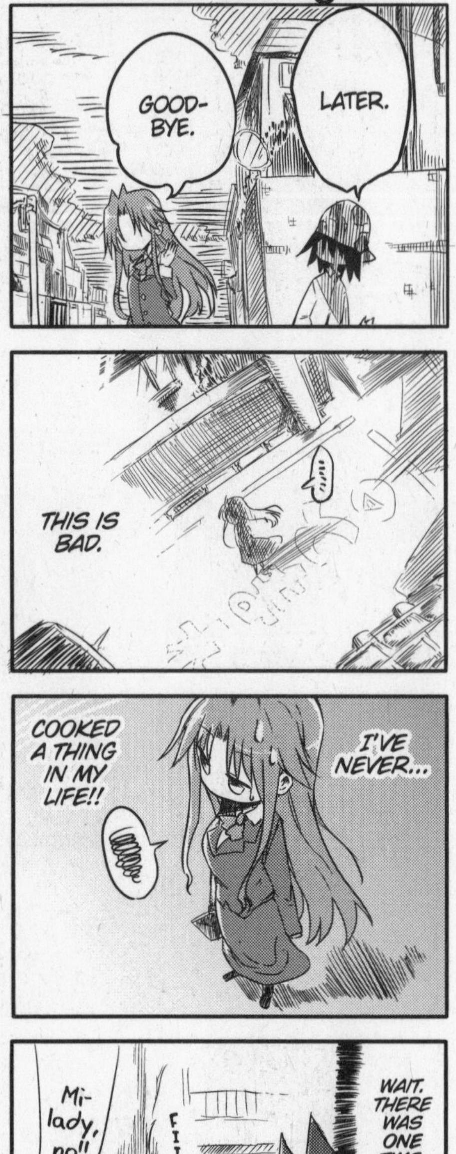
LATER.
GOOD-BYE.
THIS IS BAD.
I'VE NEVER...
COOKED A THING IN MY LIFE!!
WAIT. THERE WAS ONE TIME, WHEN I WAS A KID...
FIIIRE!
Mi-lady, no!!

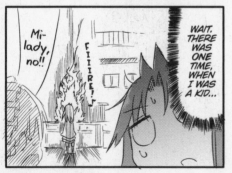

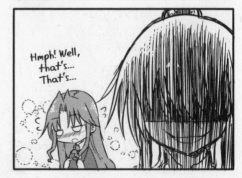

Going All Out

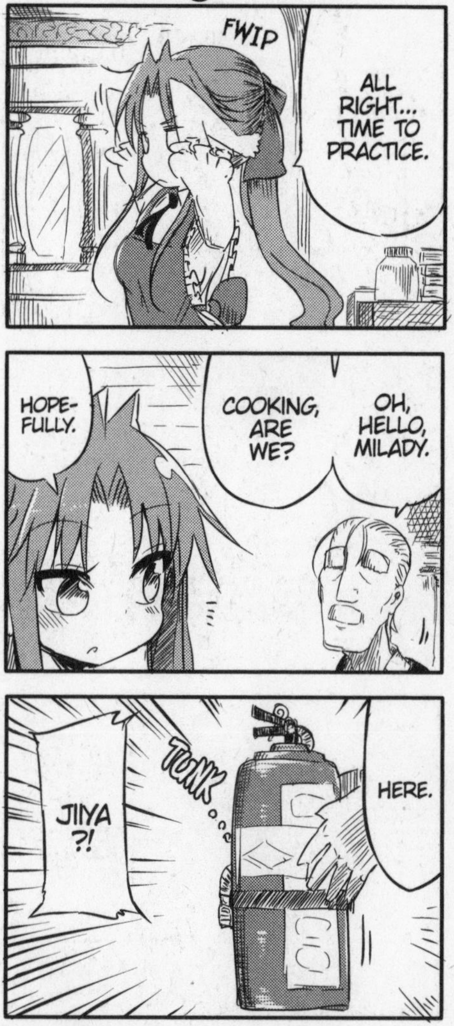
FWIP
ALL RIGHT... TIME TO PRACTICE.
OH, HELLO, MILADY.
COOKING, ARE WE?
HOPE-FULLY.
HERE.
TUNK
JIIYA ?!
SHOULD I CALL THE FIRE DEPART-MENT IN AD-VANCE?
JUST LEAVE THE EXTIN-GUISHER AND GET OUT!!

Fire

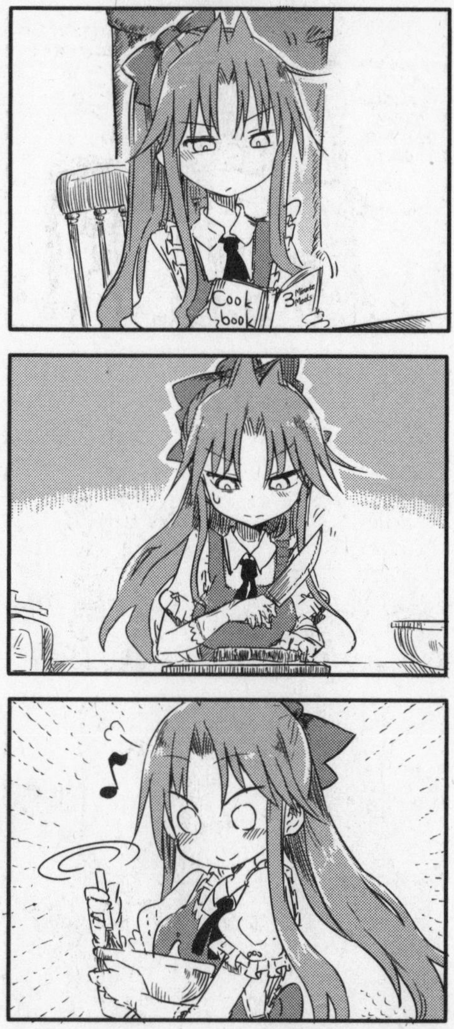
3 Minute Meals
Cook book
FWOOOOOSH
Oh. Fire...

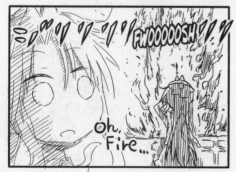

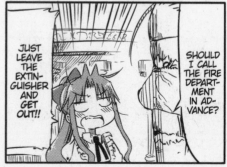

Yes but No

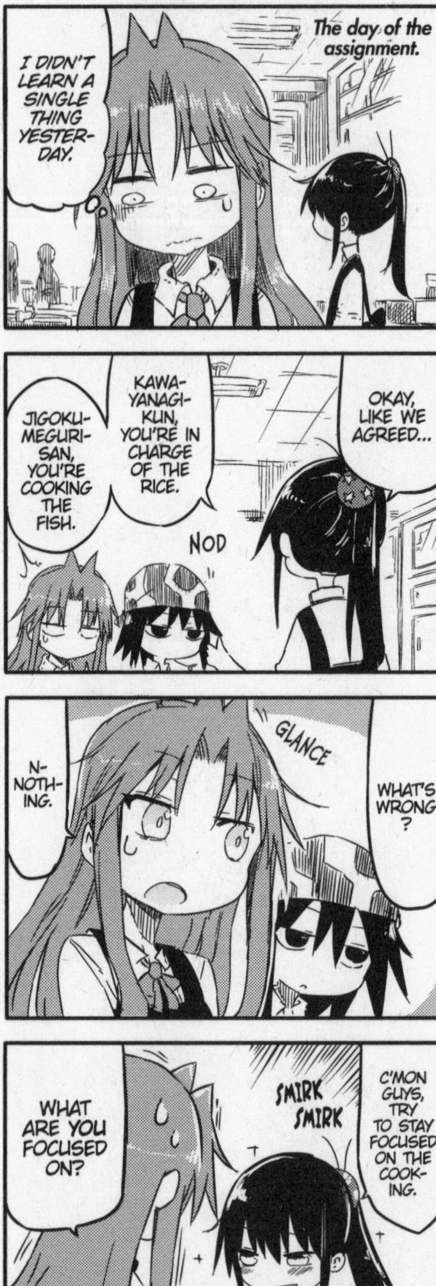
The day of the assignment.
I DIDN'T LEARN A SINGLE THING YESTERDAY.
OKAY, LIKE WE AGREED...
KAWAYANAGI-KUN, YOU'RE IN CHARGE OF THE RICE.
JIGOKUMEGURI-SAN, YOU'RE COOKING THE FISH.
NOD
WHAT'S WRONG?
GLANCE
N-NOTHING.
C'MON GUYS, TRY TO STAY FOCUSED ON THE COOKING.
SMIRK SMIRK
WHAT ARE YOU FOCUSED ON?

The Hawk That Can't Be Bothered to Use Its Talons

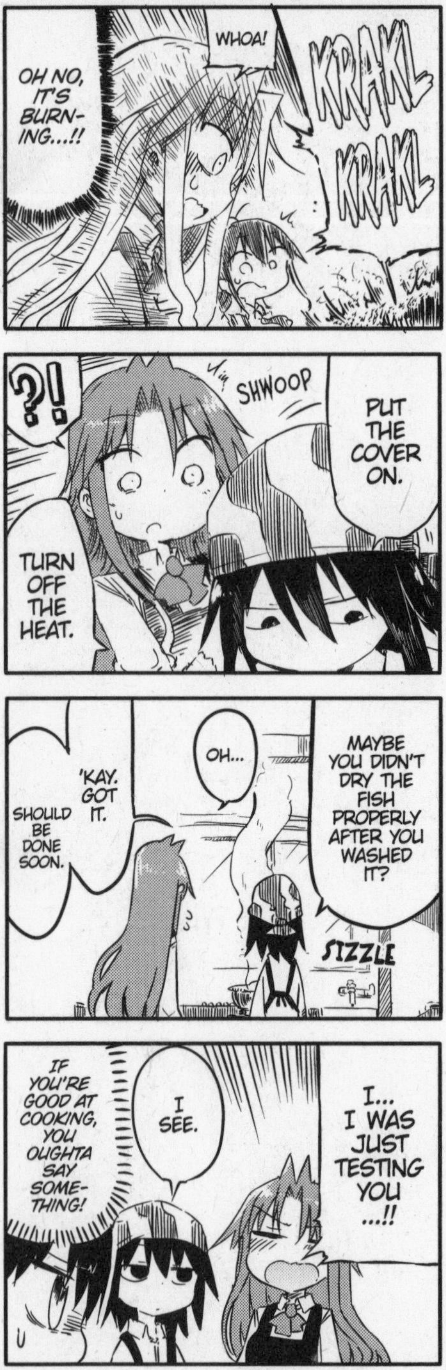
KRAKL
KRAKL
WHOA!
OH NO, IT'S BURNING...!!
PUT THE COVER ON.
SHWOOP
?!
TURN OFF THE HEAT.
MAYBE YOU DIDN'T DRY THE FISH PROPERLY AFTER YOU WASHED IT?
OH...
'KAY. GOT IT.
SHOULD BE DONE SOON.
SIZZLE
I... I WAS JUST TESTING YOU ...!!
I SEE.
IF YOU'RE GOOD AT COOKING, YOU OUGHTA SAY SOMETHING!

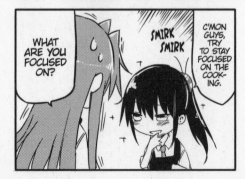

Burnt Salmon, Burning Love

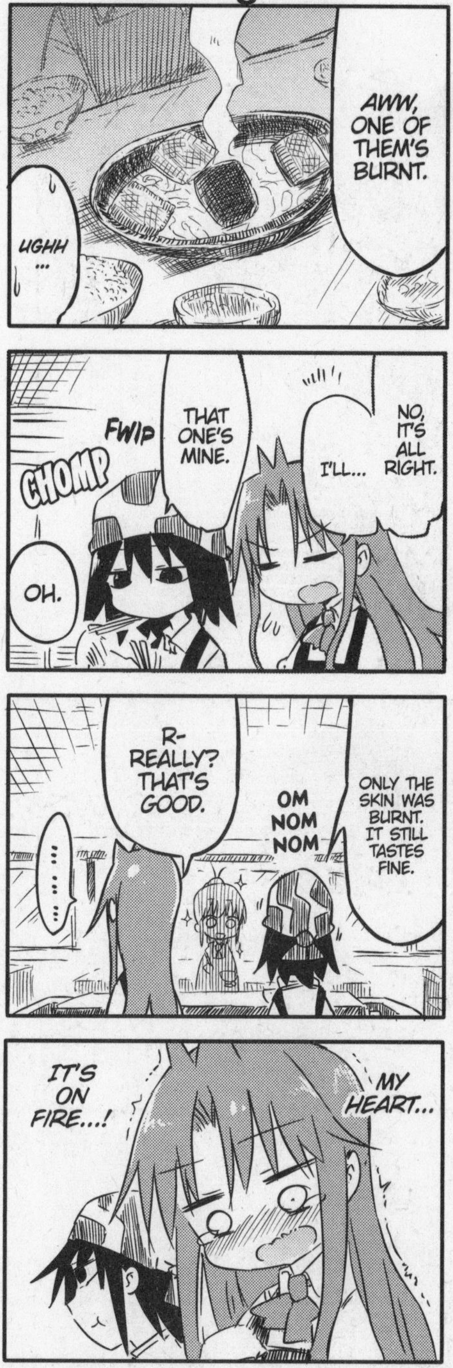
AWW, ONE OF THEM'S BURNT.
UGHH...
NO, IT'S ALL RIGHT.
I'LL...
FWIP
THAT ONE'S MINE.
CHOMP
OH.
ONLY THE SKIN WAS BURNT. IT STILL TASTES FINE.
OM NOM NOM
R-REALLY? THAT'S GOOD.
......
MY HEART...
IT'S ON FIRE...!

Burning Love, and Burning Home

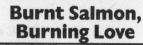

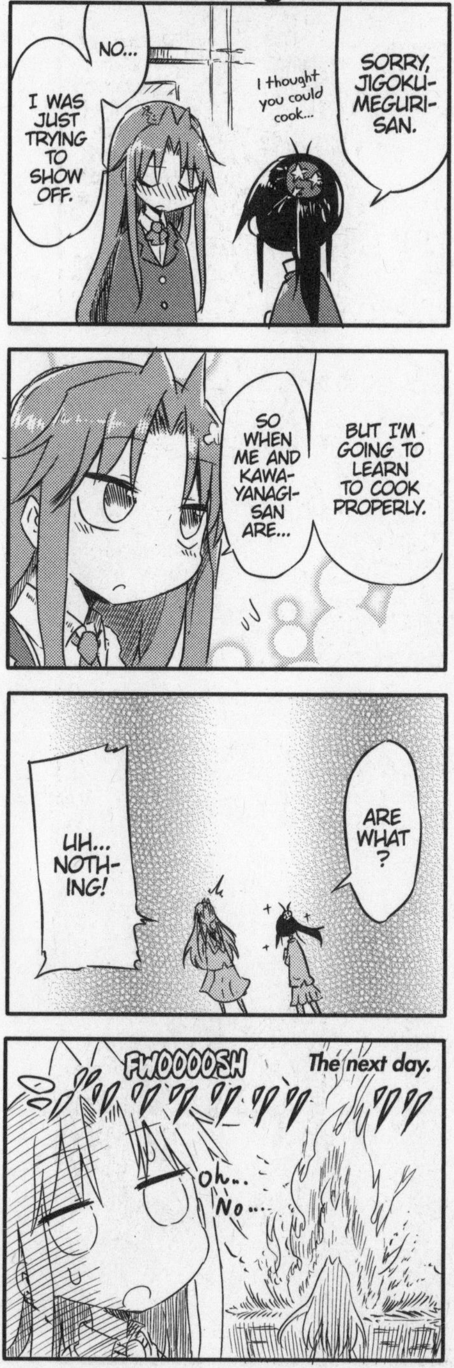
SORRY, JIGOKU-MEGURI-SAN.
I thought you could cook...
NO...
I WAS JUST TRYING TO SHOW OFF.
BUT I'M GOING TO LEARN TO COOK PROPERLY.
SO WHEN ME AND KAWA-YANAGI-SAN ARE...
ARE WHAT?
UH... NOTHING!
The next day.
FWOOOOSH
Oh... No...

The Distance Between Them

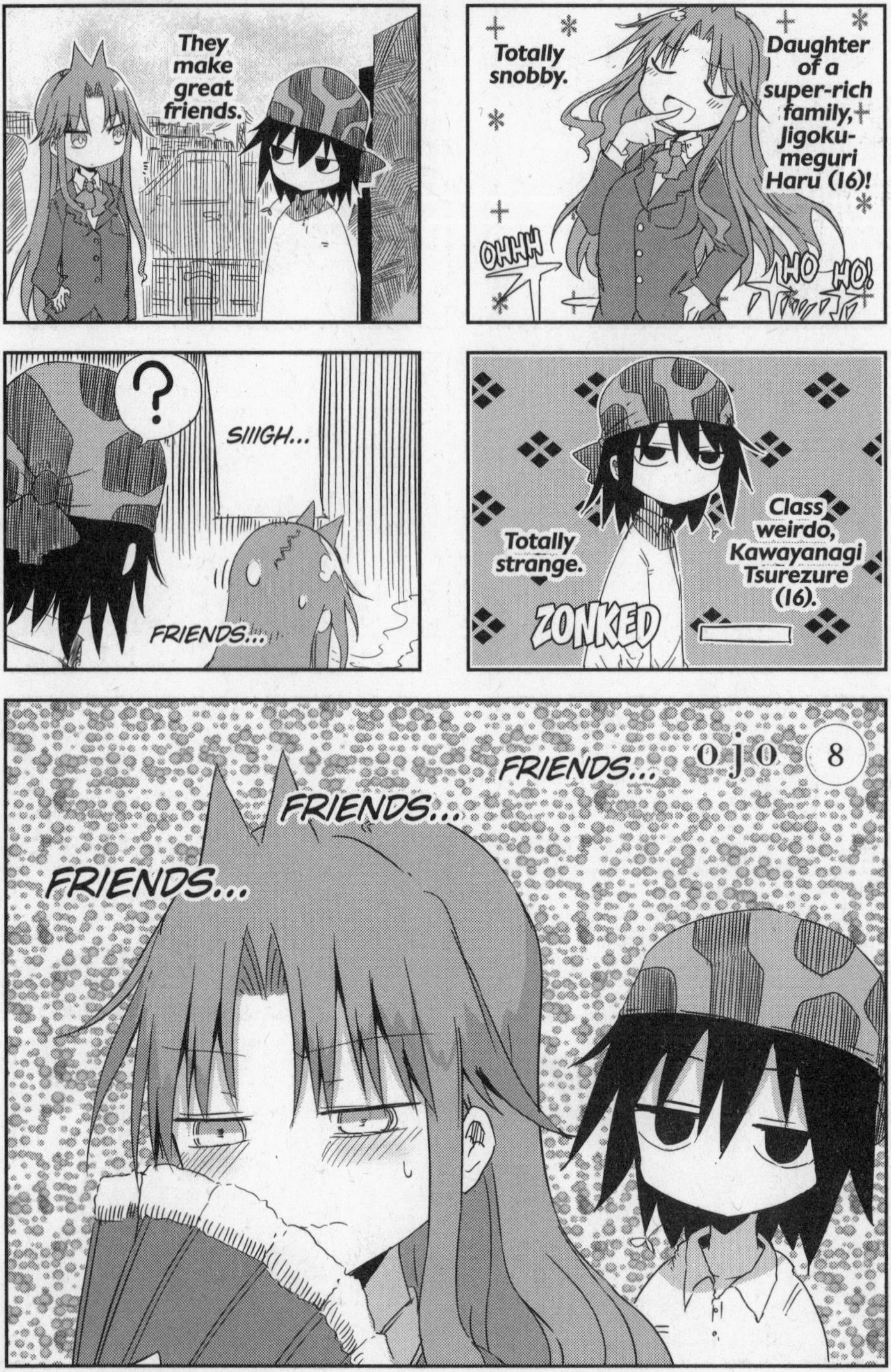
Daughter of a super-rich family, Jigoku-meguri Haru (16)!
Totally snobby.
OHHH
HO HO!
They make great friends.
Class weirdo, Kawayanagi Tsurezure (16).
Totally strange.
ZONKED
?
SIIGH...
FRIENDS...
ojo 8
FRIENDS...
FRIENDS...
FRIENDS...

Snob-dere

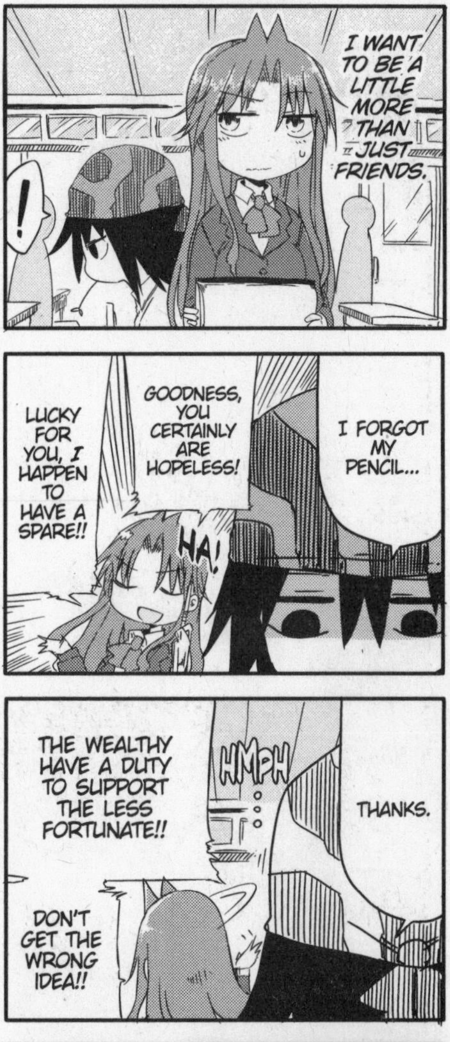
I WANT TO BE A LITTLE MORE THAN JUST FRIENDS.
!
I FORGOT MY PENCIL...
GOODNESS, YOU CERTAINLY ARE HOPELESS!
LUCKY FOR YOU, I HAPPEN TO HAVE A SPARE!!
HA!
THANKS.
HMPH
THE WEALTHY HAVE A DUTY TO SUPPORT THE LESS FORTUNATE!!
DON'T GET THE WRONG IDEA!!
?
Still working on it.

Watching the Watcher

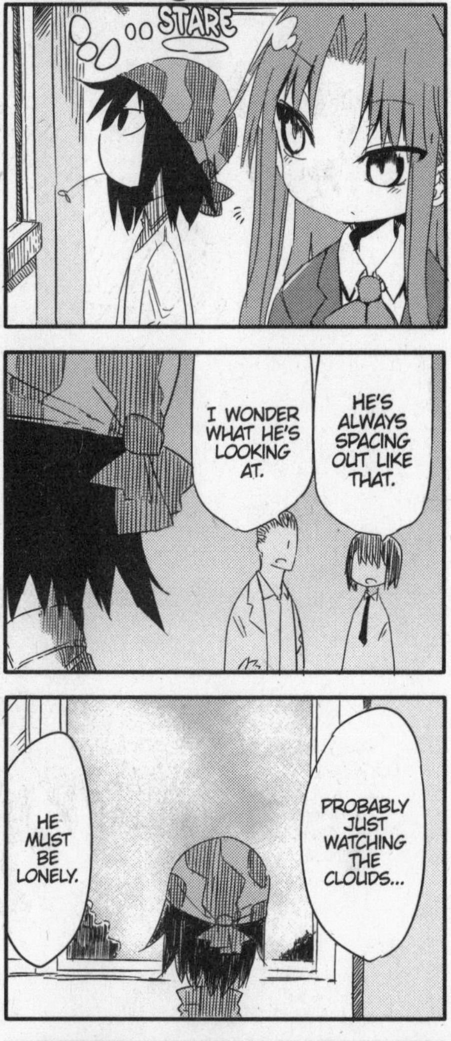
STARE
HE'S ALWAYS SPACING OUT LIKE THAT.
I WONDER WHAT HE'S LOOKING AT.
PROBABLY JUST WATCHING THE CLOUDS...
HE MUST BE LONELY.
I BET HE'S LOOKING AT SPIDERS AGAIN.

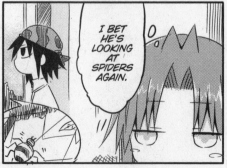

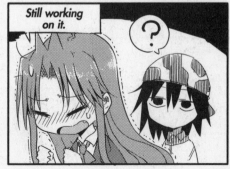

Where Did You Get That?

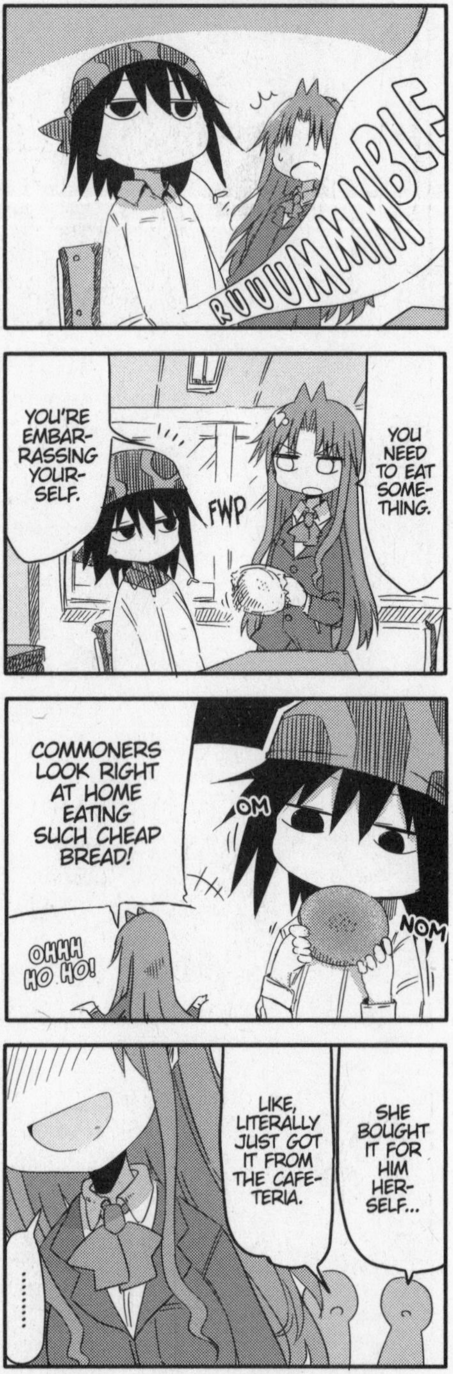
RUUUMMMBLE
YOU NEED TO EAT SOMETHING.
FWP
YOU'RE EMBARRASSING YOURSELF.
COMMONERS LOOK RIGHT AT HOME EATING SUCH CHEAP BREAD!
OM
NOM
OHHH HO HO!
SHE BOUGHT IT FOR HIM HERSELF...
LIKE, LITERALLY JUST GOT IT FROM THE CAFETERIA.
......

The War Between Great and Small

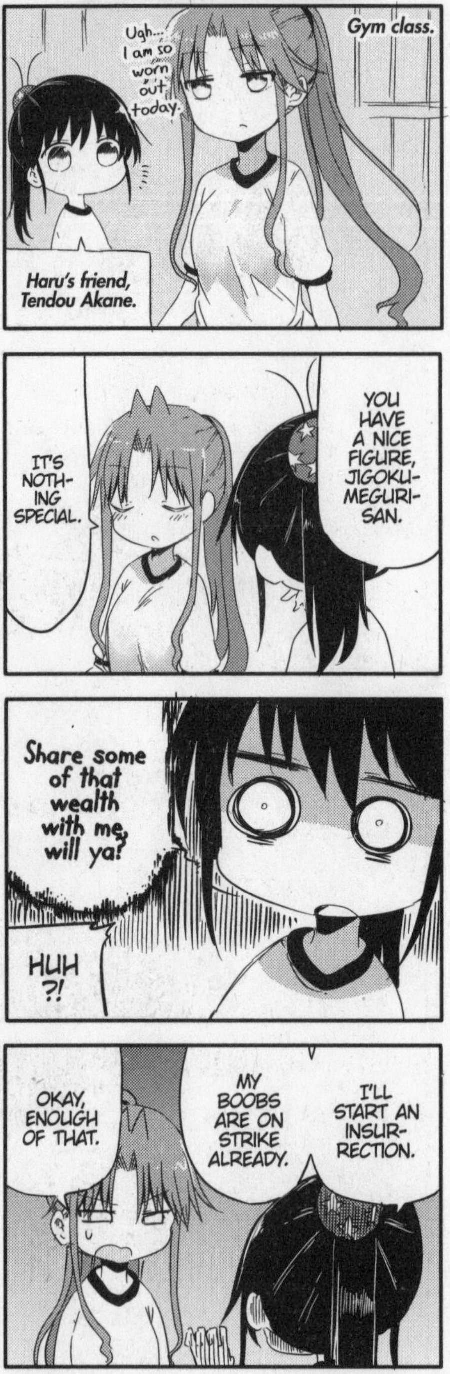
Gym class.
Ugh... I am so worn out today.
Haru's friend, Tendou Akane.
YOU HAVE A NICE FIGURE, JIGOKUMEGURI-SAN.
IT'S NOTHING SPECIAL.
Share some of that wealth with me, will ya?
HUH ?!
I'LL START AN INSURRECTION.
MY BOOBS ARE ON STRIKE ALREADY.
OKAY, ENOUGH OF THAT.

This Is Too Close

YOU CAN HAVE THIS BACK.
From this morning...
HM... I CAN'T SEEM TO CLOSE THE DISTANCE BETWEEN US.
Thanks.
TA-
TUP...
FLINCH
MEEP!
HUFF!
HUFF!
IT SEEMS I MAY NEED SOME OUTSIDE ASSISTANCE WITH THIS.

A Problem of Trust

WELCOME HOME, MILADY.
JIIYA...
HOW DO I IMPROVE MY RELATIONSHIP WITH PEOPLE?
HO HO HO...
I'M SURE THERE'S A WALK-THROUGH ONLINE IF YOU'RE STRUGGLING WITH A PARTICULAR CHARACTER.
GRIN...
JIIYA!
REAL PEOPLE! NOT VIDEO GAME ONES!!
HEH HEH!
CAN'T DISTINGUISH FANTASY FROM REALITY, I SEE.

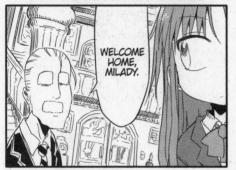

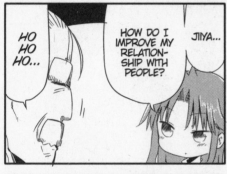

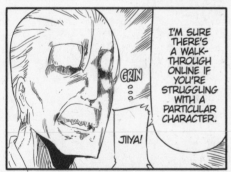

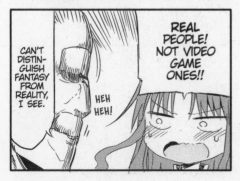

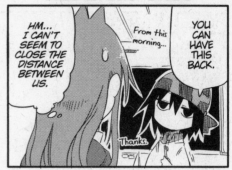

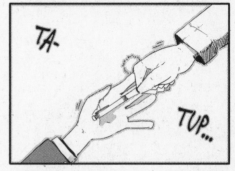

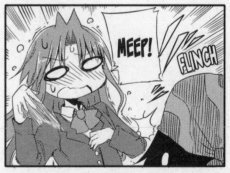

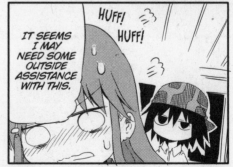

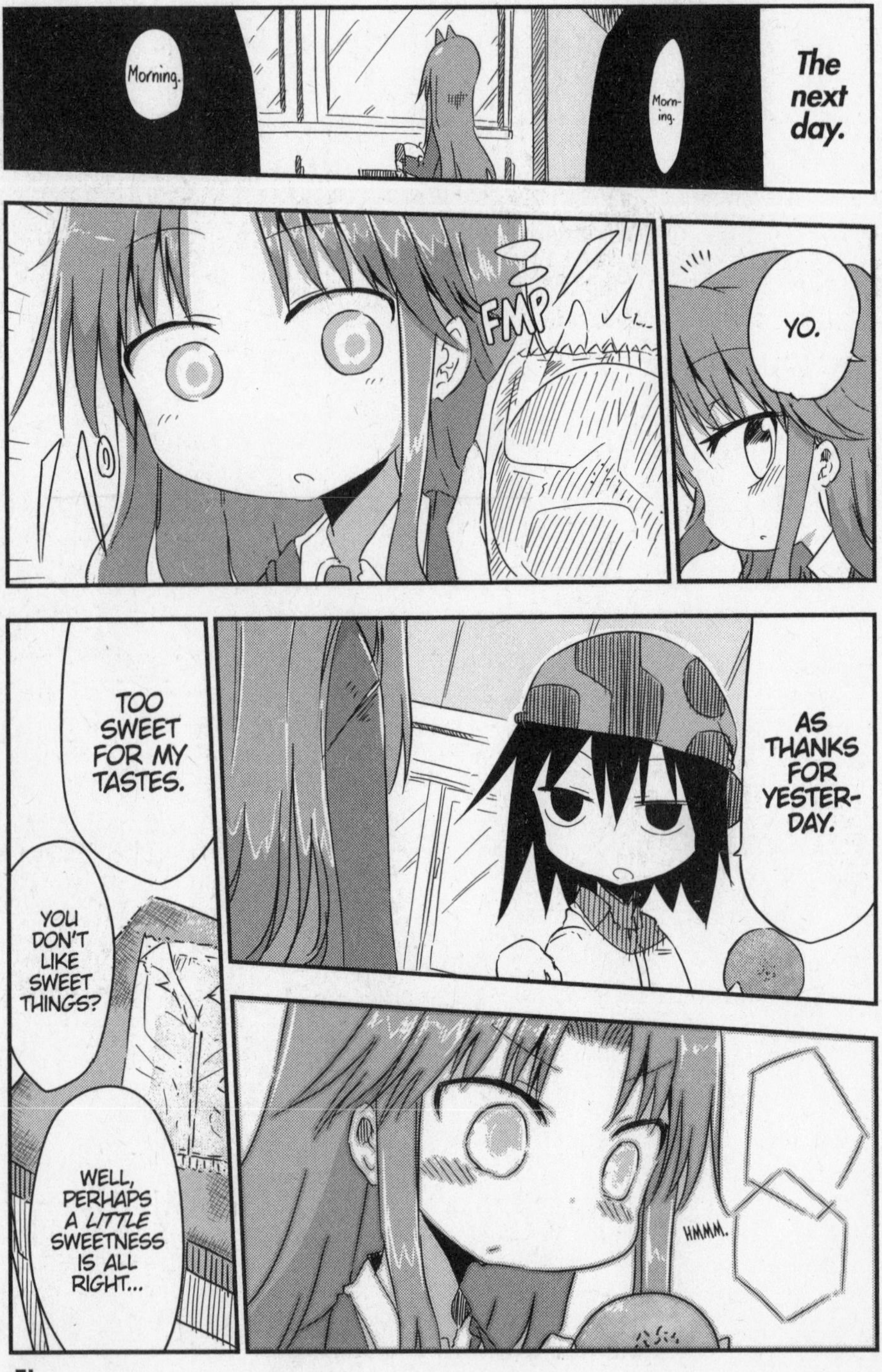
The next day.
Morn-ing.
Morning.
YO.
FMP
AS THANKS FOR YESTER-DAY.
TOO SWEET FOR MY TASTES.
YOU DON'T LIKE SWEET THINGS?
HMMM.
WELL, PERHAPS A *LITTLE* SWEETNESS IS ALL RIGHT...

Jigokumeguri
Haru

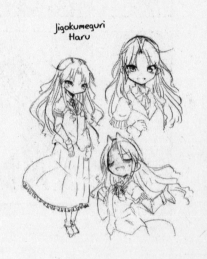

Kawayanagi
Tsurezure

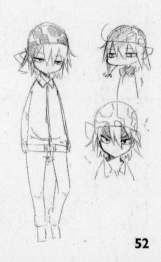

Same Way You'd Use a Balcony

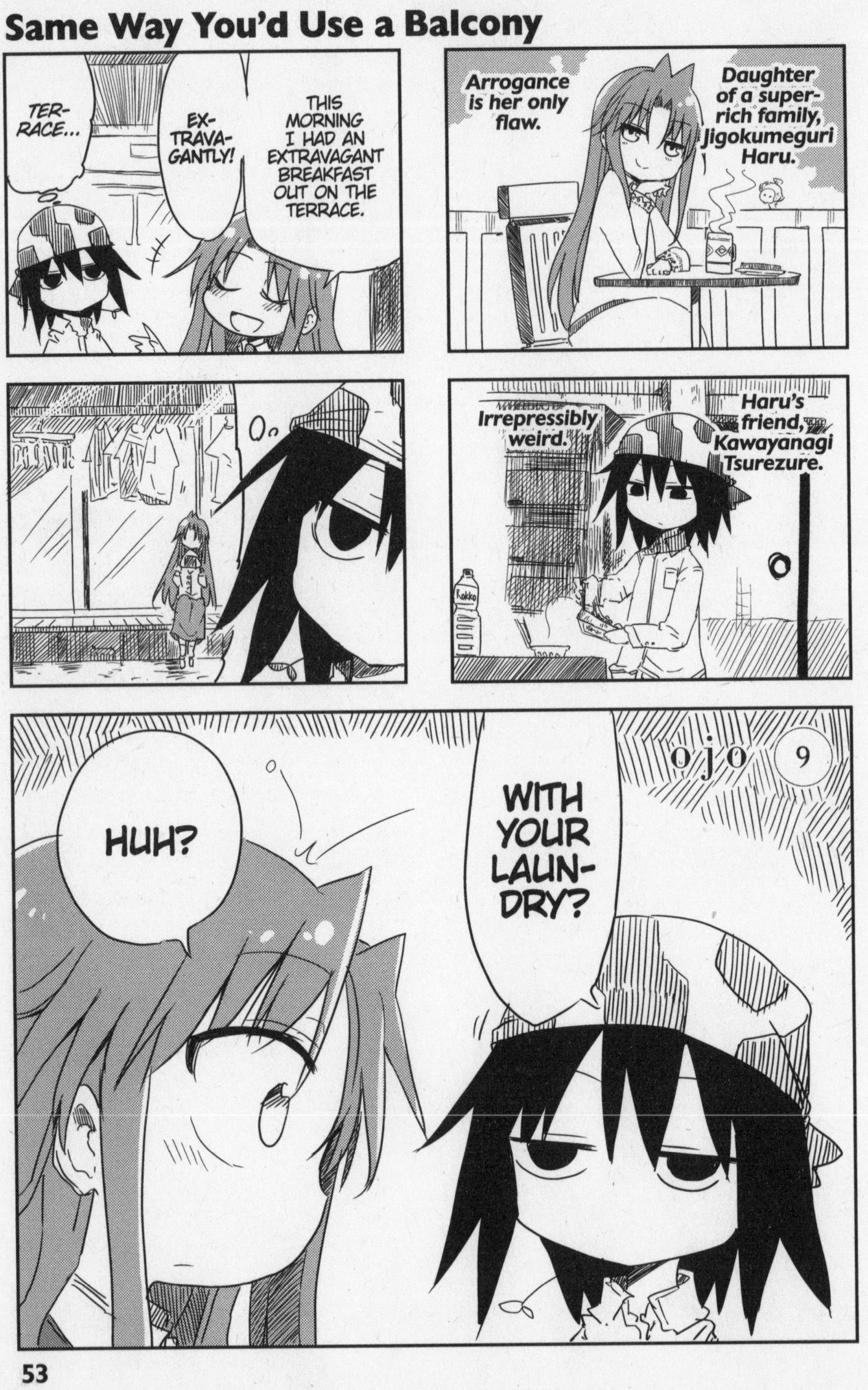
Daughter of a super-rich family, Jigokumeguri Haru.
Arrogance is her only flaw.
THIS MORNING I HAD AN EXTRAVAGANT BREAKFAST OUT ON THE TERRACE.
EX-TRAVA-GANTLY!
TER-RACE...
Haru's friend, Kawayanagi Tsurezure.
Irrepressibly weird.
Rokko
ojo 9
WITH YOUR LAUN-DRY?
HUH?

Haru's House

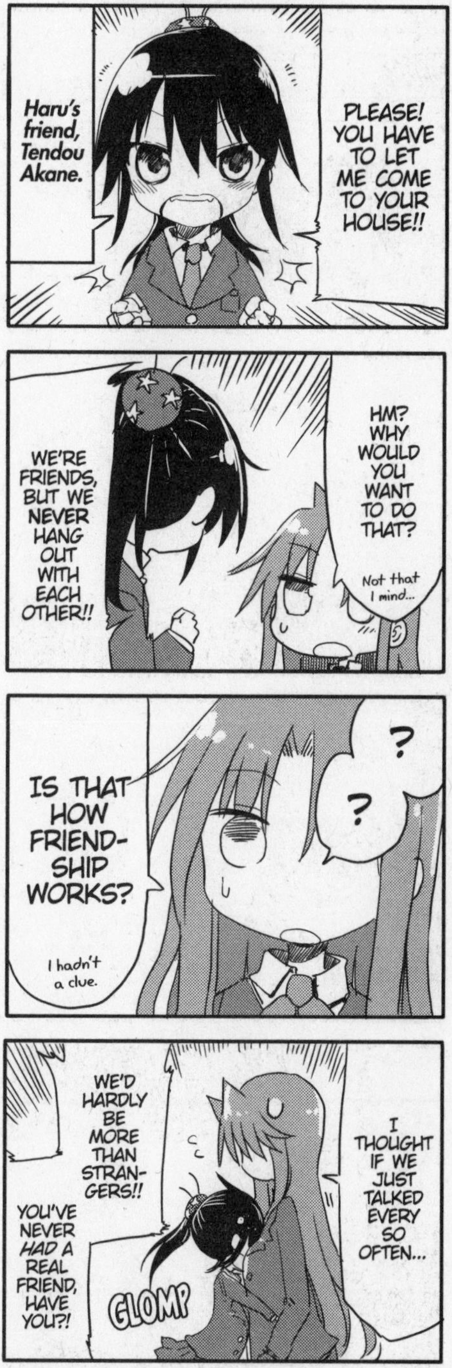
PLEASE! YOU HAVE TO LET ME COME TO YOUR HOUSE!!
Haru's friend, Tendou Akane.
HM? WHY WOULD YOU WANT TO DO THAT?
Not that I mind...
WE'RE FRIENDS, BUT WE NEVER HANG OUT WITH EACH OTHER!!
? ?
IS THAT HOW FRIENDSHIP WORKS?
I hadn't a clue.
I THOUGHT IF WE JUST TALKED EVERY SO OFTEN...
WE'D HARDLY BE MORE THAN STRANGERS!!
YOU'VE NEVER HAD A REAL FRIEND, HAVE YOU?!
GLOMP

Say Her Name Already

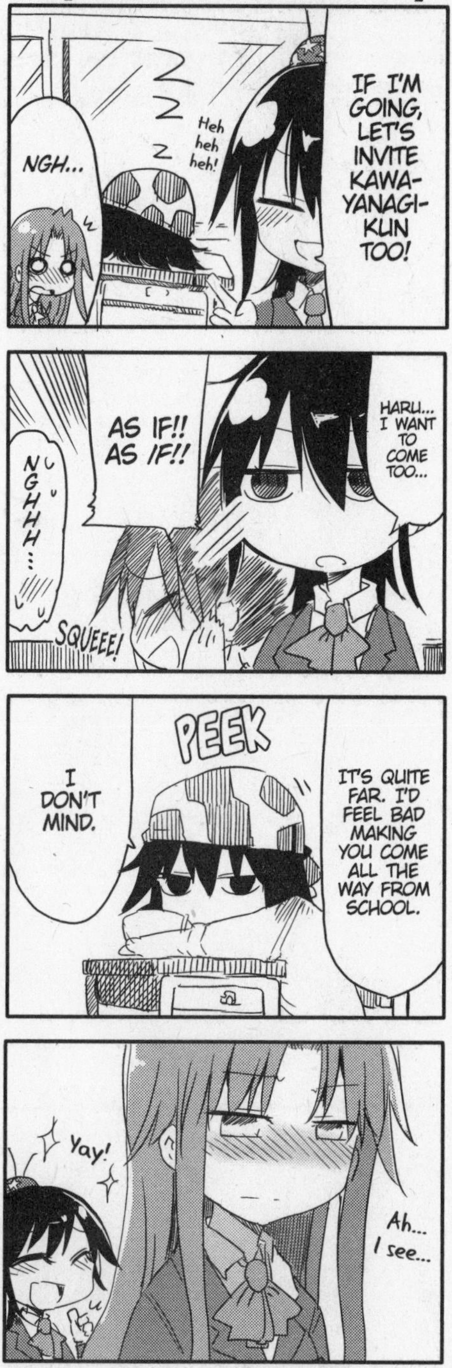
IF I'M GOING, LET'S INVITE KAWA-YANAGI-KUN TOO!
Heh heh heh!
Z Z Z
NGH...
HARU... I WANT TO COME TOO...
AS IF!! AS IF!!
NGHHH...
SQUEEE!
IT'S QUITE FAR. I'D FEEL BAD MAKING YOU COME ALL THE WAY FROM SCHOOL.
PEEK
I DON'T MIND.
Ah... I see...
Yay!

A Chance of Air Friends

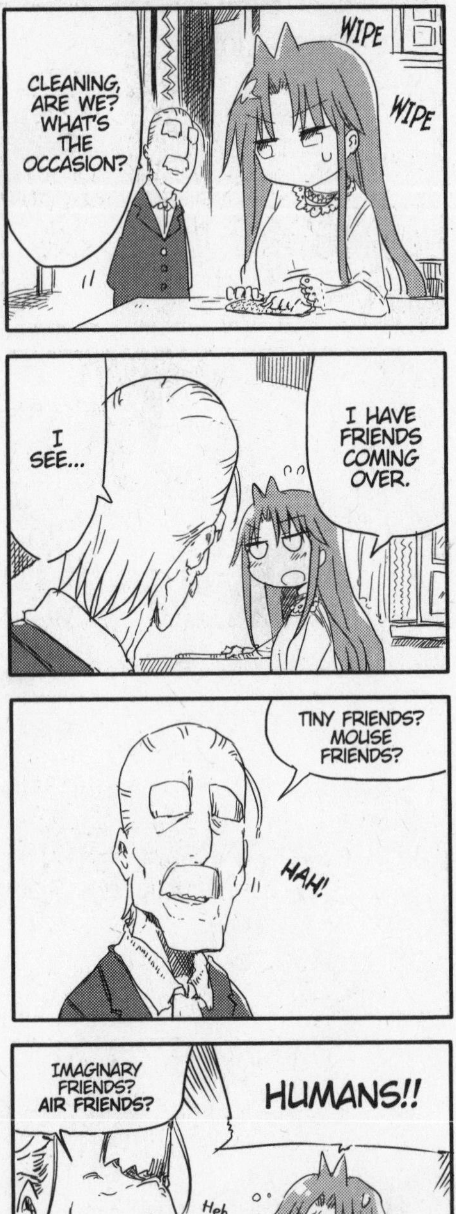
WIPE
WIPE
CLEANING, ARE WE? WHAT'S THE OCCASION?
I HAVE FRIENDS COMING OVER.
I SEE...
TINY FRIENDS? MOUSE FRIENDS?
HAH!
IMAGINARY FRIENDS? AIR FRIENDS?
HUMANS!!
Heh heh!

An Understanding

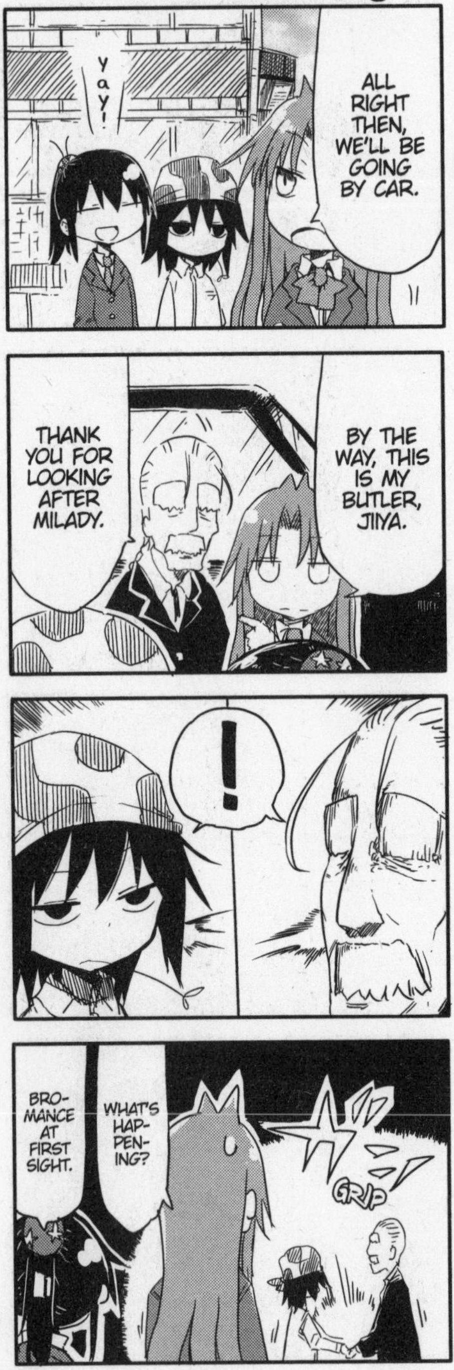
ALL RIGHT THEN, WE'LL BE GOING BY CAR.
yay!
BY THE WAY, THIS IS MY BUTLER, JIYA.
THANK YOU FOR LOOKING AFTER MILADY.
!
WHAT'S HAP-PEN-ING?
BRO-MANCE AT FIRST SIGHT.
GRIP

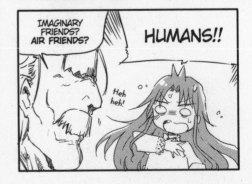

Food

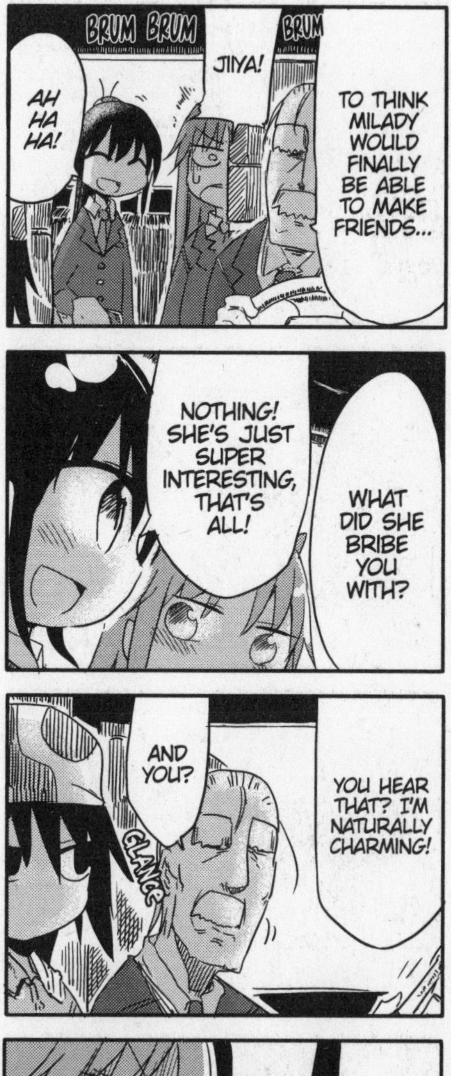
BRUM
TO THINK MILADY WOULD FINALLY BE ABLE TO MAKE FRIENDS...
JIIYA!
BRUM BRUM
AH HA HA!
WHAT DID SHE BRIBE YOU WITH?
NOTHING! SHE'S JUST SUPER INTERESTING, THAT'S ALL!
YOU HEAR THAT? I'M NATURALLY CHARMING!
AND YOU?
GLANCE
SWEET BREAD.
?!
I KNEW IT...

Waiting for the Line

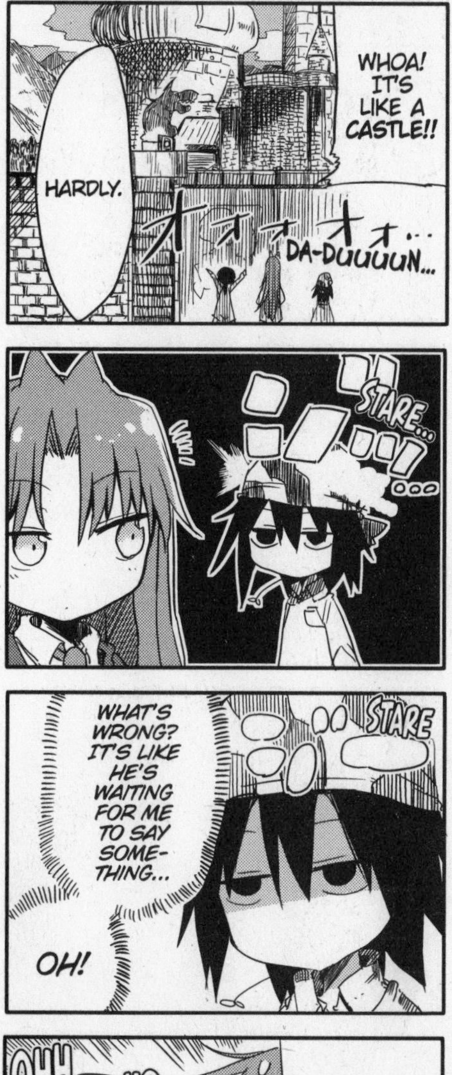
WHOA! IT'S LIKE A CASTLE!!
HARDLY.
DA-DUUUUN...
オォォオォ...
STARE...
...
STARE
WHAT'S WRONG? IT'S LIKE HE'S WAITING FOR ME TO SAY SOME-THING...
OH!
A FAR CRY FROM THE FILTHY DOG HOUSES YOU LIVE IN!!
OHH—HO HO!
Whoaaa!

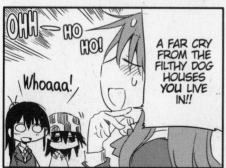

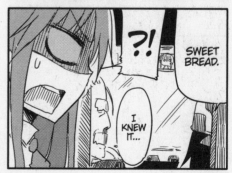

Hmmm...

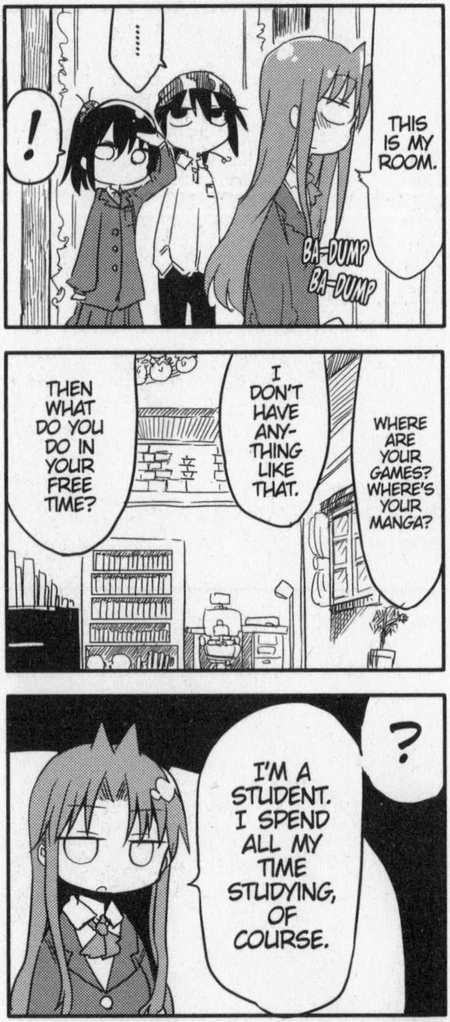
THIS IS MY ROOM.
BA-DUMP BA-DUMP
……
!
WHERE ARE YOUR GAMES? WHERE'S YOUR MANGA?
I DON'T HAVE ANYTHING LIKE THAT.
THEN WHAT DO YOU DO IN YOUR FREE TIME?
?
I'M A STUDENT. I SPEND ALL MY TIME STUDYING, OF COURSE.
HUH?
WHA?
WHAT?

Not a Good First Impression

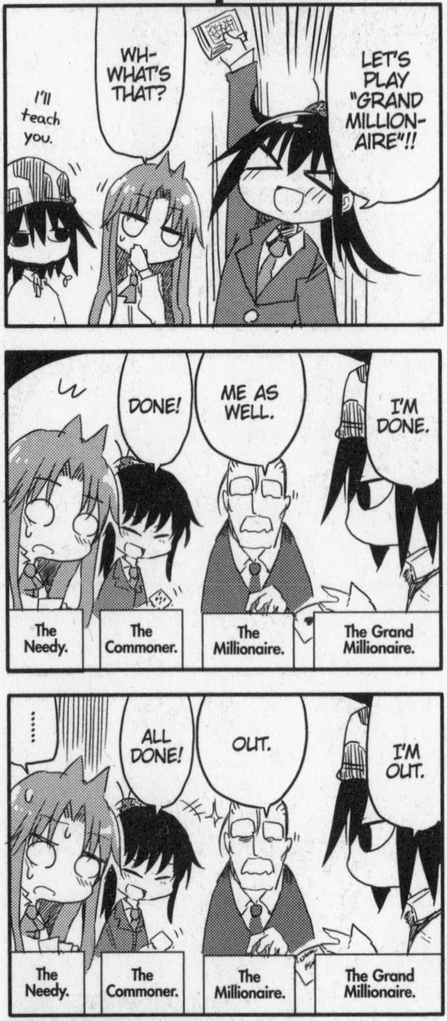
LET'S PLAY "GRAND MILLIONAIRE"!!
WH-WHAT'S THAT?
I'll teach you.
I'M DONE.
ME AS WELL.
DONE!
The Grand Millionaire.
The Millionaire.
The Commoner.
The Needy.
I'M OUT.
OUT.
ALL DONE!
……
The Grand Millionaire.
The Millionaire.
The Commoner.
The Needy.
SHOWING MERCY TO THE COMMONERS?
GRRR...

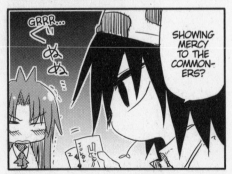

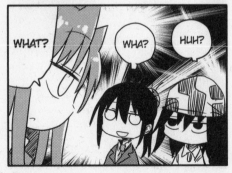

And You Still Are Today

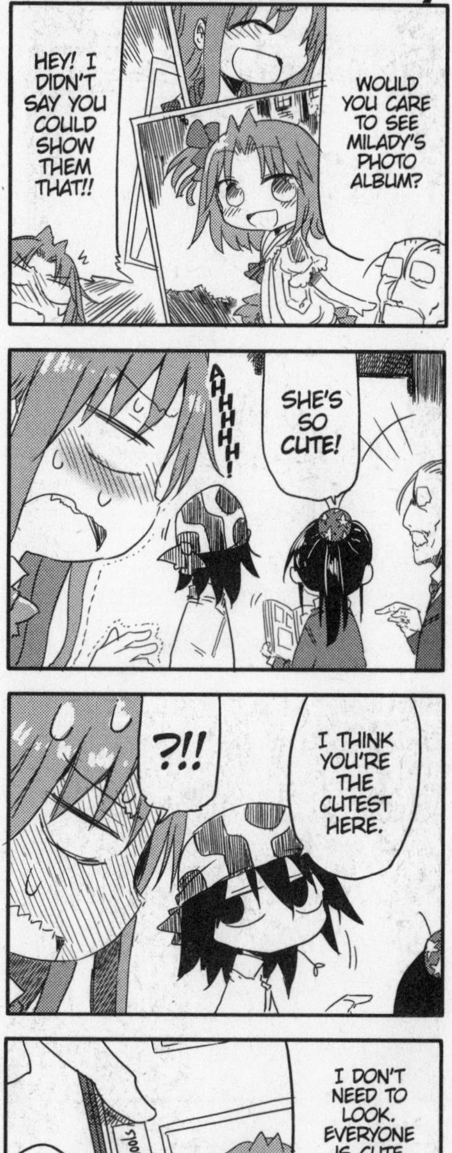
WOULD YOU CARE TO SEE MILADY'S PHOTO ALBUM?
HEY! I DIDN'T SAY YOU COULD SHOW THEM THAT!!
SHE'S SO CUTE!
AHHHHH!
I THINK YOU'RE THE CUTEST HERE.
?!!
I DON'T NEED TO LOOK. EVERYONE IS CUTE WHEN THEY'RE A CHILD!
Transferred schools
IF YOU SAY SO...

Those Words

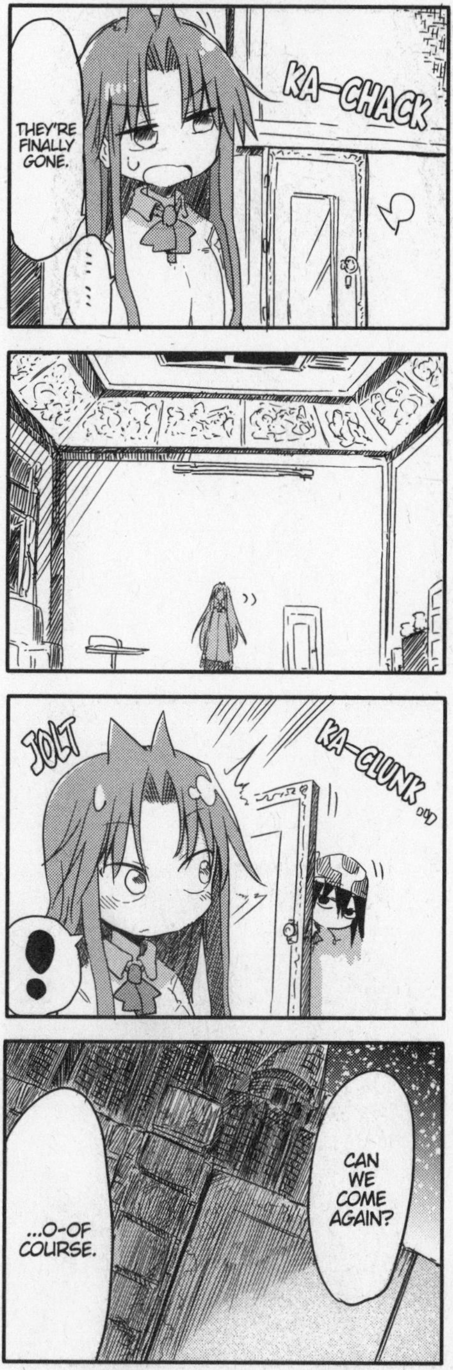
KA-CHACK
THEY'RE FINALLY GONE.
...
KA-CLUNK
JOLT
!
CAN WE COME AGAIN?
...O-OF COURSE.

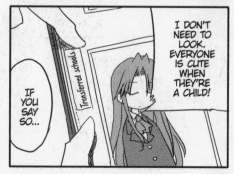

A Quartet of Two

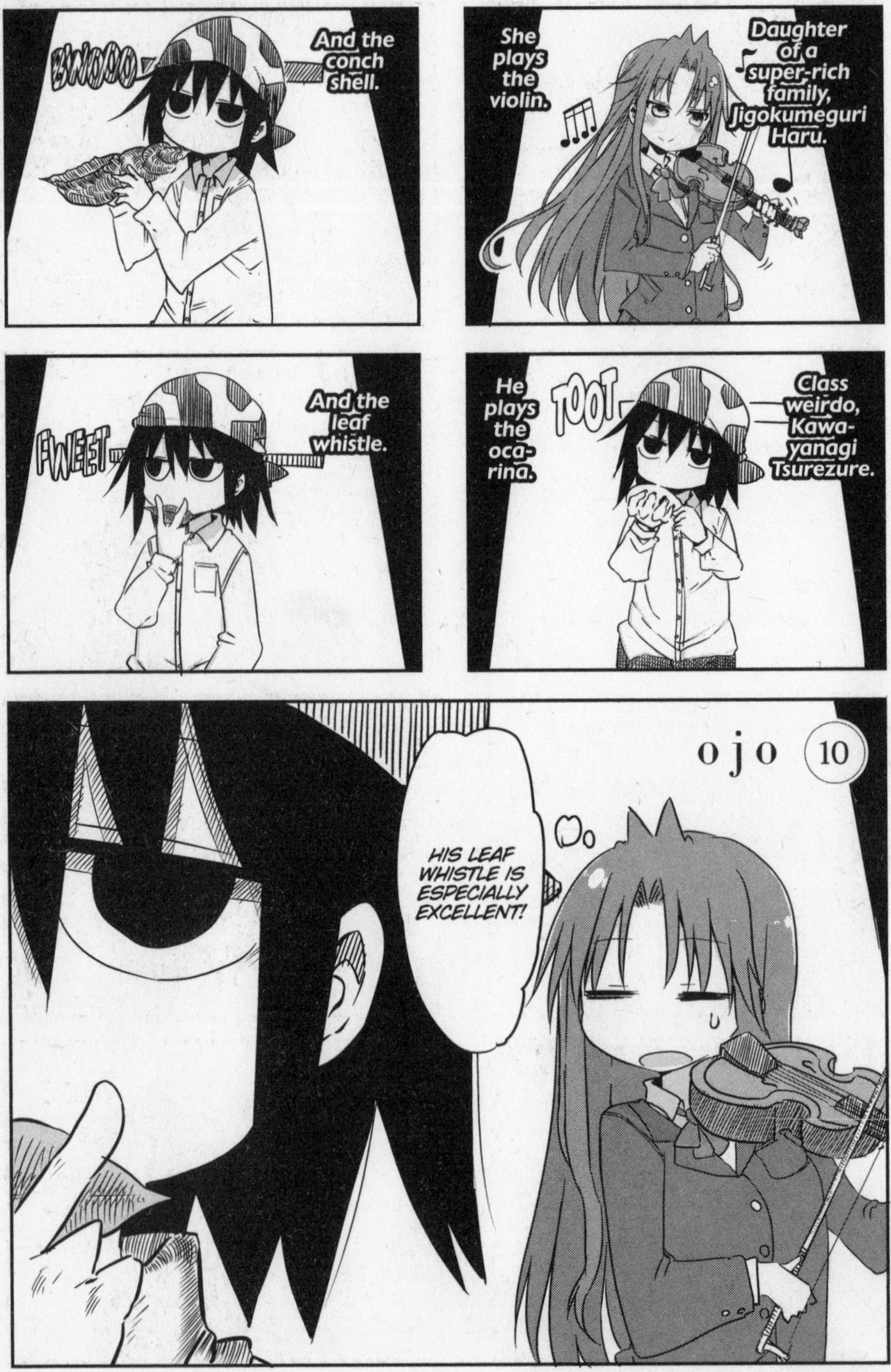
Daughter of a super-rich family, Jigokumeguri Haru.
She plays the violin.
And the conch shell.
BWOOO
Class weirdo, Kawa-yanagi Tsurezure.
TOOT
He plays the oca-rina.
And the leaf whistle.
FWEET
ojo 10
HIS LEAF WHISTLE IS ESPECIALLY EXCELLENT!

Living in the Information Age

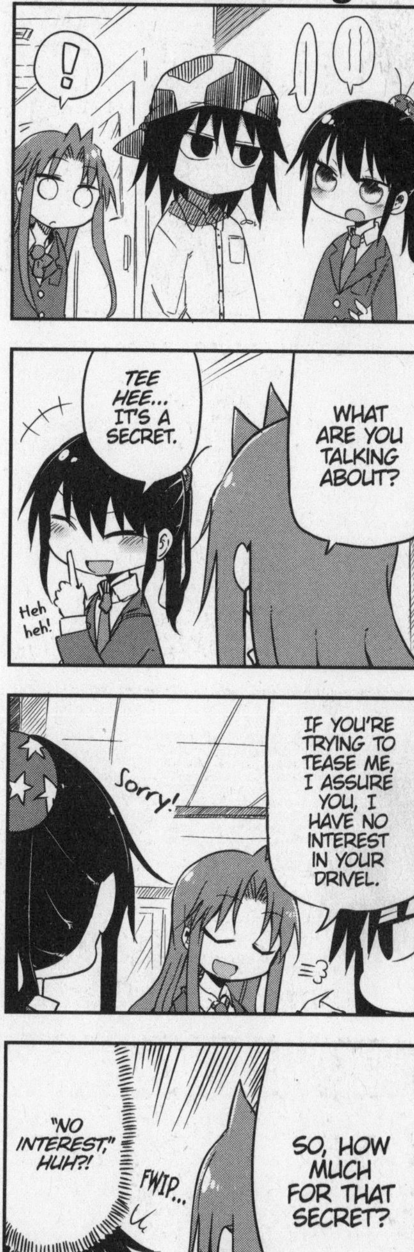
WHAT ARE YOU TALKING ABOUT?
TEE HEE... IT'S A SECRET.
Heh heh!
IF YOU'RE TRYING TO TEASE ME, I ASSURE YOU, I HAVE NO INTEREST IN YOUR DRIVEL.
Sorry!
SO, HOW MUCH FOR THAT SECRET?
FWIP...
"NO INTEREST," HUH?!

Off-duty Request

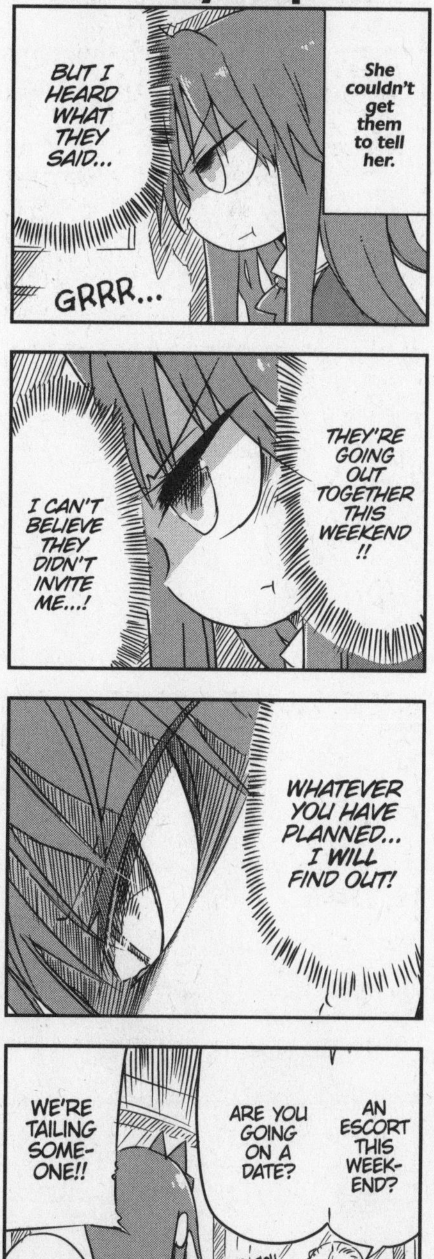
She couldn't get them to tell her.
BUT I HEARD WHAT THEY SAID...
GRRR...
THEY'RE GOING OUT TOGETHER THIS WEEKEND!!
I CAN'T BELIEVE THEY DIDN'T INVITE ME...!
WHATEVER YOU HAVE PLANNED... I WILL FIND OUT!
AN ESCORT THIS WEEKEND?
ARE YOU GOING ON A DATE?
WE'RE TAILING SOME-ONE!!
SCRATCH SCRATCH
So you're a stalker now?

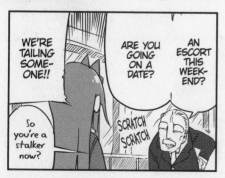

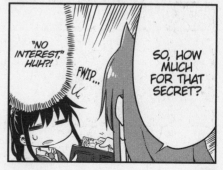

Doesn't Tuck in His Shirt

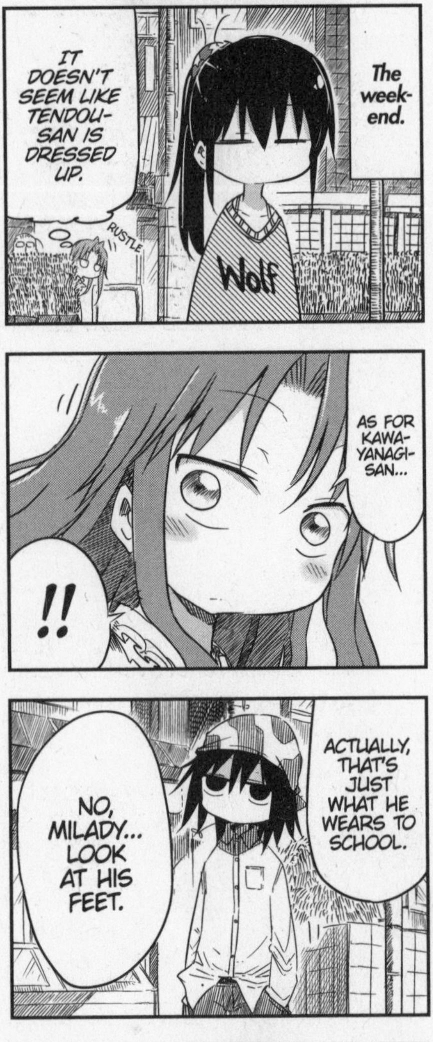
The weekend.
IT DOESN'T SEEM LIKE TENDOU-SAN IS DRESSED UP.
RUSTLE
Wolf
AS FOR KAWAYANAGI-SAN...
!!
ACTUALLY, THAT'S JUST WHAT HE WEARS TO SCHOOL.
NO, MILADY... LOOK AT HIS FEET.
WHY IS HE WEARING PLATFORM SHOES?!
BELL-BOTTOMED JEANS WITH PLATFORMS, HUH? MUST BE A MIDLIFE CRISIS.

Came Prepared

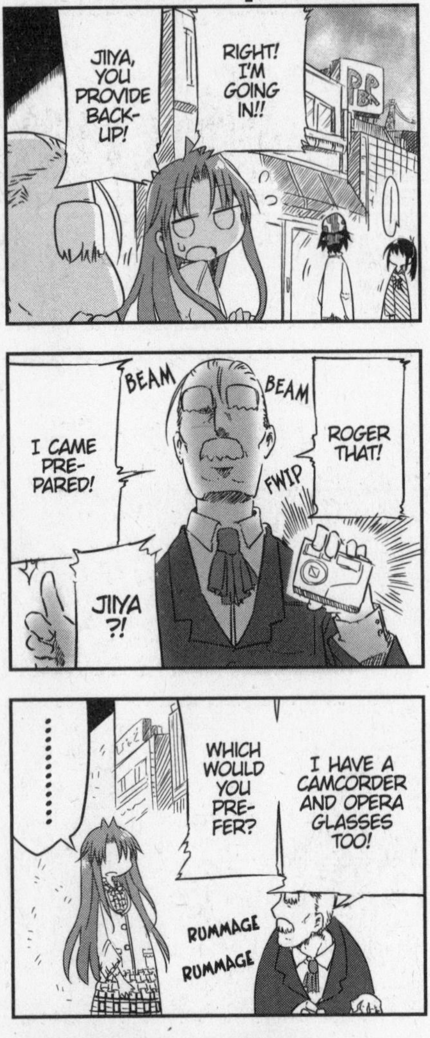
RIGHT! I'M GOING IN!!
JIIYA, YOU PROVIDE BACK-UP!
ROGER THAT!
BEAM
BEAM
I CAME PREPARED!
FWIP
JIIYA?!
I HAVE A CAMCORDER AND OPERA GLASSES TOO!
WHICH WOULD YOU PREFER?
RUMMAGE
RUMMAGE
....
THE CAMCORDER.
ROGER!

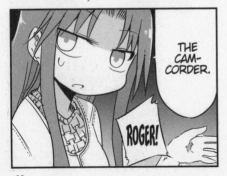

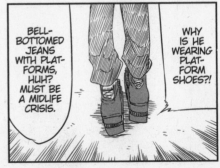

They're Close...

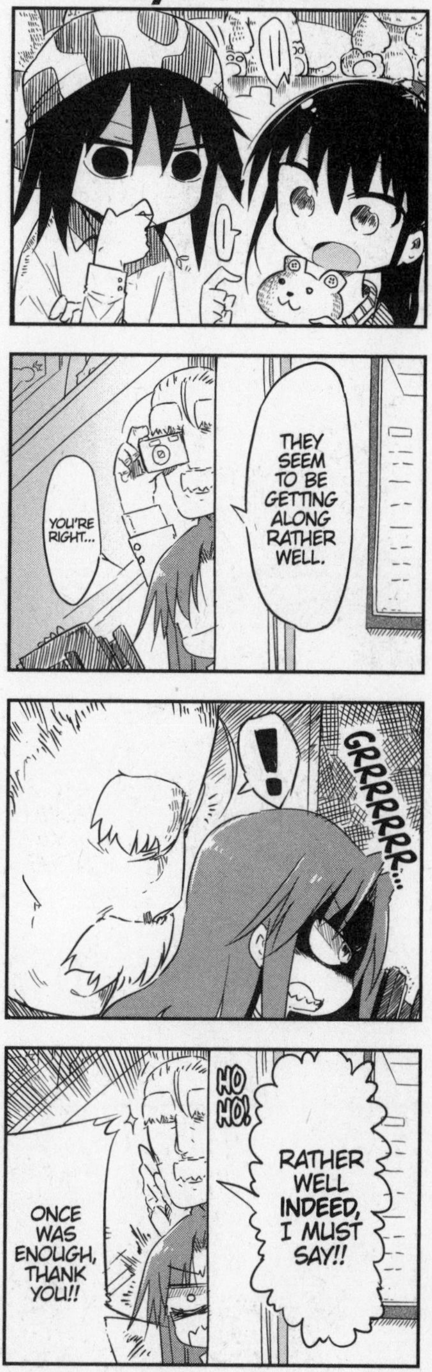
!
...
THEY SEEM TO BE GETTING ALONG RATHER WELL.
YOU'RE RIGHT...
GRRRRRRR...
!
HO HO!
RATHER WELL INDEED, I MUST SAY!!
ONCE WAS ENOUGH, THANK YOU!!

Round and Round

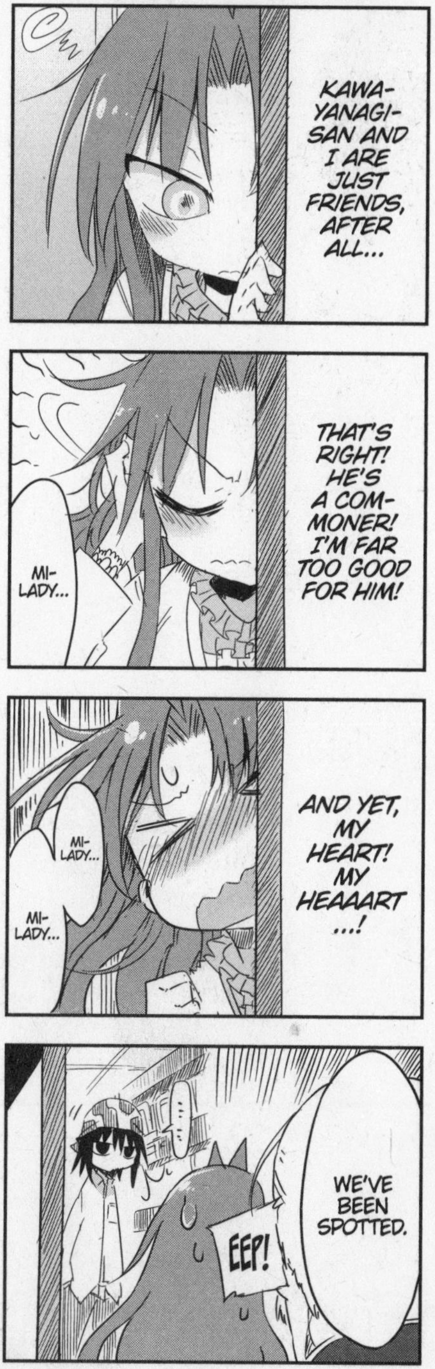
KAWA-YANAGI-SAN AND I ARE JUST FRIENDS, AFTER ALL...
THAT'S RIGHT! HE'S A COM-MONER! I'M FAR TOO GOOD FOR HIM!
MI-LADY...
AND YET, MY HEART! MY HEAAART ...!
MI-LADY...
MI-LADY...
WE'VE BEEN SPOTTED.
EEP!
...

Not Drooling at All

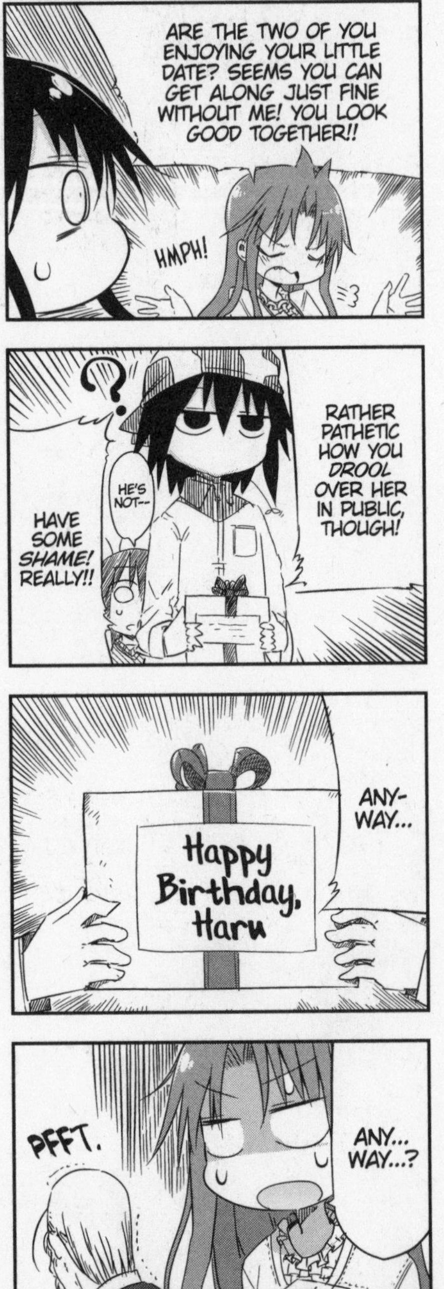
ARE THE TWO OF YOU ENJOYING YOUR LITTLE DATE? SEEMS YOU CAN GET ALONG JUST FINE WITHOUT ME! YOU LOOK GOOD TOGETHER!!
HMPH!
RATHER PATHETIC HOW YOU *DROOL* OVER HER IN PUBLIC, THOUGH!
?
HE'S NOT--
HAVE SOME *SHAME*! REALLY!!
ANY-WAY...
Happy Birthday, Haru
ANY... WAY...?
PFFT.

And Now She Finds Out

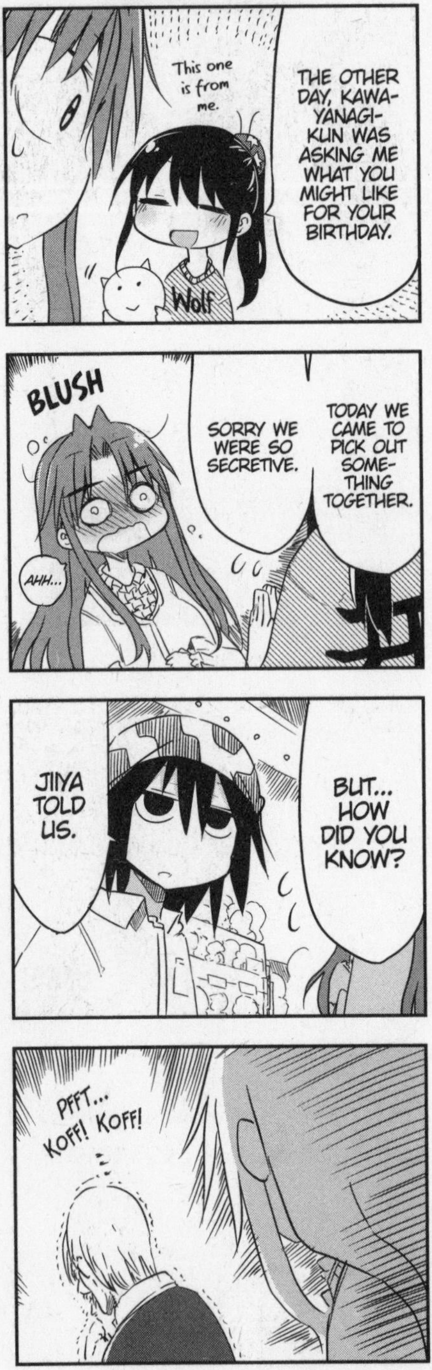
THE OTHER DAY, KAWA-YANAGI-KUN WAS ASKING ME WHAT YOU MIGHT LIKE FOR YOUR BIRTHDAY.
This one is from me.
Wolf
TODAY WE CAME TO PICK OUT SOME-THING TOGETHER.
SORRY WE WERE SO SECRETIVE.
BLUSH
AHH...
BUT... HOW DID YOU KNOW?
JIIYA TOLD US.
PFFT... KOFF! KOFF!

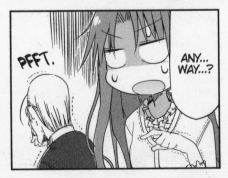

It Means Something

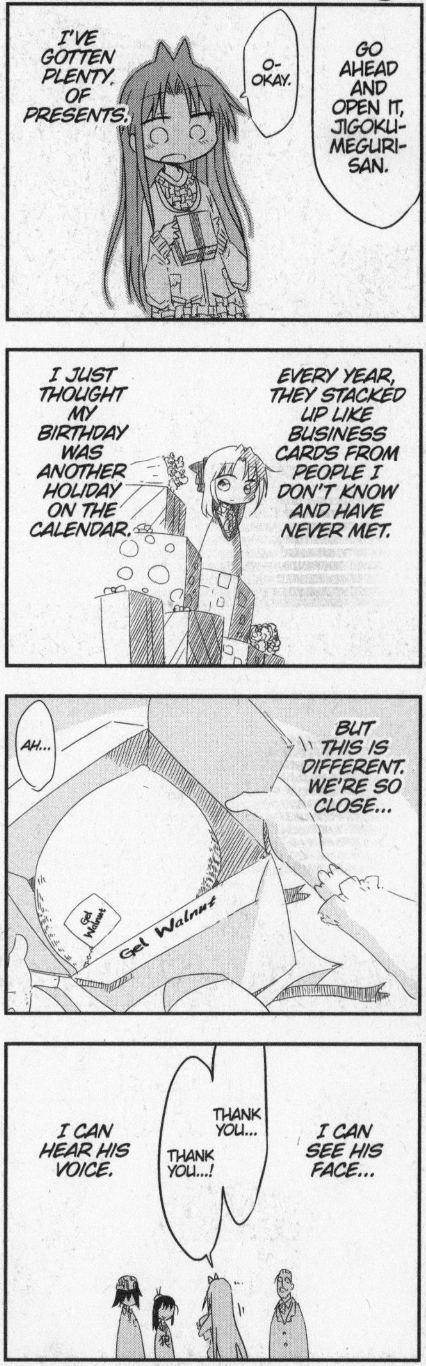
GO AHEAD AND OPEN IT, JIGOKU-MEGURI-SAN.
O-OKAY.
I'VE GOTTEN PLENTY OF PRESENTS.
EVERY YEAR, THEY STACKED UP LIKE BUSINESS CARDS FROM PEOPLE I DON'T KNOW AND HAVE NEVER MET.
I JUST THOUGHT MY BIRTHDAY WAS ANOTHER HOLIDAY ON THE CALENDAR.
BUT THIS IS DIFFERENT. WE'RE SO CLOSE...
AH...
Gel Walnut
Gel Walnut
I CAN SEE HIS FACE...
THANK YOU...
THANK YOU...!
I CAN HEAR HIS VOICE.

Awkward

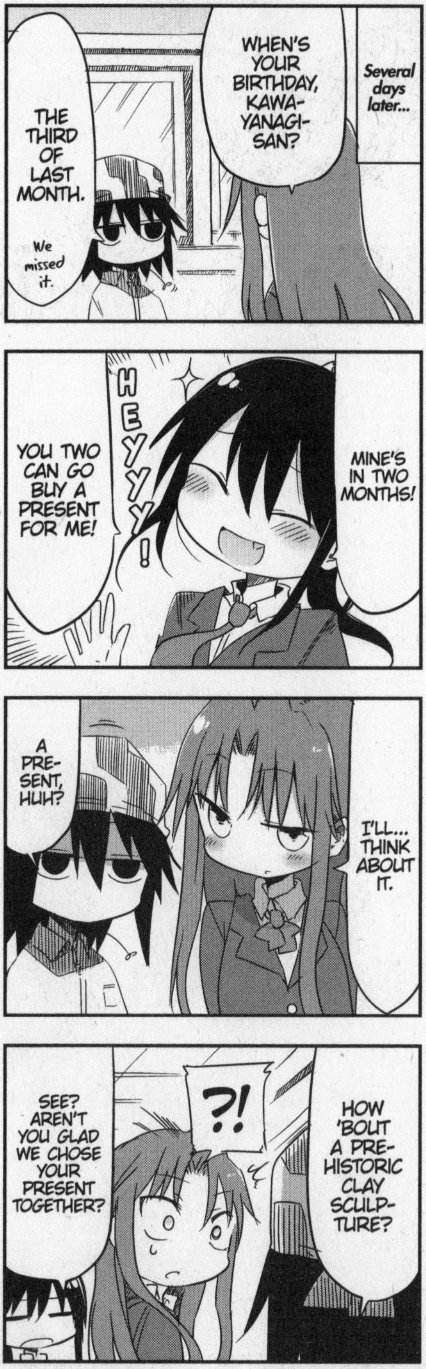
Several days later...
WHEN'S YOUR BIRTHDAY, KAWA-YANAGI-SAN?
THE THIRD OF LAST MONTH.
We missed it.
MINE'S IN TWO MONTHS!
HEYYY!
YOU TWO CAN GO BUY A PRESENT FOR ME!
I'LL... THINK ABOUT IT.
A PRE-SENT, HUH?
HOW 'BOUT A PRE-HISTORIC CLAY SCULP-TURE?
?!
SEE? AREN'T YOU GLAD WE CHOSE YOUR PRESENT TOGETHER?

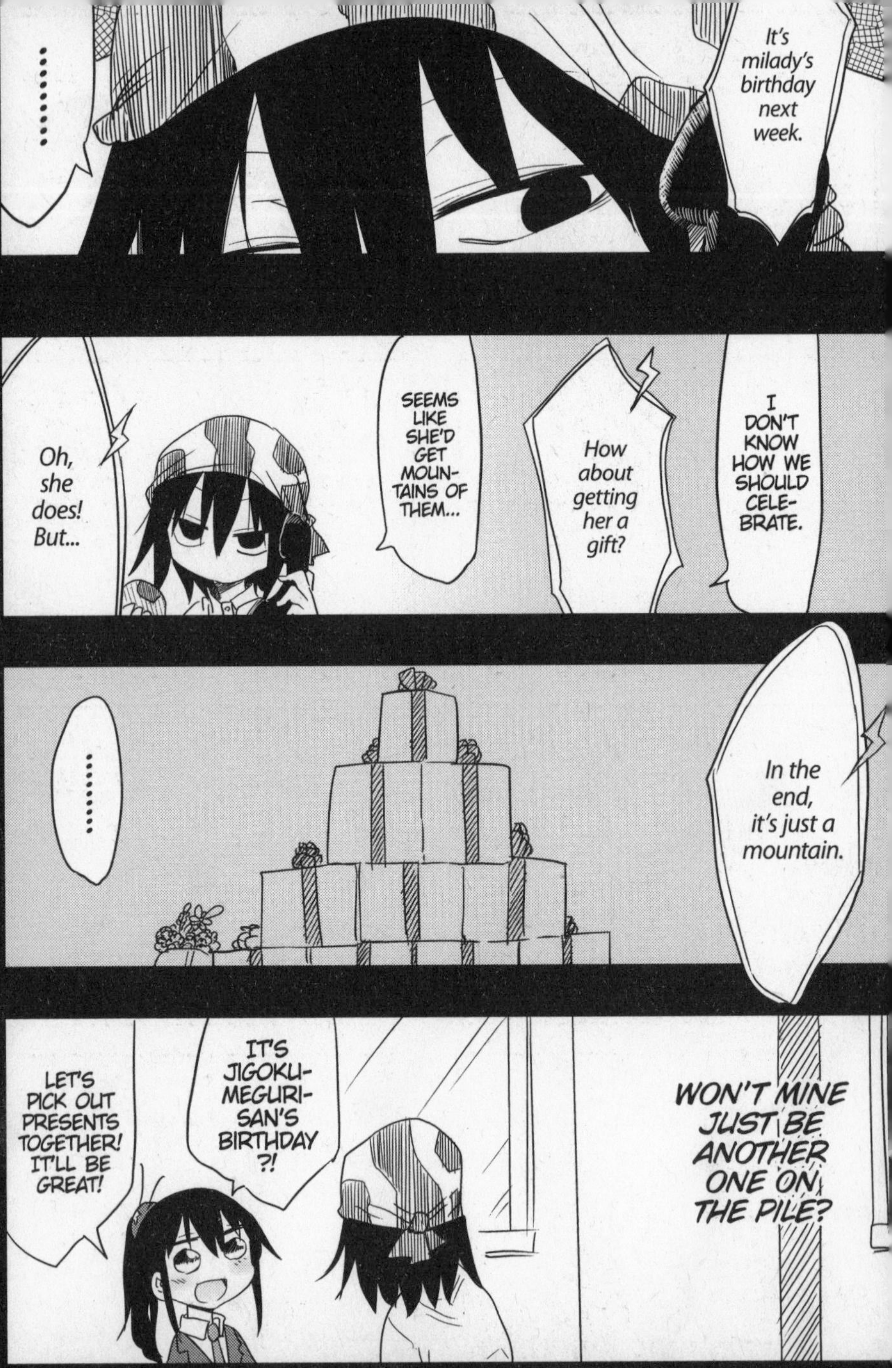
It's milady's birthday next week.
……
I DON'T KNOW HOW WE SHOULD CELEBRATE.
How about getting her a gift?
SEEMS LIKE SHE'D GET MOUNTAINS OF THEM...
Oh, she does! But...
In the end, it's just a mountain.
……
WON'T MINE JUST BE ANOTHER ONE ON THE PILE?
IT'S JIGOKUMEGURI-SAN'S BIRTHDAY?!
LET'S PICK OUT PRESENTS TOGETHER! IT'LL BE GREAT!

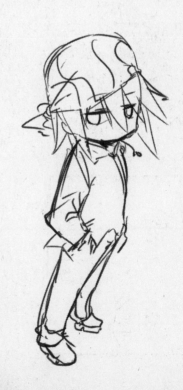

Opening Act

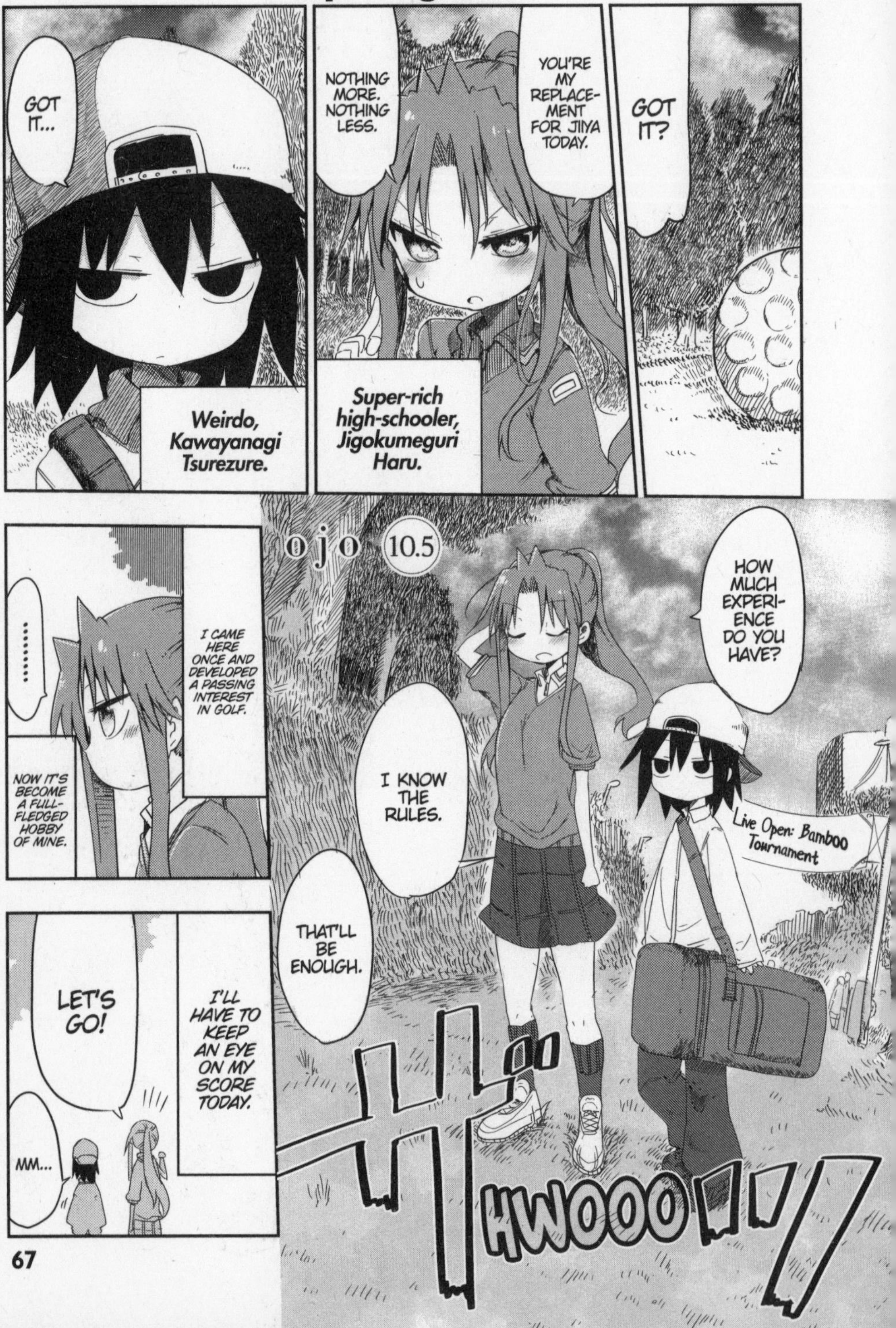
GOT IT?
YOU'RE MY REPLACEMENT FOR JIIYA TODAY.
NOTHING MORE. NOTHING LESS.
Super-rich high-schooler, Jigokumeguri Haru.
GOT IT...
Weirdo, Kawayanagi Tsurezure.
ojo 10.5
HOW MUCH EXPERIENCE DO YOU HAVE?
I KNOW THE RULES.
THAT'LL BE ENOUGH.
Live Open: Bamboo Tournament
HWOOO
I CAME HERE ONCE AND DEVELOPED A PASSING INTEREST IN GOLF.
....
NOW IT'S BECOME A FULL-FLEDGED HOBBY OF MINE.
I'LL HAVE TO KEEP AN EYE ON MY SCORE TODAY.
LET'S GO!
MM...

Silver-medal Haru

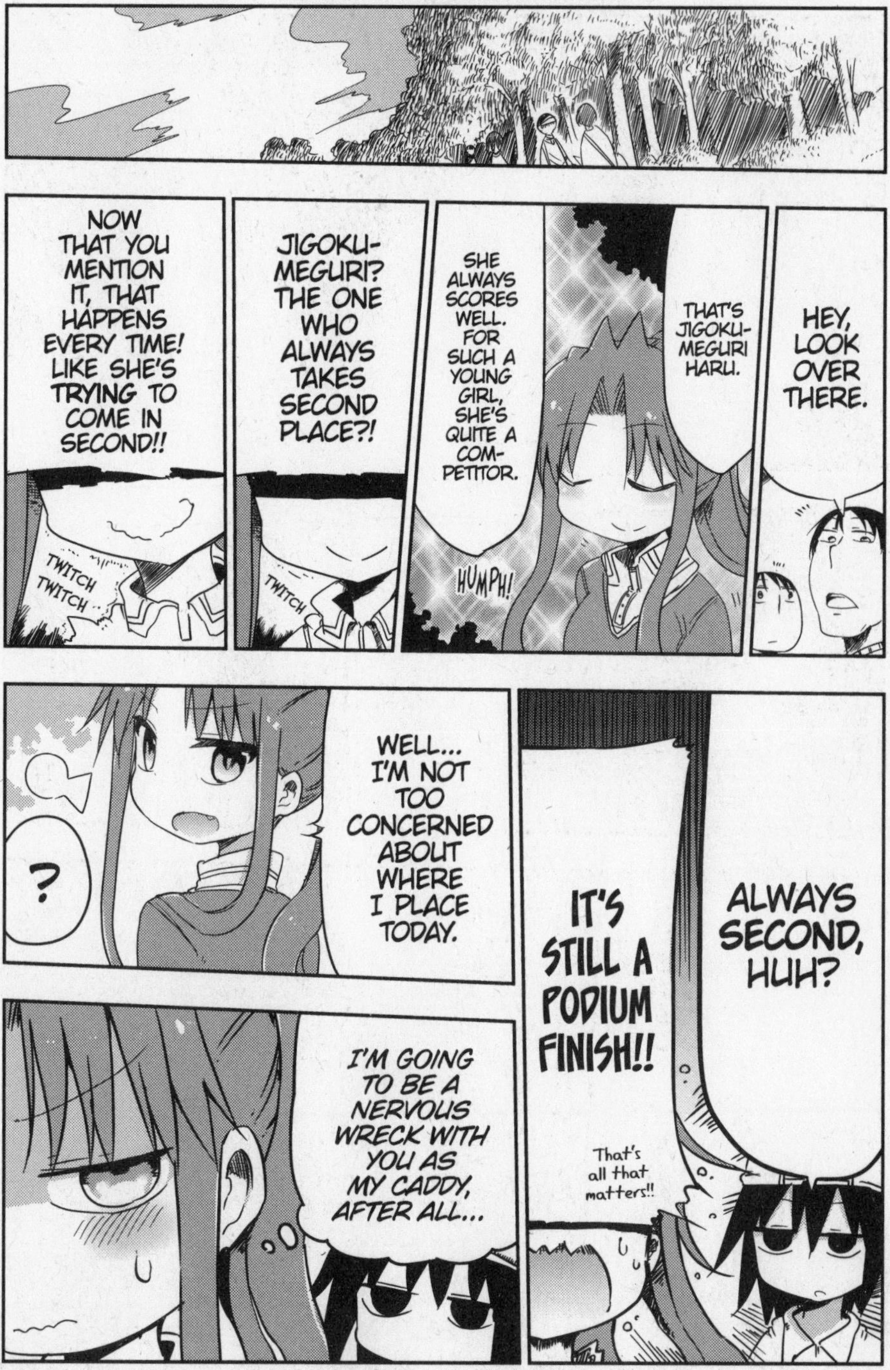
HEY, LOOK OVER THERE.
THAT'S JIGOKU-MEGURI HARU.
SHE ALWAYS SCORES WELL. FOR SUCH A YOUNG GIRL, SHE'S QUITE A COMPETITOR.
HUMPH!
JIGOKU-MEGURI? THE ONE WHO ALWAYS TAKES SECOND PLACE?!
TWITCH
NOW THAT YOU MENTION IT, THAT HAPPENS EVERY TIME! LIKE SHE'S TRYING TO COME IN SECOND!!
TWITCH TWITCH
ALWAYS SECOND, HUH?
IT'S STILL A PODIUM FINISH!!
That's all that matters!!
WELL... I'M NOT TOO CONCERNED ABOUT WHERE I PLACE TODAY.
?
I'M GOING TO BE A NERVOUS WRECK WITH YOU AS MY CADDY, AFTER ALL...

I Don't Want You to Leave

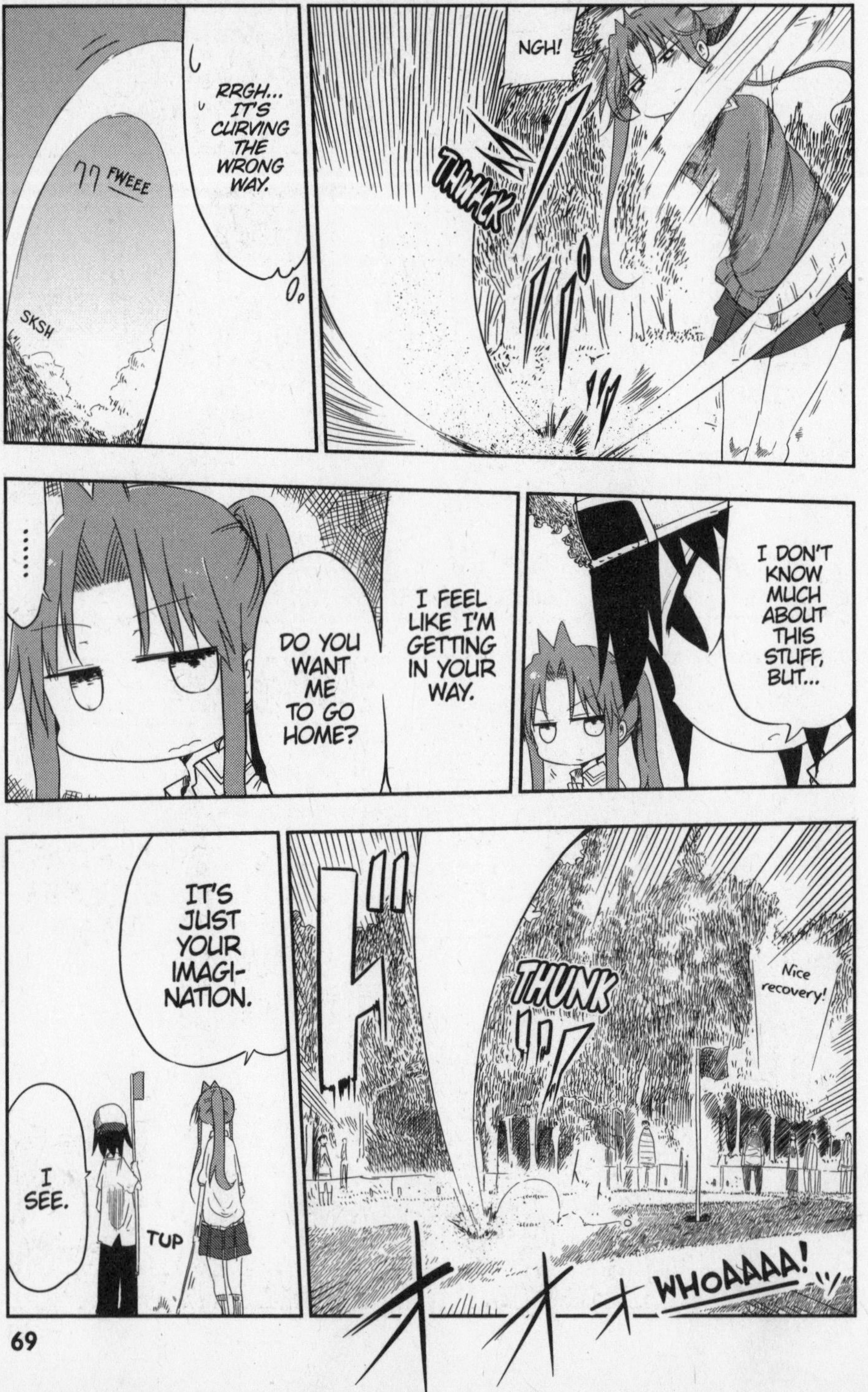
NGH!
THWACK
RRGH... IT'S CURVING THE WRONG WAY.
FWEEE
SKSH
I DON'T KNOW MUCH ABOUT THIS STUFF, BUT...
I FEEL LIKE I'M GETTING IN YOUR WAY.
DO YOU WANT ME TO GO HOME?
......
THUNK
Nice recovery!
WHOAAAA!
IT'S JUST YOUR IMAGINATION.
I SEE.
TUP

Why Didn't You Tell Me This Before We Started?

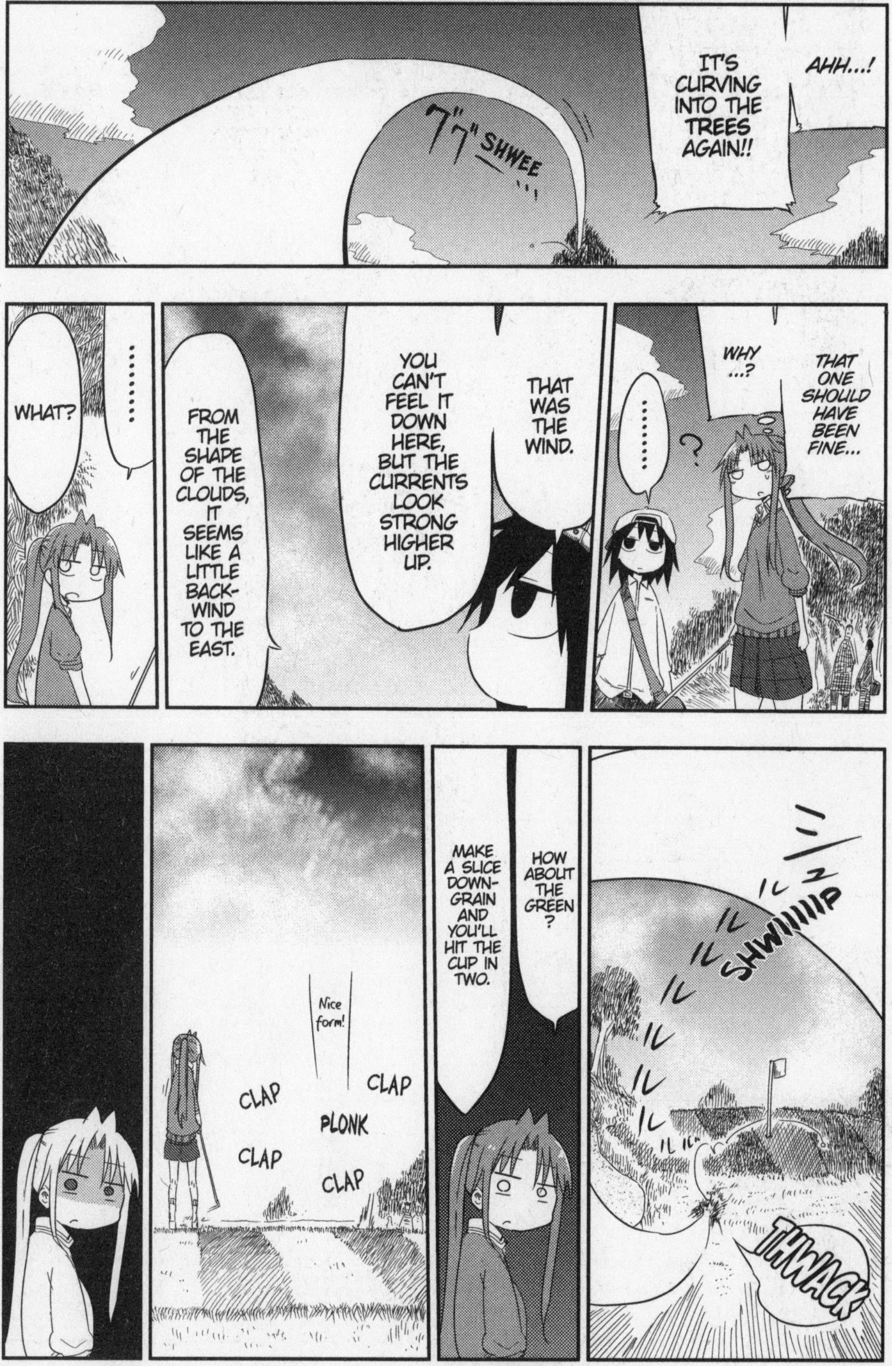

AHH...!
IT'S CURVING INTO THE TREES AGAIN!!
SHWEE
THAT ONE SHOULD HAVE BEEN FINE...
WHY ...?
....
?
THAT WAS THE WIND.
YOU CAN'T FEEL IT DOWN HERE, BUT THE CURRENTS LOOK STRONG HIGHER UP.
FROM THE SHAPE OF THE CLOUDS, IT SEEMS LIKE A LITTLE BACK-WIND TO THE EAST.
....
WHAT?
SHWIIIIIP
THWACK
HOW ABOUT THE GREEN?
MAKE A SLICE DOWN-GRAIN AND YOU'LL HIT THE CUP IN TWO.
Nice form!
CLAP
CLAP
PLONK
CLAP
CLAP

Does Her Worst When She's Ahead

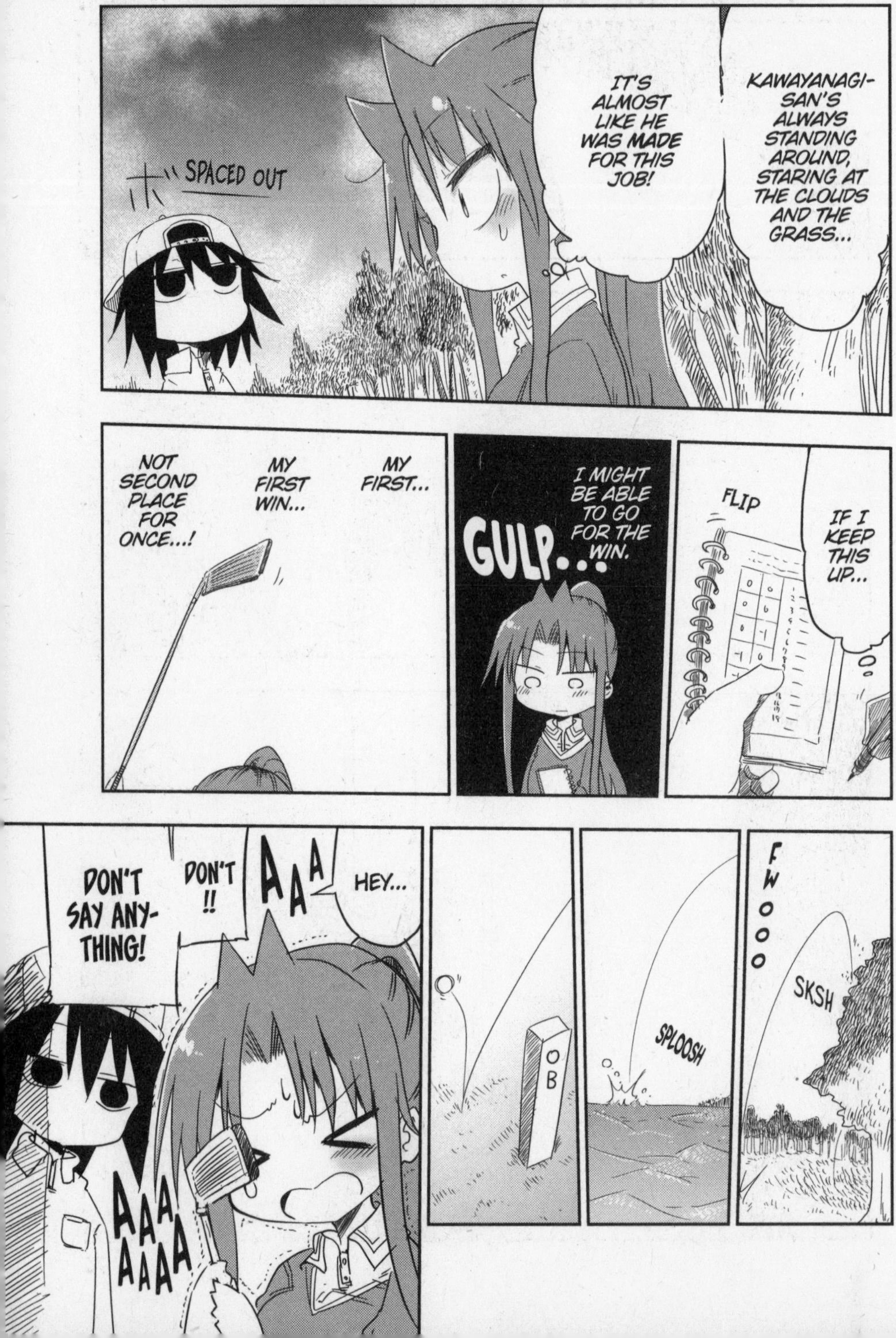
KAWAYANAGI-SAN'S ALWAYS STANDING AROUND, STARING AT THE CLOUDS AND THE GRASS...
IT'S ALMOST LIKE HE WAS MADE FOR THIS JOB!
SPACED OUT
FLIP
IF I KEEP THIS UP...
I MIGHT BE ABLE TO GO FOR THE WIN.
GULP...
MY FIRST...
MY FIRST WIN...
NOT SECOND PLACE FOR ONCE...!
FWOOO
SKSH
SPLOOSH
OB
HEY...
AAA
DON'T !!
DON'T SAY ANY-THING!
AAAAAAA

Cool as a Cucumber

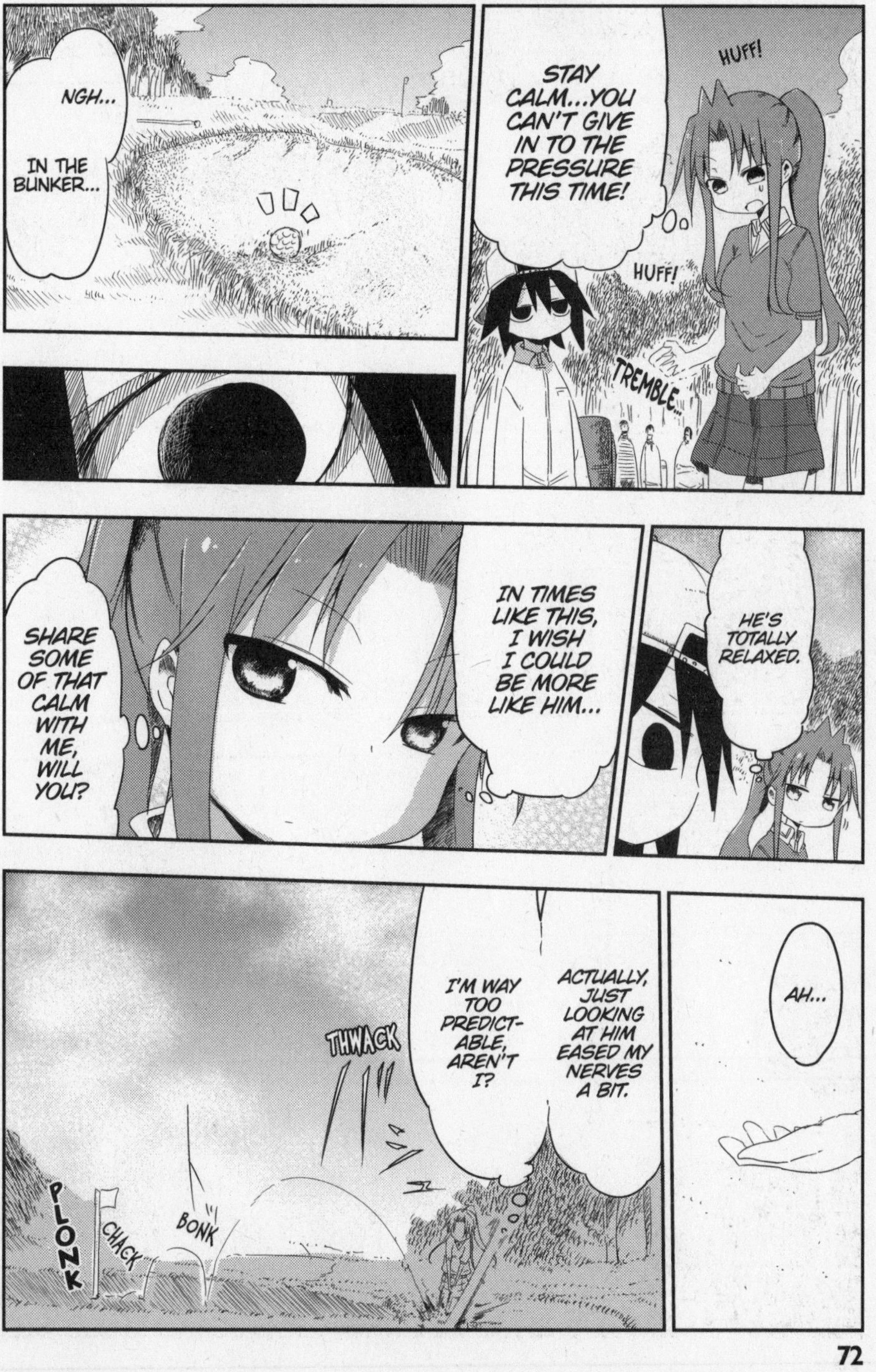

HUFF!
STAY CALM...YOU CAN'T GIVE IN TO THE PRESSURE THIS TIME!
HUFF!
TREMBLE...
NGH...
IN THE BUNKER...
HE'S TOTALLY RELAXED.
IN TIMES LIKE THIS, I WISH I COULD BE MORE LIKE HIM...
SHARE SOME OF THAT CALM WITH ME, WILL YOU?
AH...
ACTUALLY, JUST LOOKING AT HIM EASED MY NERVES A BIT.
I'M WAY TOO PREDICT-ABLE, AREN'T I?
THWACK
BONK
CHACK
PLONK

The Power of Trust

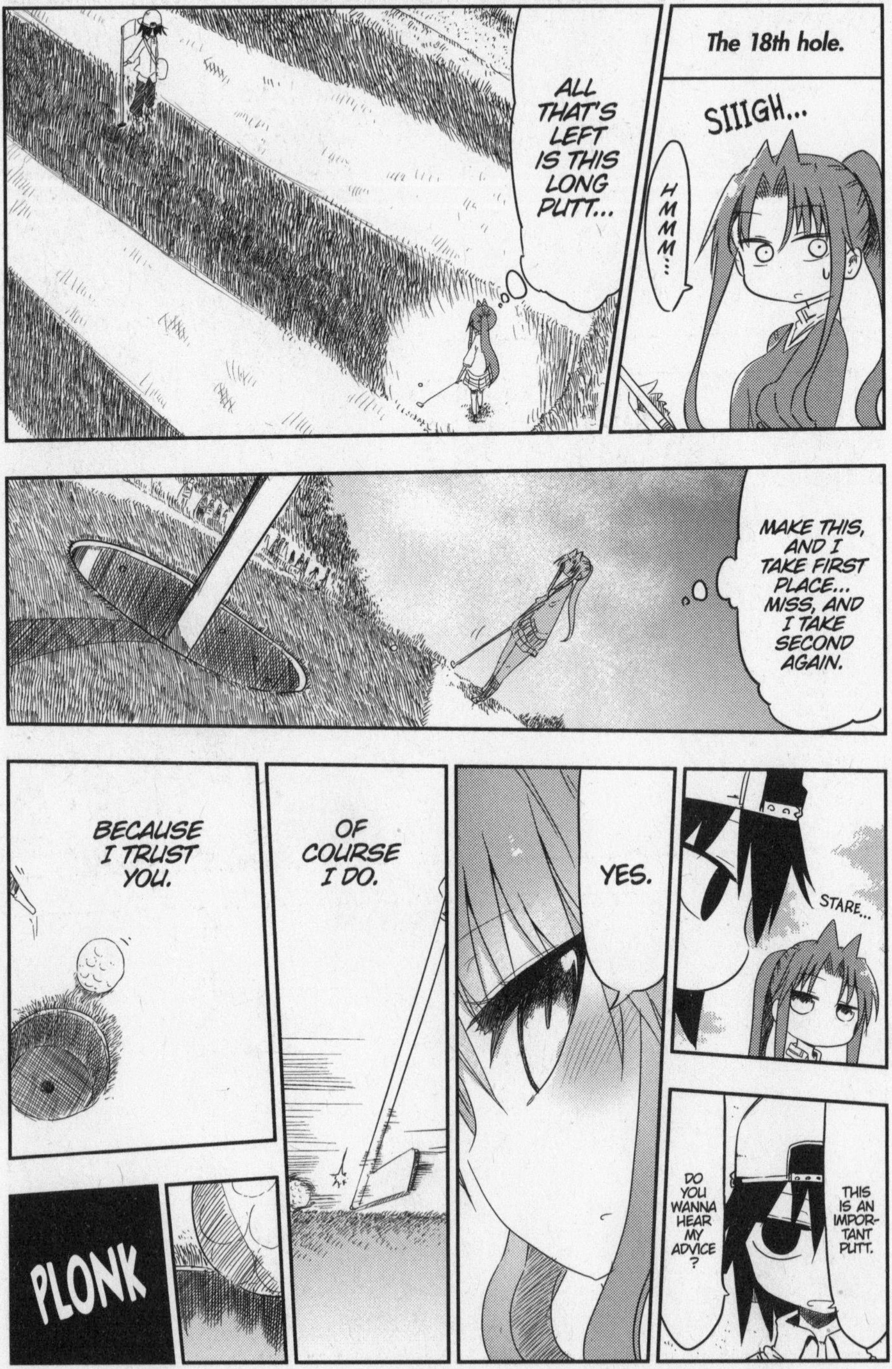
The 18th hole.
SIIIGH...
HMMM...
ALL THAT'S LEFT IS THIS LONG PUTT...
MAKE THIS, AND I TAKE FIRST PLACE... MISS, AND I TAKE SECOND AGAIN.
STARE...
THIS IS AN IMPORTANT PUTT.
DO YOU WANNA HEAR MY ADVICE?
YES.
OF COURSE I DO.
BECAUSE I TRUST YOU.
PLONK

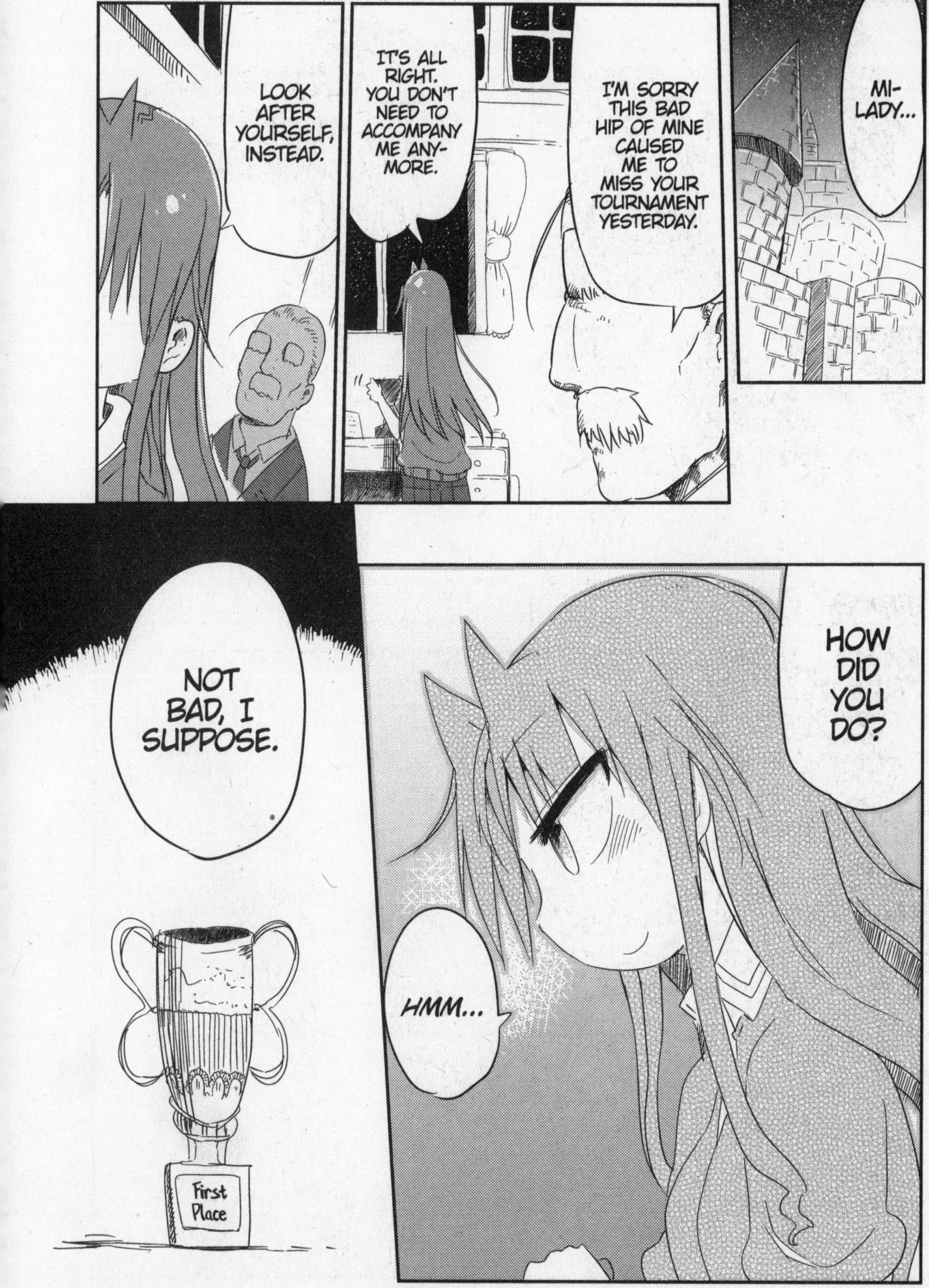
MI-LADY...
I'M SORRY THIS BAD HIP OF MINE CAUSED ME TO MISS YOUR TOURNAMENT YESTERDAY.
IT'S ALL RIGHT. YOU DON'T NEED TO ACCOMPANY ME ANY-MORE.
LOOK AFTER YOURSELF, INSTEAD.
HOW DID YOU DO?
HMM...
NOT BAD, I SUPPOSE.
First Place

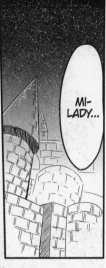

Eye to Eye Docking

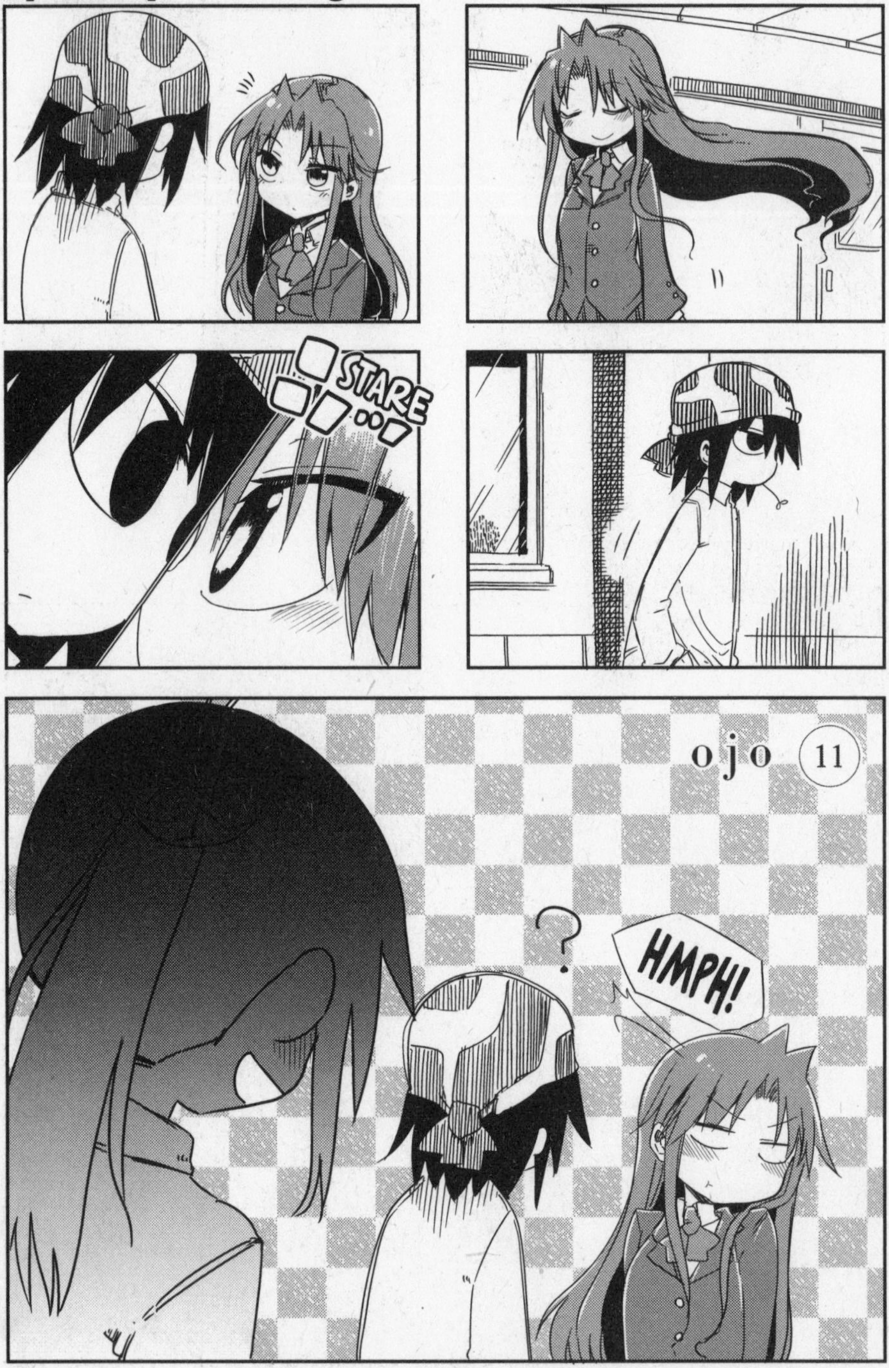
STARE
ojo 11
HMPH!
?

Sickness

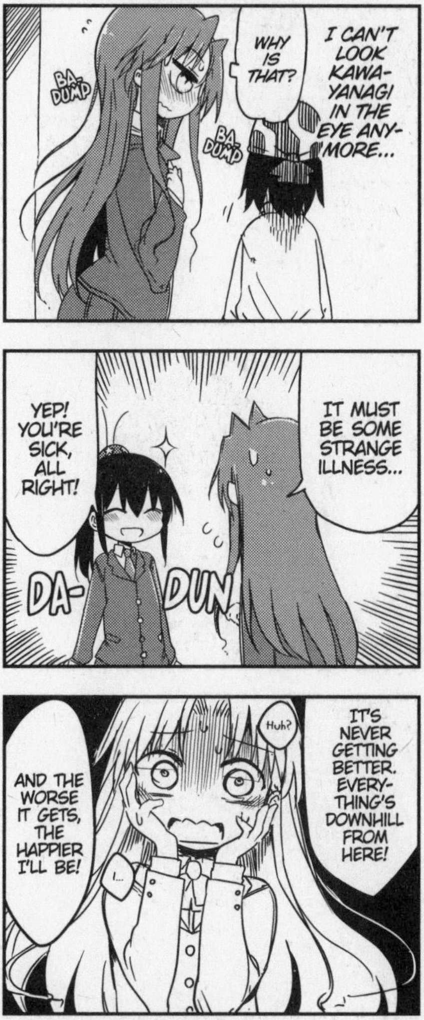
I CAN'T LOOK KAWAYANAGI IN THE EYE ANYMORE...
WHY IS THAT?
BA-DUMP
BA-DUMP
IT MUST BE SOME STRANGE ILLNESS...
YEP! YOU'RE SICK, ALL RIGHT!
DA-DUN
IT'S NEVER GETTING BETTER. EVERYTHING'S DOWNHILL FROM HERE!
Huh?
AND THE WORSE IT GETS, THE HAPPIER I'LL BE!
I...
BEFORE YOU KNOW IT, YOU'LL TOTALLY EXPLODE!
I CAN'T WAIT!
EXPLODE?!!

Imagination is Everything

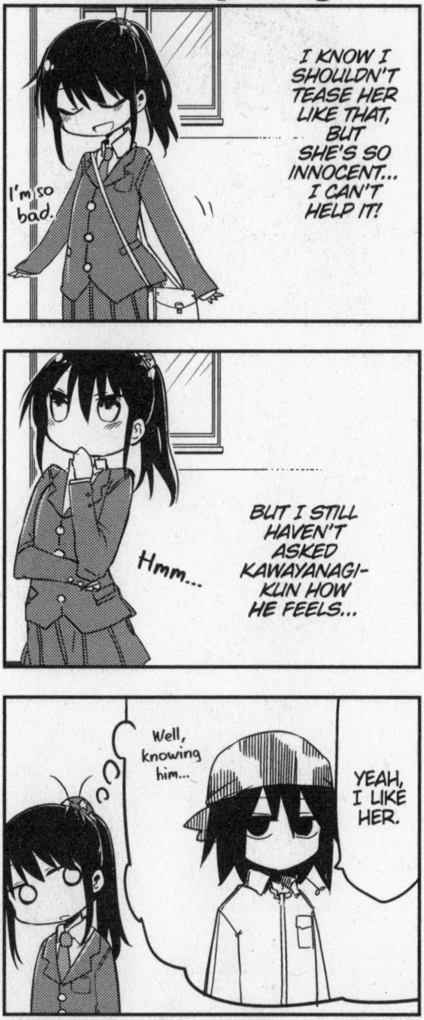
I KNOW I SHOULDN'T TEASE HER LIKE THAT, BUT SHE'S SO INNOCENT... I CAN'T HELP IT!
I'm so bad.
BUT I STILL HAVEN'T ASKED KAWAYANAGI-KUN HOW HE FEELS...
Hmm...
YEAH, I LIKE HER.
Well, knowing him...
IT'S CRAZY MELTY LOVE, BABY!
Only in my dreams.

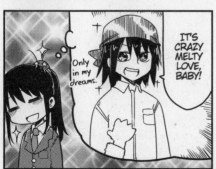

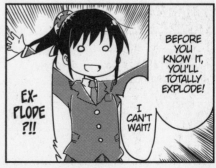

How Do You Feel?

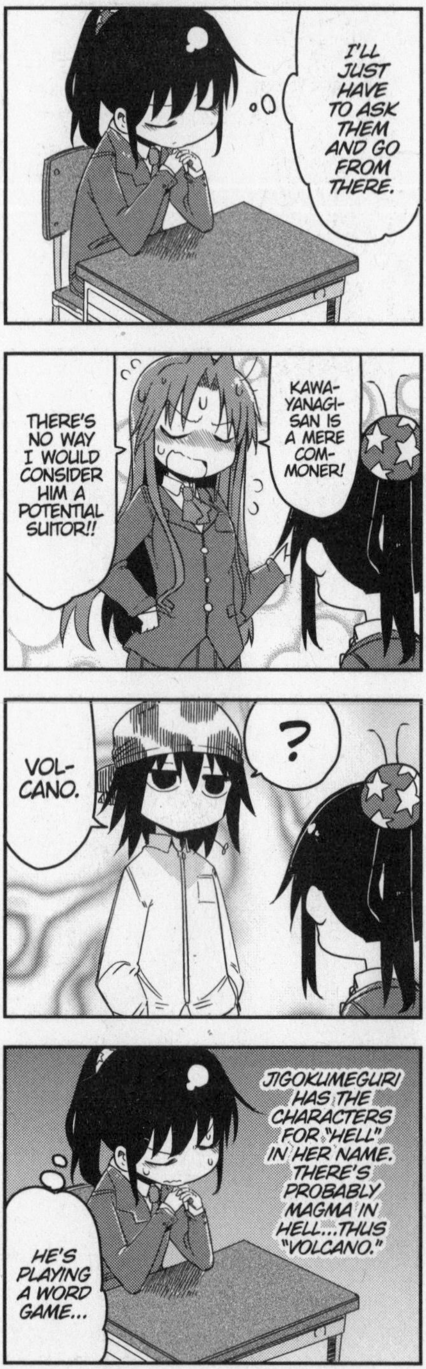
I'LL JUST HAVE TO ASK THEM AND GO FROM THERE.
KAWA-YANAGI-SAN IS A MERE COM-MONER!
THERE'S NO WAY I WOULD CONSIDER HIM A POTENTIAL SUITOR!!
?
VOL-CANO.
JIGOKUMEGURI HAS THE CHARACTERS FOR "HELL" IN HER NAME. THERE'S PROBABLY MAGMA IN HELL...THUS "VOLCANO."
HE'S PLAYING A WORD GAME...

Lost in Her Head

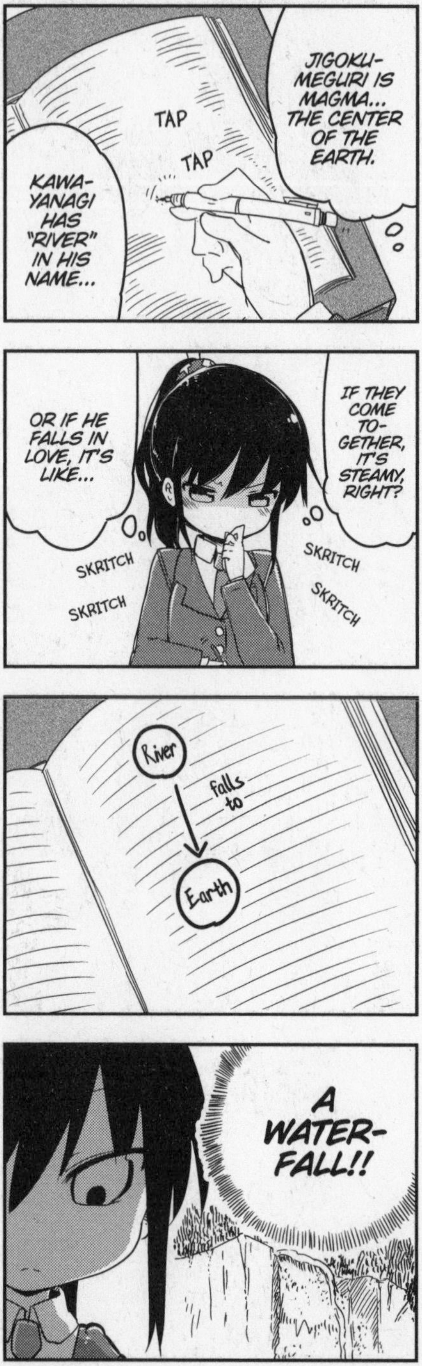
JIGOKU-MEGURI IS MAGMA... THE CENTER OF THE EARTH.
TAP
TAP
KAWA-YANAGI HAS "RIVER" IN HIS NAME...
IF THEY COME TO-GETHER, IT'S STEAMY, RIGHT?
SKRITCH
SKRITCH
OR IF HE FALLS IN LOVE, IT'S LIKE...
SKRITCH
SKRITCH
River
falls to
Earth
A WATER-FALL!!

It's Too Late

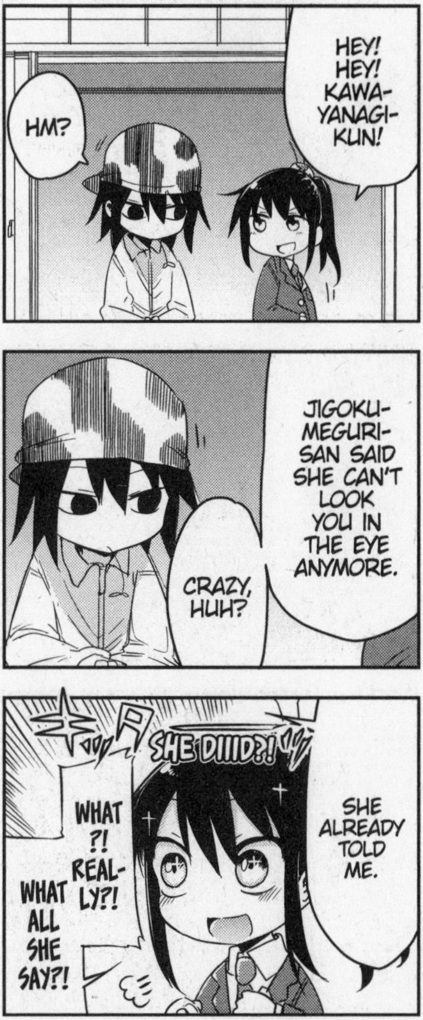
HEY! HEY! KAWA-YANAGI-KUN!
HM?
JIGOKU-MEGURI-SAN SAID SHE CAN'T LOOK YOU IN THE EYE ANYMORE.
CRAZY, HUH?
SHE DIIID?!
SHE ALREADY TOLD ME.
WHAT?! REALLY?!
WHAT ALL SHE SAY?!
JUST THAT SHE'S SICK.
GONNA EXPLODE, APPARENTLY.
WHAT HAVE I DONE?

A Flash of Demonic Wrath

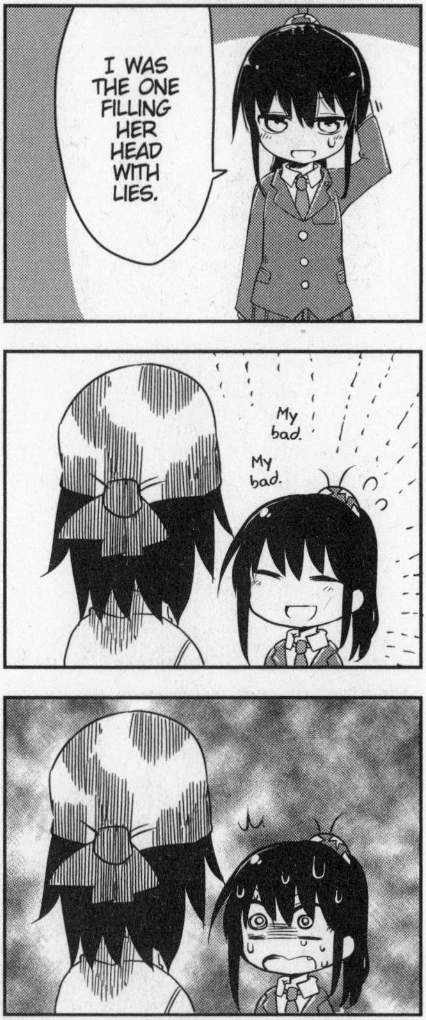
I WAS THE ONE FILLING HER HEAD WITH LIES.
My bad.
My bad.
I'M SORRY!!
REALLY SORRY!!
TELL THAT TO JIGOKUMEGURI.
She was scared.

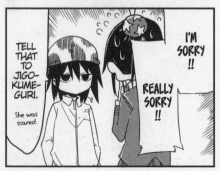

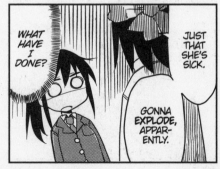

True Evil

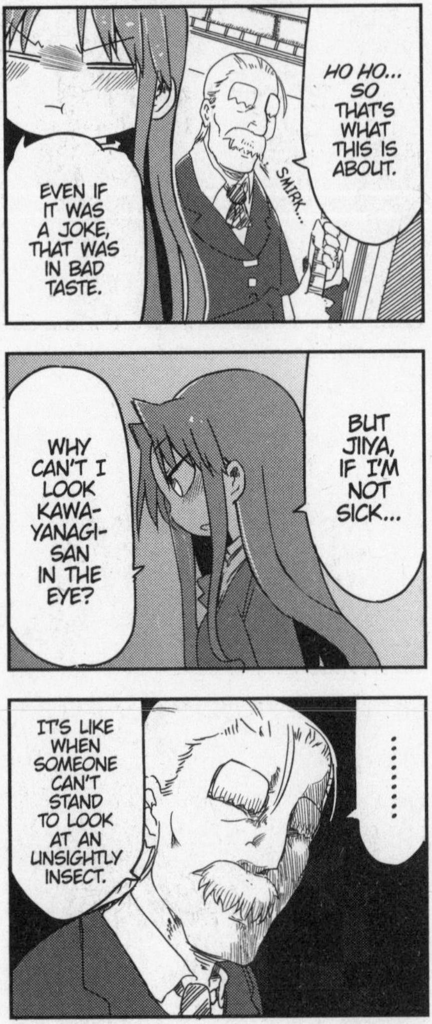
HO HO... SO THAT'S WHAT THIS IS ABOUT.
SMIRK...
EVEN IF IT WAS A JOKE, THAT WAS IN BAD TASTE.
BUT JIIYA, IF I'M NOT SICK...
WHY CAN'T I LOOK KAWAYANAGI-SAN IN THE EYE?
....
IT'S LIKE WHEN SOMEONE CAN'T STAND TO LOOK AT AN UNSIGHTLY INSECT.
I KNEW YOU WERE A SNOB, BUT THAT REALLY IS QUITE HARSH!
WHA...?!
THAT IS NOT THE REASON!!

Dark Past

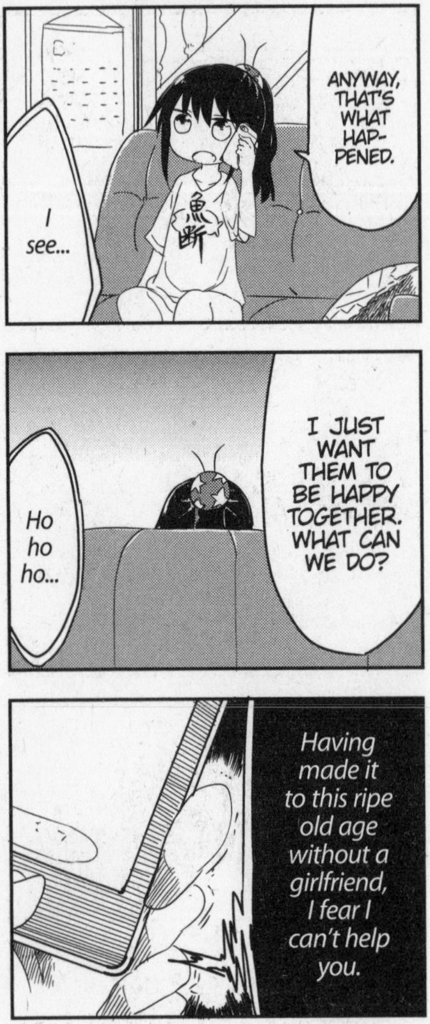
ANYWAY, THAT'S WHAT HAPPENED.
I see...
I JUST WANT THEM TO BE HAPPY TOGETHER. WHAT CAN WE DO?
Ho ho ho...
Having made it to this ripe old age without a girlfriend, I fear I can't help you.
SILENCE...
JIIYA-SAN...
CHIRP
CHIRP
CHIRP

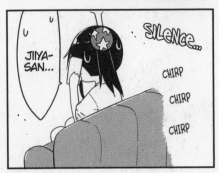

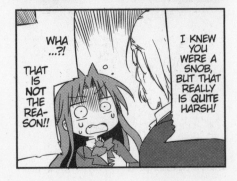

Pushing on Regardless

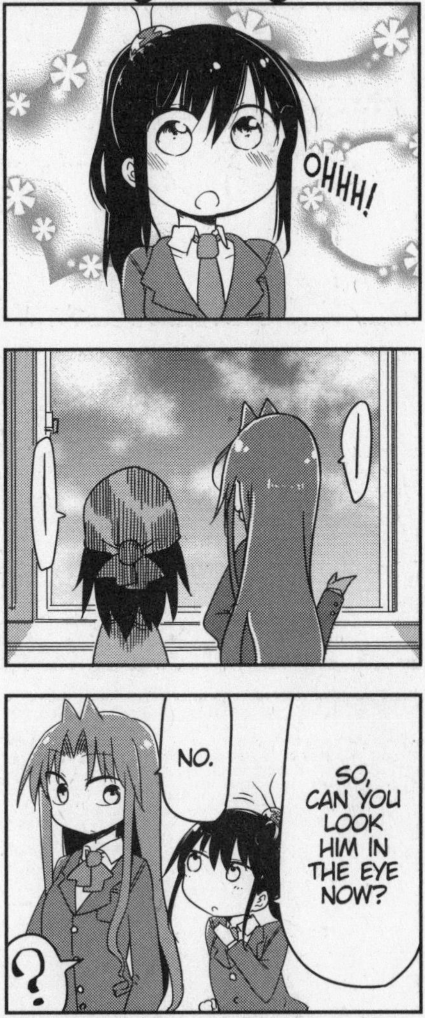
OHHHH!
SO, CAN YOU LOOK HIM IN THE EYE NOW?
NO.
?
BUT WE CAN TALK JUST FINE WITHOUT LOOKING AT EACH OTHER!!
HO!
HO
OH
NOTH-ING STOPS YOU, HUH ...?

Eruption

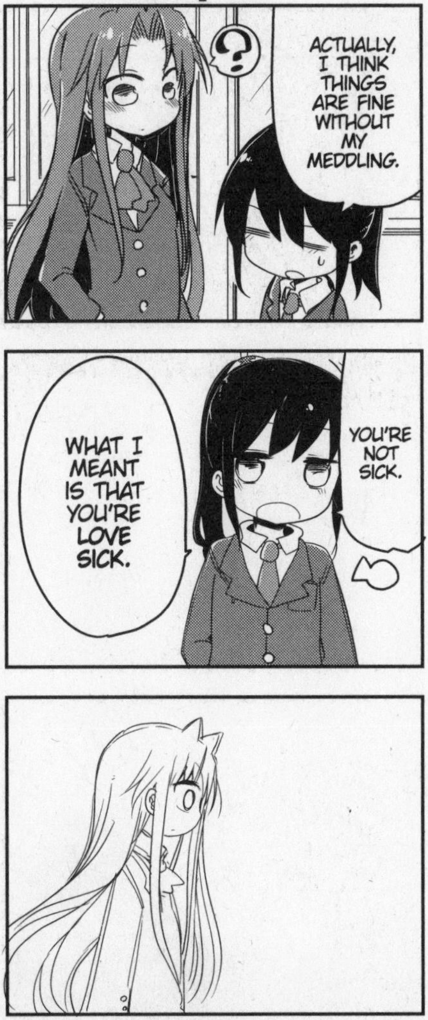
ACTUALLY, I THINK THINGS ARE FINE WITHOUT MY MEDDLING.
?
YOU'RE NOT SICK.
WHAT I MEANT IS THAT YOU'RE LOVE SICK.
Volcano...

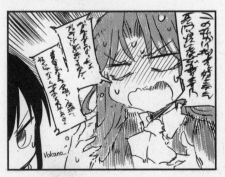

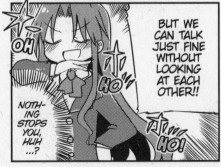

Can I Use This?

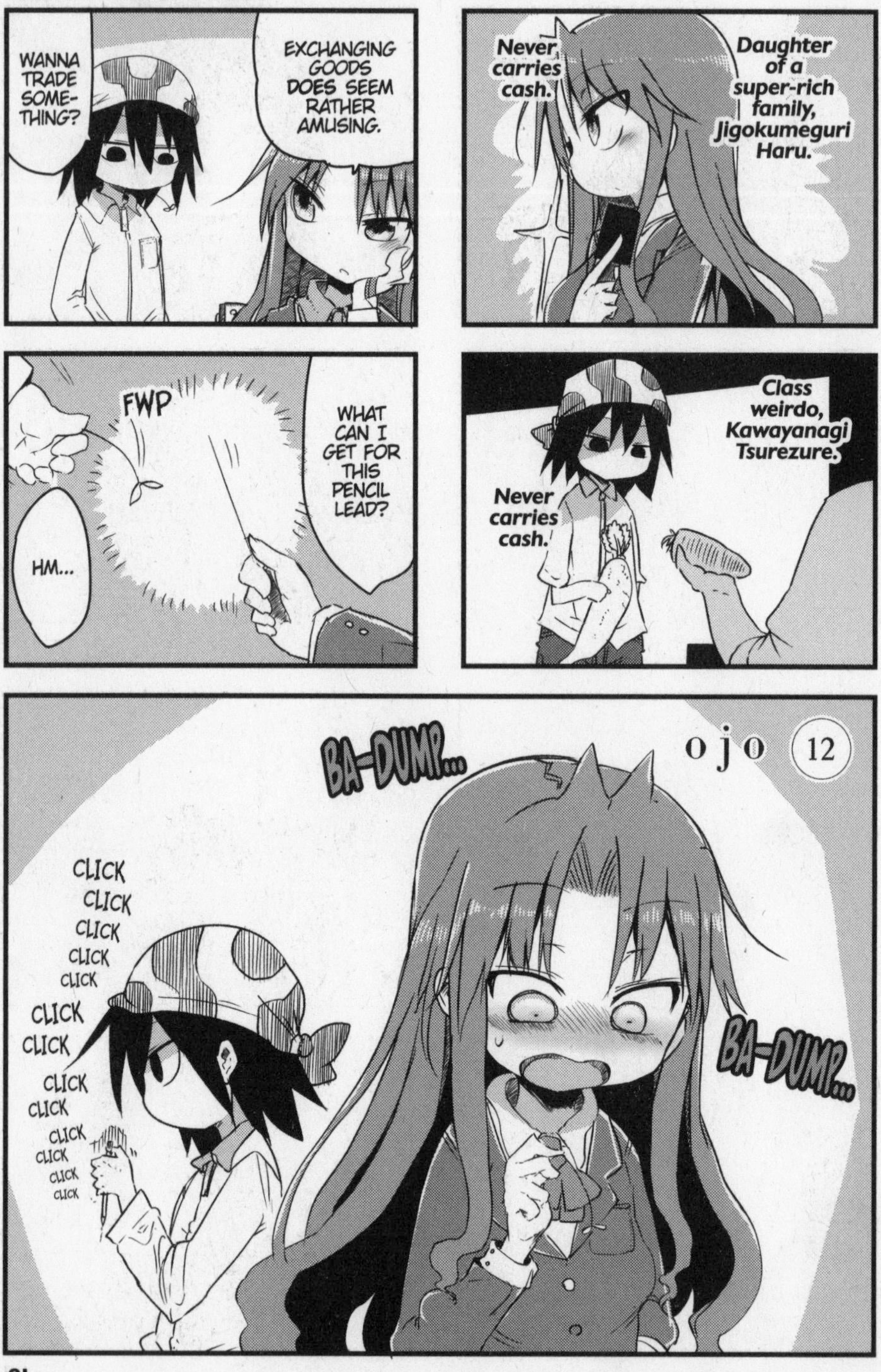
Daughter of a super-rich family, Jigokumeguri Haru.
Never carries cash.
EXCHANGING GOODS DOES SEEM RATHER AMUSING.
WANNA TRADE SOME-THING?
Class weirdo, Kawayanagi Tsurezure.
Never carries cash.
WHAT CAN I GET FOR THIS PENCIL LEAD?
FWP
HM...
ojo 12
BA-DUMP...
BA-DUMP...
CLICK CLICK CLICK CLICK CLICK CLICK CLICK CLICK CLICK CLICK CLICK CLICK CLICK

Something Wrong

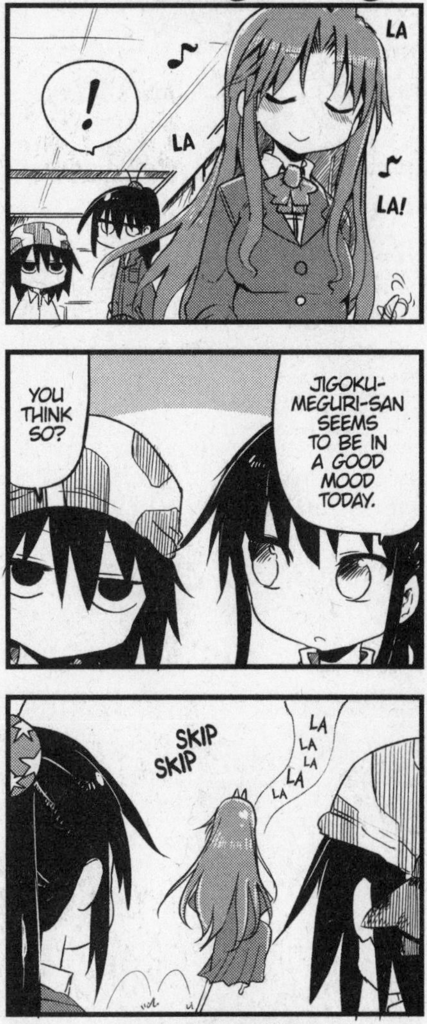
LA
LA
LA!
!
JIGOKU-MEGURI-SAN SEEMS TO BE IN A GOOD MOOD TODAY.
YOU THINK SO?
LA LA LA LA LA LA
SKIP SKIP
LIKE A SUPER GOOD MOOD.
I GUESS.

The King

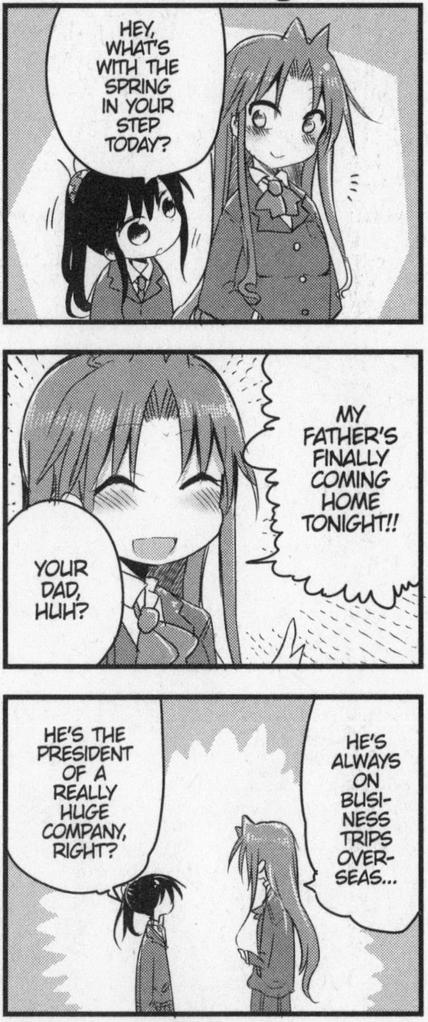
HEY, WHAT'S WITH THE SPRING IN YOUR STEP TODAY?
MY FATHER'S FINALLY COMING HOME TONIGHT!!
YOUR DAD, HUH?
HE'S ALWAYS ON BUSINESS TRIPS OVERSEAS...
HE'S THE PRESIDENT OF A REALLY HUGE COMPANY, RIGHT?
I WOULDN'T SAY THAT. IT'S MORE LIKE HE'S A...
KING!
KING?!

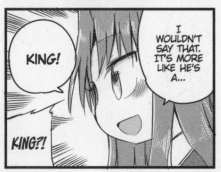

King of Hell

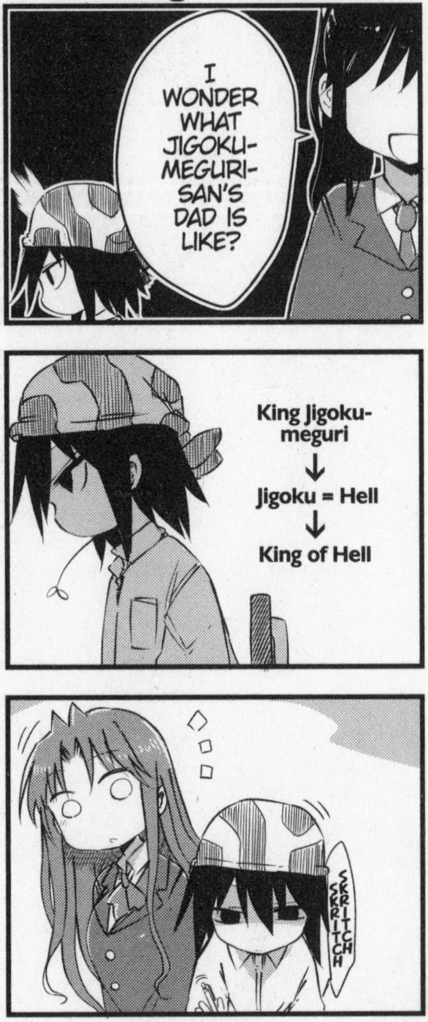
I WONDER WHAT JIGOKU-MEGURI-SAN'S DAD IS LIKE?
King Jigoku-meguri
↓
Jigoku = Hell
↓
King of Hell
SKRITCH SKRITCH
Hell
IS THAT A DEMON?
Not bad.

This is My...

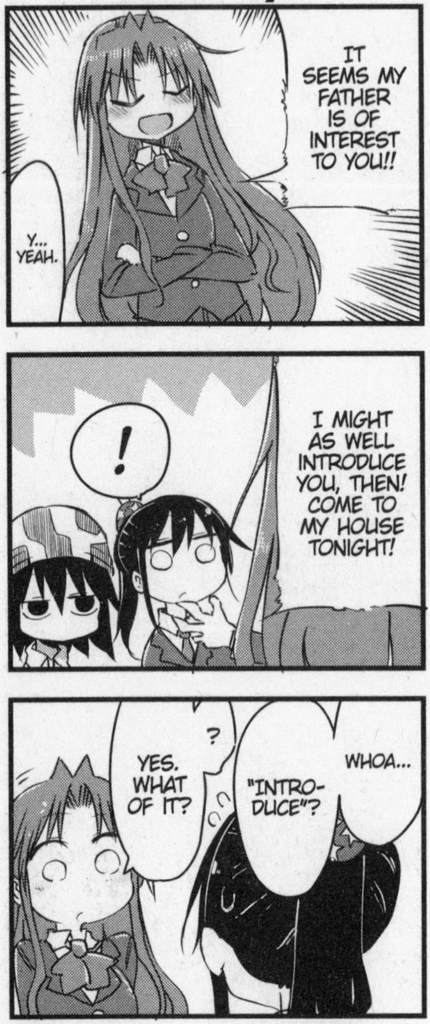
IT SEEMS MY FATHER IS OF INTEREST TO YOU!!
Y... YEAH.
I MIGHT AS WELL INTRODUCE YOU, THEN! COME TO MY HOUSE TONIGHT!
!
WHOA...
"INTRO-DUCE"?
?
YES. WHAT OF IT?
THEN IT'S OFFI-CIAL!
?
NO!

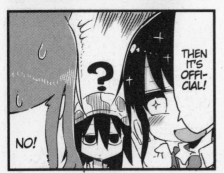

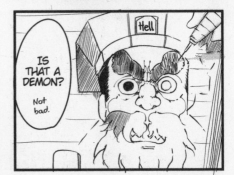

You'll Die

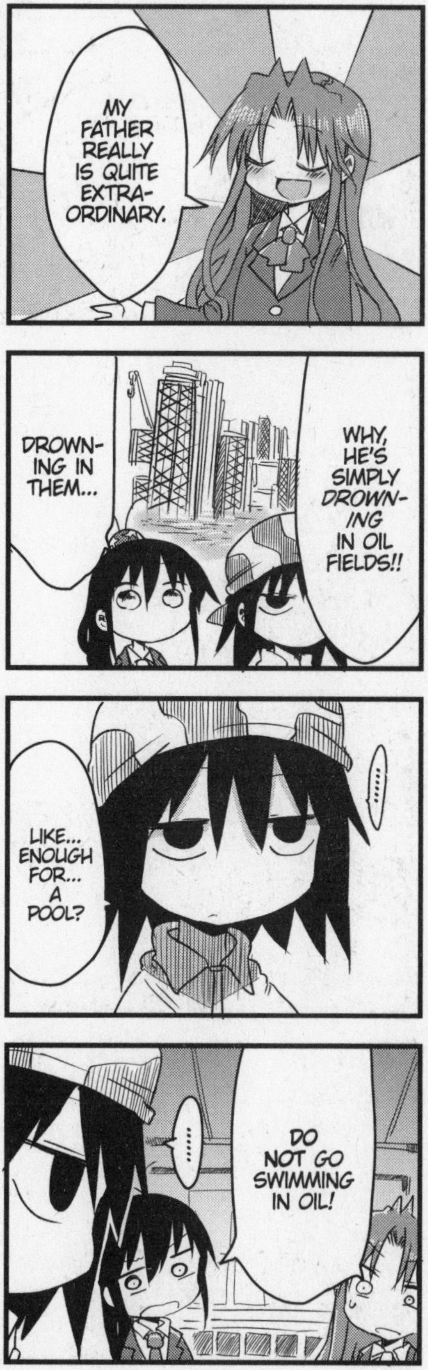
MY FATHER REALLY IS QUITE EXTRA-ORDINARY.
WHY, HE'S SIMPLY DROWNING IN OIL FIELDS!!
DROWNING IN THEM...
......
LIKE... ENOUGH FOR... A POOL?
DO NOT GO SWIMMING IN OIL!
......

International CEO

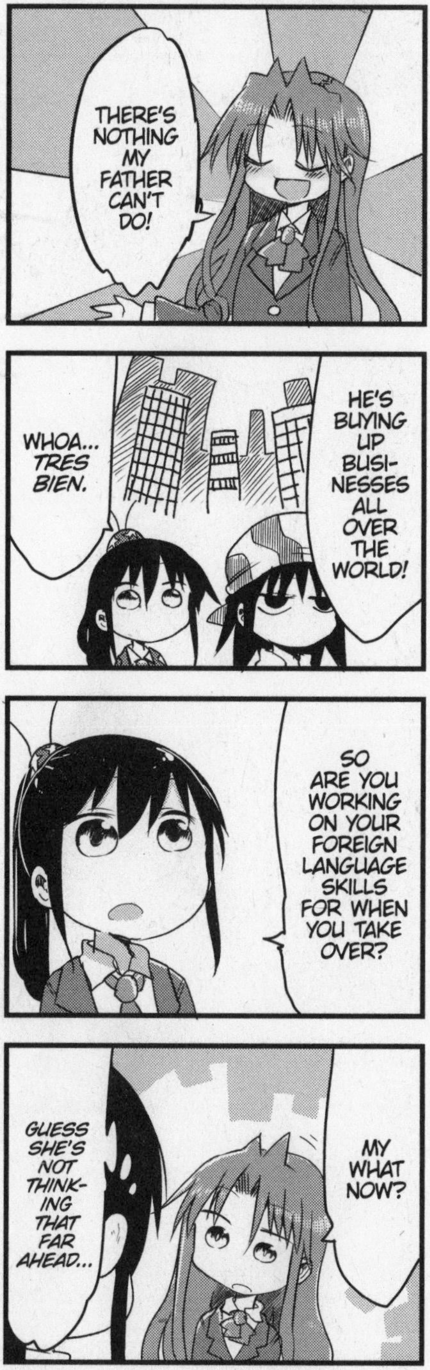
THERE'S NOTHING MY FATHER CAN'T DO!
HE'S BUYING UP BUSINESSES ALL OVER THE WORLD!
WHOA... TRES BIEN.
SO ARE YOU WORKING ON YOUR FOREIGN LANGUAGE SKILLS FOR WHEN YOU TAKE OVER?
MY WHAT NOW?
GUESS SHE'S NOT THINKING THAT FAR AHEAD...

One Moment...

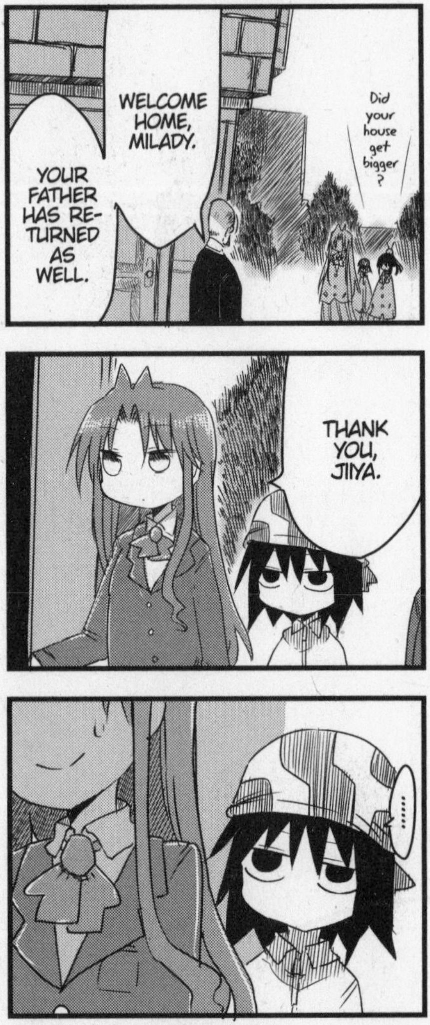
Did your house get bigger?
WELCOME HOME, MILADY.
YOUR FATHER HAS RE-TURNED AS WELL.
THANK YOU, JIIYA.
......
ARE YOU OKAY?
HM? WHY WOULDN'T I BE?

A Different Smile

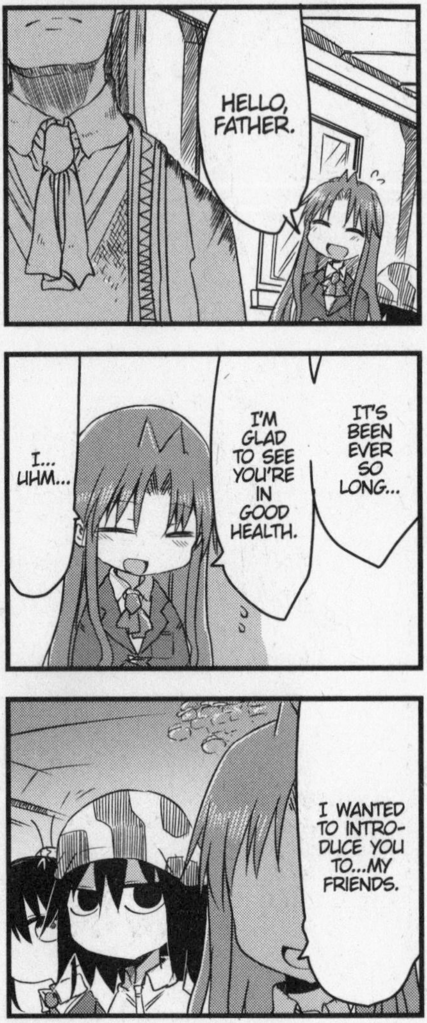
HELLO, FATHER.
IT'S BEEN EVER SO LONG...
I'M GLAD TO SEE YOU'RE IN GOOD HEALTH.
I... UHM...
I WANTED TO INTRO-DUCE YOU TO...MY FRIENDS.
HELLO...
THANK YOU FOR TREATING MY DAUGHTER KINDLY.
PLEASE, MAKE YOURSELVES AT HOME.

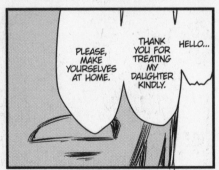

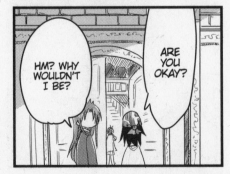

The Usual Smile

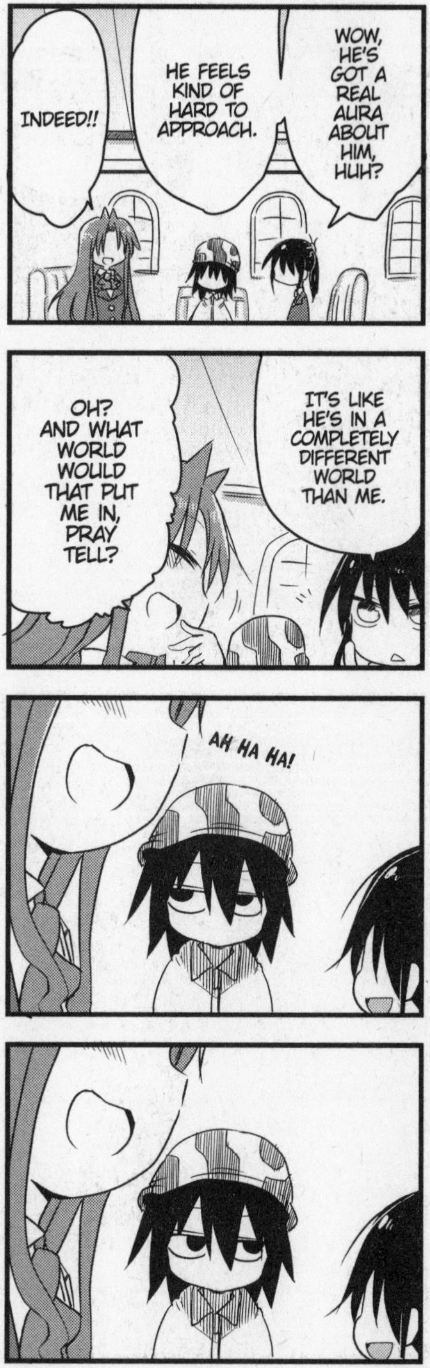
WOW, HE'S GOT A REAL AURA ABOUT HIM, HUH?
HE FEELS KIND OF HARD TO APPROACH.
INDEED!!
IT'S LIKE HE'S IN A COMPLETELY DIFFERENT WORLD THAN ME.
OH? AND WHAT WORLD WOULD THAT PUT ME IN, PRAY TELL?
AH HA HA!

Rules

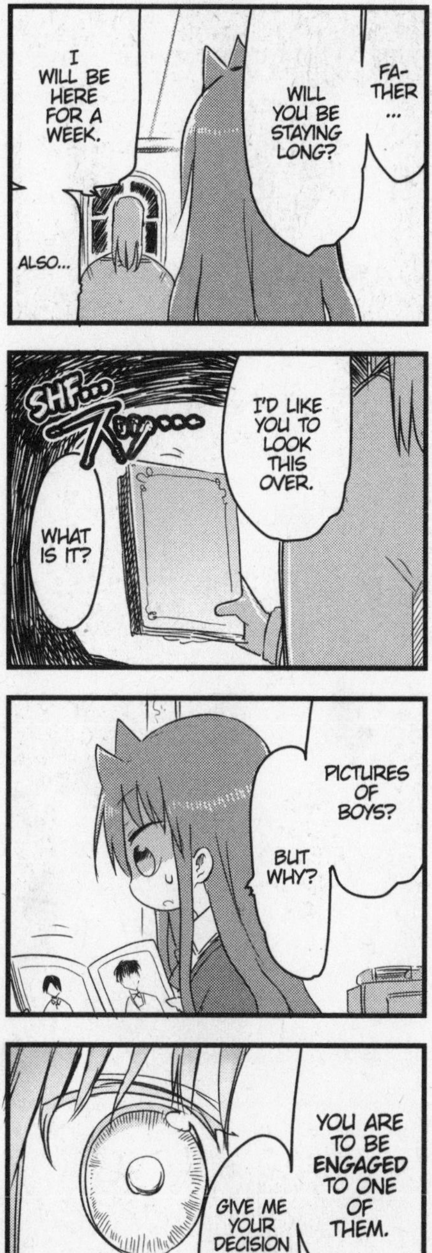
FA-THER ...
WILL YOU BE STAYING LONG?
I WILL BE HERE FOR A WEEK.
ALSO...
I'D LIKE YOU TO LOOK THIS OVER.
SHF...
WHAT IS IT?
PICTURES OF BOYS?
BUT WHY?
YOU ARE TO BE ENGAGED TO ONE OF THEM.
GIVE ME YOUR DECISION BY THE END OF THE WEEK.

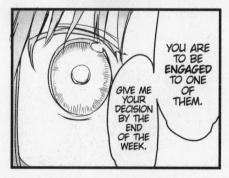

The Noble

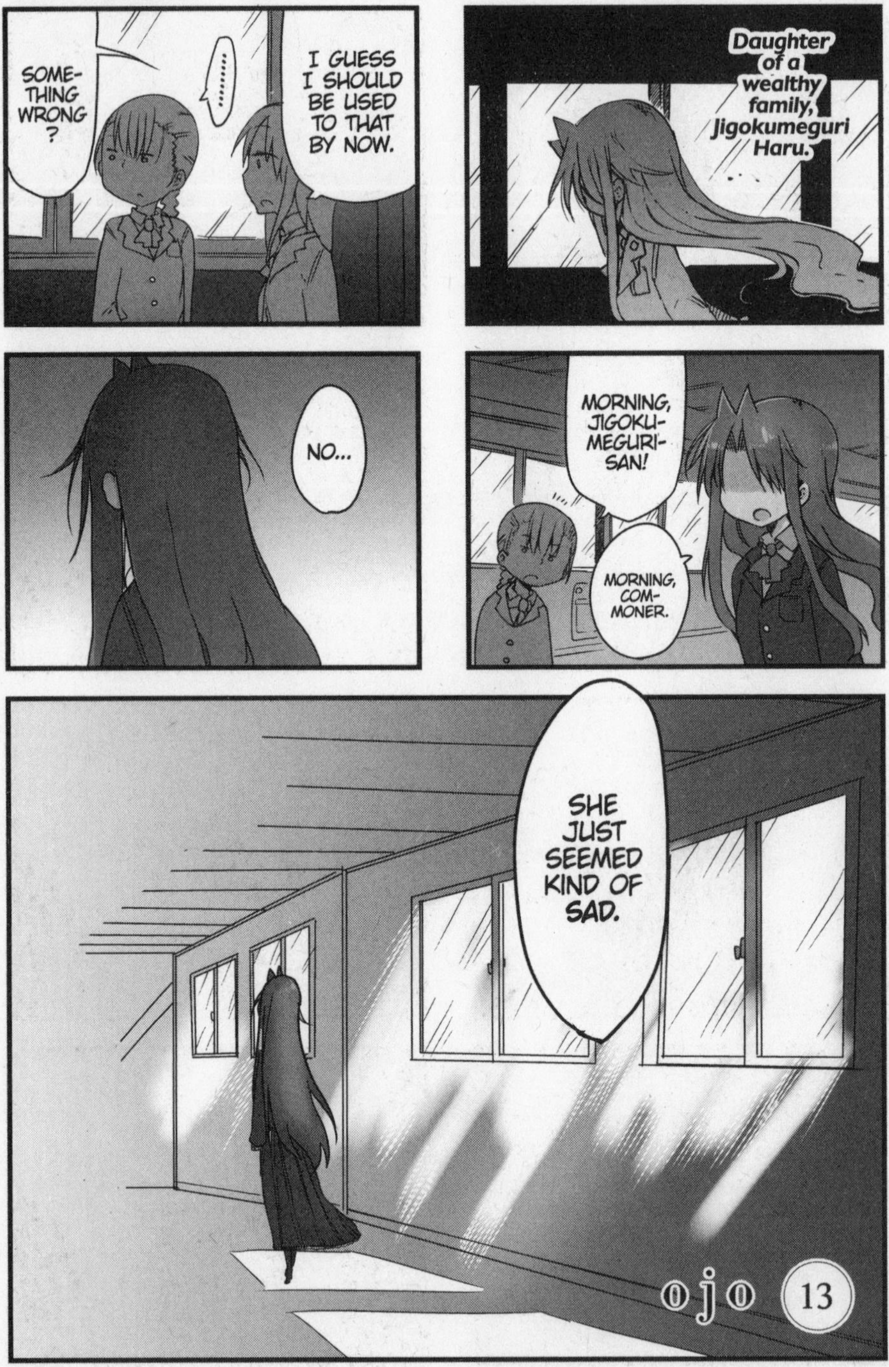

Daughter of a wealthy family, Jigokumeguri Haru.
I GUESS I SHOULD BE USED TO THAT BY NOW.
......
SOME-THING WRONG?
MORNING, JIGOKU-MEGURI-SAN!
MORNING, COM-MONER.
NO...
SHE JUST SEEMED KIND OF SAD.
ojo 13

When All Is Said and Done

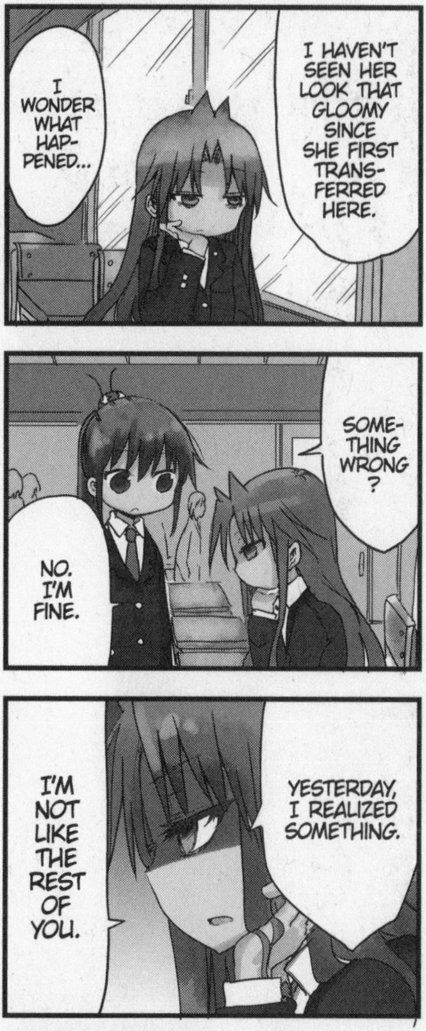
I HAVEN'T SEEN HER LOOK THAT GLOOMY SINCE SHE FIRST TRANS-FERRED HERE.
I WONDER WHAT HAP-PENED...
SOME-THING WRONG?
NO. I'M FINE.
YESTERDAY, I REALIZED SOMETHING.
I'M NOT LIKE THE REST OF YOU.
I DON'T NEED YOU WORRYING ABOUT ME OR TRYING TO MAKE ME FEEL BETTER.
THIS ISN'T SOMETHING A COMMONER CAN HELP WITH.

Jigokumeguri-san Can't Decline!

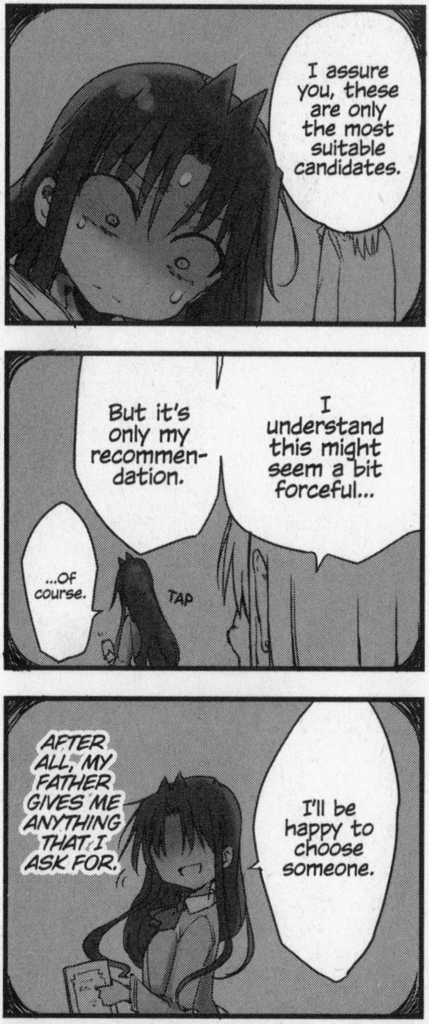
I assure you, these are only the most suitable candidates.
I understand this might seem a bit forceful...
But it's only my recommen-dation.
...of course.
TAP
I'll be happy to choose someone.
AFTER ALL, MY FATHER GIVES ME ANYTHING THAT I ASK FOR.
HOW COULD I POSSIBLY REFUSE?

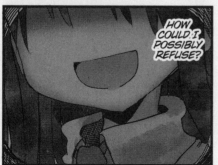

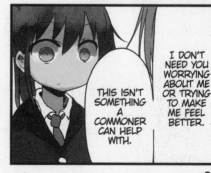

Take This!!

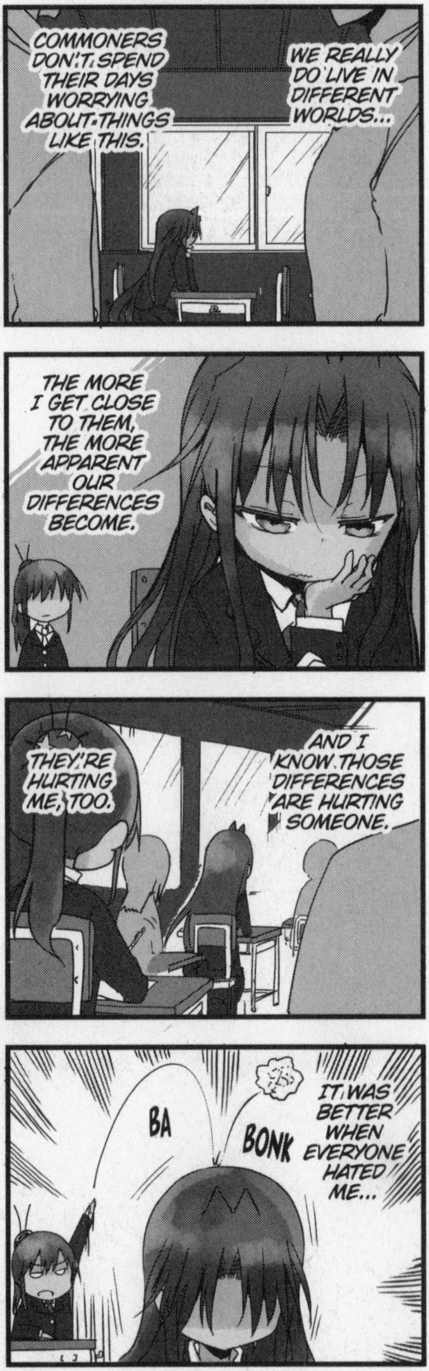
WE REALLY DO LIVE IN DIFFERENT WORLDS...
COMMONERS DON'T SPEND THEIR DAYS WORRYING ABOUT THINGS LIKE THIS.
THE MORE I GET CLOSE TO THEM, THE MORE APPARENT OUR DIFFERENCES BECOME.
AND I KNOW THOSE DIFFERENCES ARE HURTING SOMEONE.
THEY'RE HURTING ME, TOO.
IT WAS BETTER WHEN EVERYONE HATED ME...
BONK
BA

He's Right There Next to You

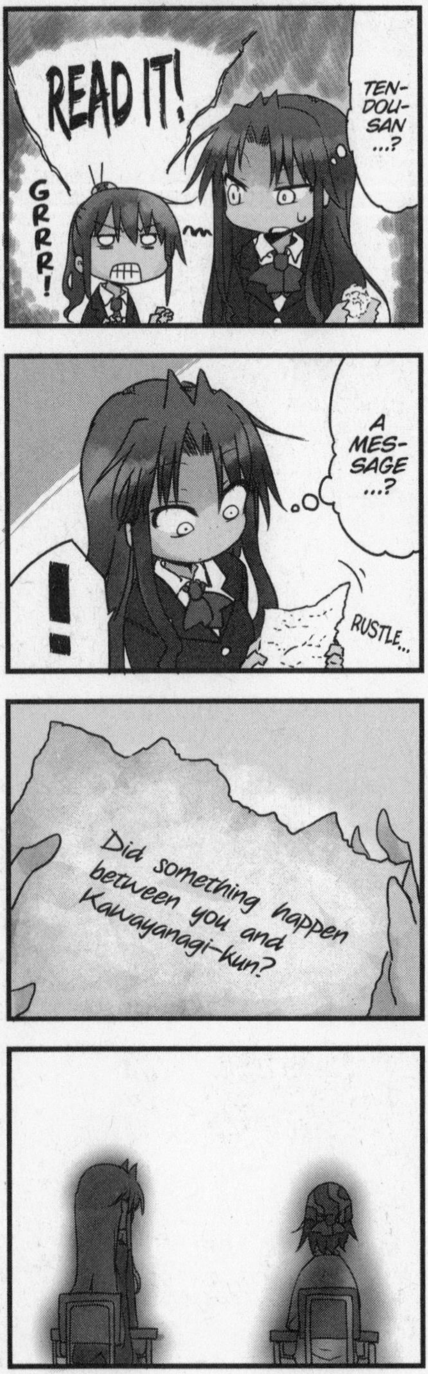
TEN-DOU-SAN ...?
READ IT!
GRRR!
A MES-SAGE ...?
RUSTLE...
!
Did something happen between you and Kawayanagi-kun?

Just Like Normal

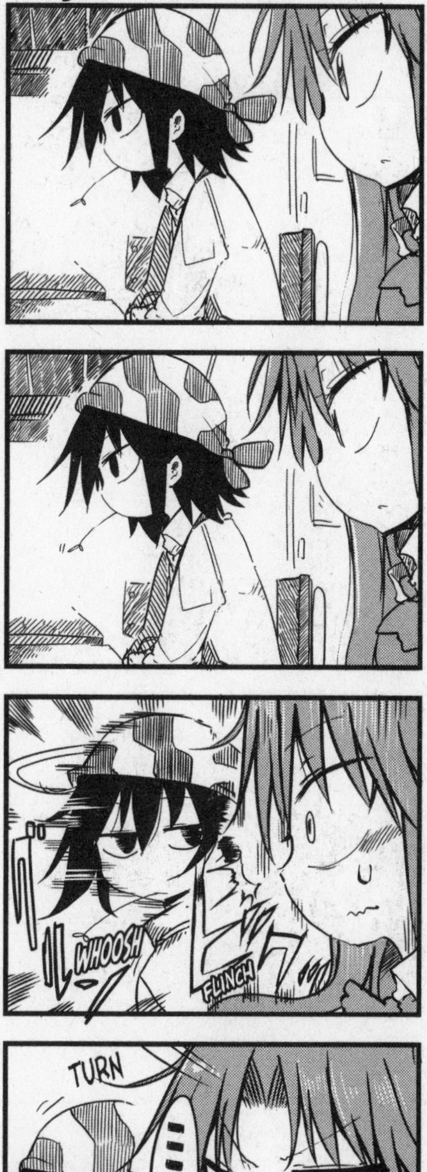
WHOOSH
FLINCH
TURN

Nothing Today, Either

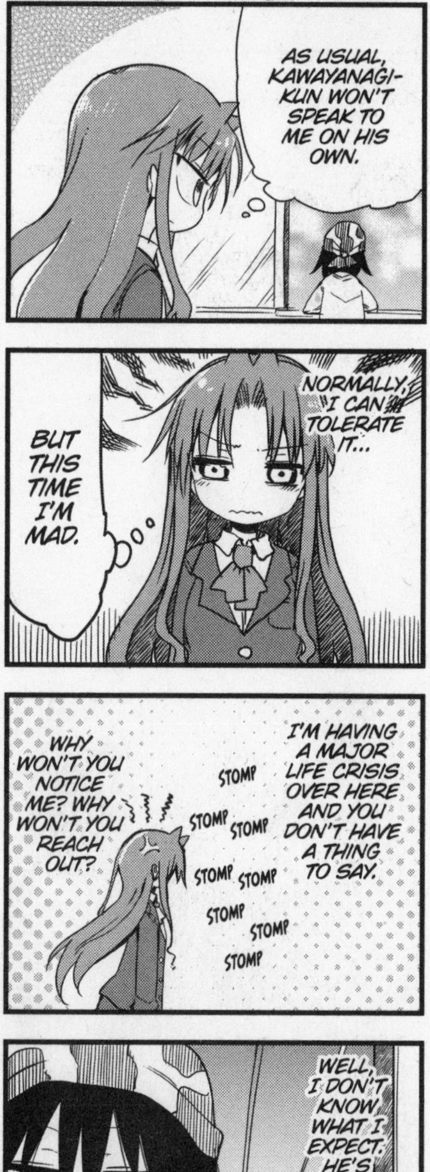
AS USUAL, KAWAYANAGI-KUN WON'T SPEAK TO ME ON HIS OWN.
NORMALLY, I CAN TOLERATE IT...
BUT THIS TIME I'M MAD.
I'M HAVING A MAJOR LIFE CRISIS OVER HERE AND YOU DON'T HAVE A THING TO SAY.
STOMP STOMP STOMP STOMP STOMP STOMP STOMP STOMP
WHY WON'T YOU NOTICE ME? WHY WON'T YOU REACH OUT?
WELL, I DON'T KNOW WHAT I EXPECT. HE'S ALWAYS LIKE THIS.

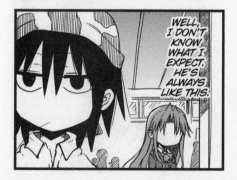

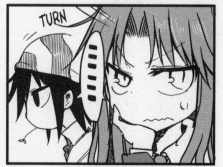

Still Next to You...

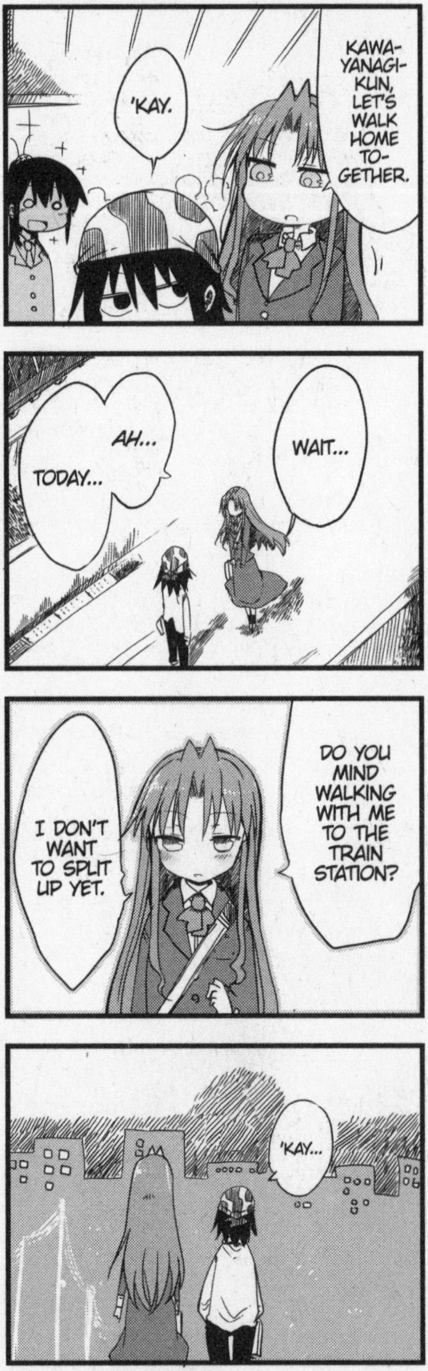
KAWA-YANAGI-KUN, LET'S WALK HOME TO-GETHER.
'KAY.
WAIT...
AH...
TODAY...
DO YOU MIND WALKING WITH ME TO THE TRAIN STATION?
I DON'T WANT TO SPLIT UP YET.
'KAY...

Straight

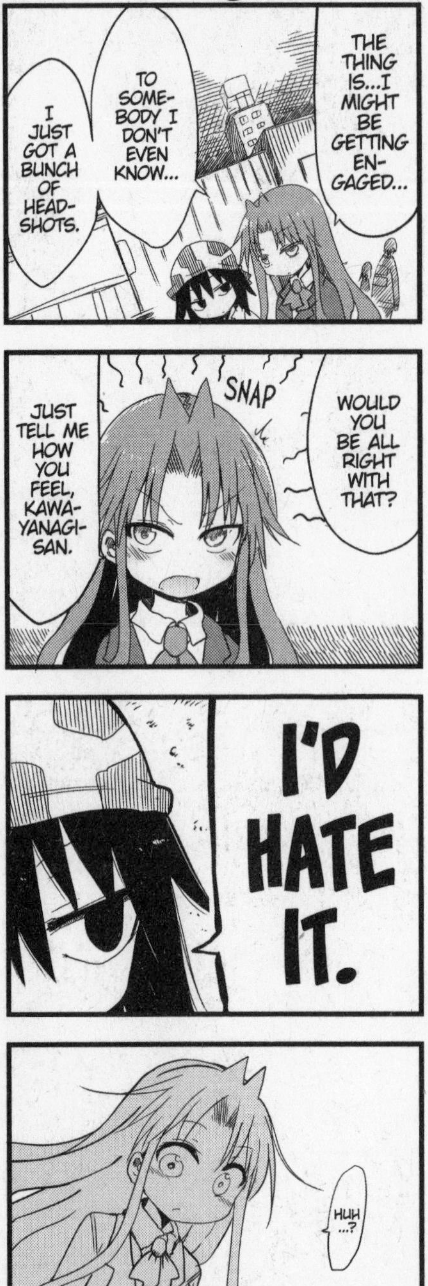
THE THING IS...I MIGHT BE GETTING EN-GAGED...
TO SOME-BODY I DON'T EVEN KNOW...
I JUST GOT A BUNCH OF HEAD-SHOTS.
WOULD YOU BE ALL RIGHT WITH THAT?
SNAP
JUST TELL ME HOW YOU FEEL, KAWA-YANAGI-SAN.
I'D HATE IT.
HUH ...?

Now I Know

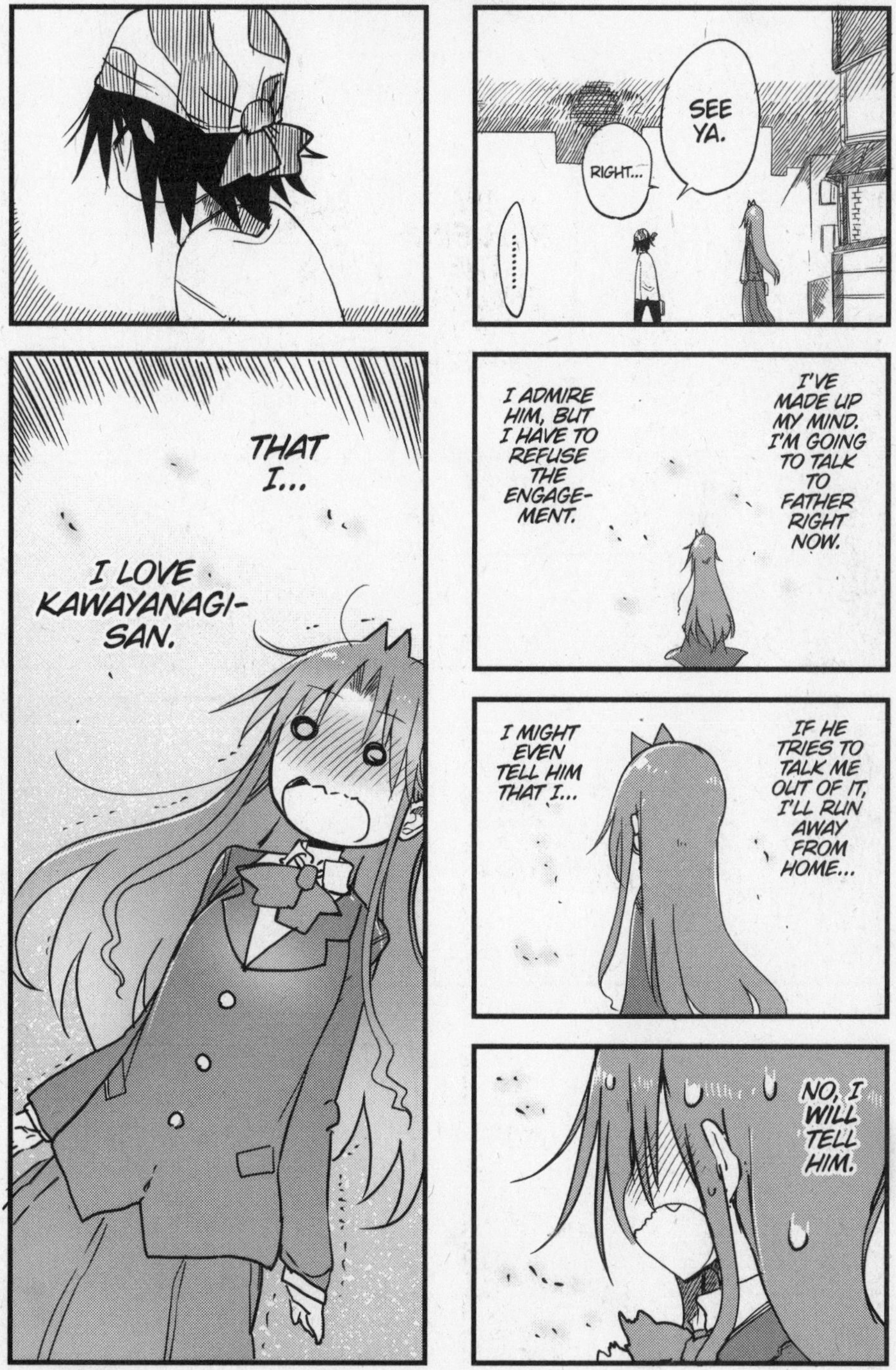

SEE YA.
RIGHT...
......
I'VE MADE UP MY MIND. I'M GOING TO TALK TO FATHER RIGHT NOW.
I ADMIRE HIM, BUT I HAVE TO REFUSE THE ENGAGE-MENT.
IF HE TRIES TO TALK ME OUT OF IT, I'LL RUN AWAY FROM HOME...
I MIGHT EVEN TELL HIM THAT I...
NO, I WILL TELL HIM.
THAT I...
I LOVE KAWAYANAGI-SAN.

Her Will

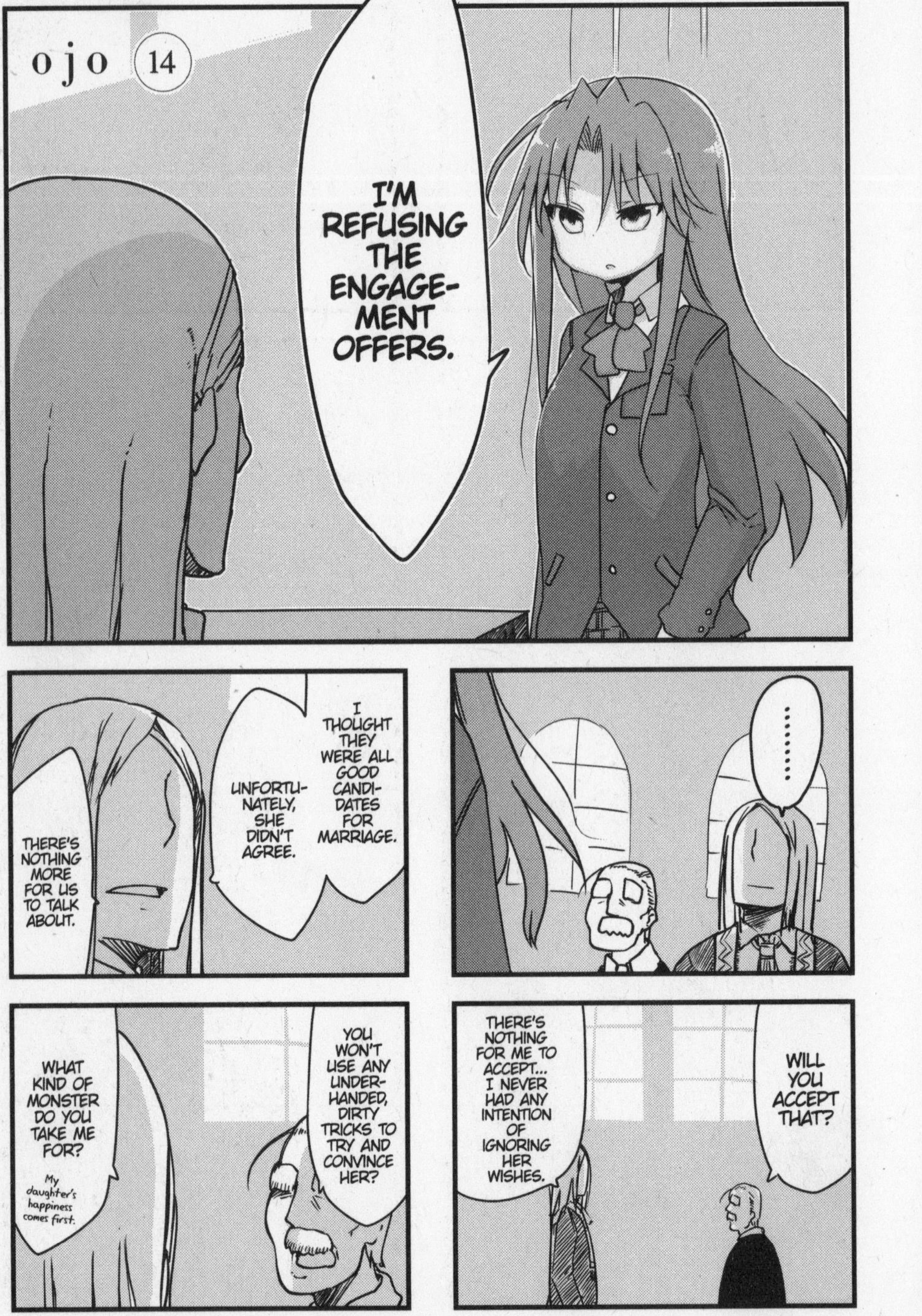
ojo 14
I'M REFUSING THE ENGAGEMENT OFFERS.
……
I THOUGHT THEY WERE ALL GOOD CANDIDATES FOR MARRIAGE.
UNFORTUNATELY, SHE DIDN'T AGREE.
THERE'S NOTHING MORE FOR US TO TALK ABOUT.
WILL YOU ACCEPT THAT?
THERE'S NOTHING FOR ME TO ACCEPT... I NEVER HAD ANY INTENTION OF IGNORING HER WISHES.
YOU WON'T USE ANY UNDERHANDED, DIRTY TRICKS TO TRY AND CONVINCE HER?
WHAT KIND OF MONSTER DO YOU TAKE ME FOR?
My daughter's happiness comes first.

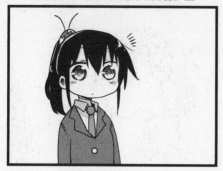

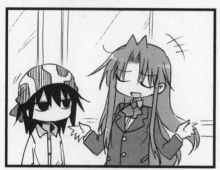

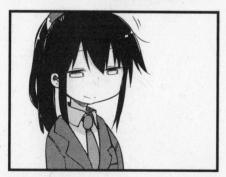

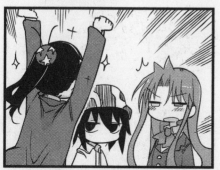

Back to Normal

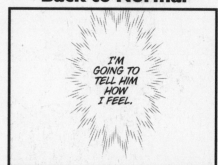

I'M GOING TO TELL HIM HOW I FEEL.
BUT WHEN? WHERE?
HOW SHOULD I DO IT?
IS IT ENOUGH TO SIMPLY BLURT IT OUT?
JUST BE NORMAL!
WAIT, HOW AM I SUPPOSED TO ACT AROUND HIM AGAIN?
Good morning, commoner.

Back to Normal 2

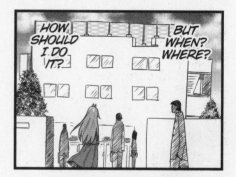

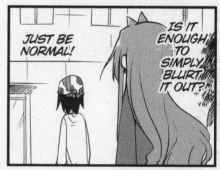

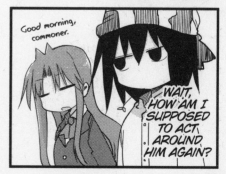

It's Finally Here!

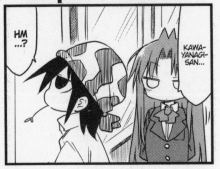

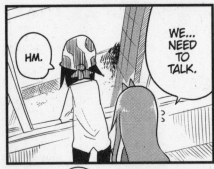

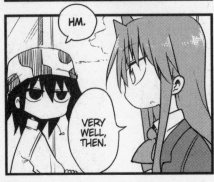

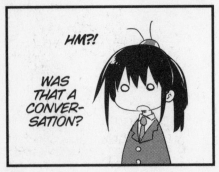

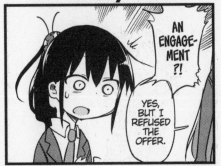

AN ENGAGEMENT?!
YES, BUT I REFUSED THE OFFER.
AND YOUR DAD WAS OKAY WITH THAT?
YES. IT'S FINE.
BUT NOW...
I FEAR...
THERE'S SOMETHING EVEN MORE TERRIFYING THAT I MUST CONTEND WITH.
HUH? WAIT, I'M NOT SURE I'M READY TO HEAR THIS!!
OH.

Telepathic Abilities

KAWAYANAGI-SAN...
HM...?
WE... NEED TO TALK.
HM.
HM.
VERY WELL, THEN.
HM?!
WAS THAT A CONVERSATION?

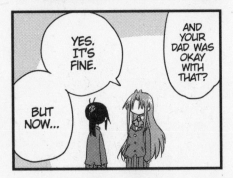

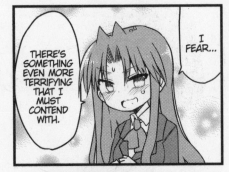

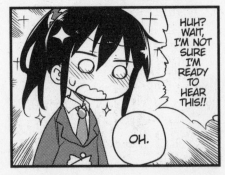

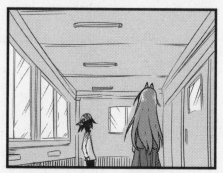

That's Just Who She Is

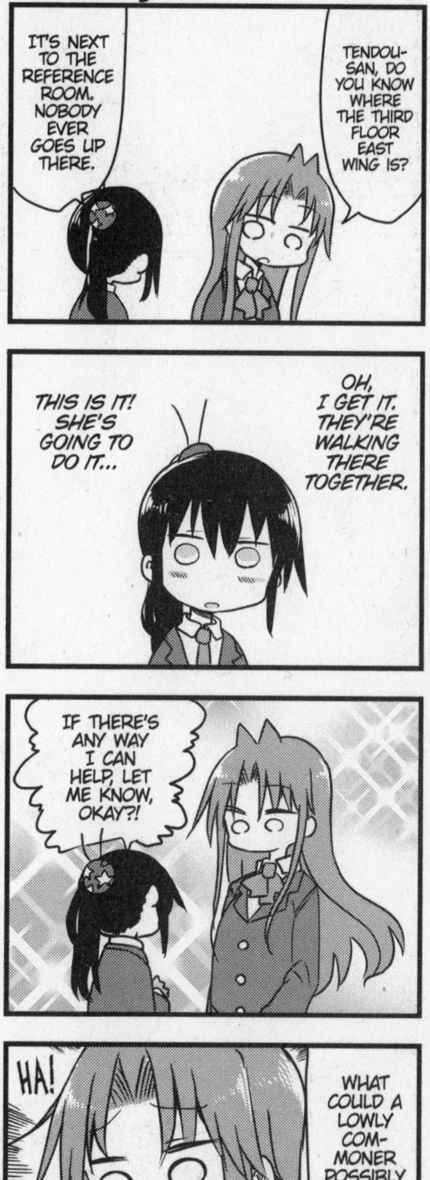
TENDOU-SAN, DO YOU KNOW WHERE THE THIRD FLOOR EAST WING IS?
IT'S NEXT TO THE REFERENCE ROOM. NOBODY EVER GOES UP THERE.
OH, I GET IT. THEY'RE WALKING THERE TOGETHER.
THIS IS IT! SHE'S GOING TO DO IT...
IF THERE'S ANY WAY I CAN HELP, LET ME KNOW, OKAY?!
WHAT COULD A LOWLY COMMONER POSSIBLY DO FOR ME?
HA!
SCREW YOU, TOO!

Going to Talk to Him

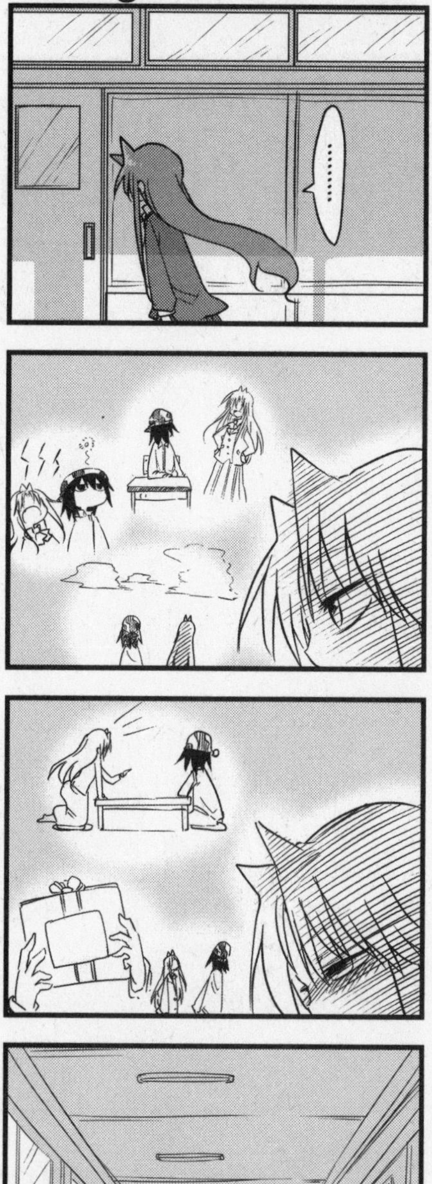
......

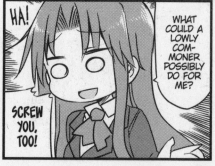

Say It

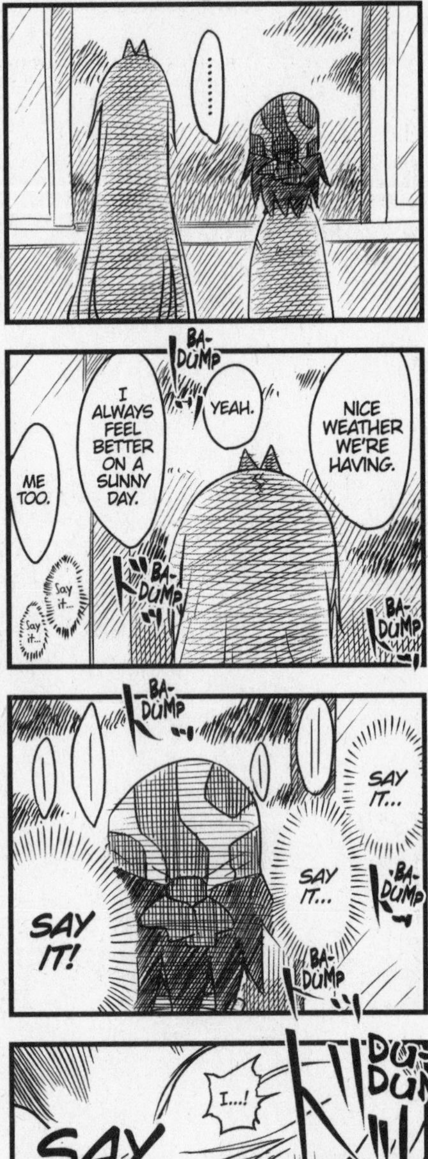
......
BA-DUMP
NICE WEATHER WE'RE HAVING.
YEAH.
I ALWAYS FEEL BETTER ON A SUNNY DAY.
ME TOO.
BA-DUMP
BA-DUMP
Say it...
Say it...
BA-DUMP
SAY IT...
SAY IT...
BA-DUMP
BA-DUMP
SAY IT!
DU-DUN
I...!
SAY IT!

Her Words

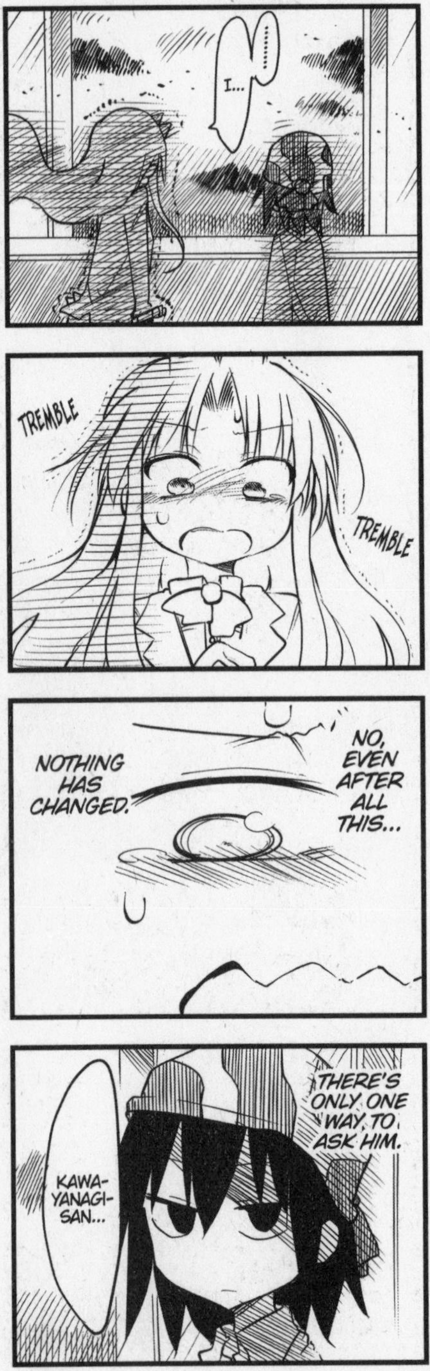
......
I...
TREMBLE
TREMBLE
NO, EVEN AFTER ALL THIS...
NOTHING HAS CHANGED.
THERE'S ONLY ONE WAY TO ASK HIM.
KAWA-YANAGI-SAN...

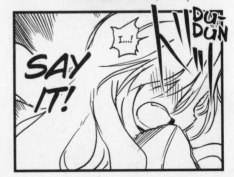

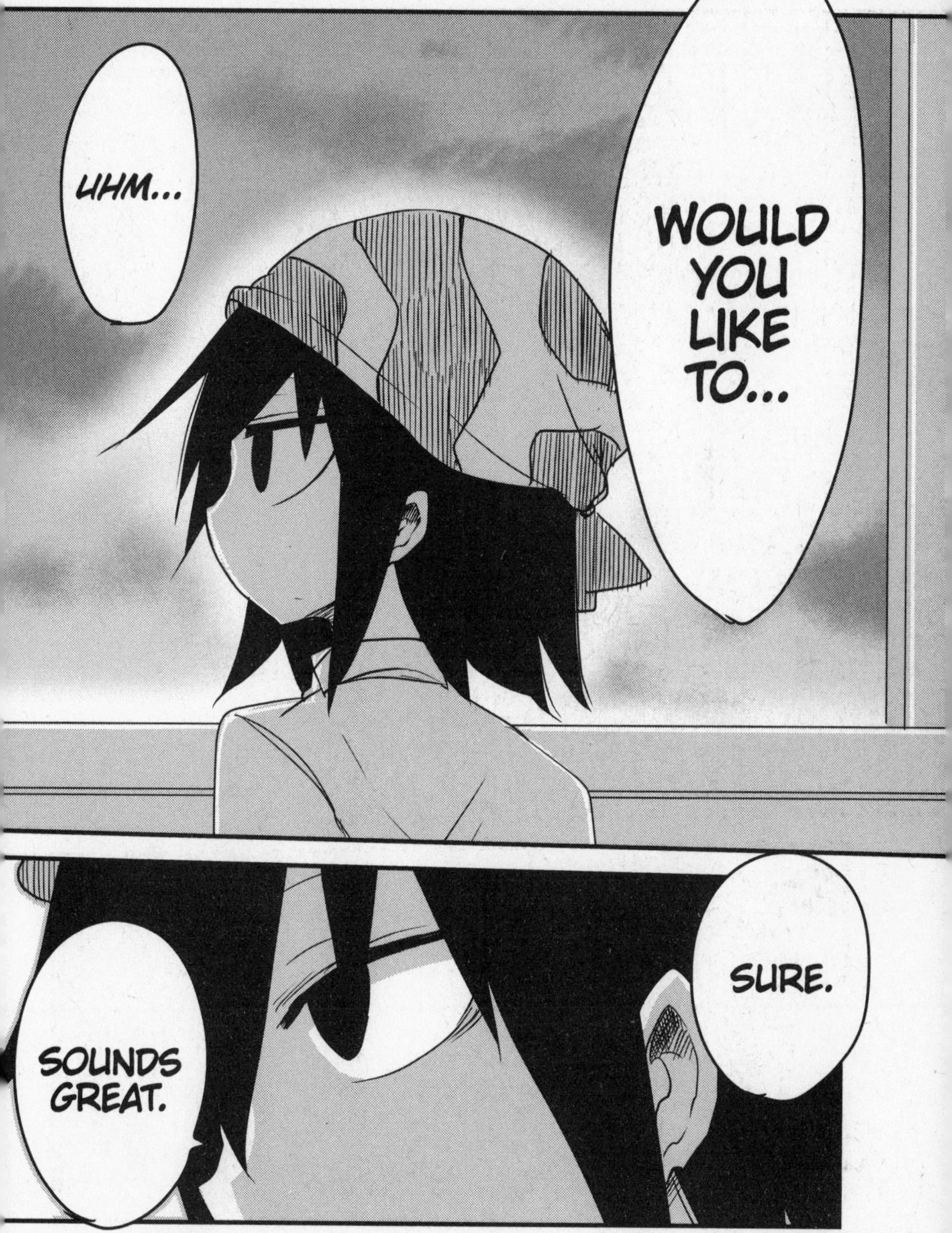
WOULD YOU LIKE TO...
UHM...
SURE.
SOUNDS GREAT.

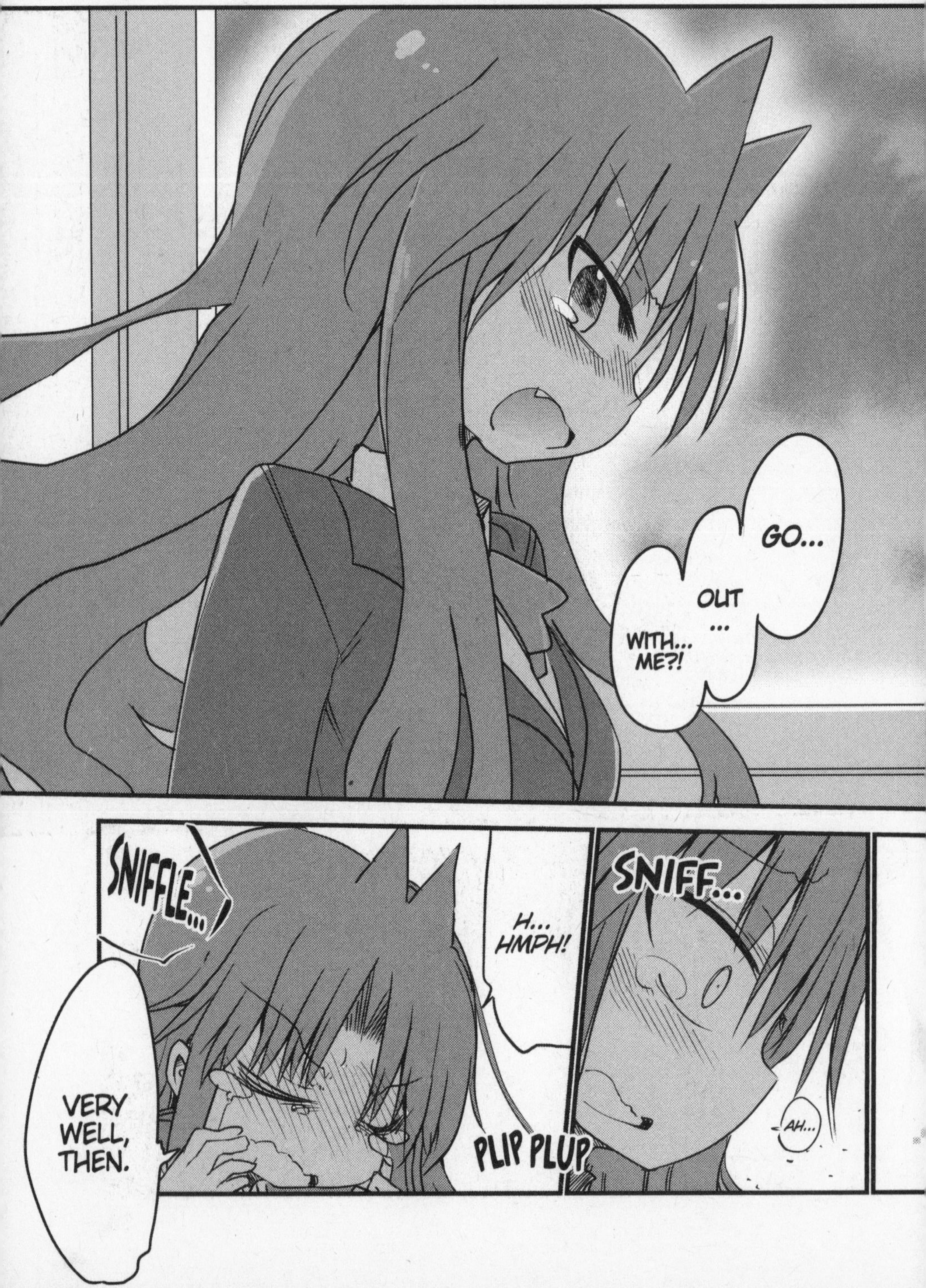
GO... OUT... WITH... ME?!
SNIFF...
AH...
H... HMPH!
SNIFFLE...
PLIP PLUP
VERY WELL, THEN.

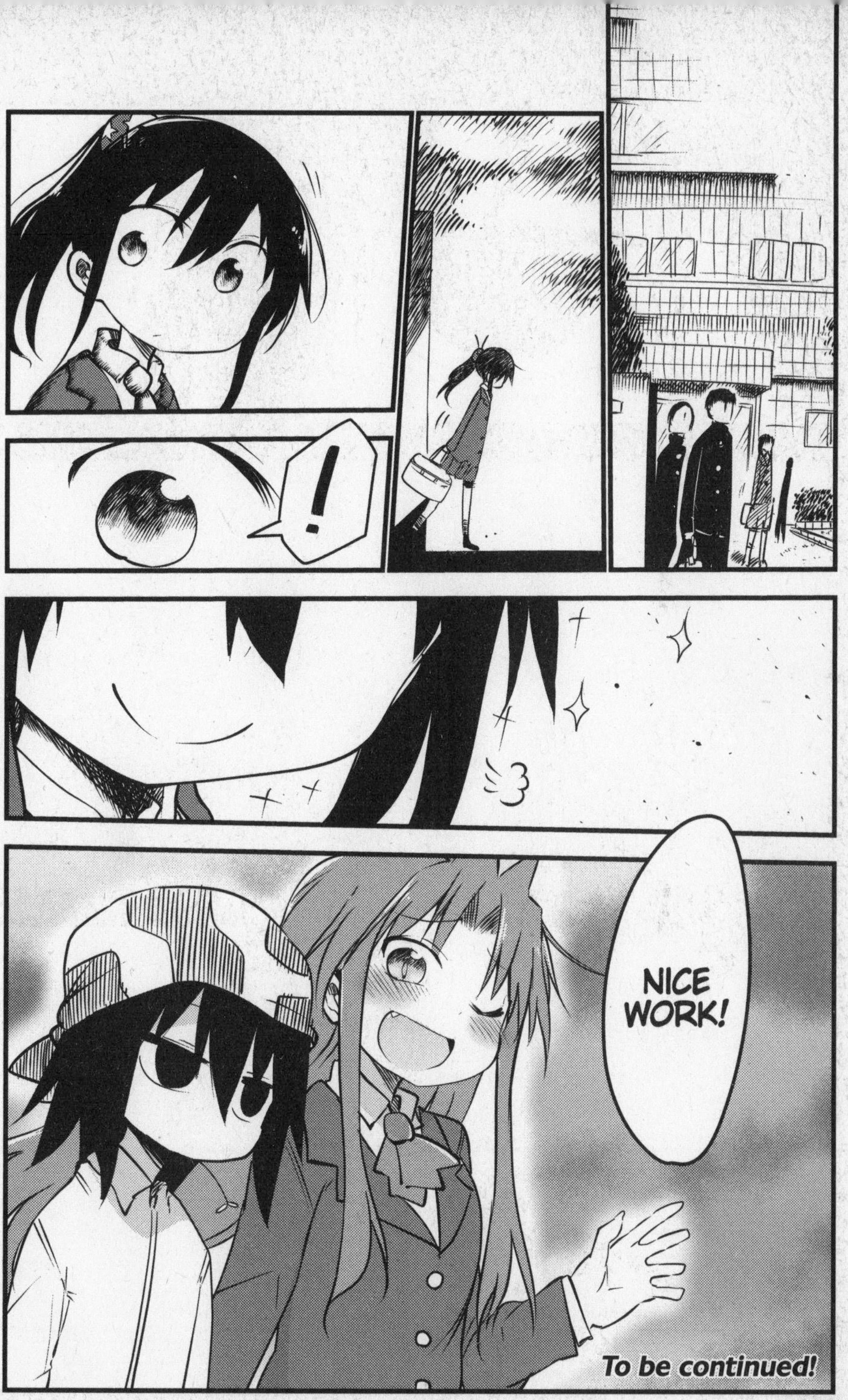
!
NICE WORK!
To be continued!

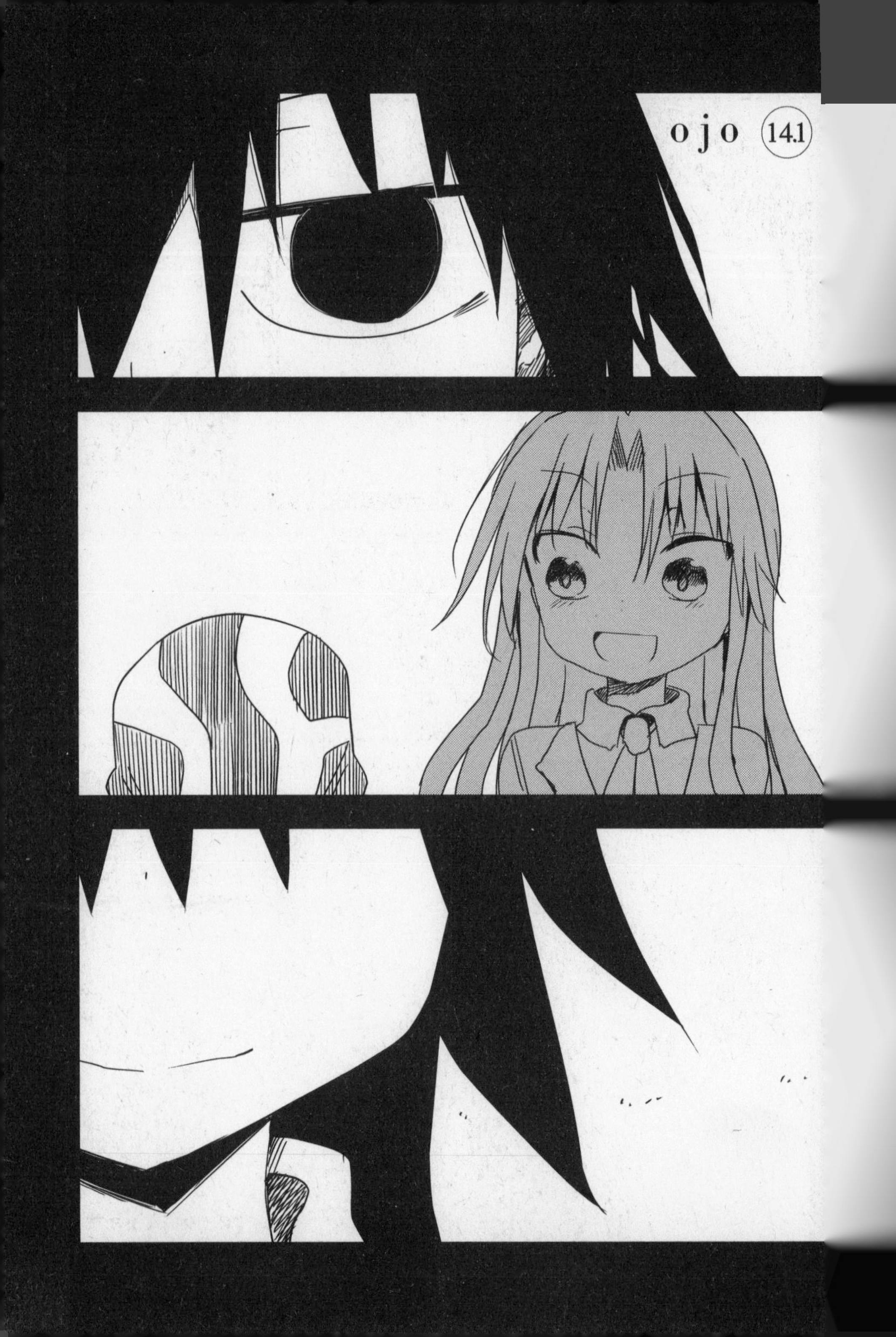
ojo 14.1

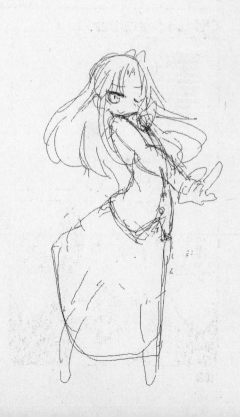

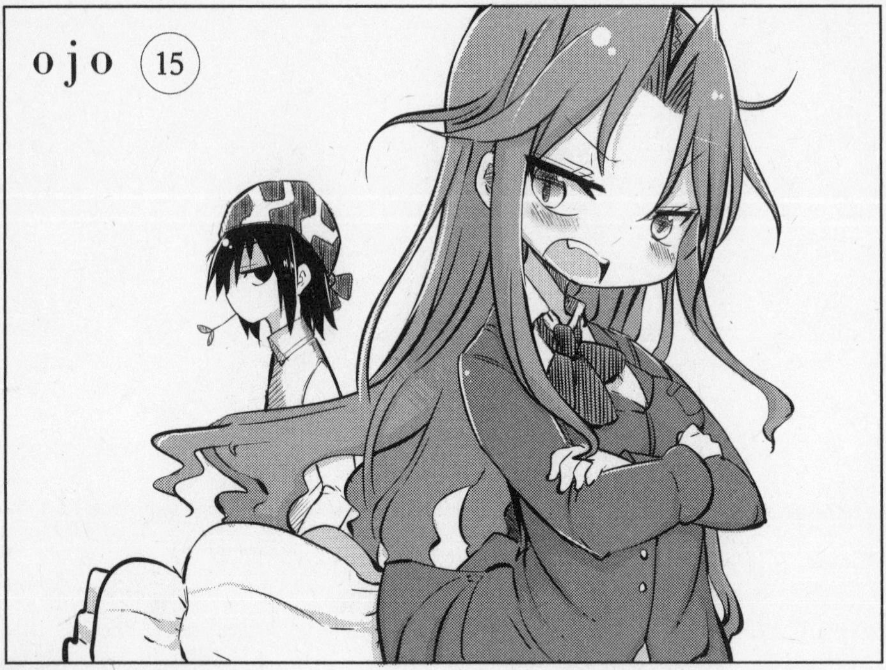
ojo 15

Oil and Water

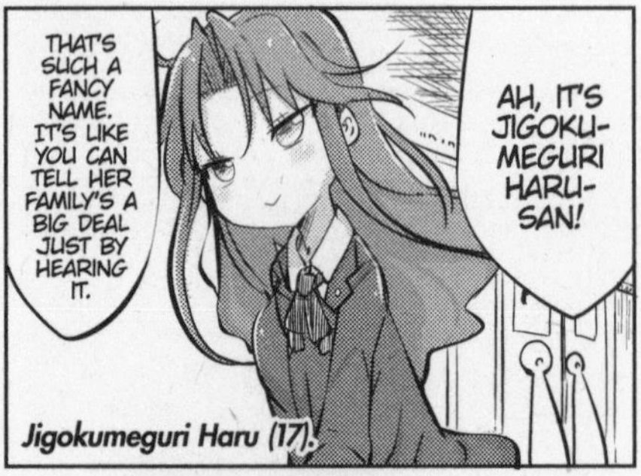
AH, IT'S JIGOKUMEGURI HARU-SAN!
THAT'S SUCH A FANCY NAME. IT'S LIKE YOU CAN TELL HER FAMILY'S A BIG DEAL JUST BY HEARING IT.
Jigokumeguri Haru (17).

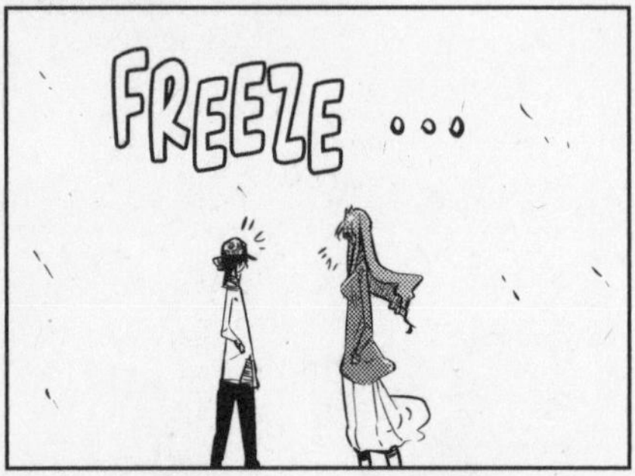
FREEZE ...

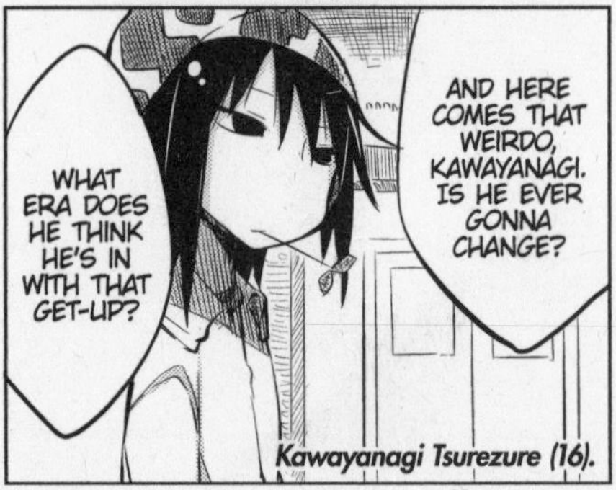
AND HERE COMES THAT WEIRDO, KAWAYANAGI. IS HE EVER GONNA CHANGE?
WHAT ERA DOES HE THINK HE'S IN WITH THAT GET-UP?
Kawayanagi Tsurezure (16).

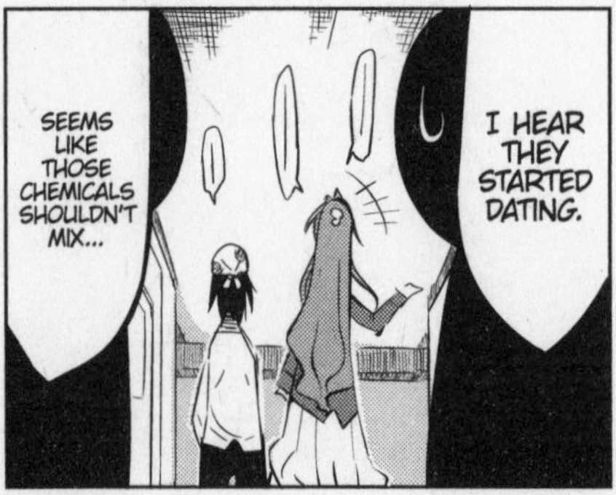
I HEAR THEY STARTED DATING.
SEEMS LIKE THOSE CHEMICALS SHOULDN'T MIX...

Still Has Her Pride

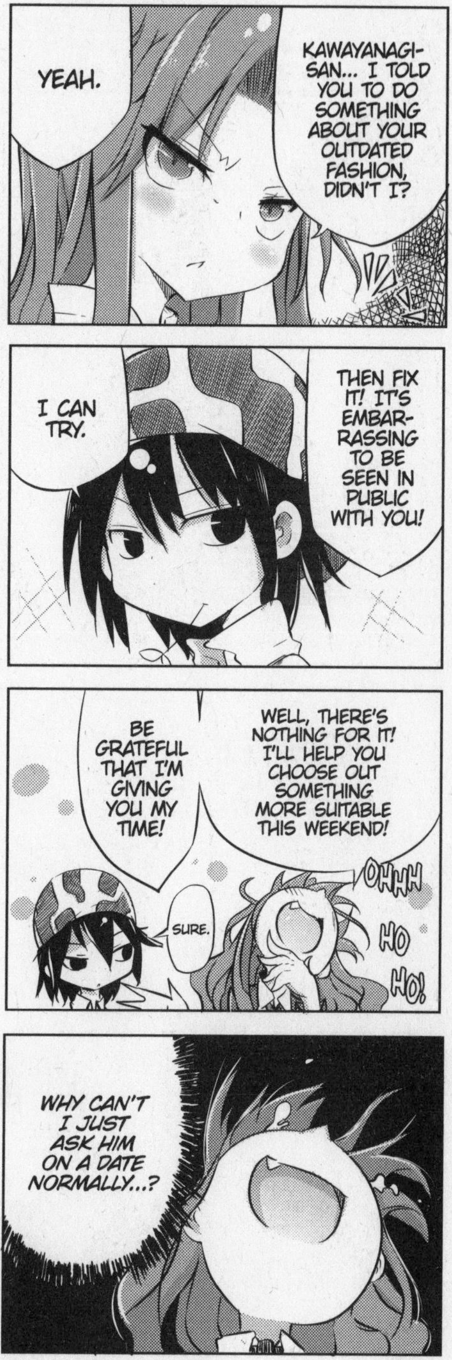
KAWAYANAGI-SAN... I TOLD YOU TO DO SOMETHING ABOUT YOUR OUTDATED FASHION, DIDN'T I?
YEAH.
THEN FIX IT! IT'S EMBARRASSING TO BE SEEN IN PUBLIC WITH YOU!
I CAN TRY.
WELL, THERE'S NOTHING FOR IT! I'LL HELP YOU CHOOSE OUT SOMETHING MORE SUITABLE THIS WEEKEND!
BE GRATEFUL THAT I'M GIVING YOU MY TIME!
OHHH HO HO!
SURE.
WHY CAN'T I JUST ASK HIM ON A DATE NORMALLY...?

Long Years of Observation

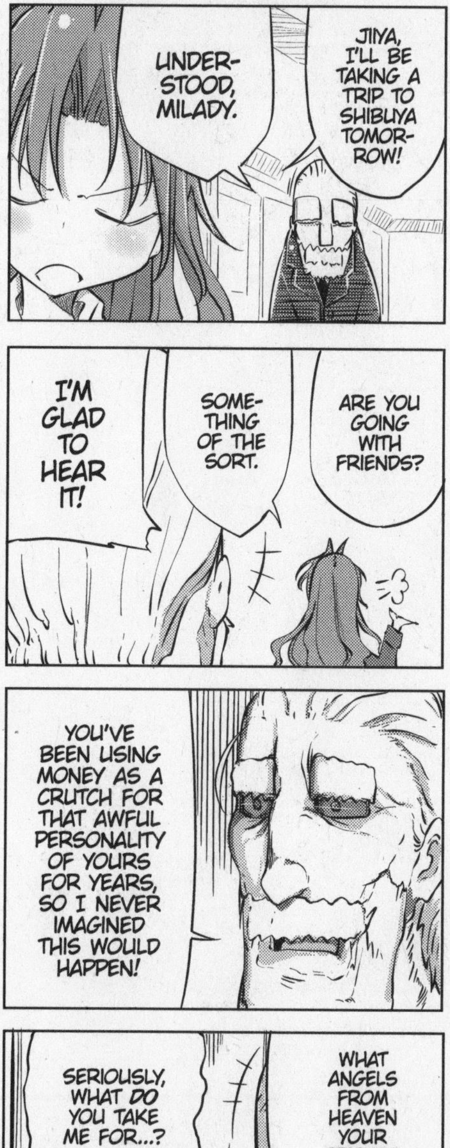
JIIYA, I'LL BE TAKING A TRIP TO SHIBUYA TOMORROW!
UNDERSTOOD, MILADY.
ARE YOU GOING WITH FRIENDS?
SOMETHING OF THE SORT.
I'M GLAD TO HEAR IT!
YOU'VE BEEN USING MONEY AS A CRUTCH FOR THAT AWFUL PERSONALITY OF YOURS FOR YEARS, SO I NEVER IMAGINED THIS WOULD HAPPEN!
WHAT ANGELS FROM HEAVEN YOUR FRIENDS MUST BE!
SERIOUSLY, WHAT DO YOU TAKE ME FOR...?

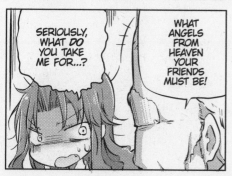

Translation

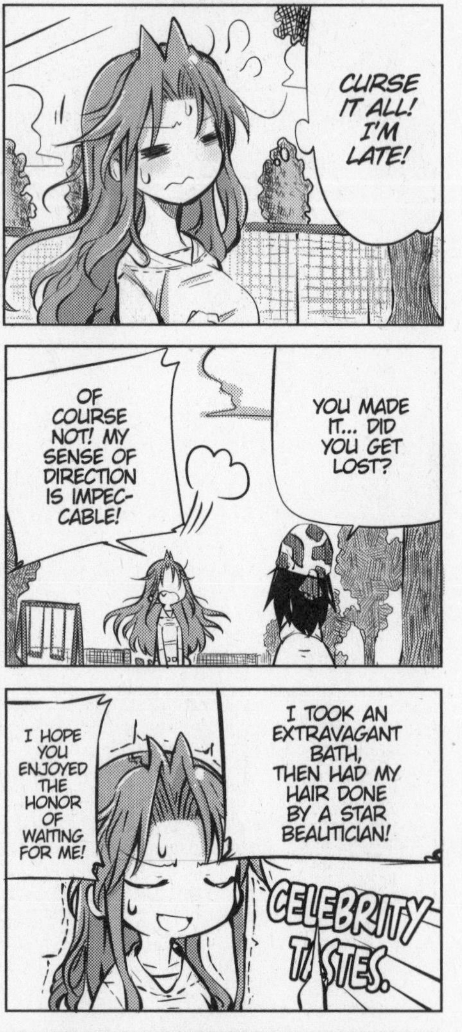
CURSE IT ALL! I'M LATE!
YOU MADE IT... DID YOU GET LOST?
OF COURSE NOT! MY SENSE OF DIRECTION IS IMPECCABLE!
I TOOK AN EXTRAVAGANT BATH, THEN HAD MY HAIR DONE BY A STAR BEAUTICIAN!
I HOPE YOU ENJOYED THE HONOR OF WAITING FOR ME!
CELEBRITY TASTES.
I SEE... YOU REALLY WENT ALL OUT TODAY.
N-NONSENSE! THIS IS MY LIFESTYLE!

He Sleeps in a Monk's Robe

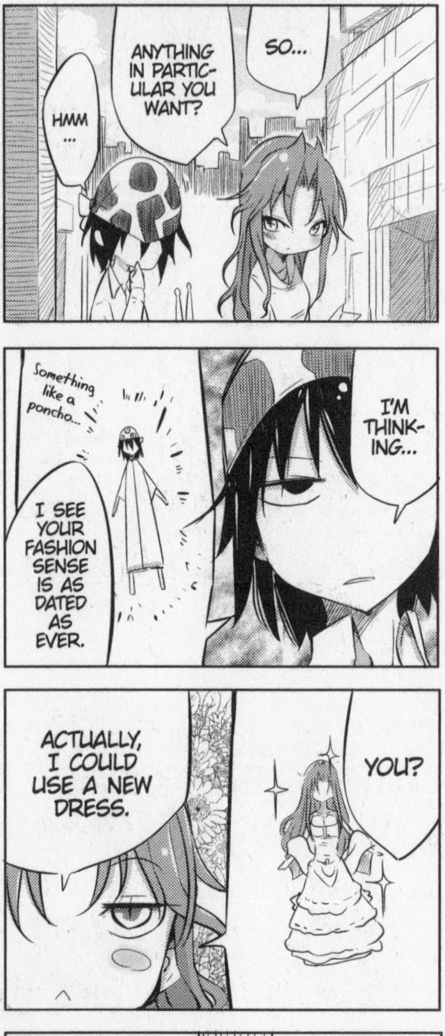
SO...
ANYTHING IN PARTICULAR YOU WANT?
HMM ...
I'M THINKING...
Something like a poncho...
I SEE YOUR FASHION SENSE IS AS DATED AS EVER.
YOU?
ACTUALLY, I COULD USE A NEW DRESS.
A PONCHO'S LIKE A DRESS. WE WANT THE SAME THING.
THAT'S HOW YOU'RE RATIONALIZING IT?!

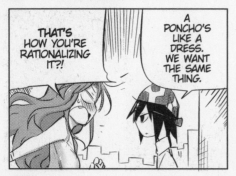

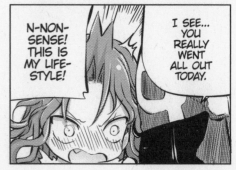

Student Date Spot

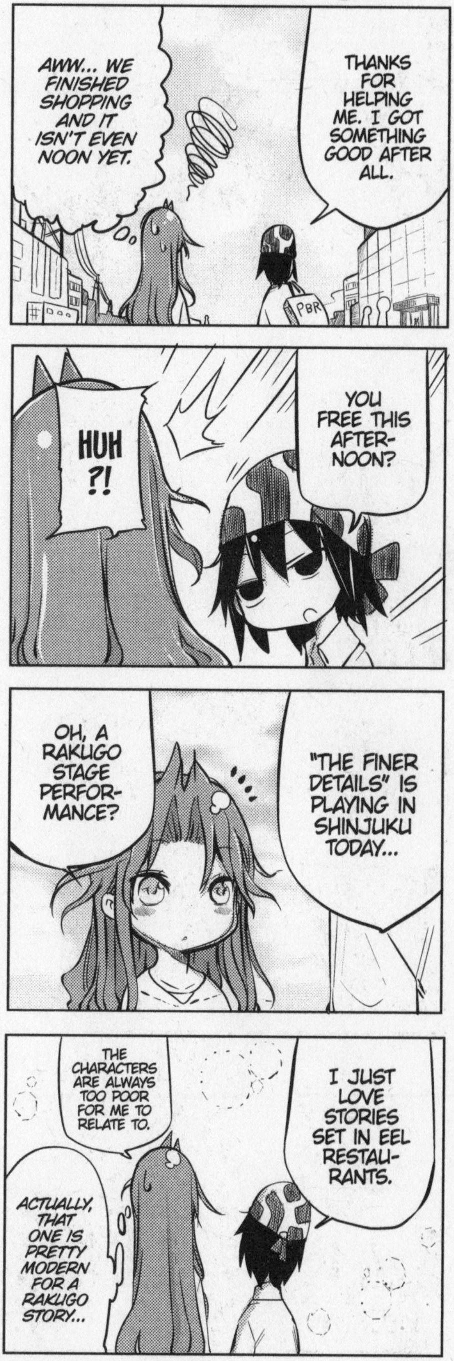

THANKS FOR HELPING ME. I GOT SOMETHING GOOD AFTER ALL.
AWW... WE FINISHED SHOPPING AND IT ISN'T EVEN NOON YET.
PBR
YOU FREE THIS AFTER-NOON?
HUH ?!
"THE FINER DETAILS" IS PLAYING IN SHINJUKU TODAY...
OH, A RAKUGO STAGE PERFOR-MANCE?
I JUST LOVE STORIES SET IN EEL RESTAU-RANTS.
THE CHARACTERS ARE ALWAYS TOO POOR FOR ME TO RELATE TO.
ACTUALLY, THAT ONE IS PRETTY MODERN FOR A RAKUGO STORY...

It Was Beautiful

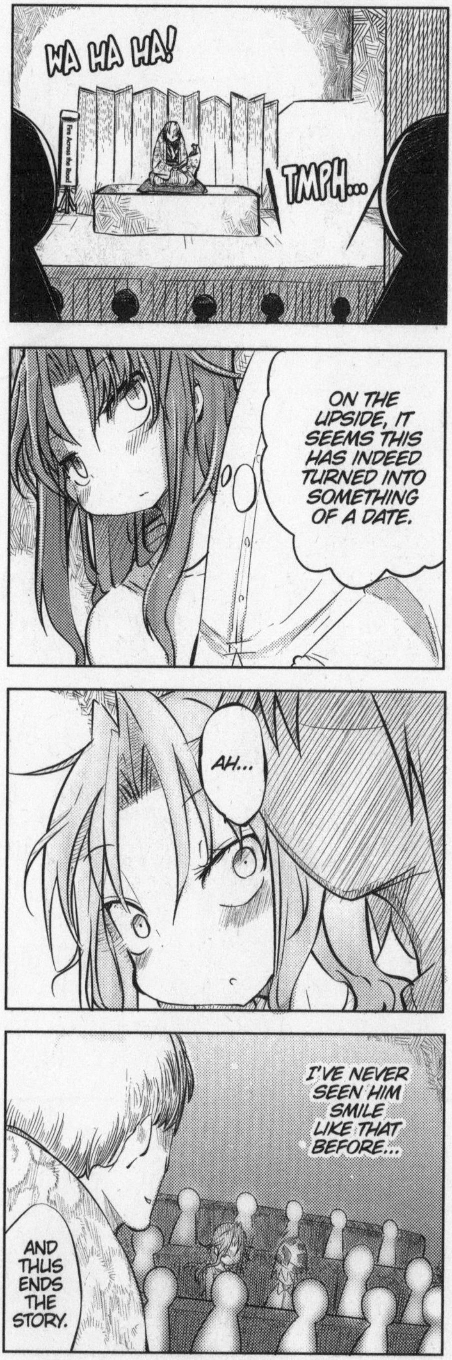

WA HA HA!
TMPH...
ON THE UPSIDE, IT SEEMS THIS HAS INDEED TURNED INTO SOMETHING OF A DATE.
AH...
I'VE NEVER SEEN HIM SMILE LIKE THAT BEFORE...
AND THUS ENDS THE STORY.

Home Cooking

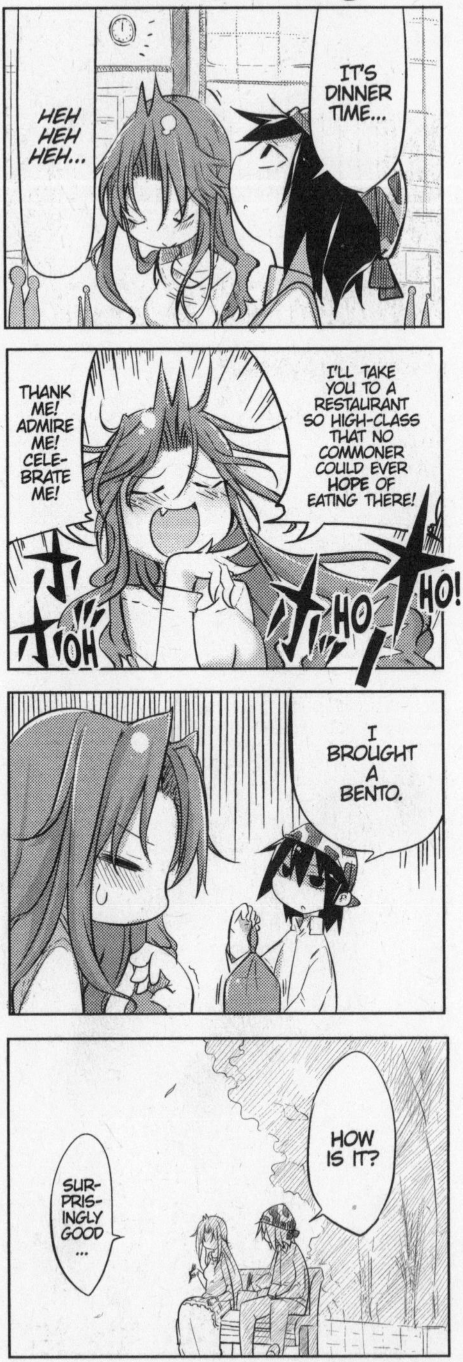

IT'S DINNER TIME...
HEH HEH HEH...
I'LL TAKE YOU TO A RESTAURANT SO HIGH-CLASS THAT NO COMMONER COULD EVER HOPE OF EATING THERE!
THANK ME! ADMIRE ME! CELEBRATE ME!
HO!
HO
OH
I BROUGHT A BENTO.
HOW IS IT?
SURPRISINGLY GOOD ...

Puppy Mentality

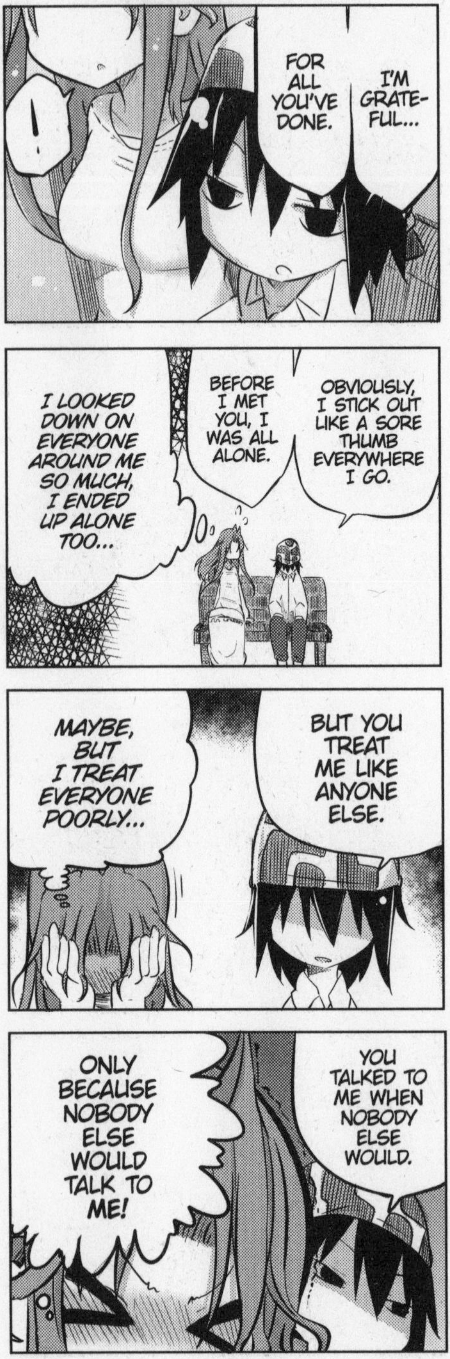

I'M GRATEFUL...
FOR ALL YOU'VE DONE.
!
OBVIOUSLY, I STICK OUT LIKE A SORE THUMB EVERYWHERE I GO.
BEFORE I MET YOU, I WAS ALL ALONE.
I LOOKED DOWN ON EVERYONE AROUND ME SO MUCH, I ENDED UP ALONE TOO...
BUT YOU TREAT ME LIKE ANYONE ELSE.
MAYBE, BUT I TREAT EVERYONE POORLY...
YOU TALKED TO ME WHEN NOBODY ELSE WOULD.
ONLY BECAUSE NOBODY ELSE WOULD TALK TO ME!

Just as Tsurezure Would

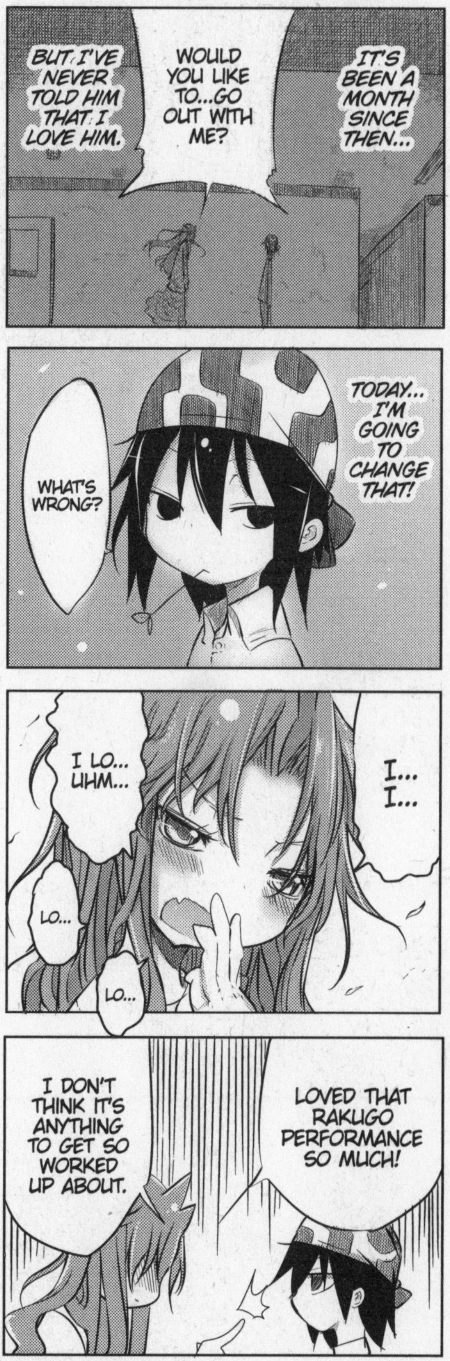
IT'S BEEN A MONTH SINCE THEN...
WOULD YOU LIKE TO...GO OUT WITH ME?
BUT I'VE NEVER TOLD HIM THAT I LOVE HIM.
TODAY... I'M GOING TO CHANGE THAT!
WHAT'S WRONG?
I... I...
I LO... UHM...
LO...
LO...
LOVED THAT RAKUGO PERFORMANCE SO MUCH!
I DON'T THINK IT'S ANYTHING TO GET SO WORKED UP ABOUT.

From Jigoku to Kawayanagi

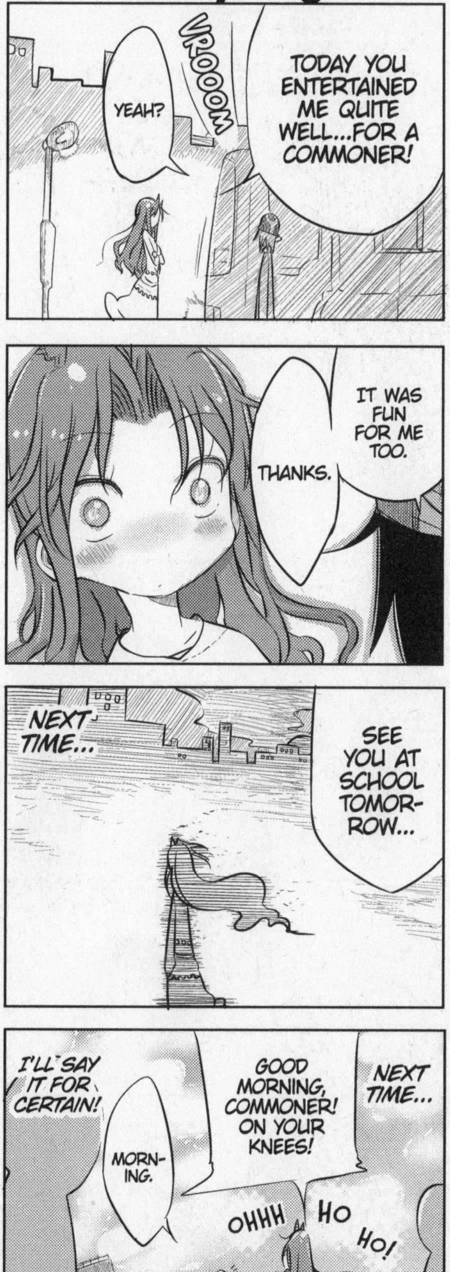
TODAY YOU ENTERTAINED ME QUITE WELL...FOR A COMMONER!
VROOOM
YEAH?
IT WAS FUN FOR ME TOO.
THANKS.
SEE YOU AT SCHOOL TOMORROW...
NEXT TIME...
NEXT TIME...
GOOD MORNING, COMMONER! ON YOUR KNEES!
I'LL SAY IT FOR CERTAIN!
MORNING.
OHHH HO HO!

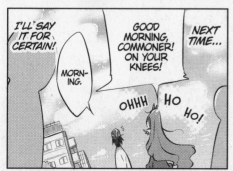

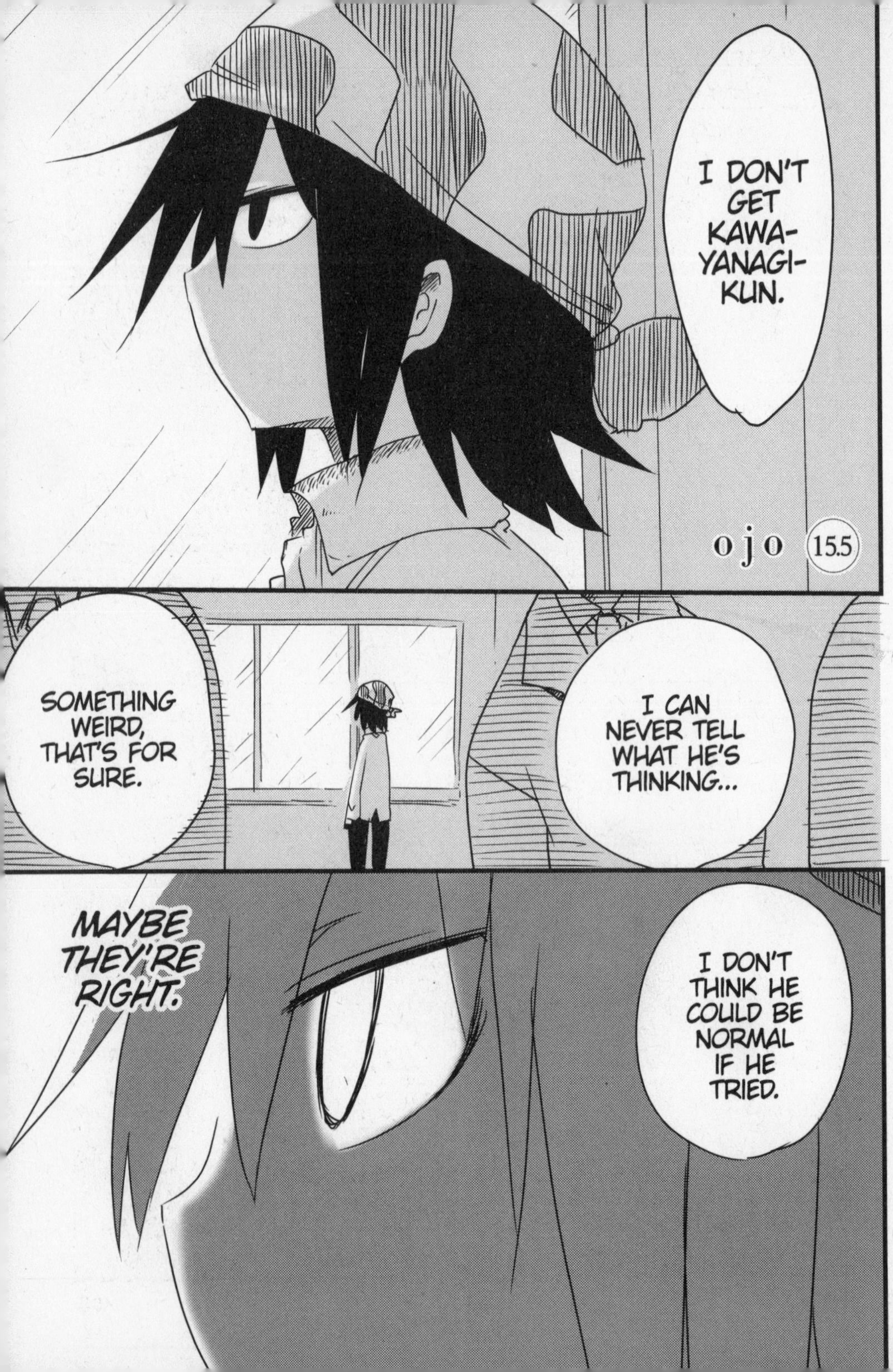
I DON'T GET KAWA-YANAGI-KUN.
ojo 15.5
I CAN NEVER TELL WHAT HE'S THINKING...
SOMETHING WEIRD, THAT'S FOR SURE.
I DON'T THINK HE COULD BE NORMAL IF HE TRIED.
MAYBE THEY'RE RIGHT.

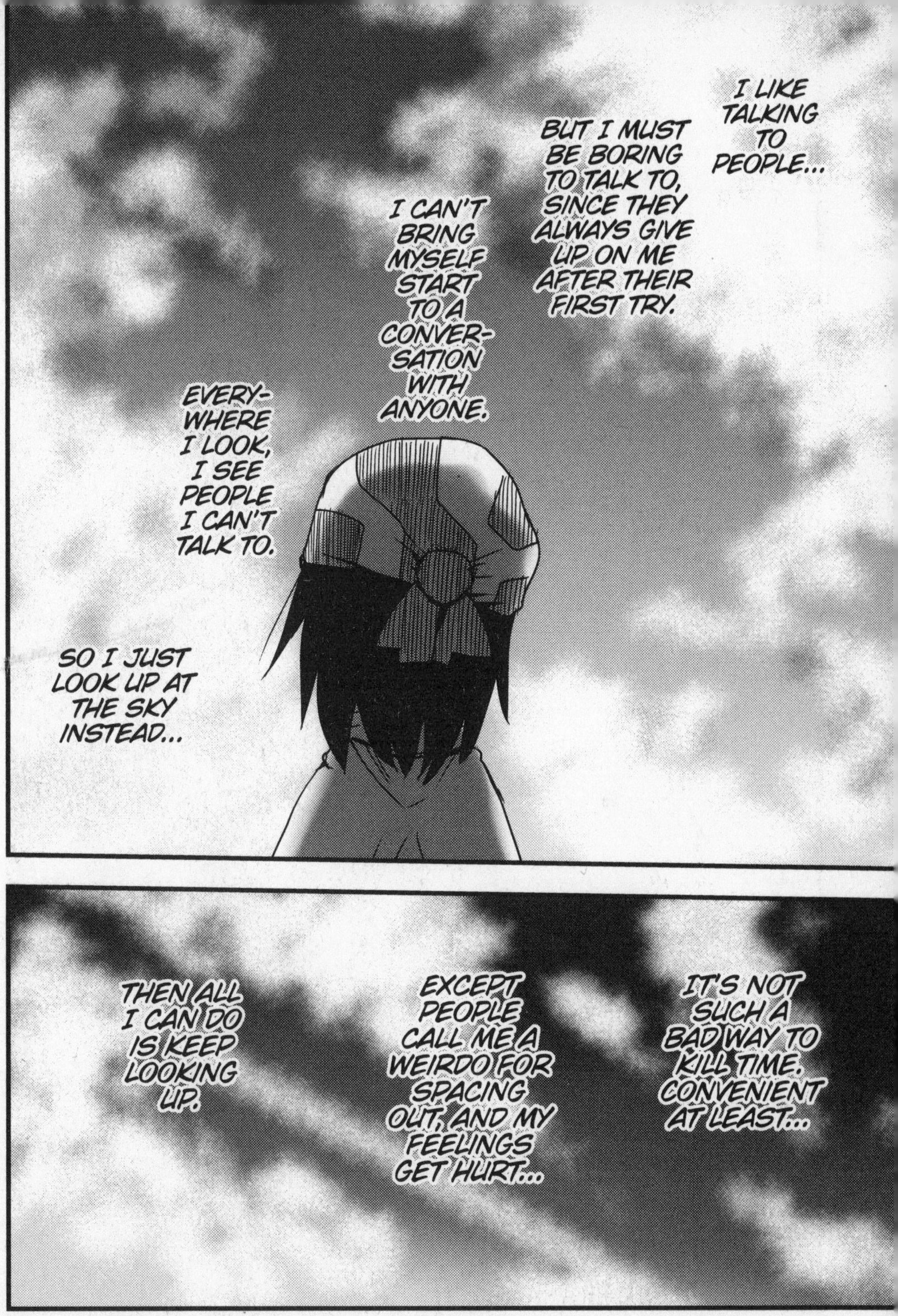
I LIKE TALKING TO PEOPLE...
BUT I MUST BE BORING TO TALK TO, SINCE THEY ALWAYS GIVE UP ON ME AFTER THEIR FIRST TRY.
I CAN'T BRING MYSELF START TO A CONVERSATION WITH ANYONE.
EVERYWHERE I LOOK, I SEE PEOPLE I CAN'T TALK TO.
SO I JUST LOOK UP AT THE SKY INSTEAD...
IT'S NOT SUCH A BAD WAY TO KILL TIME. CONVENIENT AT LEAST...
EXCEPT PEOPLE CALL ME A WEIRDO FOR SPACING OUT, AND MY FEELINGS GET HURT...
THEN ALL I CAN DO IS KEEP LOOKING UP.

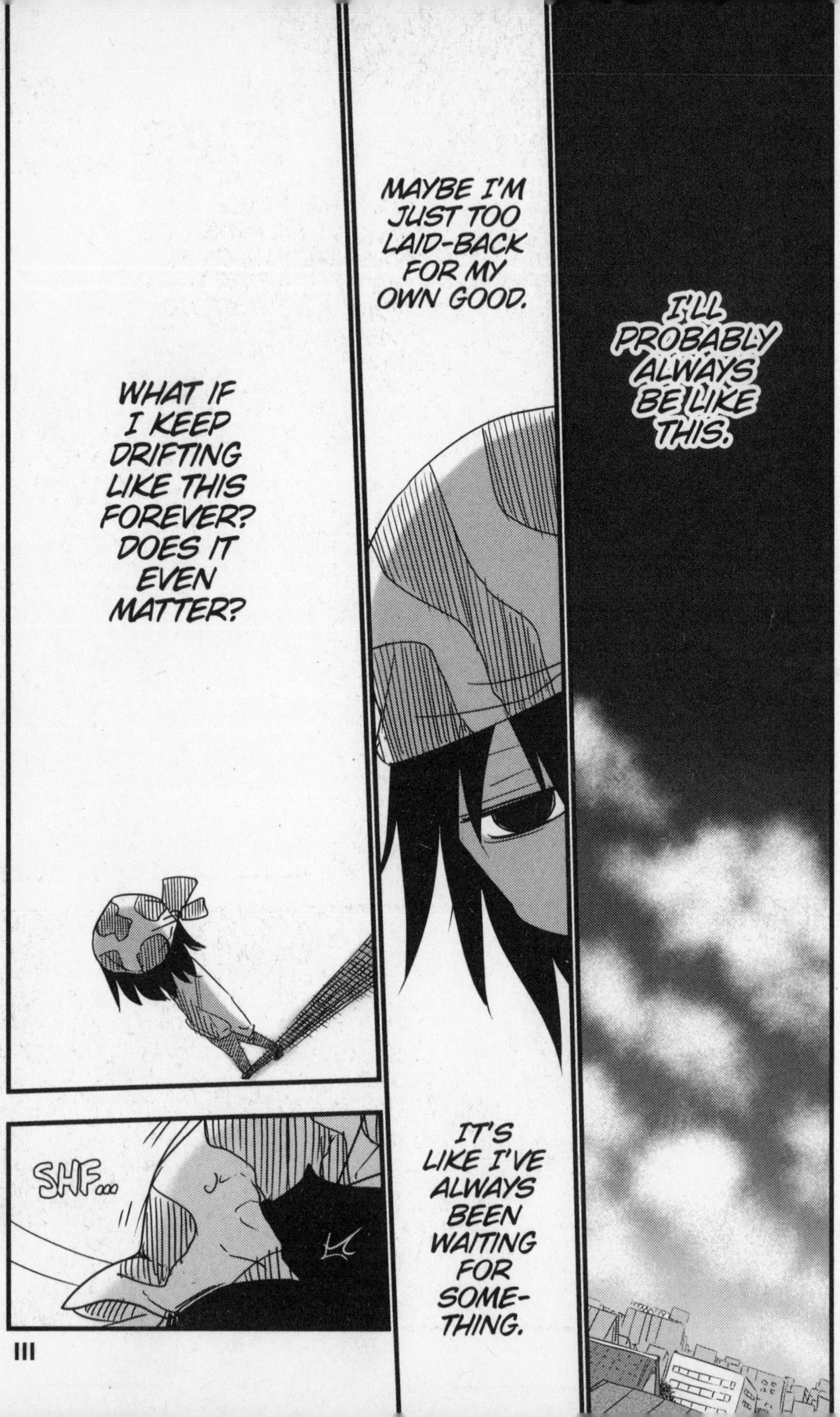
I'LL PROBABLY ALWAYS BE LIKE THIS.
MAYBE I'M JUST TOO LAID-BACK FOR MY OWN GOOD.
IT'S LIKE I'VE ALWAYS BEEN WAITING FOR SOME-THING.
WHAT IF I KEEP DRIFTING LIKE THIS FOREVER? DOES IT EVEN MATTER?
SHF...

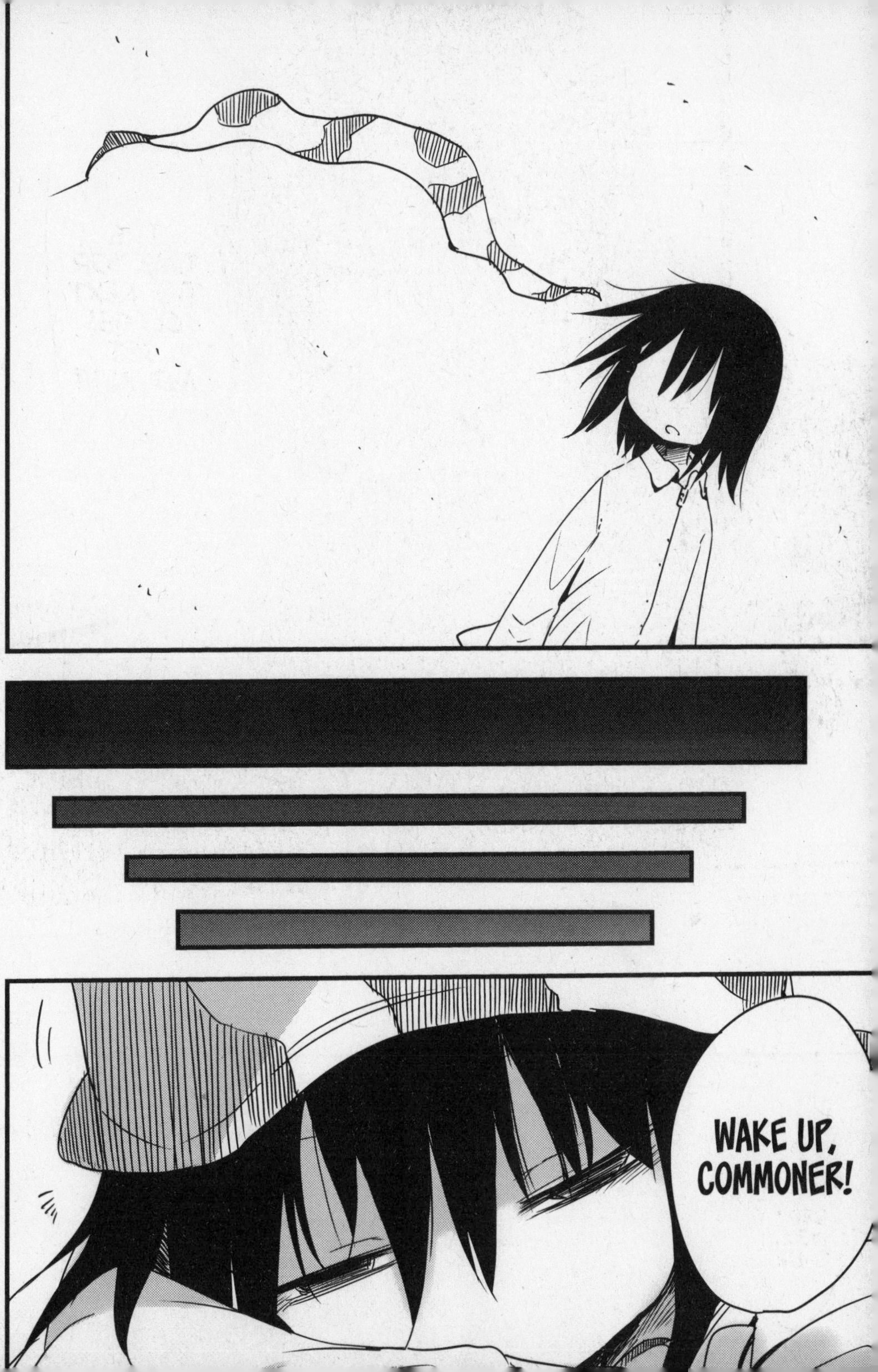
WAKE UP, COMMONER!

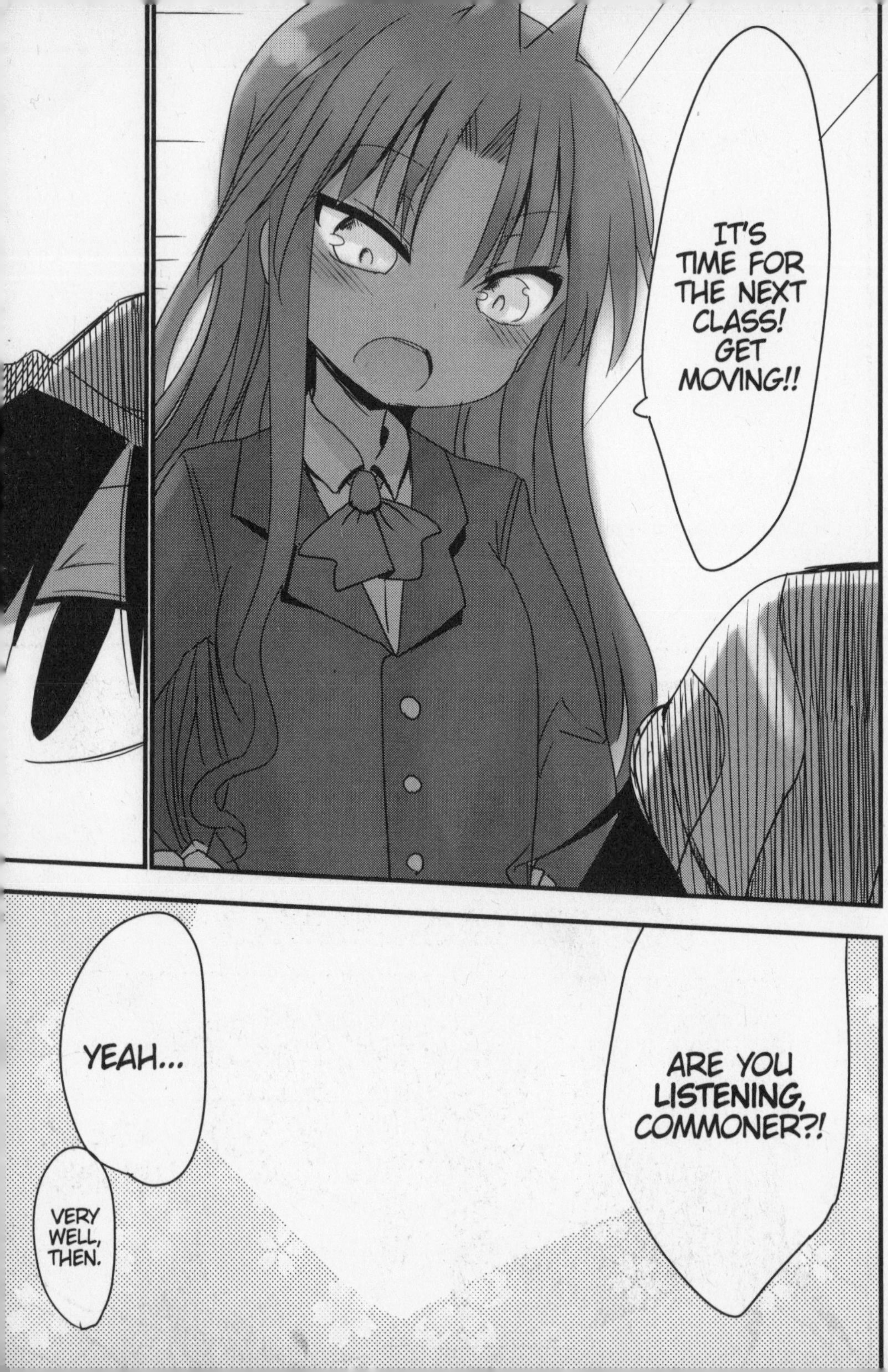
IT'S TIME FOR THE NEXT CLASS! GET MOVING!!
ARE YOU LISTENING, COMMONER?!
YEAH...
VERY WELL, THEN.

ojojojo

ojojojo 2

story & art
coolkyousinnjya

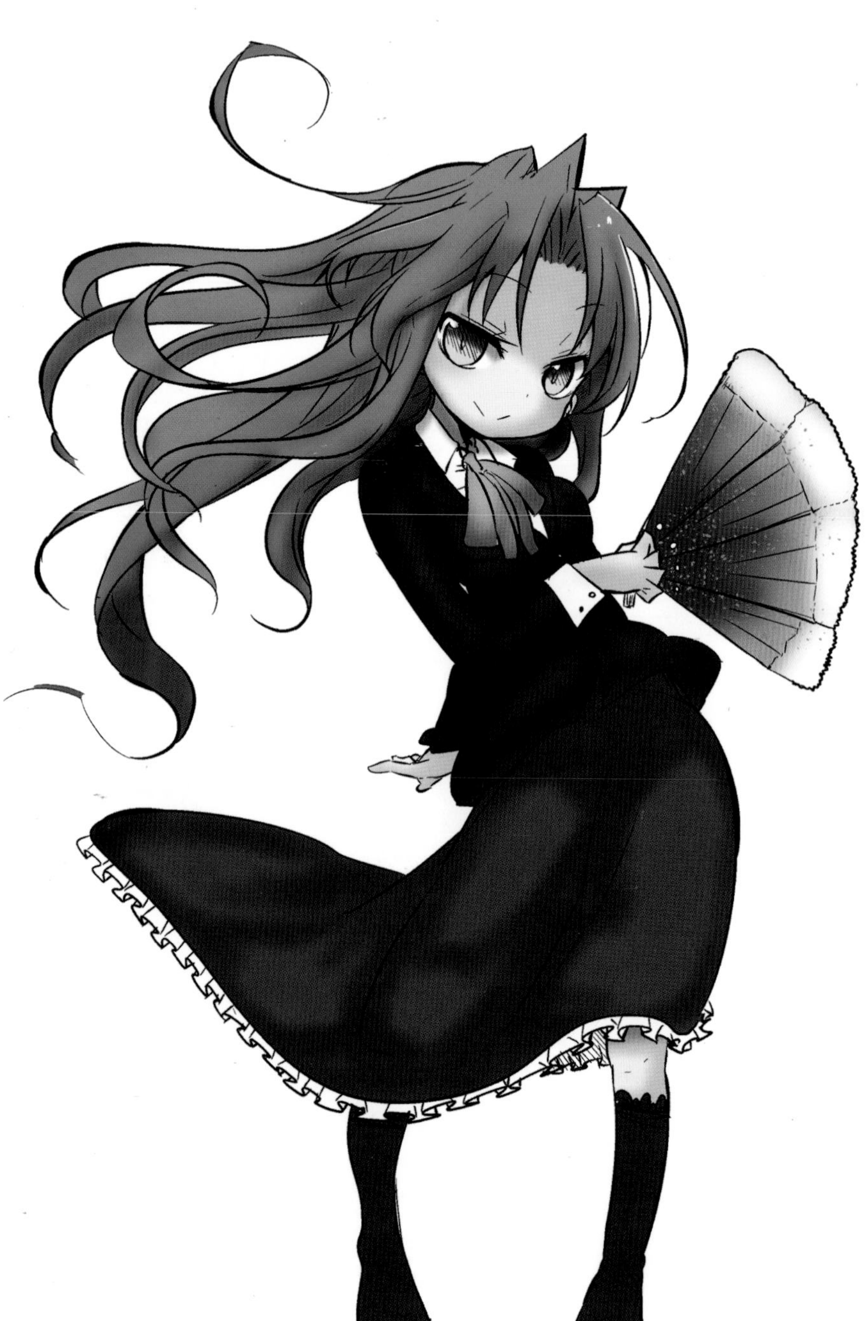

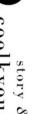

Ojojojo 2 – CHARACTERS

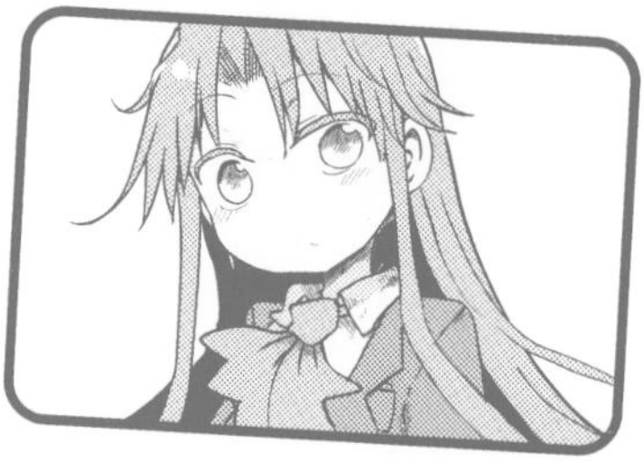

Jigokumeguri Haru

Daughter of the richest family in Japan. Her snobbish attitude has caused her to be isolated from her classmates. However, after meeting Kawayanagi and Tendou, she seems to be changing, bit by bit.

Kawayanagi Tsurezure

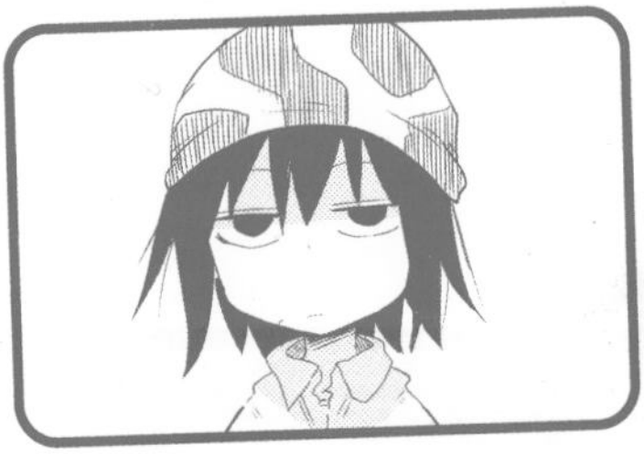

Recently started going out with Haru. His odd clothes and silent demeanor have earned him a reputation as the class weirdo.

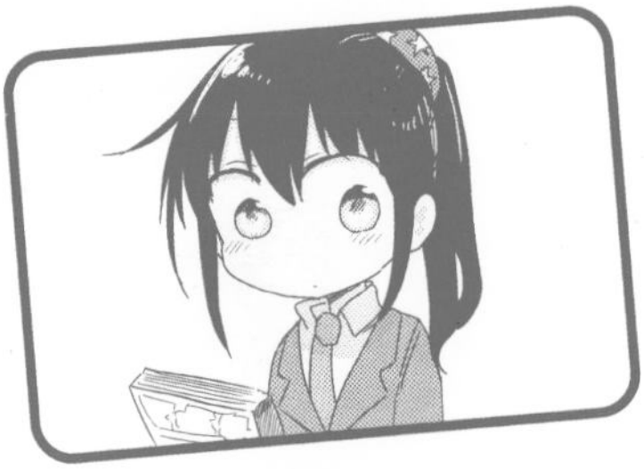

Tendou Akane

Haru's classmate. She's in support of Haru and Tsurezure's relationship, and is always trying to help them out.

Jiiya

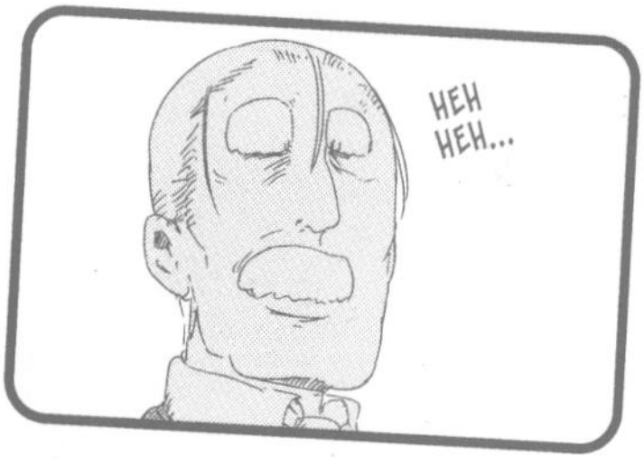
HEH
HEH...

Haru's butler. Although he has a sharp tongue and a tendency to be painfully blunt, he actually cares for Haru very much.

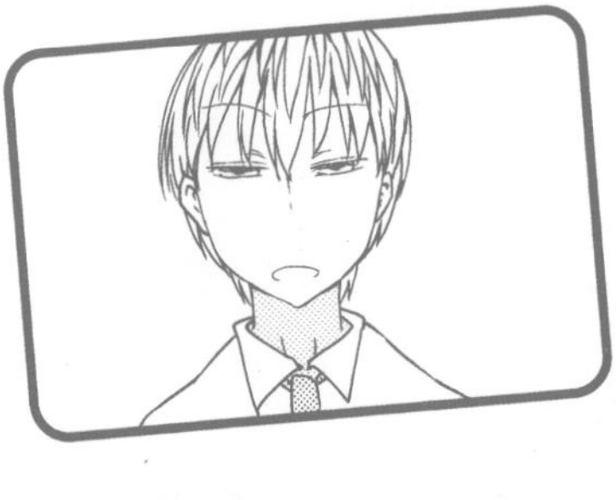

Chris Portman

Son of a noble family, he has recently transferred schools from the UK. He's handsome, athletic, intelligent, and amiable, with seemingly no flaws to speak of. *Seemingly...*

Their Relationship

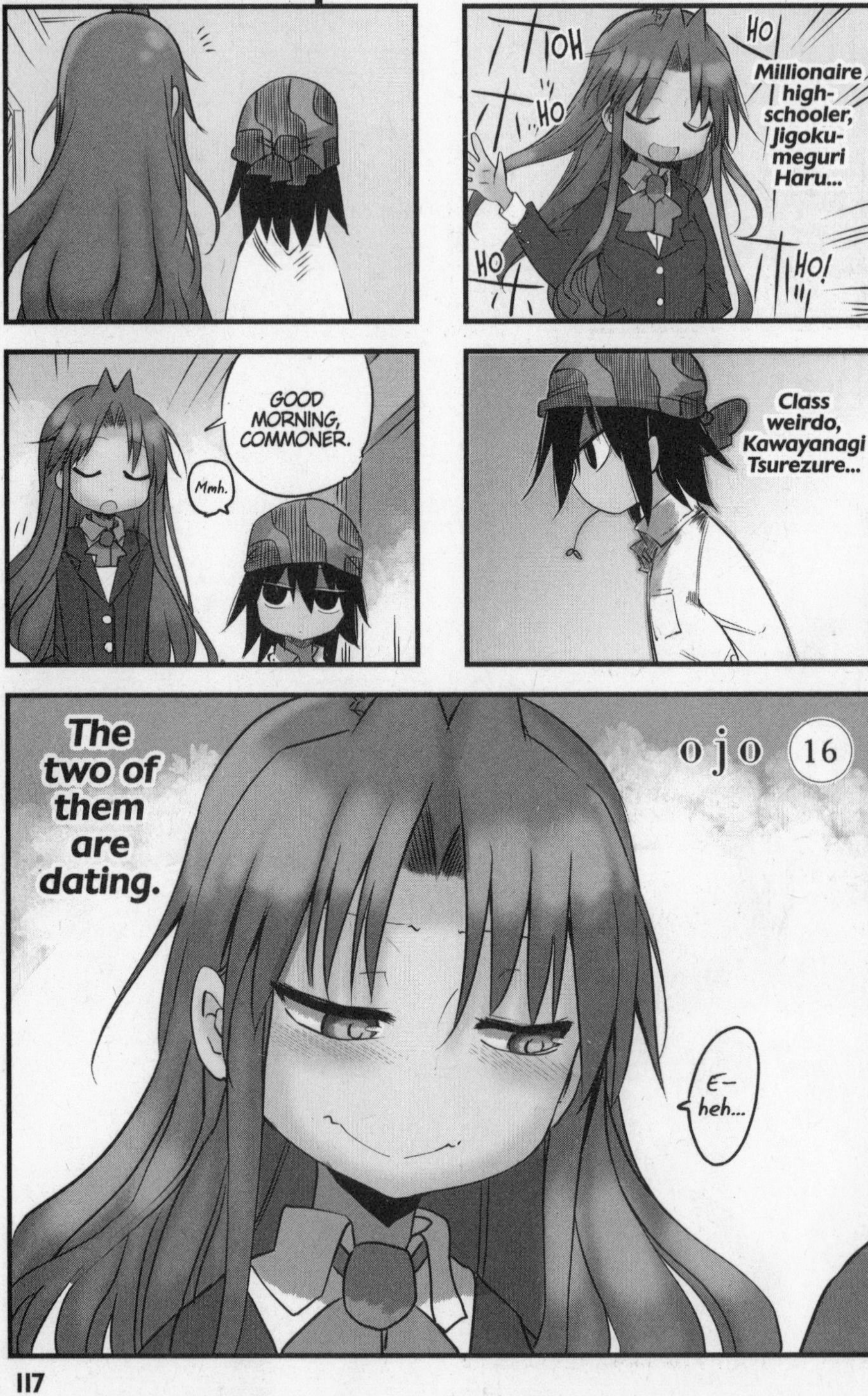
HO
HOH
Millionaire high-schooler, Jigoku-meguri Haru...
HO
HO!
HO
Class weirdo, Kawayanagi Tsurezure...
GOOD MORNING, COMMONER.
Mmh.
ojo 16
The two of them are dating.
E-heh...

Right?!

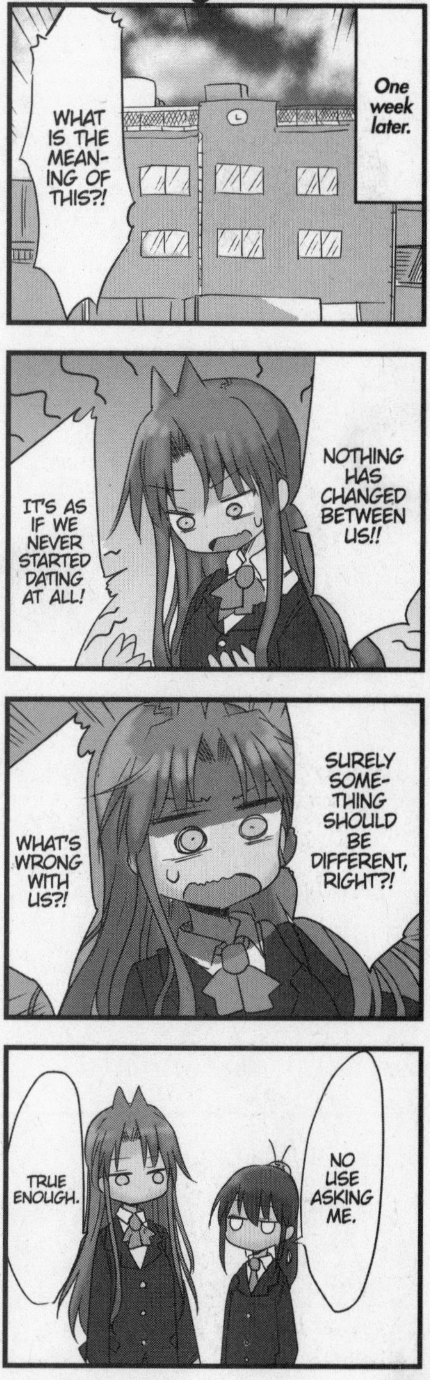
One week later.
WHAT IS THE MEANING OF THIS?!
NOTHING HAS CHANGED BETWEEN US!!
IT'S AS IF WE NEVER STARTED DATING AT ALL!
SURELY SOMETHING SHOULD BE DIFFERENT, RIGHT?!
WHAT'S WRONG WITH US?!
NO USE ASKING ME.
TRUE ENOUGH.

Tendou-san Has Zero Experience

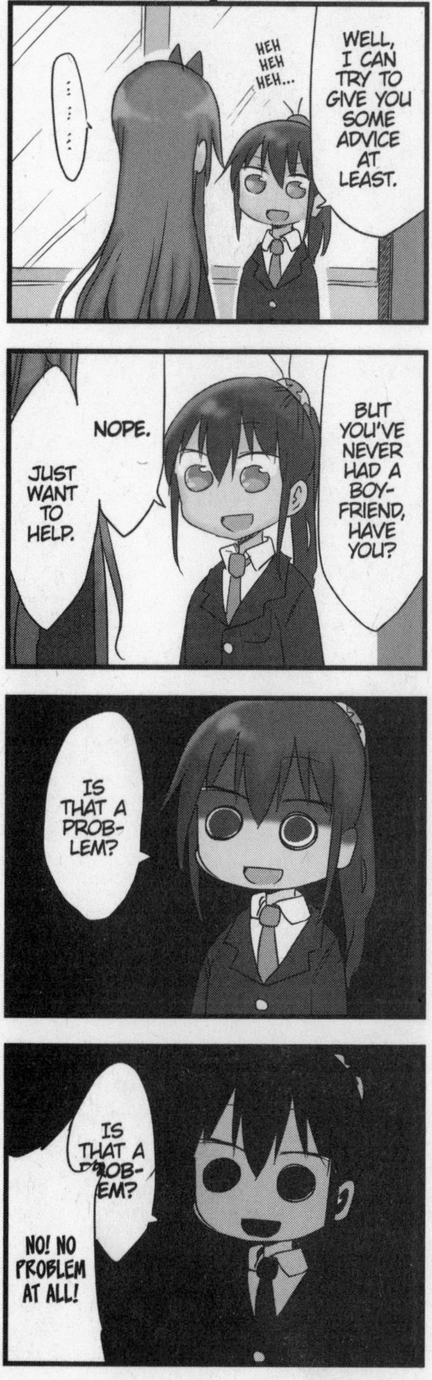
WELL, I CAN TRY TO GIVE YOU SOME ADVICE AT LEAST.
HEH HEH HEH...
......
BUT YOU'VE NEVER HAD A BOYFRIEND, HAVE YOU?
NOPE.
JUST WANT TO HELP.
IS THAT A PROBLEM?
IS THAT A PROBLEM?
NO! NO PROBLEM AT ALL!

Deep Breath

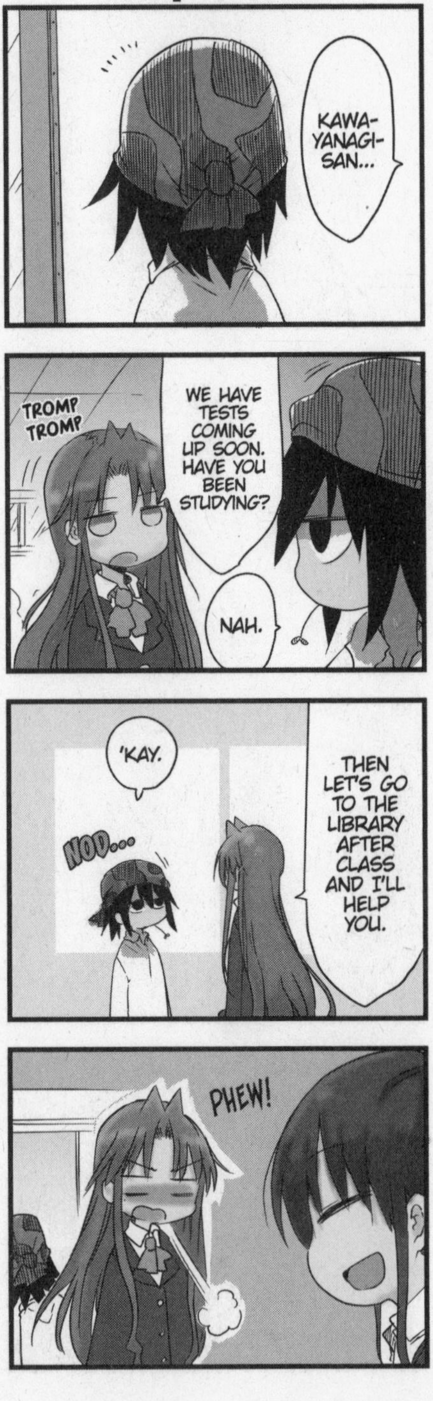
KAWA-YANAGI-SAN...
WE HAVE TESTS COMING UP SOON. HAVE YOU BEEN STUDYING?
TROMP TROMP
NAH.
THEN LET'S GO TO THE LIBRARY AFTER CLASS AND I'LL HELP YOU.
'KAY.
NOD...
PHEW!

What Is a Girlfriend?

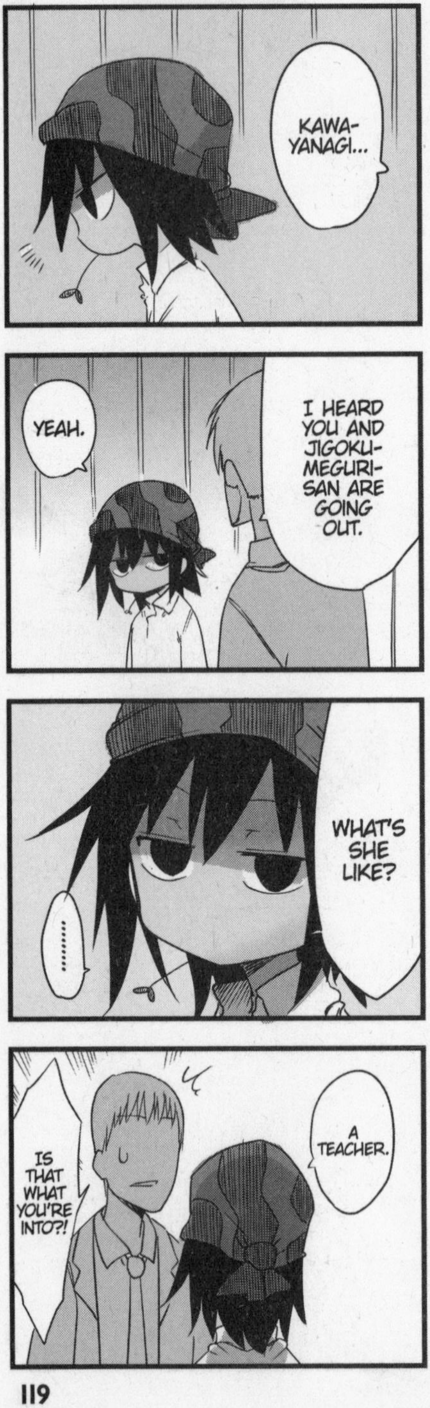
KAWA-YANAGI...
I HEARD YOU AND JIGOKU-MEGURI-SAN ARE GOING OUT.
YEAH.
WHAT'S SHE LIKE?
......
A TEACHER.
IS THAT WHAT YOU'RE INTO?!

Example

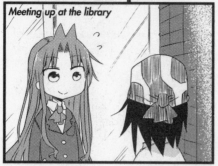

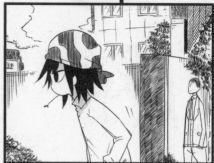

I DON'T REALLY GET WHAT IT MEANS TO GO OUT WITH SOMEONE.
LOVEY DOVEY
MAYBE WE AREN'T A REAL COUPLE AFTER ALL...

For Example...?

Meeting up at the library
That's all wrong. We'll have to start over.
You commoners really are hopeless!
......
STARE...
!
WE ARE GOING OUT, RIGHT?
?!

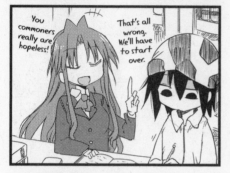

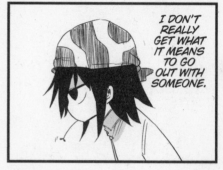

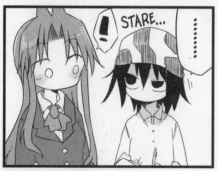

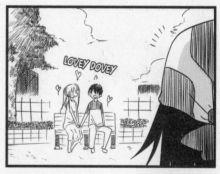

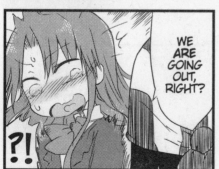

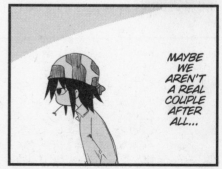

Unconfirmed

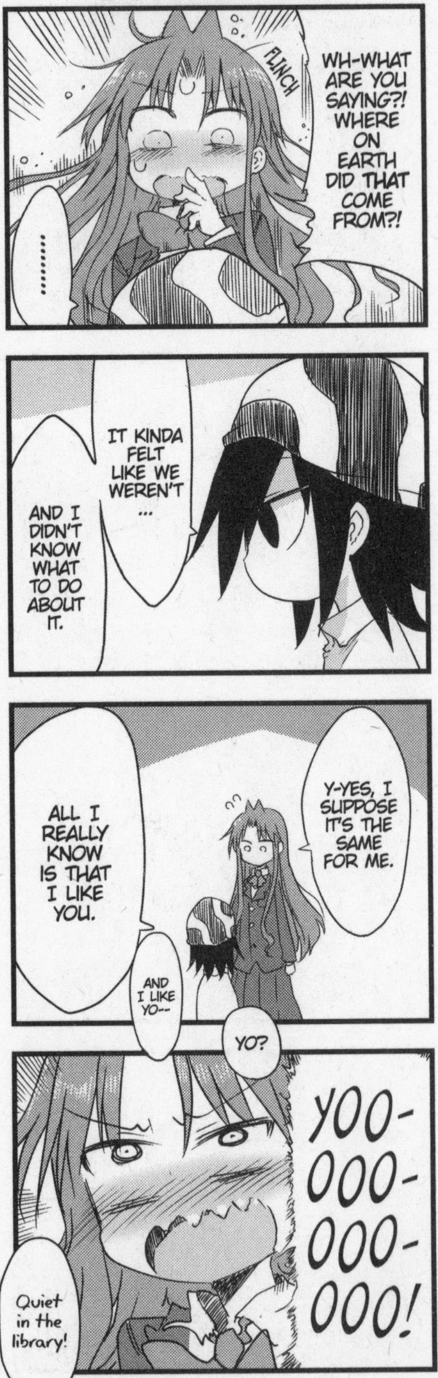
FLINCH
WH-WHAT ARE YOU SAYING?! WHERE ON EARTH DID THAT COME FROM?!
......
IT KINDA FELT LIKE WE WEREN'T ...
AND I DIDN'T KNOW WHAT TO DO ABOUT IT.
Y-YES, I SUPPOSE IT'S THE SAME FOR ME.
ALL I REALLY KNOW IS THAT I LIKE YOU.
AND I LIKE YO--
YO?
YOO-000-000-000-000!
Quiet in the library!

Longing

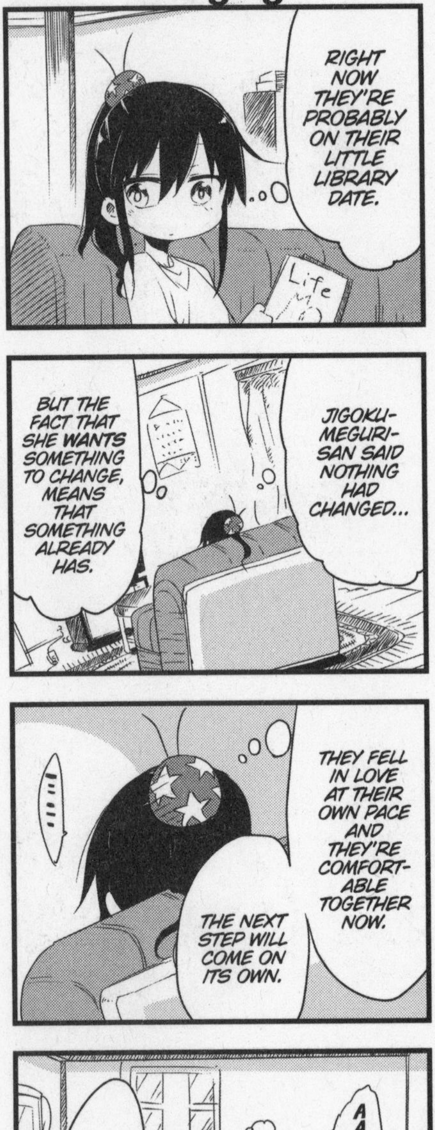
RIGHT NOW THEY'RE PROBABLY ON THEIR LITTLE LIBRARY DATE.
Life
JIGOKU-MEGURI-SAN SAID NOTHING HAD CHANGED...
BUT THE FACT THAT SHE WANTS SOMETHING TO CHANGE, MEANS THAT SOMETHING ALREADY HAS.
THEY FELL IN LOVE AT THEIR OWN PACE AND THEY'RE COMFORTABLE TOGETHER NOW.
THE NEXT STEP WILL COME ON ITS OWN.
......
AAAARRGH!
I WANNA FALL IN LOVE, TOO!

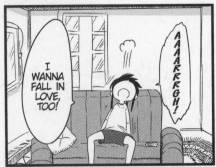

I Know He Meant It

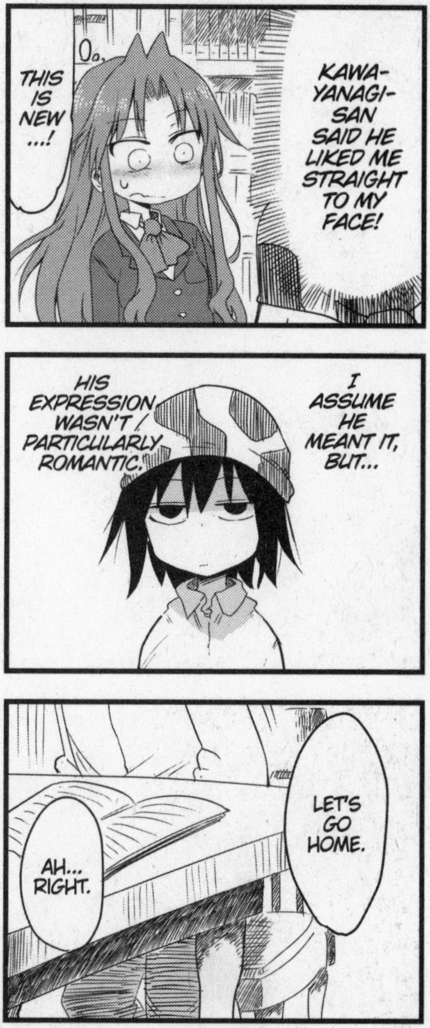
KAWA-YANAGI-SAN SAID HE LIKED ME STRAIGHT TO MY FACE!
THIS IS NEW ...!
I ASSUME HE MEANT IT, BUT...
HIS EXPRESSION WASN'T PARTICULARLY ROMANTIC.
LET'S GO HOME.
AH... RIGHT.
STILL...
I'M HAPPY.

Head in the Clouds

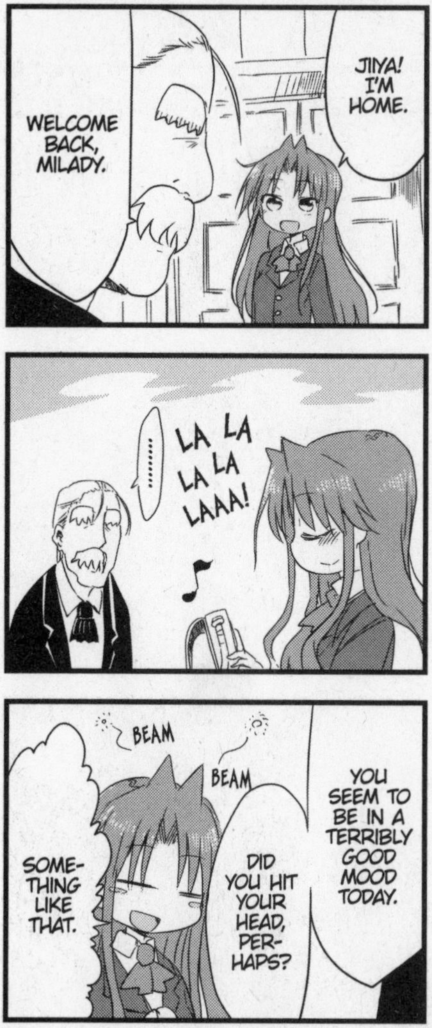
JIIYA! I'M HOME.
WELCOME BACK, MILADY.
LA LA LA LA LAAA!
......
YOU SEEM TO BE IN A TERRIBLY GOOD MOOD TODAY.
BEAM
BEAM
DID YOU HIT YOUR HEAD, PERHAPS?
SOMETHING LIKE THAT.
TRA-LA TRA-LA LA-LA!
SHE'S GETTING STRONGER.

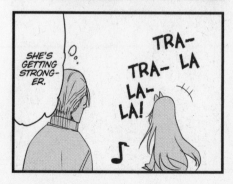

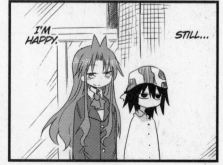

Shock

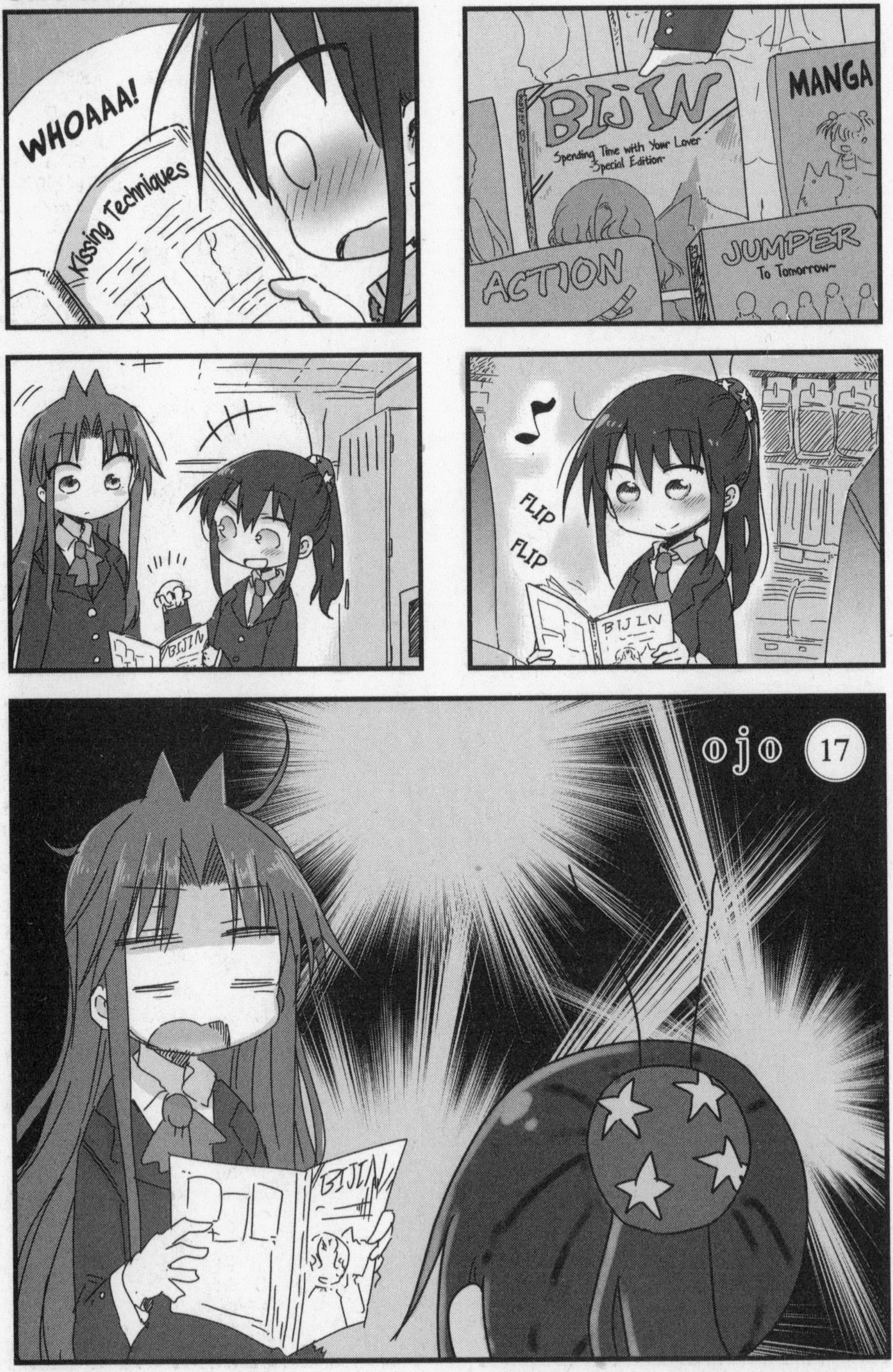

BIJIN
Spending Time with Your Lover Special Edition
MANGA
ACTION
JUMPER
To Tomorrow~
WHOAAA!
Kissing Techniques
♪
FLIP
FLIP
BIJIN
BIJIN
ojo 17
BIJIN

Unbelievable

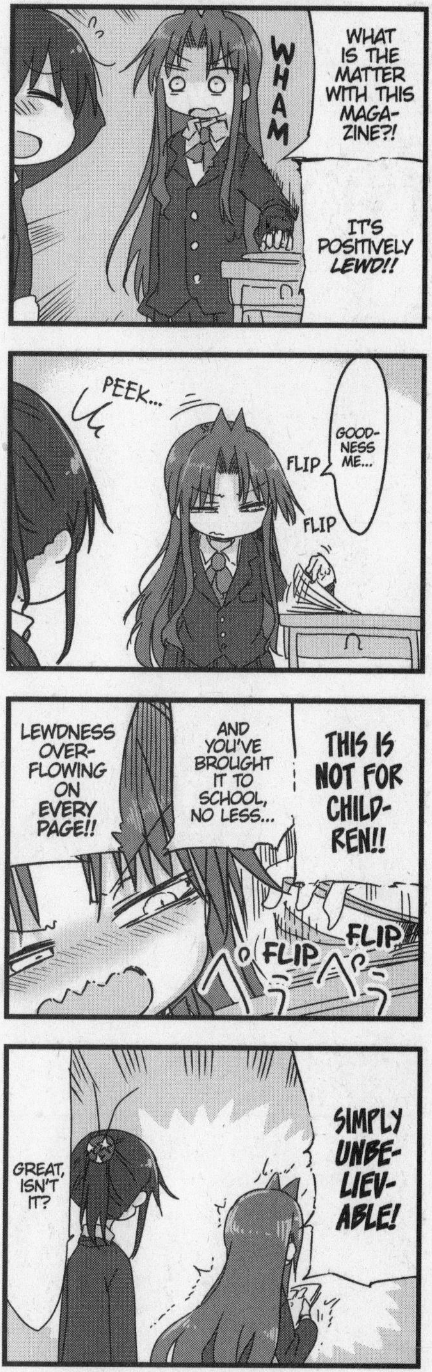
WHAT IS THE MATTER WITH THIS MAGAZINE?!
WHAM
IT'S POSITIVELY LEWD!!
GOODNESS ME...
FLIP
FLIP
PEEK...
THIS IS NOT FOR CHILDREN!!
AND YOU'VE BROUGHT IT TO SCHOOL, NO LESS...
LEWDNESS OVERFLOWING ON EVERY PAGE!!
FLIP
FLIP
SIMPLY UNBELIEVABLE!
GREAT, ISN'T IT?

Still at Lowercase A

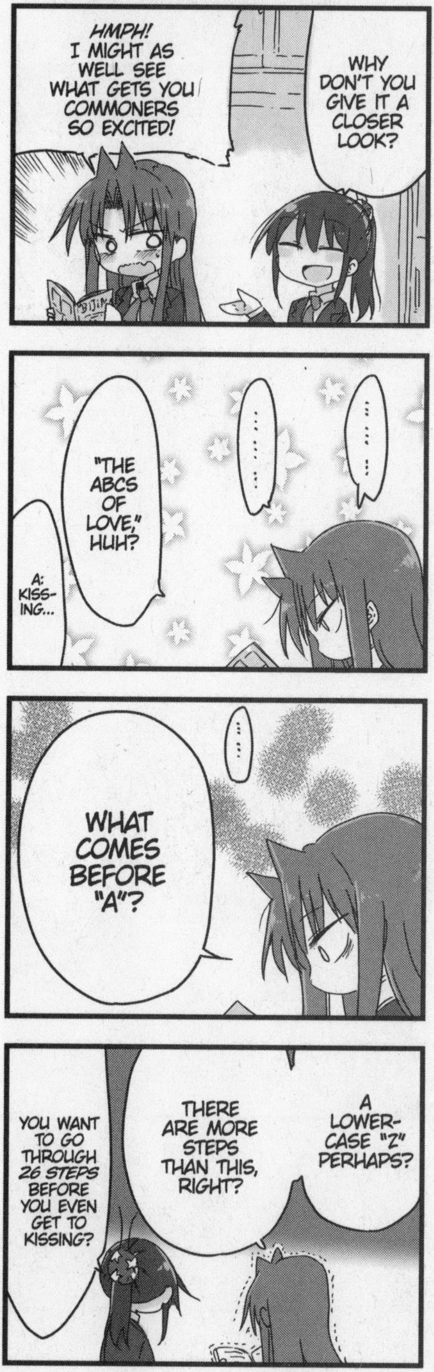
WHY DON'T YOU GIVE IT A CLOSER LOOK?
HMPH! I MIGHT AS WELL SEE WHAT GETS YOU COMMONERS SO EXCITED!
......
....
"THE ABCS OF LOVE," HUH?
A: KISSING...
......
WHAT COMES BEFORE "A"?
A LOWERCASE "Z" PERHAPS?
THERE ARE MORE STEPS THAN THIS, RIGHT?
YOU WANT TO GO THROUGH 26 STEPS BEFORE YOU EVEN GET TO KISSING?

Reaction

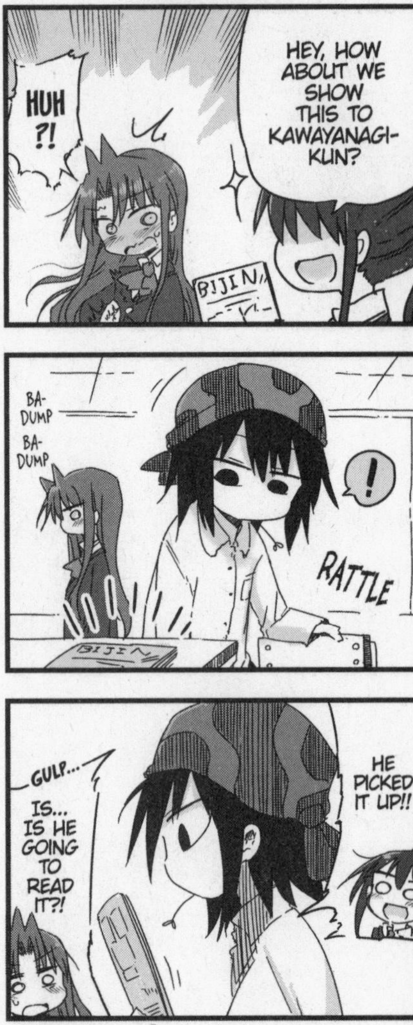
HEY, HOW ABOUT WE SHOW THIS TO KAWAYANAGI-KUN?
HUH ?!
BIJIN
!
RATTLE
BA-DUMP
BA-DUMP
BIJIN
HE PICKED IT UP!!
GULP...
IS... IS HE GOING TO READ IT?!
OH... HE PUT IT BACK ON MY DESK.
HE KNOWS YOU TOO WELL.

Indirect Touch

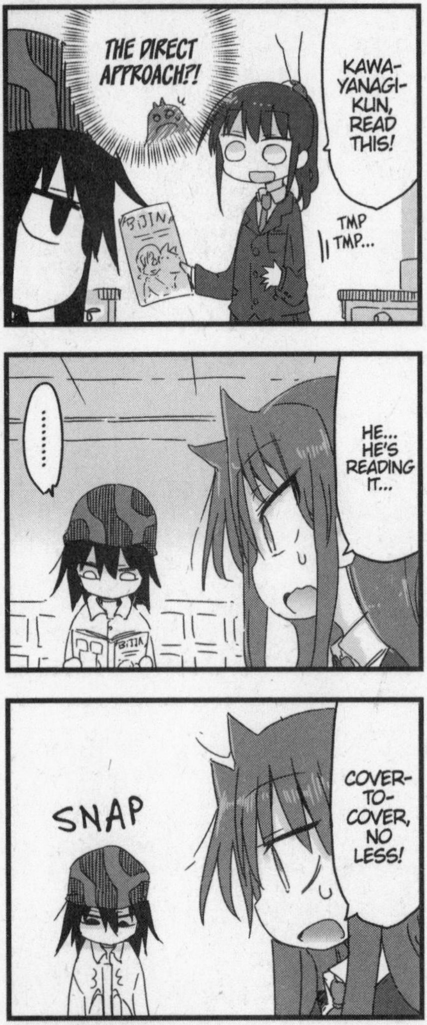
KAWA-YANAGI-KUN, READ THIS!
THE DIRECT APPROACH?!
TMP TMP...
BIJIN
HE... HE'S READING IT...
......
COVER-TO-COVER, NO LESS!
SNAP
HE TOUCHED THE SAME DIRTY BOOK THAT I DID... HE *READ* IT...
WHAT ARE YOU TALKING ABOUT?

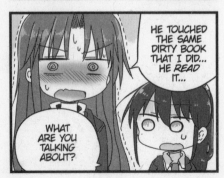

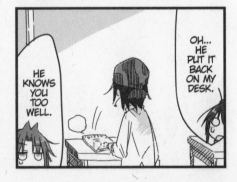

What Kawayanagi Wants

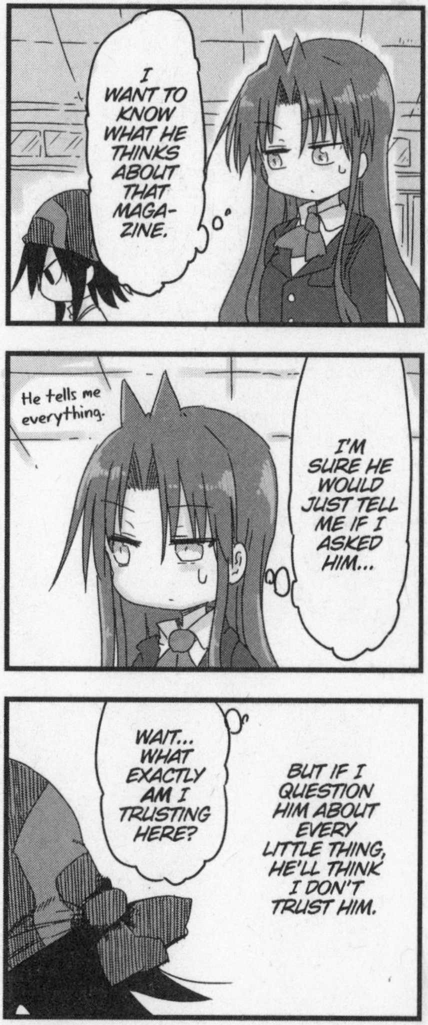
I WANT TO KNOW WHAT HE THINKS ABOUT THAT MAGAZINE.
I'M SURE HE WOULD JUST TELL ME IF I ASKED HIM...
He tells me everything.
BUT IF I QUESTION HIM ABOUT EVERY LITTLE THING, HE'LL THINK I DON'T TRUST HIM.
WAIT... WHAT EXACTLY AM I TRUSTING HERE?
THAT HE HAS LUSTFUL THOUGHTS...?!
I'M SO VULGAR!!

What She Wants to Hear

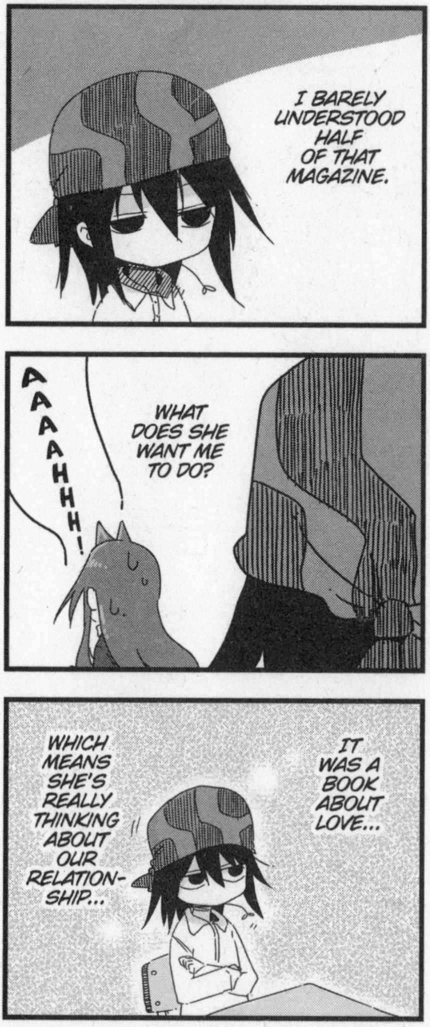
I BARELY UNDERSTOOD HALF OF THAT MAGAZINE.
WHAT DOES SHE WANT ME TO DO?
AAAAHHH!
IT WAS A BOOK ABOUT LOVE...
WHICH MEANS SHE'S REALLY THINKING ABOUT OUR RELATIONSHIP...
SHE'S SERIOUS ABOUT THIS.
I'M SO VULGAR!!

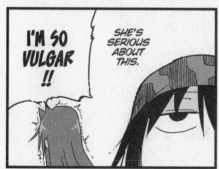

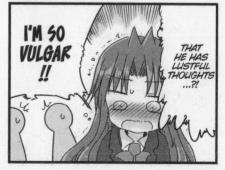

I Could Barely Hear Your Voice

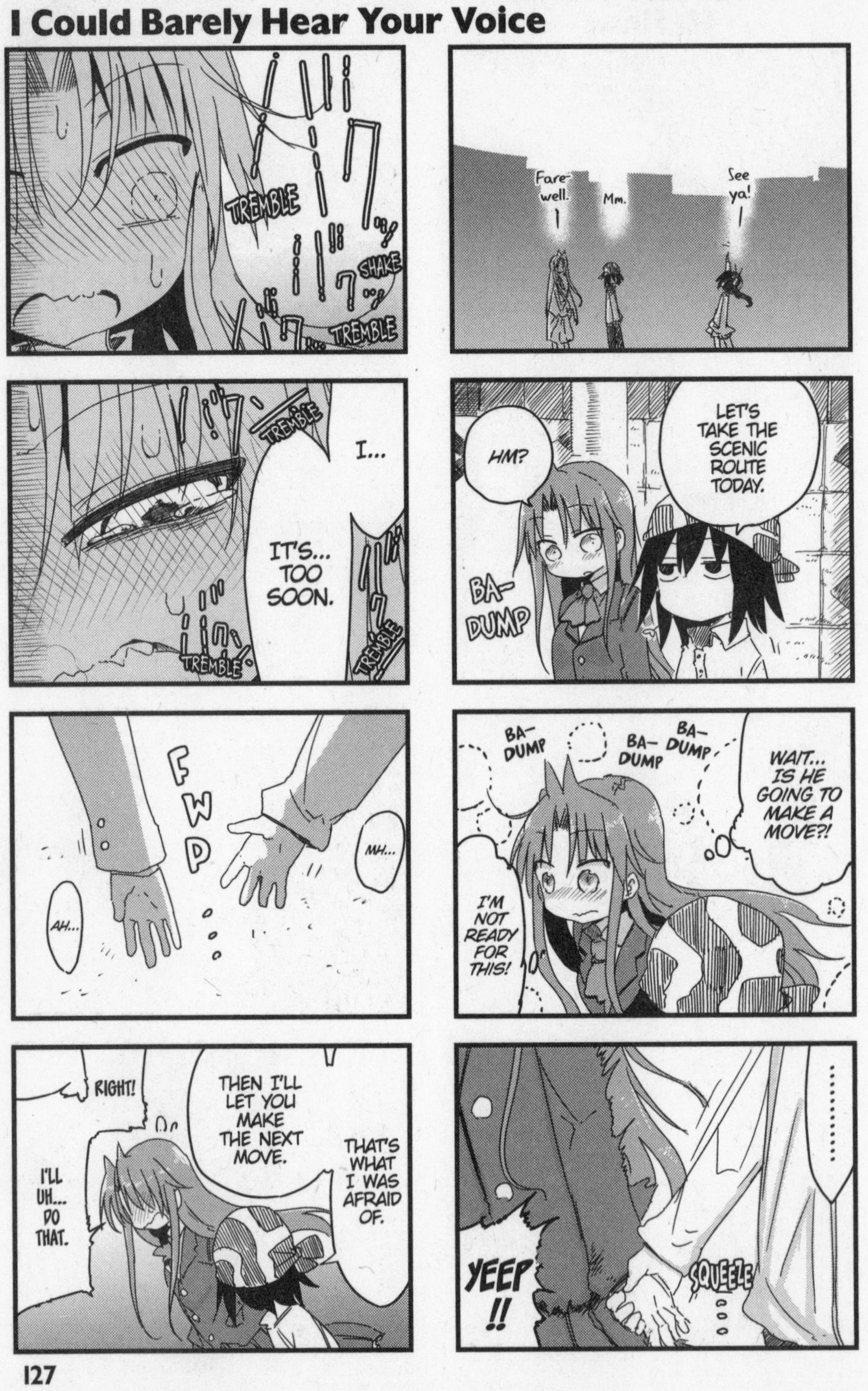
See ya!
Mm.
Fare-well.
LET'S TAKE THE SCENIC ROUTE TODAY.
HM?
BA-DUMP
WAIT... IS HE GOING TO MAKE A MOVE?!
BA-DUMP
BA-DUMP
BA-DUMP
I'M NOT READY FOR THIS!
......
SQUEEZE
YEEP!!
TREMBLE
SHAKE
TREMBLE
I...
IT'S... TOO SOON.
TREMBLE
TREMBLE
TREMBLE
MH...
FWP
AH...
THAT'S WHAT I WAS AFRAID OF.
THEN I'LL LET YOU MAKE THE NEXT MOVE.
RIGHT!
I'LL UH... DO THAT.

Getting to Lowercase B

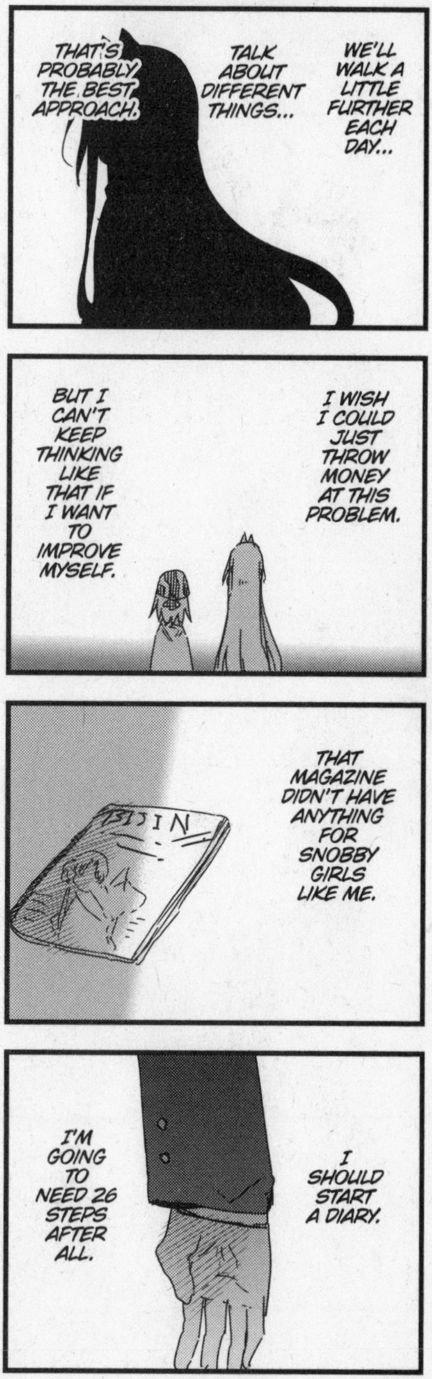
WE'LL WALK A LITTLE FURTHER EACH DAY...
TALK ABOUT DIFFERENT THINGS...
THAT'S PROBABLY THE BEST APPROACH.
I WISH I COULD JUST THROW MONEY AT THIS PROBLEM.
BUT I CAN'T KEEP THINKING LIKE THAT IF I WANT TO IMPROVE MYSELF.
BIJIN
THAT MAGAZINE DIDN'T HAVE ANYTHING FOR SNOBBY GIRLS LIKE ME.
I SHOULD START A DIARY.
I'M GOING TO NEED 26 STEPS AFTER ALL.

Not Your Typical Couple

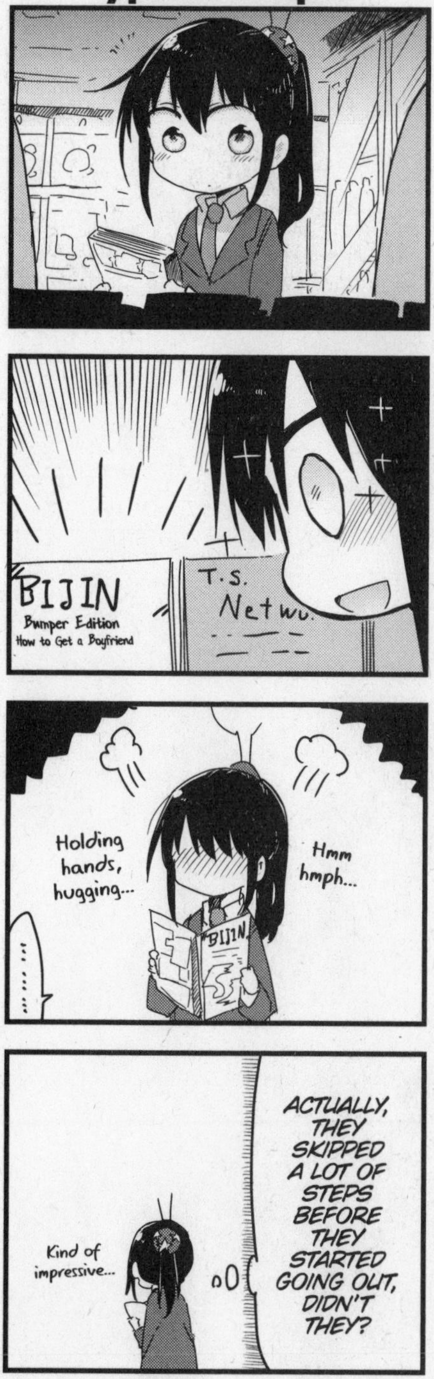
T.S.
BIJIN
Bumper Edition
How to Get a Boyfriend
Hmm hmph...
Holding hands, hugging...
BIJIN
ACTUALLY, THEY SKIPPED A LOT OF STEPS BEFORE THEY STARTED GOING OUT, DIDN'T THEY?
Kind of impressive...

Somehow, This Happened

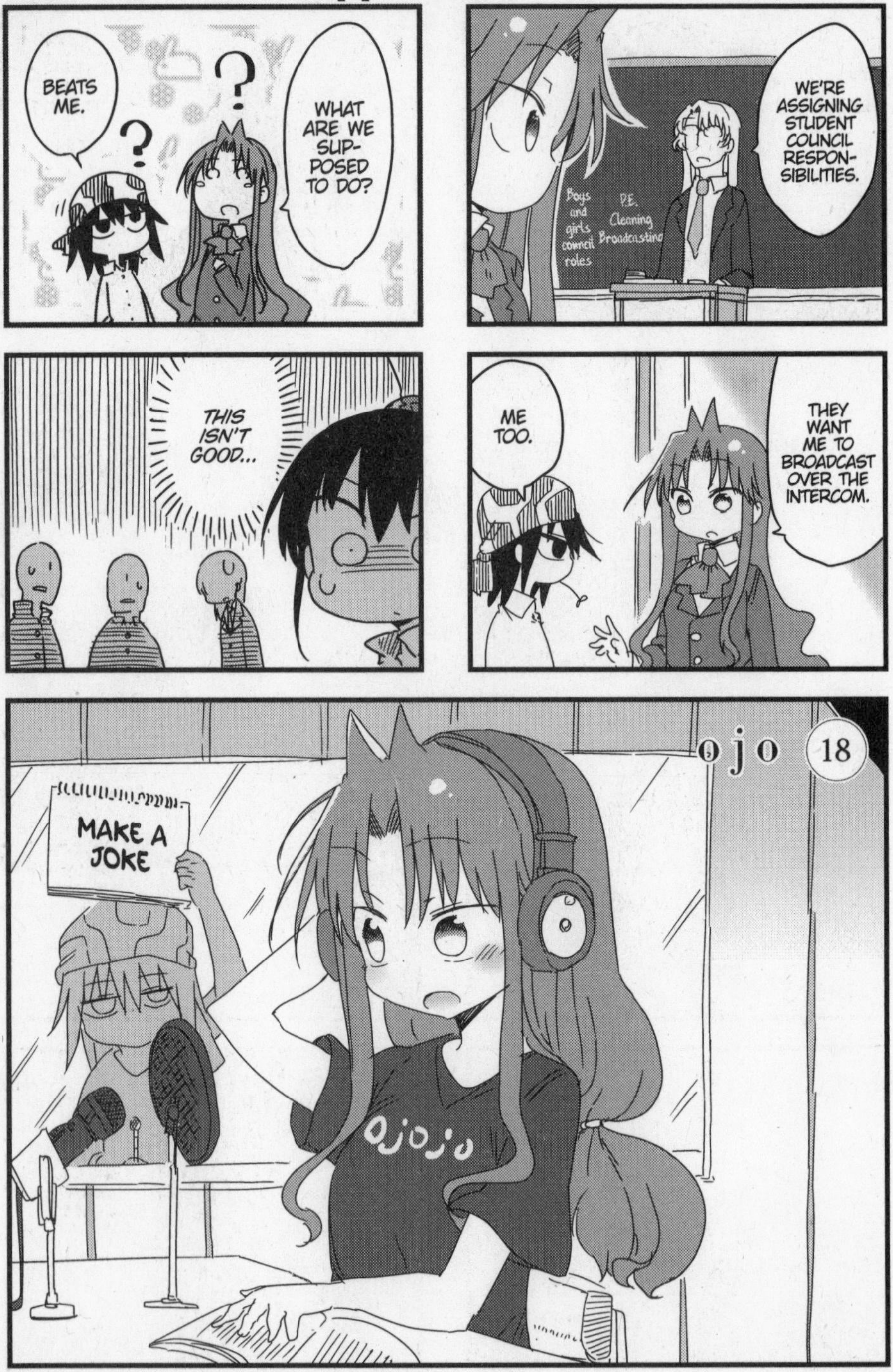
Boys and girls council roles
P.E.
Cleaning
Broadcasting
WE'RE ASSIGNING STUDENT COUNCIL RESPON-SIBILITIES.
WHAT ARE WE SUP-POSED TO DO?
BEATS ME.
THEY WANT ME TO BROADCAST OVER THE INTERCOM.
ME TOO.
THIS ISN'T GOOD...
ojo 18
MAKE A JOKE
ojojo

Good Pronunciation

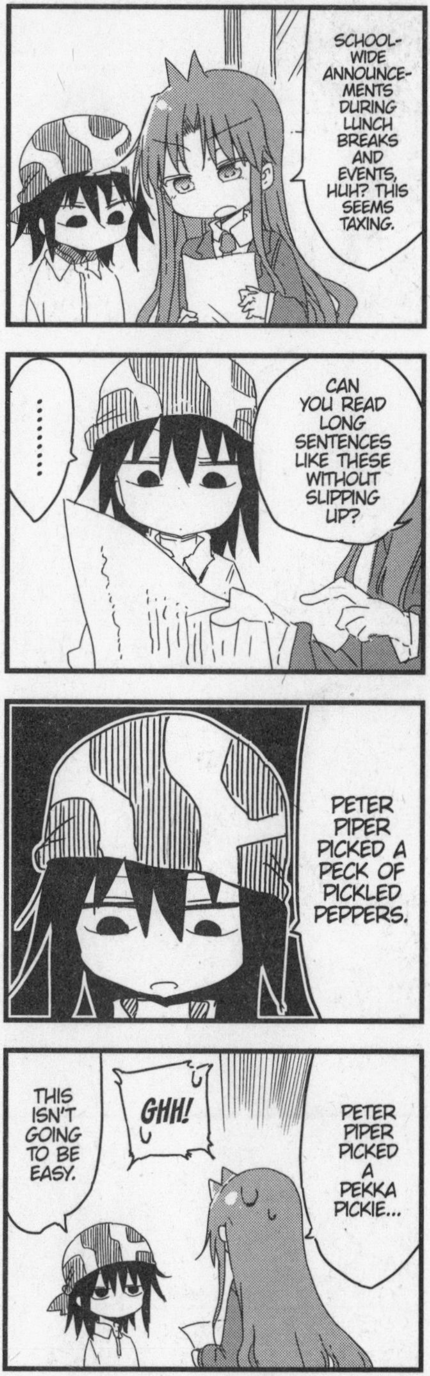

SCHOOL-WIDE ANNOUNCEMENTS DURING LUNCH BREAKS AND EVENTS, HUH? THIS SEEMS TAXING.
CAN YOU READ LONG SENTENCES LIKE THESE WITHOUT SLIPPING UP?
....
PETER PIPER PICKED A PECK OF PICKLED PEPPERS.
PETER PIPER PICKED A PEKKA PICKIE...
GHH!
THIS ISN'T GOING TO BE EASY.

Popular with Him at Least

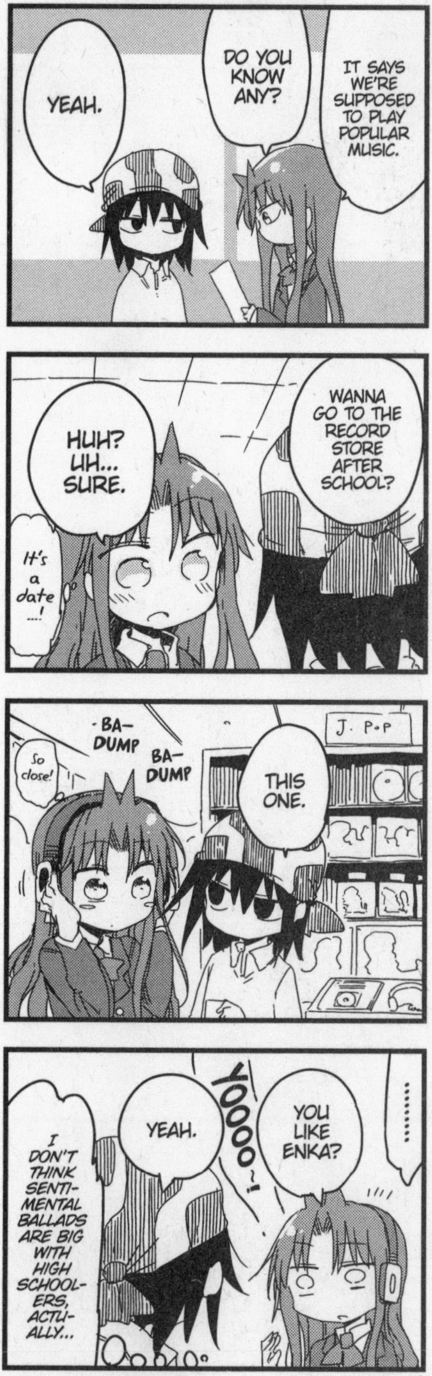

IT SAYS WE'RE SUPPOSED TO PLAY POPULAR MUSIC.
DO YOU KNOW ANY?
YEAH.
WANNA GO TO THE RECORD STORE AFTER SCHOOL?
HUH? UH... SURE.
It's a date...!
J. P•P
THIS ONE.
BA-DUMP
BA-DUMP
So close!
....
YOU LIKE ENKA?
YOOOO~!
YEAH.
I DON'T THINK SENTIMENTAL BALLADS ARE BIG WITH HIGH SCHOOLERS, ACTUALLY...

Oh No

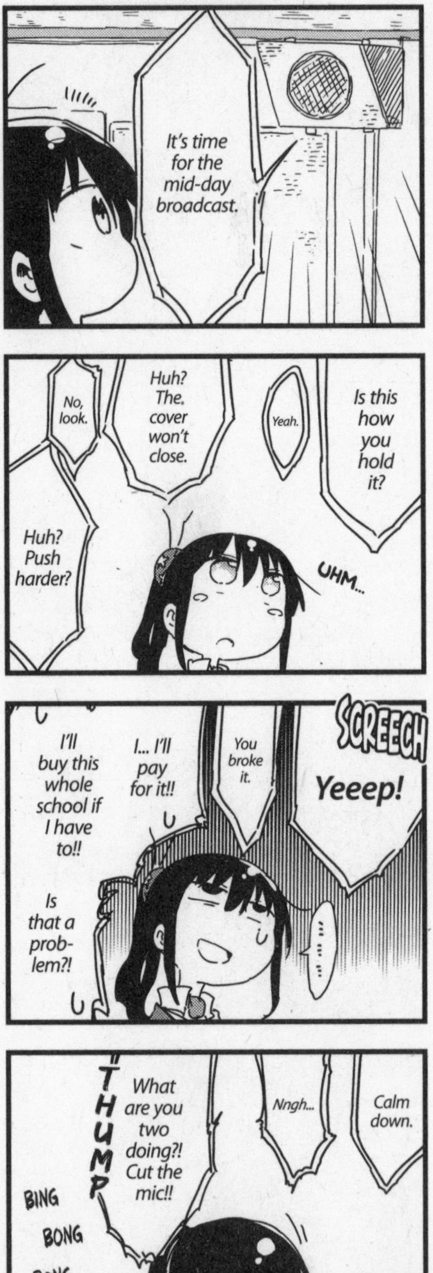
It's time for the mid-day broadcast.
Is this how you hold it?
Yeah.
Huh? The. cover won't close.
No, look.
Huh? Push harder?
UHM...
SCREECH
Yeeep!
You broke it.
I... I'll pay for it!!
I'll buy this whole school if I have to!!
Is that a problem?!
...
Calm down.
Nngh...
What are you two doing?! Cut the mic!!
THUMP
BING
BONG
BeNG
BONG

Tightening the Purse Strings

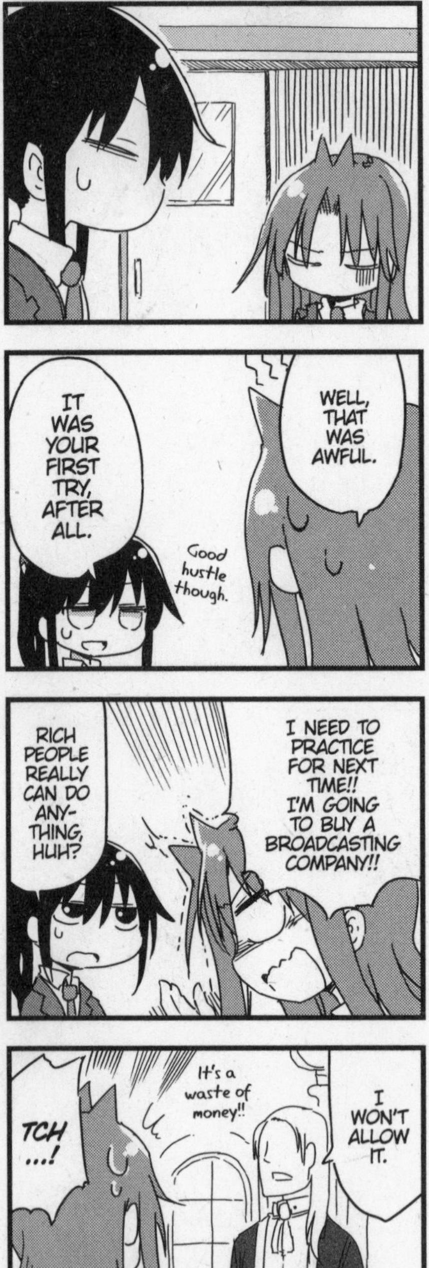
WELL, THAT WAS AWFUL.
IT WAS YOUR FIRST TRY, AFTER ALL.
Good hustle though.
I NEED TO PRACTICE FOR NEXT TIME!! I'M GOING TO BUY A BROADCASTING COMPANY!!
RICH PEOPLE REALLY CAN DO ANY-THING, HUH?
I WON'T ALLOW IT.
It's a waste of money!!
TCH ...!

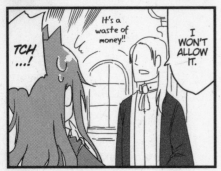

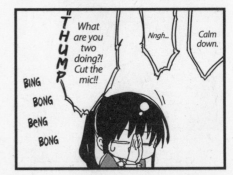

Expectations

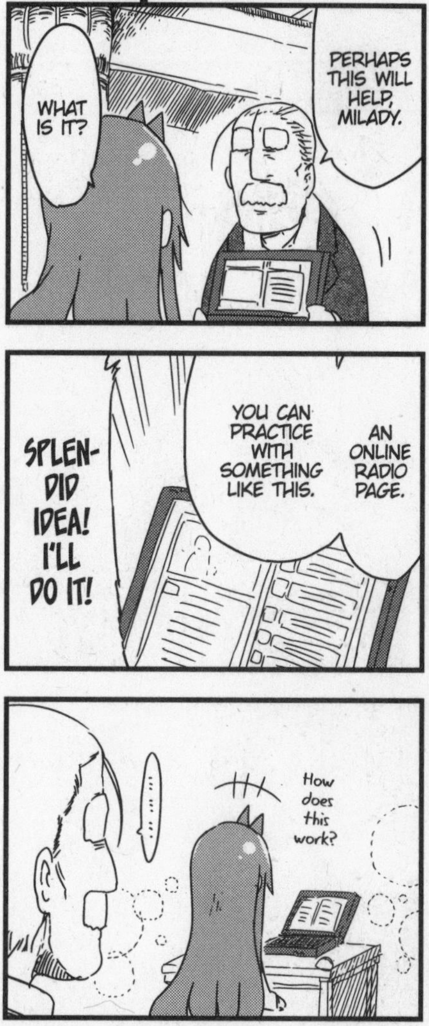
PERHAPS THIS WILL HELP, MILADY.
WHAT IS IT?
AN ONLINE RADIO PAGE.
YOU CAN PRACTICE WITH SOMETHING LIKE THIS.
SPLENDID IDEA! I'LL DO IT!
How does this work?
……
HOW LONG UNTIL THE FLAME WARS BEGIN, I WONDER...?
HEH HEH...

Making Progress

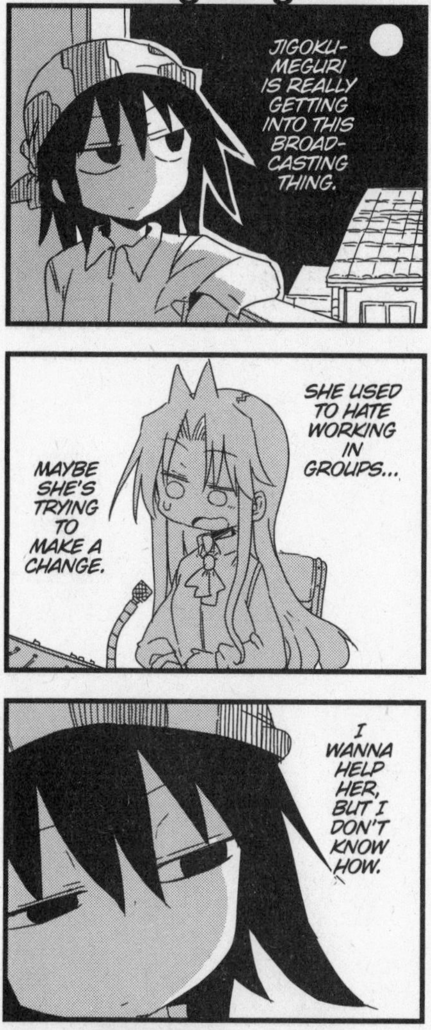
JIGOKU-MEGURI IS REALLY GETTING INTO THIS BROADCASTING THING.
SHE USED TO HATE WORKING IN GROUPS...
MAYBE SHE'S TRYING TO MAKE A CHANGE.
I WANNA HELP HER, BUT I DON'T KNOW HOW.
I GUESS MAKING SURE SHE DOESN'T SMASH ANY MORE CD COVERS MIGHT BE A GOOD START...

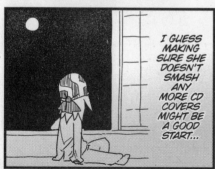

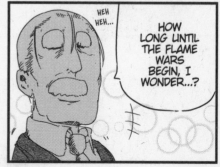

Celebrity Comedian

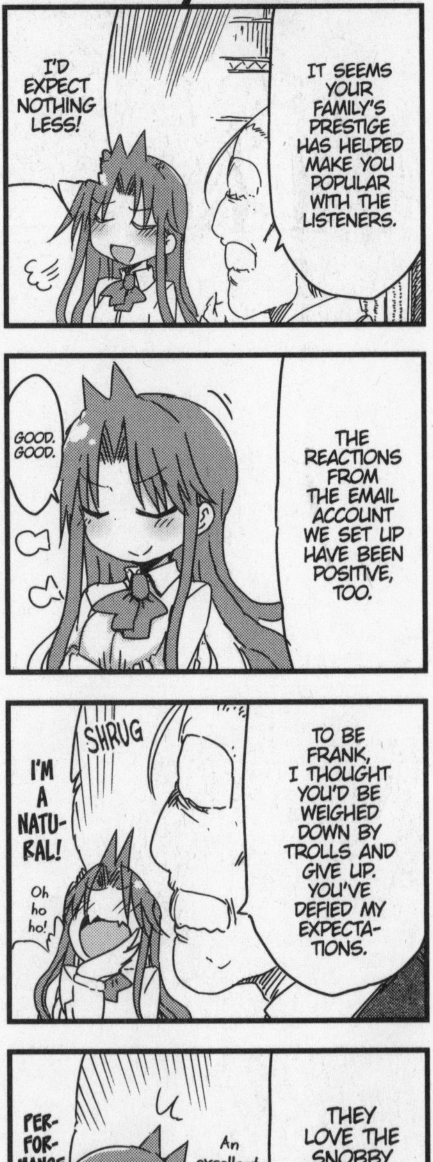
IT SEEMS YOUR FAMILY'S PRESTIGE HAS HELPED MAKE YOU POPULAR WITH THE LISTENERS.
I'D EXPECT NOTHING LESS!
THE REACTIONS FROM THE EMAIL ACCOUNT WE SET UP HAVE BEEN POSITIVE, TOO.
GOOD. GOOD.
TO BE FRANK, I THOUGHT YOU'D BE WEIGHED DOWN BY TROLLS AND GIVE UP. YOU'VE DEFIED MY EXPECTATIONS.
SHRUG
I'M A NATURAL!
Oh ho ho!
THEY LOVE THE SNOBBY RICH GIRL CHARACTER YOU'RE PLAYING.
An excellent performance.
PERFORMANCE?!

Great Minds Think Alike

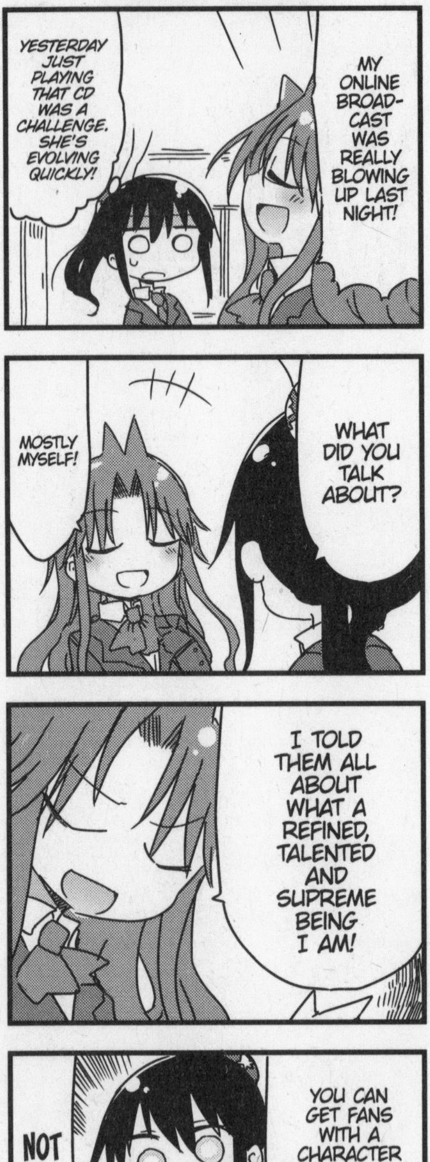
MY ONLINE BROADCAST WAS REALLY BLOWING UP LAST NIGHT!
YESTERDAY JUST PLAYING THAT CD WAS A CHALLENGE. SHE'S EVOLVING QUICKLY!
WHAT DID YOU TALK ABOUT?
MOSTLY MYSELF!
I TOLD THEM ALL ABOUT WHAT A REFINED, TALENTED AND SUPREME BEING I AM!
YOU CAN GET FANS WITH A CHARACTER LIKE THAT? I FIGURED PEOPLE WOULD JUST FLAME YOU.
NOT YOU TOO!
HA HA HA HA!

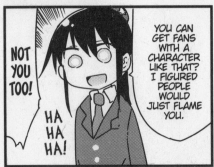

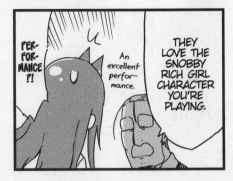

A Special Reward

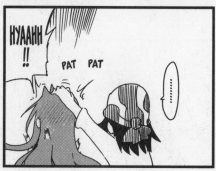

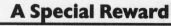

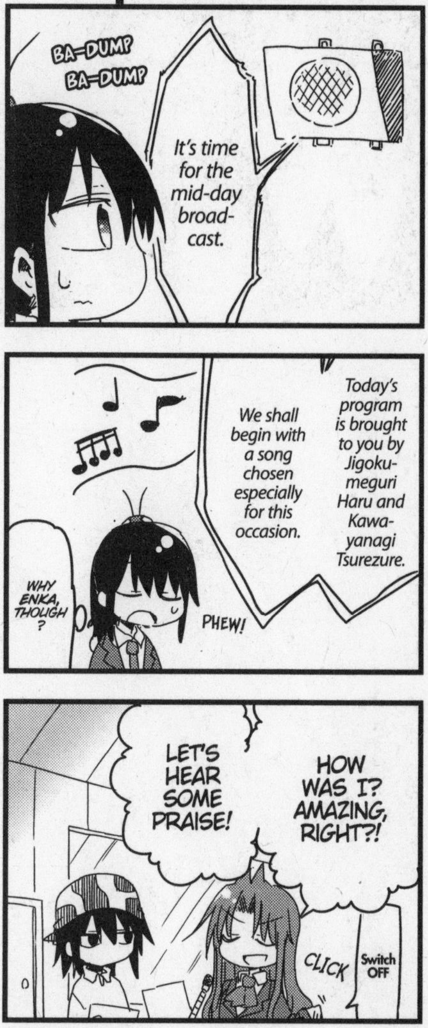
BA-DUMP
BA-DUMP
It's time for the mid-day broad-cast.
Today's program is brought to you by Jigoku-meguri Haru and Kawa-yanagi Tsurezure.
We shall begin with a song chosen especially for this occasion.
WHY ENKA, THOUGH?
PHEW!
HOW WAS I? AMAZING, RIGHT?!
LET'S HEAR SOME PRAISE!
Switch OFF
CLICK
NICE WORK.
PAT PAT
HYAH!

An Extra Special Reward

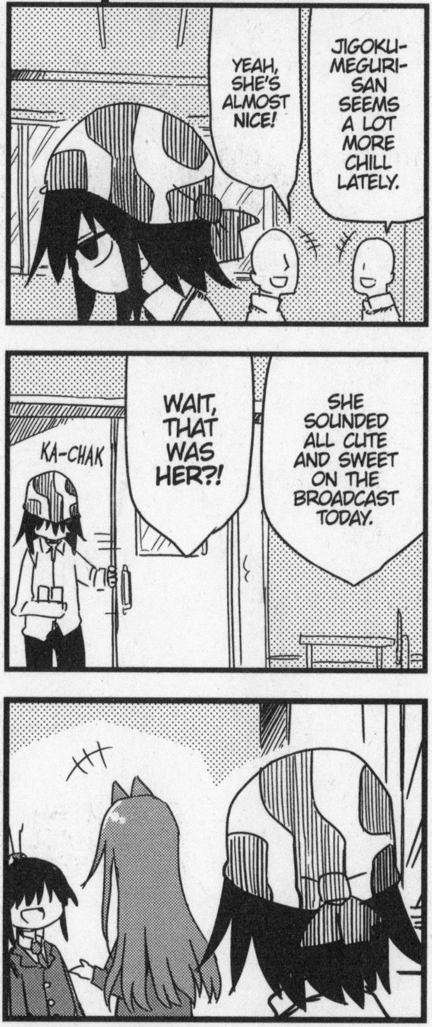
JIGOKU-MEGURI-SAN SEEMS A LOT MORE CHILL LATELY.
YEAH, SHE'S ALMOST NICE!
SHE SOUNDED ALL CUTE AND SWEET ON THE BROADCAST TODAY.
WAIT, THAT WAS HER?!
KA-CHAK
......
PAT PAT
HYAAHH!!

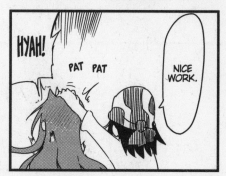

Déjà Vu

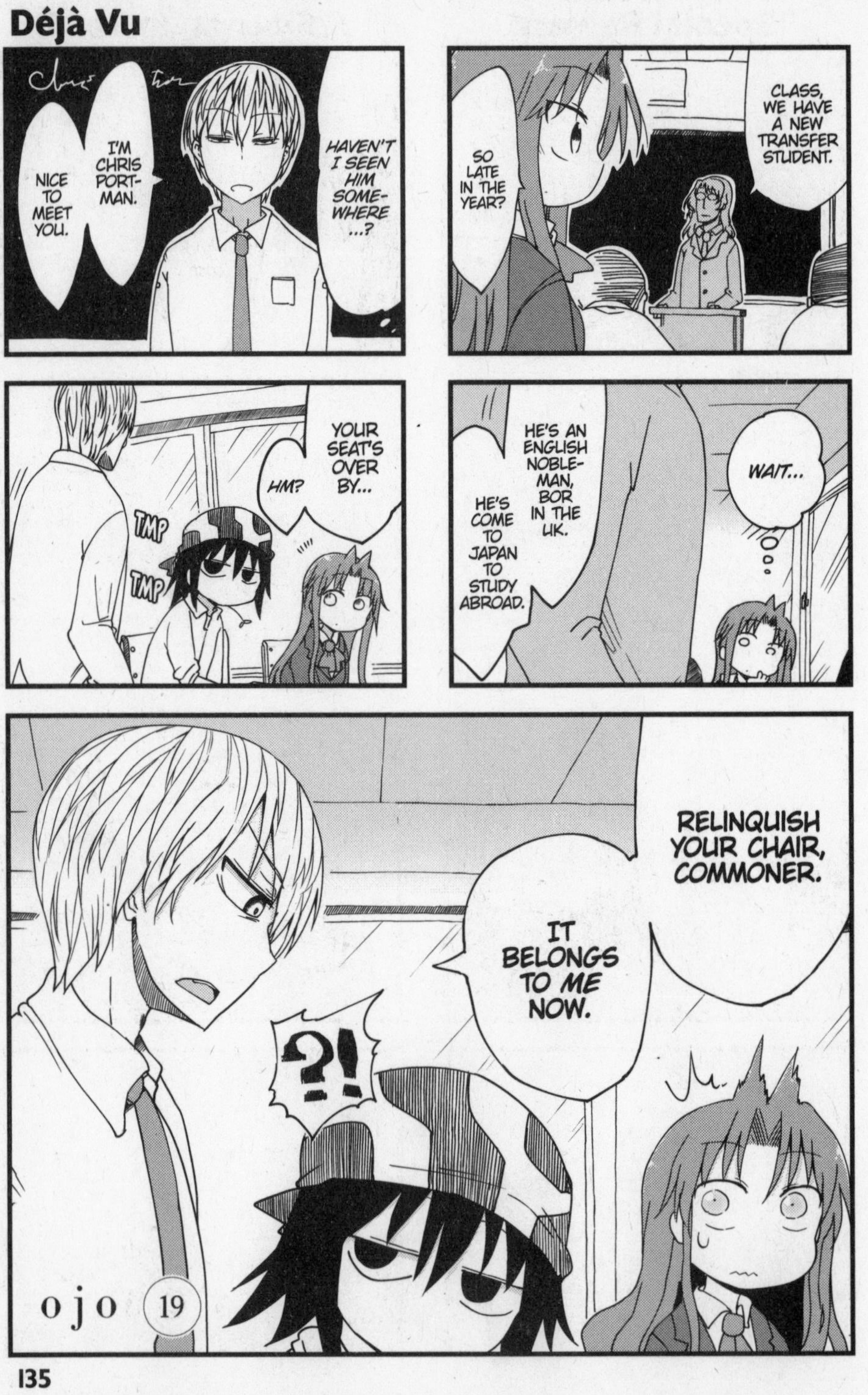

CLASS, WE HAVE A NEW TRANSFER STUDENT.
SO LATE IN THE YEAR?
HAVEN'T I SEEN HIM SOME-WHERE ...?
I'M CHRIS PORT-MAN.
NICE TO MEET YOU.
WAIT...
HE'S AN ENGLISH NOBLE-MAN, BOR IN THE UK.
HE'S COME TO JAPAN TO STUDY ABROAD.
YOUR SEAT'S OVER BY...
HM?
TMP
TMP
RELINQUISH YOUR CHAIR, COMMONER.
IT BELONGS TO ME NOW.
?!
ojo 19

Different Set of Social Skills

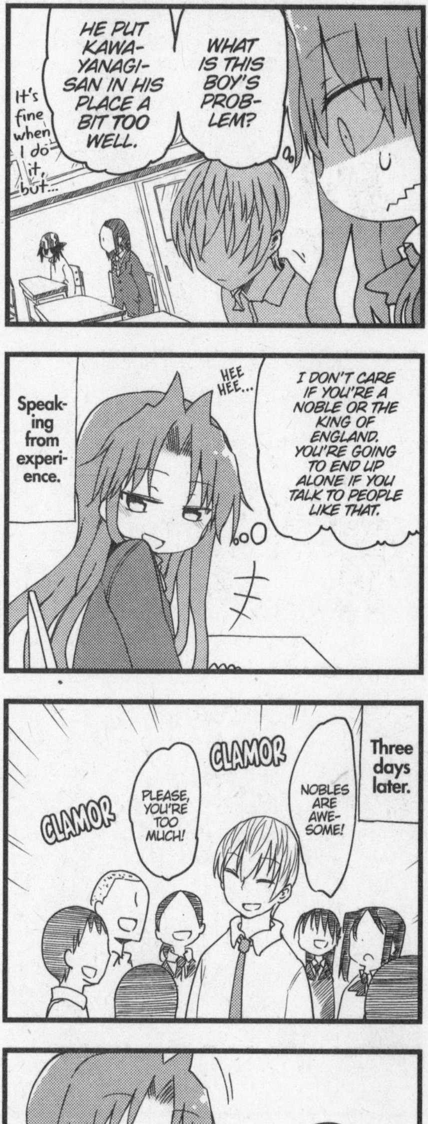
WHAT IS THIS BOY'S PROBLEM?
HE PUT KAWA-YANAGI-SAN IN HIS PLACE A BIT TOO WELL.
It's fine when I do it, but...
I DON'T CARE IF YOU'RE A NOBLE OR THE KING OF ENGLAND. YOU'RE GOING TO END UP ALONE IF YOU TALK TO PEOPLE LIKE THAT.
HEE HEE...
Speak-ing from experi-ence.
Three days later.
NOBLES ARE AWE-SOME!
CLAMOR
PLEASE, YOU'RE TOO MUCH!
CLAMOR
HUH...?

Above the Rest

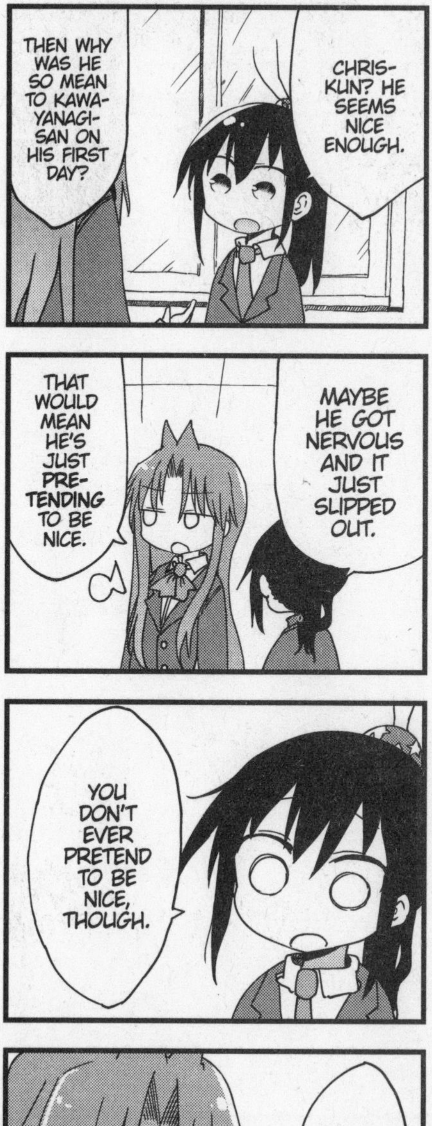
CHRIS-KUN? HE SEEMS NICE ENOUGH.
THEN WHY WAS HE SO MEAN TO KAWA-YANAGI-SAN ON HIS FIRST DAY?
MAYBE HE GOT NERVOUS AND IT JUST SLIPPED OUT.
THAT WOULD MEAN HE'S JUST PRE-TENDING TO BE NICE.
YOU DON'T EVER PRETEND TO BE NICE, THOUGH.
OF COURSE NOT. I'M TRANS-CENDENT.

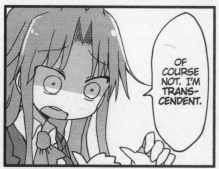

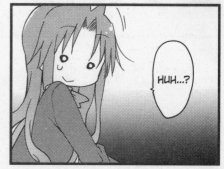

An Unfortunate Painting

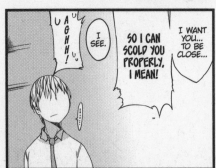

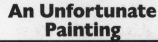

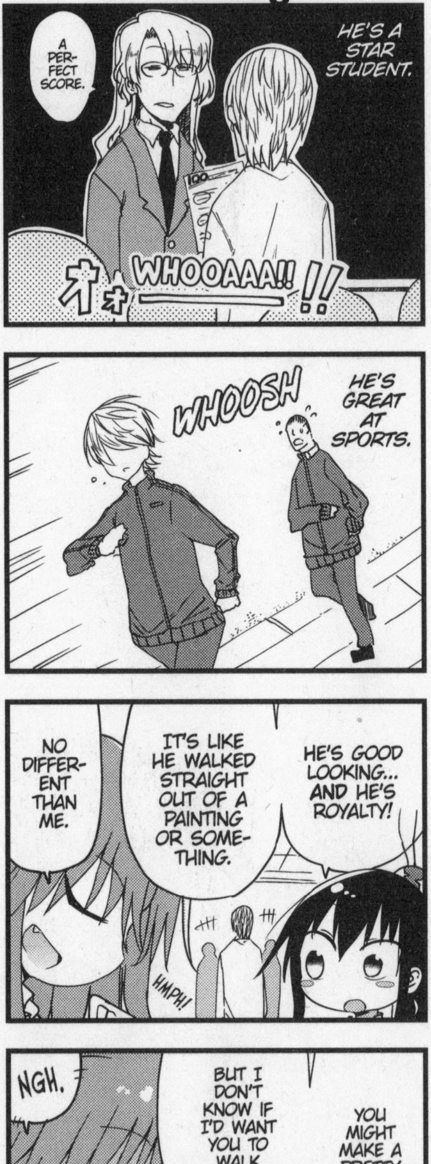
HE'S A STAR STUDENT.
A PERFECT SCORE.
オォ WHOOAAA!! !!
HE'S GREAT AT SPORTS.
WHOOSH
HE'S GOOD LOOKING... AND HE'S ROYALTY!
IT'S LIKE HE WALKED STRAIGHT OUT OF A PAINTING OR SOMETHING.
NO DIFFERENT THAN ME.
HMPH!
YOU MIGHT MAKE A PRETTY PAINTING...
BUT I DON'T KNOW IF I'D WANT YOU TO WALK OUT OF IT...
NGH.

Killer Line

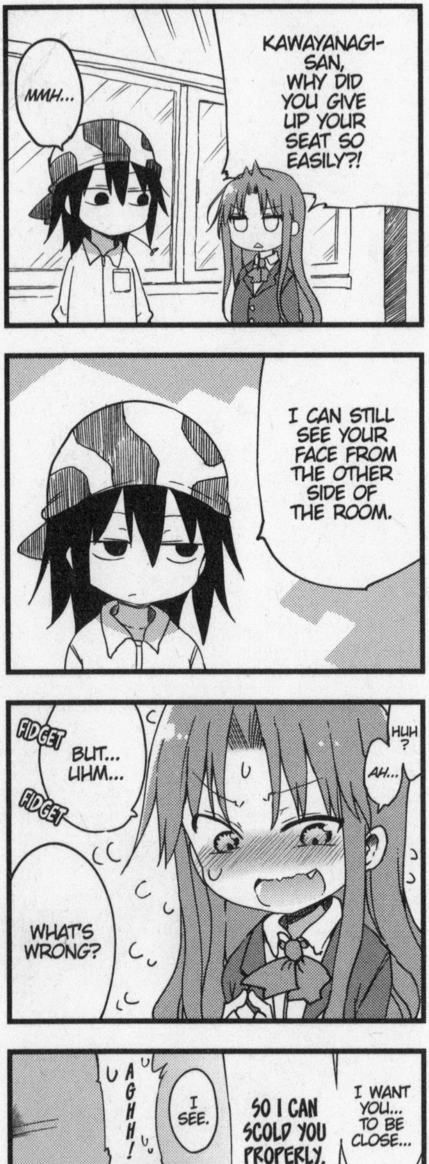
KAWAYANAGI-SAN, WHY DID YOU GIVE UP YOUR SEAT SO EASILY?!
MMH...
I CAN STILL SEE YOUR FACE FROM THE OTHER SIDE OF THE ROOM.
HUH?
AH...
BUT... UHM...
FIDGET
FIDGET
WHAT'S WRONG?
I WANT YOU... TO BE CLOSE...
SO I CAN SCOLD YOU PROPERLY, I MEAN!
I SEE.
AGHH!
......

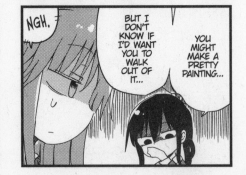

He Finally Said It!!

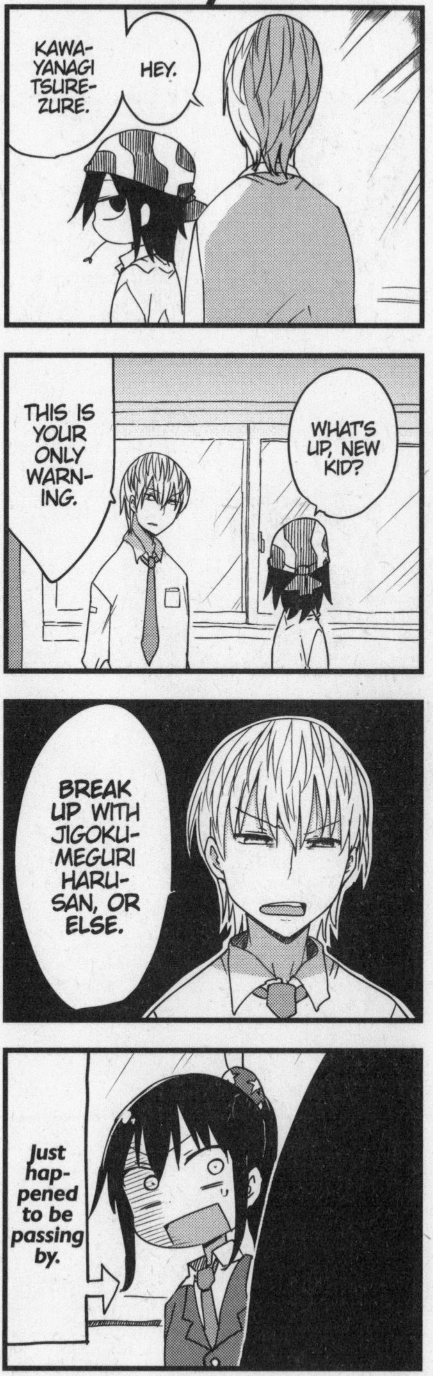
HEY.
KAWA-YANAGI TSURE-ZURE.
WHAT'S UP, NEW KID?
THIS IS YOUR ONLY WARN-ING.
BREAK UP WITH JIGOKU-MEGURI HARU-SAN, OR ELSE.
Just hap-pened to be passing by.

Forgotten in an Instant

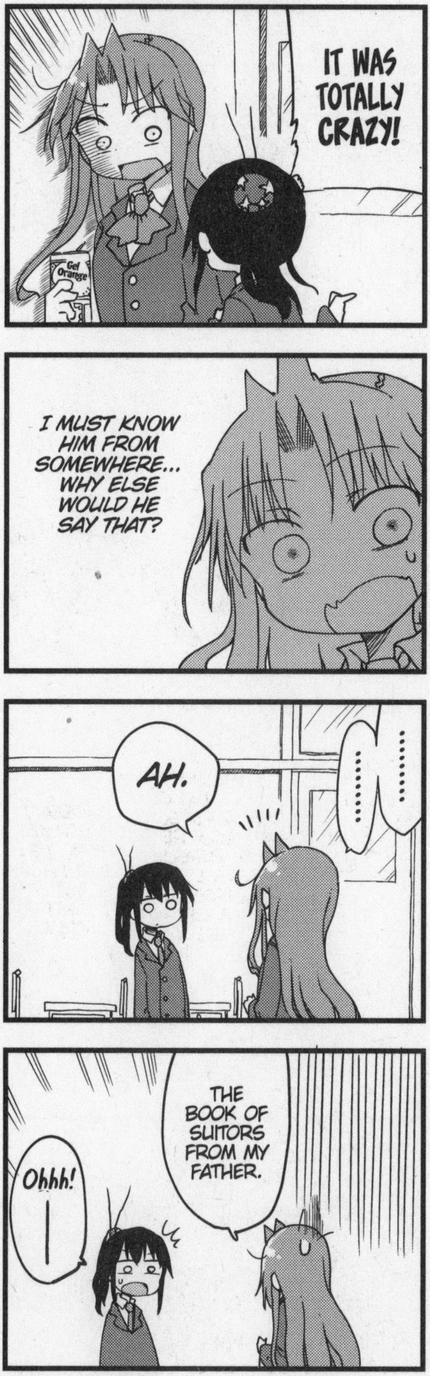
IT WAS TOTALLY CRAZY!
Gel Orange
I MUST KNOW HIM FROM SOMEWHERE... WHY ELSE WOULD HE SAY THAT?
....
AH.
THE BOOK OF SUITORS FROM MY FATHER.
Ohhh!—

Why?

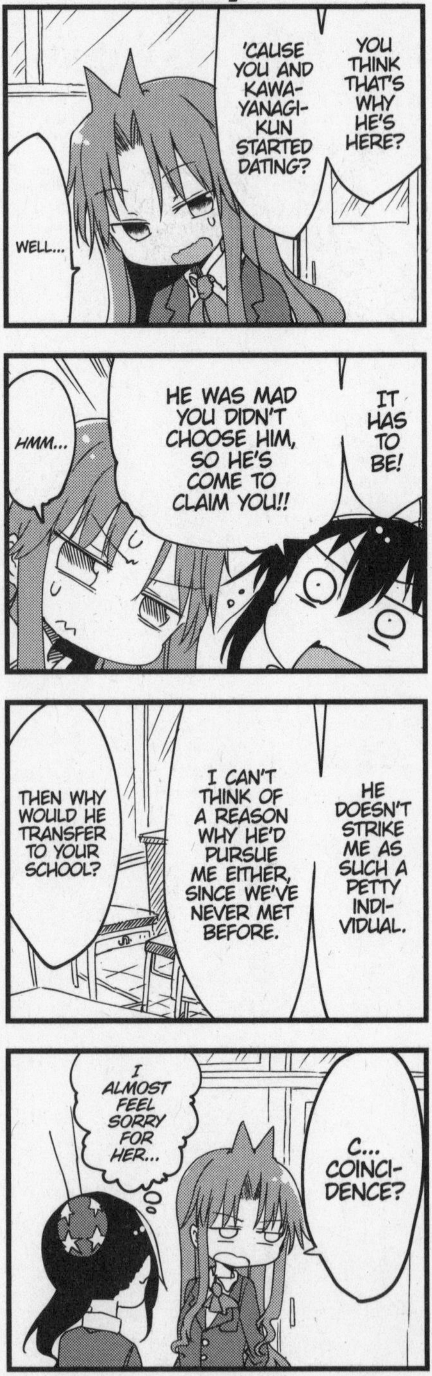
YOU THINK THAT'S WHY HE'S HERE?
'CAUSE YOU AND KAWAYANAGI-KUN STARTED DATING?
WELL...
IT HAS TO BE!
HE WAS MAD YOU DIDN'T CHOOSE HIM, SO HE'S COME TO CLAIM YOU!!
HMM...
HE DOESN'T STRIKE ME AS SUCH A PETTY INDIVIDUAL.
I CAN'T THINK OF A REASON WHY HE'D PURSUE ME EITHER, SINCE WE'VE NEVER MET BEFORE.
THEN WHY WOULD HE TRANSFER TO YOUR SCHOOL?
C... COINCIDENCE?
I ALMOST FEEL SORRY FOR HER...

He Wouldn't Say That!

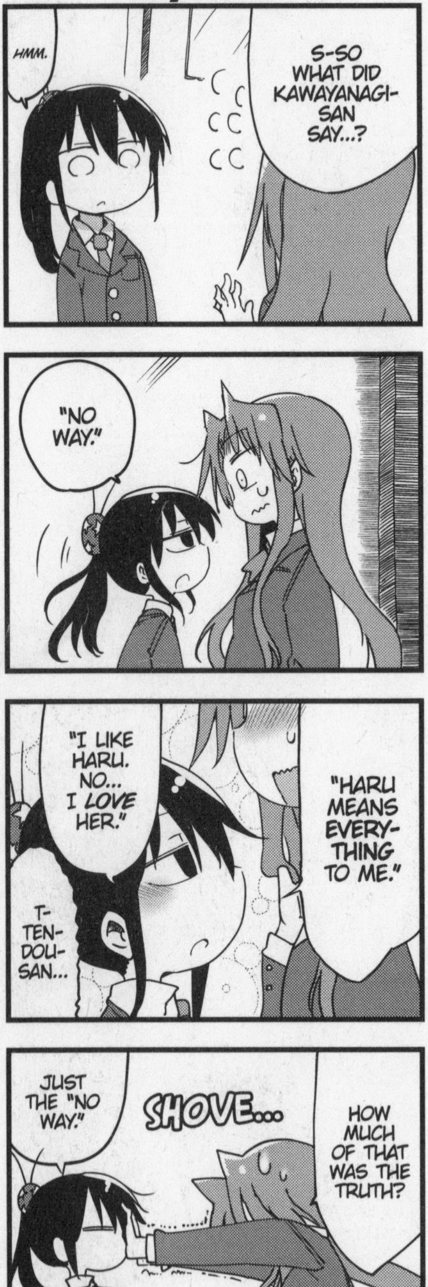
S-SO WHAT DID KAWAYANAGI-SAN SAY...?
HMM.
"NO WAY."
"HARU MEANS EVERYTHING TO ME."
"I LIKE HARU. NO... I *LOVE* HER."
T-TENDOU-SAN...
HOW MUCH OF THAT WAS THE TRUTH?
SHOVE...
JUST THE "NO WAY."

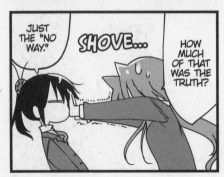

Petty

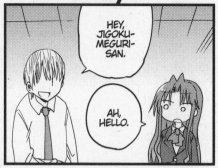

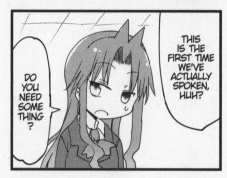

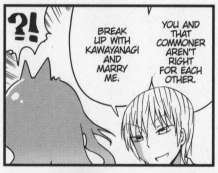

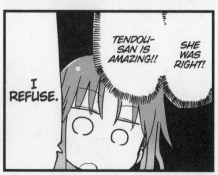

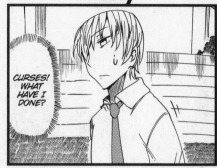

CURSES! WHAT HAVE I DONE?
JIGOKUMEGURI HARU... I ASKED FOR YOUR HAND IN MARRIAGE ONLY TO FIND THAT YOUR HEART ALREADY BELONGS TO ANOTHER!
WHAT A BLOW TO MY PRIDE...
I'M HOME, BAAYA.
WELCOME HOME, MASTER CHRIS.
I WILL CLAIM HER YET... BY ANY MEANS NECESSARY.
PETTY, AS USUAL.
Ooo

Petty 2

HEY, JIGOKUMEGURI-SAN.
AH, HELLO.
THIS IS THE FIRST TIME WE'VE ACTUALLY SPOKEN, HUH?
DO YOU NEED SOMETHING?
?!
YOU AND THAT COMMONER AREN'T RIGHT FOR EACH OTHER.
BREAK UP WITH KAWAYANAGI AND MARRY ME.
SHE WAS RIGHT!
TENDOU-SAN IS AMAZING!!
I REFUSE.

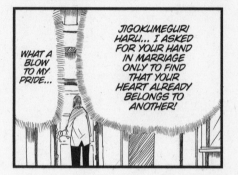

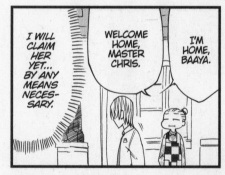

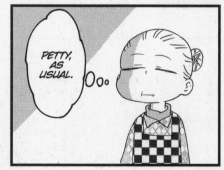

Because He's There for Me

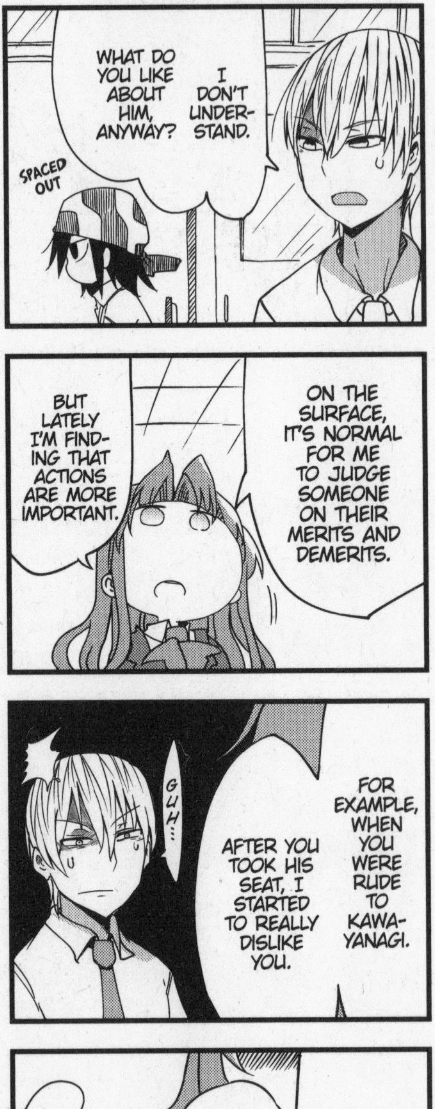
I DON'T UNDER-STAND.
WHAT DO YOU LIKE ABOUT HIM, ANYWAY?
SPACED OUT
ON THE SURFACE, IT'S NORMAL FOR ME TO JUDGE SOMEONE ON THEIR MERITS AND DEMERITS.
BUT LATELY I'M FIND-ING THAT ACTIONS ARE MORE IMPORTANT.
FOR EXAMPLE, WHEN YOU WERE RUDE TO KAWA-YANAGI.
AFTER YOU TOOK HIS SEAT, I STARTED TO REALLY DISLIKE YOU.
GUH...
I'VE ALSO COME TO REALIZE THAT I MADE A LOT OF MISTAKES IN THE PAST.
BUT KAWAYANAGI-SAN ACCEPTED ME AND HAS HELPED ME TO GROW.
THAT'S ALL I HAVE TO SAY.

An Elder's Perspective

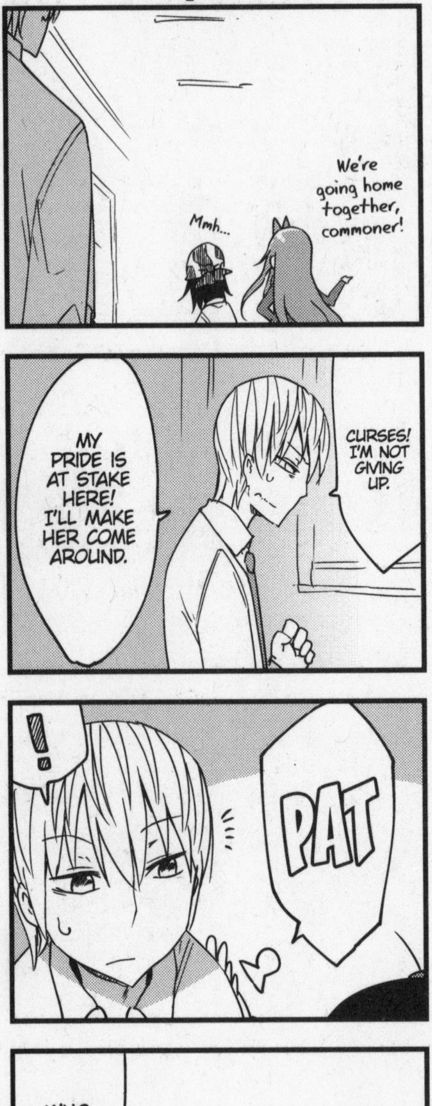
We're going home together, commoner!
Mmh...
CURSES! I'M NOT GIVING UP.
MY PRIDE IS AT STAKE HERE! I'LL MAKE HER COME AROUND.
PAT
!
Ah, to be young.
There there.
WHO ARE YOU AGAIN?

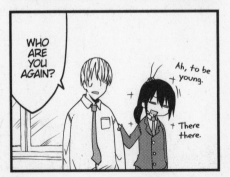

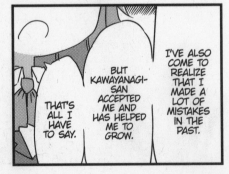

Sorry...

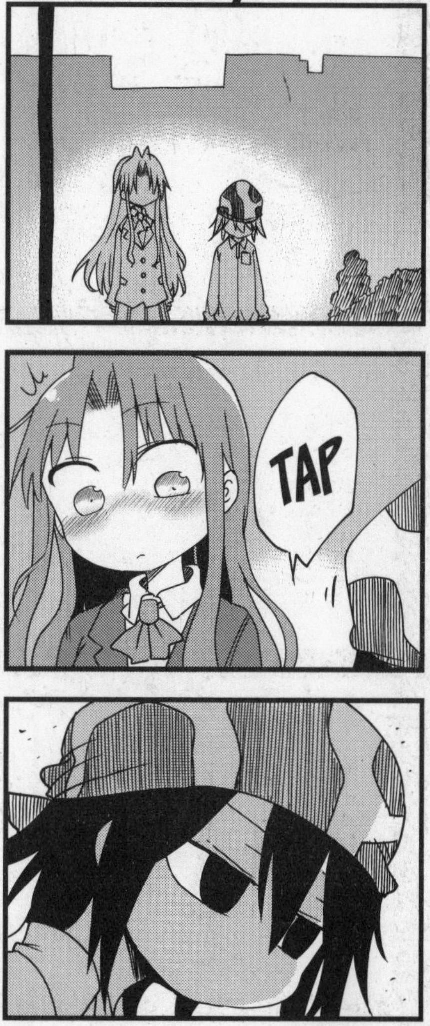
TAP
!

Homecoming

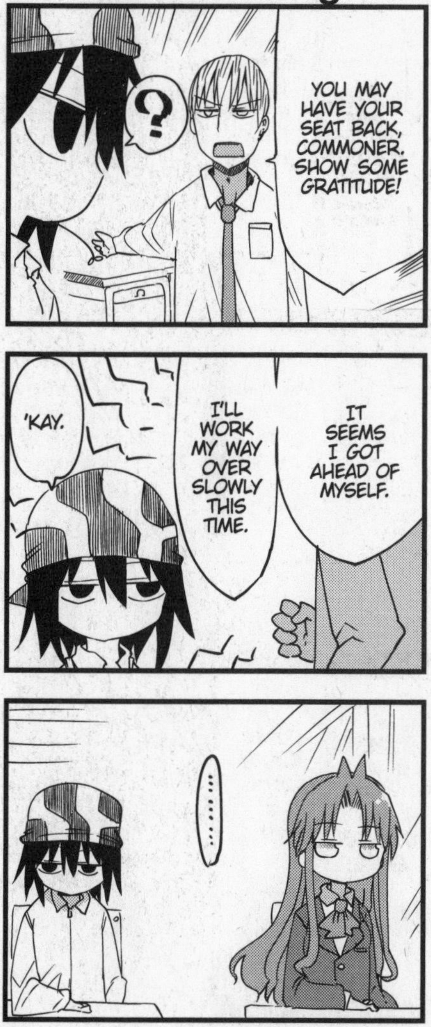
?
YOU MAY HAVE YOUR SEAT BACK, COMMONER. SHOW SOME GRATITUDE!
IT SEEMS I GOT AHEAD OF MYSELF.
I'LL WORK MY WAY OVER SLOWLY THIS TIME.
'KAY.
......
WEL-COME BACK.
GLAD TO BE BACK.
Next to you now, huh?
What's up?

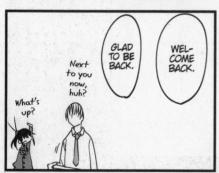

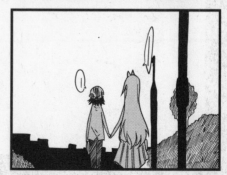

ojo 19.1

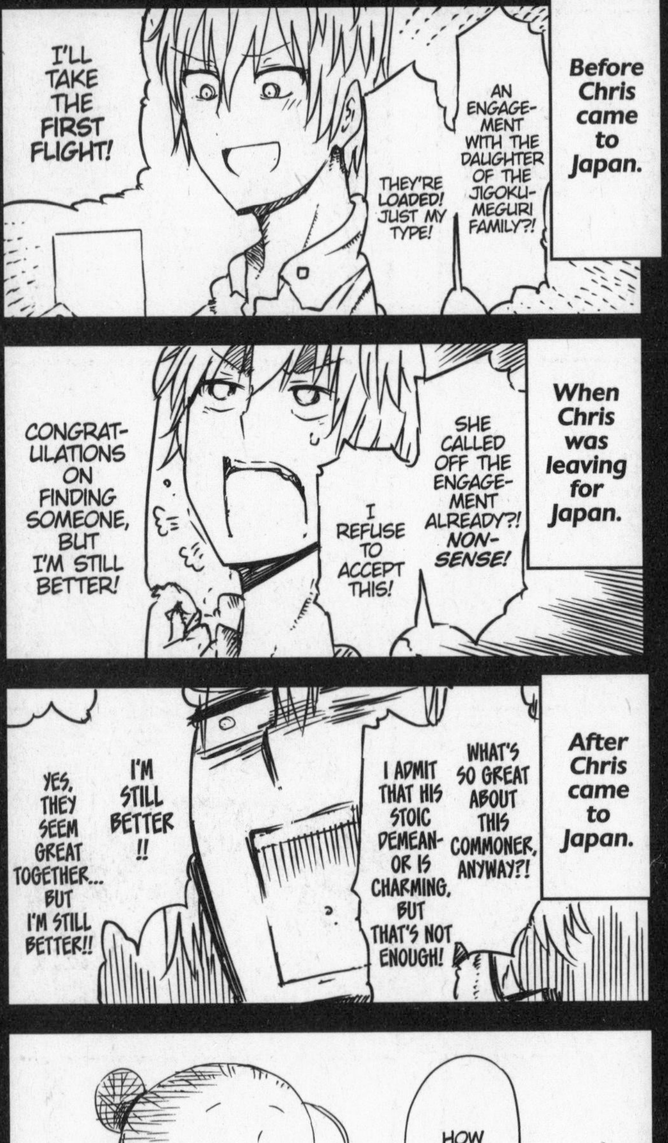
Before Chris came to Japan.
AN ENGAGEMENT WITH THE DAUGHTER OF THE JIGOKUMEGURI FAMILY?!
THEY'RE LOADED! JUST MY TYPE!
I'LL TAKE THE FIRST FLIGHT!
When Chris was leaving for Japan.
SHE CALLED OFF THE ENGAGEMENT ALREADY?! NONSENSE!
I REFUSE TO ACCEPT THIS!
CONGRATULATIONS ON FINDING SOMEONE, BUT I'M STILL BETTER!
After Chris came to Japan.
WHAT'S SO GREAT ABOUT THIS COMMONER, ANYWAY?!
I ADMIT THAT HIS STOIC DEMEANOR IS CHARMING, BUT THAT'S NOT ENOUGH!
I'M STILL BETTER!!
YES, THEY SEEM GREAT TOGETHER... BUT I'M STILL BETTER!!
HOW PETTY.

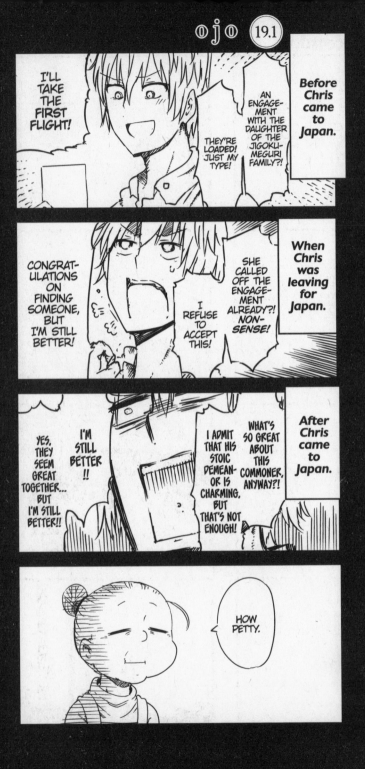

OJOJOJO

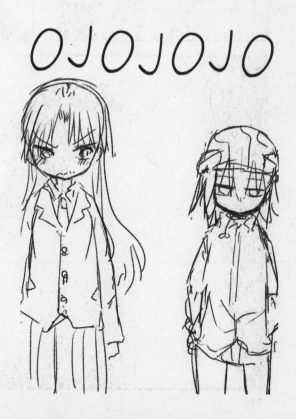

Akane's Job

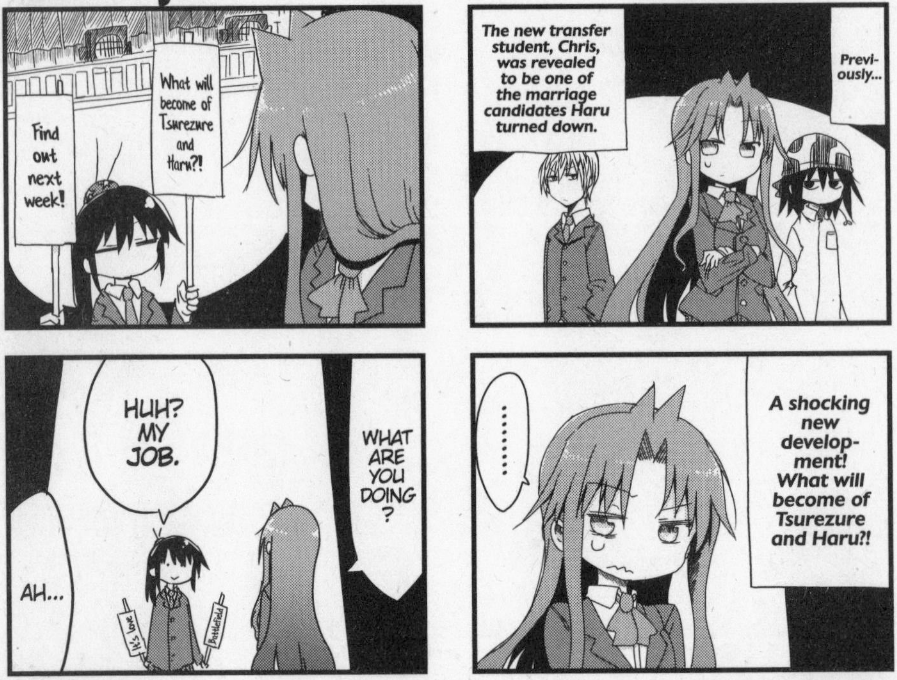

Previously...
The new transfer student, Chris, was revealed to be one of the marriage candidates Haru turned down.
What will become of Tsurezure and Haru?!
Find out next week!
A shocking new development! What will become of Tsurezure and Haru?!
....
WHAT ARE YOU DOING?
HUH? MY JOB.
Battlefield
It's love
AH...

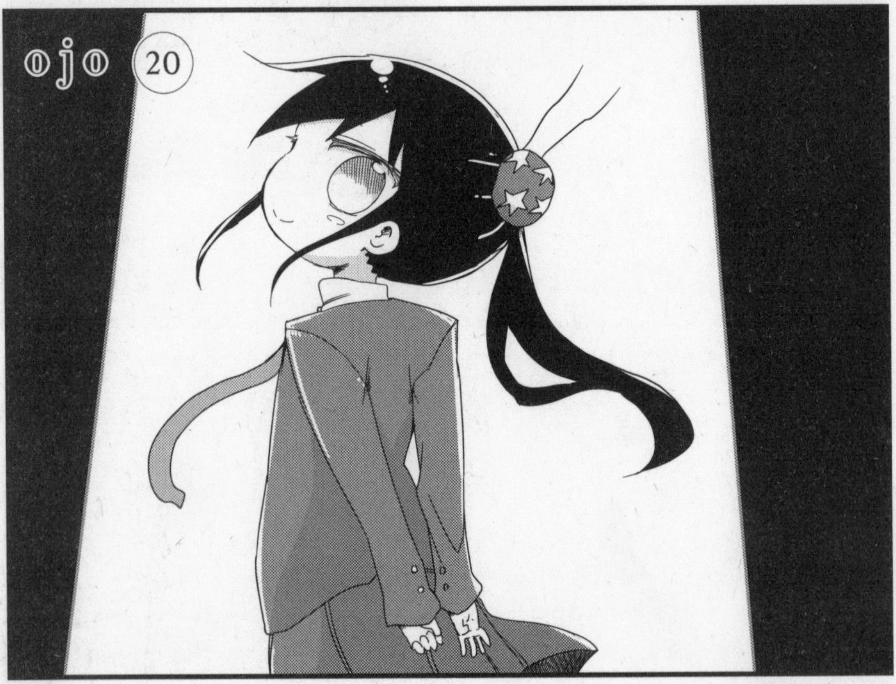

ojo 20

In the End

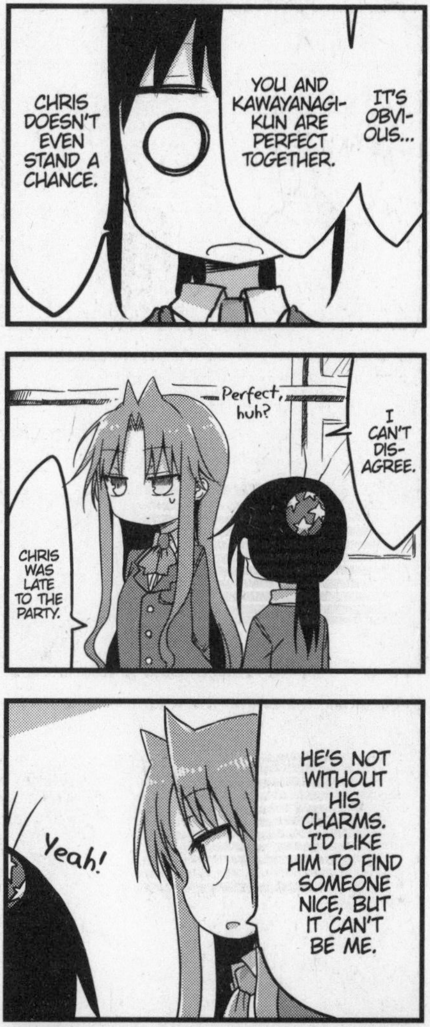
IT'S OBVIOUS...
YOU AND KAWAYANAGI-KUN ARE PERFECT TOGETHER.
CHRIS DOESN'T EVEN STAND A CHANCE.
I CAN'T DISAGREE.
Perfect, huh?
CHRIS WAS LATE TO THE PARTY.
HE'S NOT WITHOUT HIS CHARMS. I'D LIKE HIM TO FIND SOMEONE NICE, BUT IT CAN'T BE ME.
Yeah!
WHY DO I FEEL AS IF THE BATTLE HAS ENDED BEFORE I'VE EVEN BEGUN TO FIGHT?

Watch and Wait

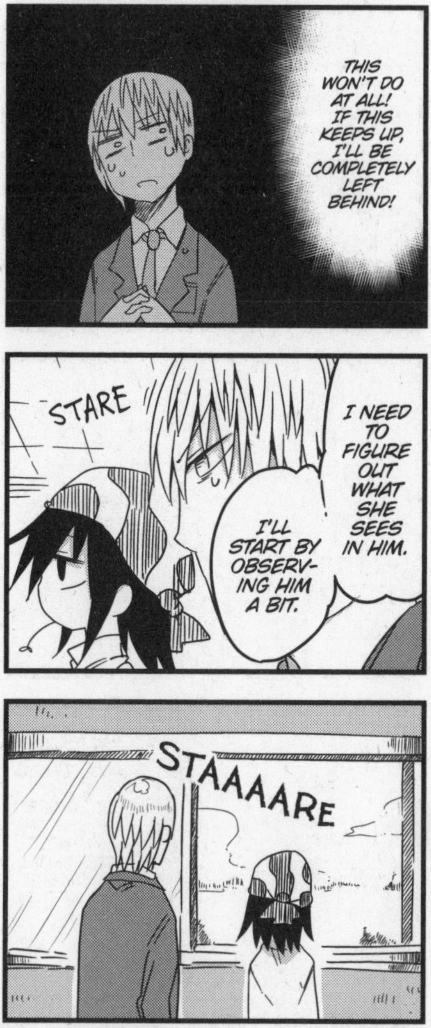
THIS WON'T DO AT ALL! IF THIS KEEPS UP, I'LL BE COMPLETELY LEFT BEHIND!
I NEED TO FIGURE OUT WHAT SHE SEES IN HIM.
I'LL START BY OBSERVING HIM A BIT.
STARE
STAAAAARE
...
HE ISN'T DOING ANYTHING.

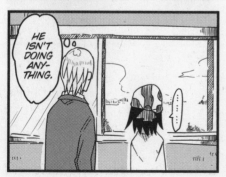

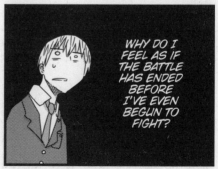

Questionable Taste

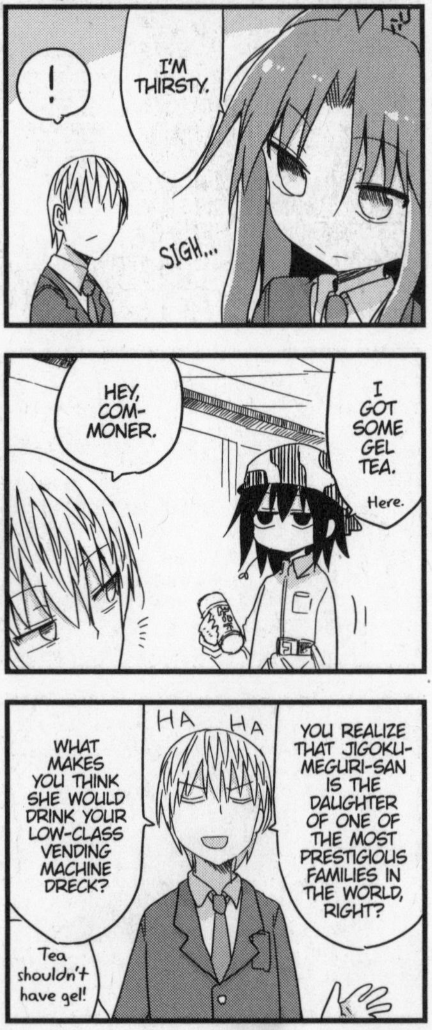
I'M THIRSTY.
!
SIGH...
I GOT SOME GEL TEA.
Here.
HEY, COMMONER.
YOU REALIZE THAT JIGOKU-MEGURI-SAN IS THE DAUGHTER OF ONE OF THE MOST PRESTIGIOUS FAMILIES IN THE WORLD, RIGHT?
HA HA
WHAT MAKES YOU THINK SHE WOULD DRINK YOUR LOW-CLASS VENDING MACHINE DRECK?
Tea shouldn't have gel!
RIGHT, JIGOKU-MEGURI-SAN?!
RIGHT ?!
MMMGH...

Can't Remember Her Face

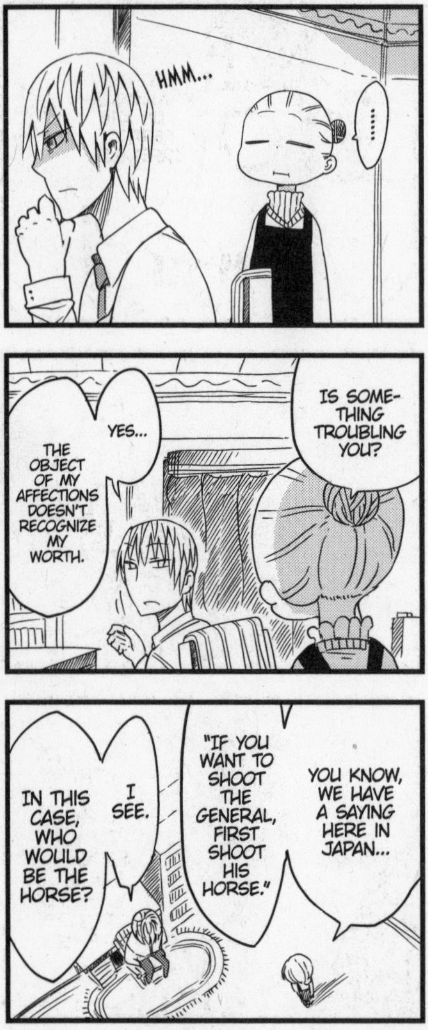
......
HMM...
IS SOME-THING TROUBLING YOU?
YES... THE OBJECT OF MY AFFECTIONS DOESN'T RECOGNIZE MY WORTH.
YOU KNOW, WE HAVE A SAYING HERE IN JAPAN...
"IF YOU WANT TO SHOOT THE GENERAL, FIRST SHOOT HIS HORSE."
I SEE.
IN THIS CASE, WHO WOULD BE THE HORSE?
IT MUST BE HER.

※ *In other words, to accomplish a bigger goal, you should start by dealing with the smaller issues surrounding it.*

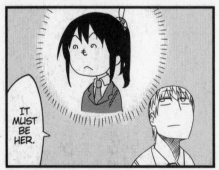

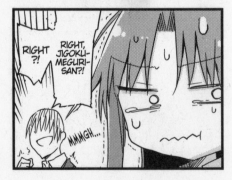

Hmph

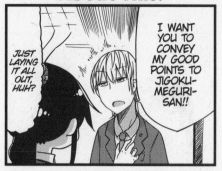

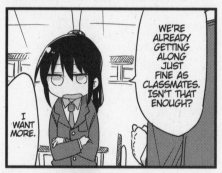

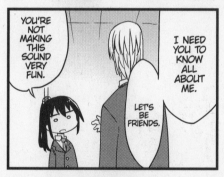

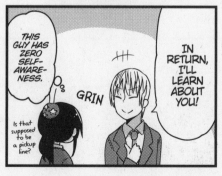

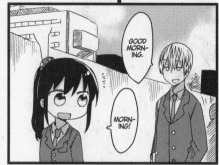

GOOD MORNING.
MORNING!
SAY, CHRIS-KUN... WHY DON'T YOU JUST GIVE UP ON JIGOKUMEGURI-SAN?
YOU SHOULDN'T BUTT IN ON OTHER PEOPLES' RELATIONSHIPS.
SORRY, BUT I'VE COME UP WITH A PLAN.
I'M GOING TO BECOME FRIENDS WITH YOU.

What Do You Think About This?

I WANT YOU TO CONVEY MY GOOD POINTS TO JIGOKUMEGURI-SAN!!
JUST LAYING IT ALL OUT, HUH?
WE'RE ALREADY GETTING ALONG JUST FINE AS CLASSMATES. ISN'T THAT ENOUGH?
I WANT MORE.
I NEED YOU TO KNOW ALL ABOUT ME.
LET'S BE FRIENDS.
YOU'RE NOT MAKING THIS SOUND VERY FUN.
IN RETURN, I'LL LEARN ABOUT YOU!
GRIN
THIS GUY HAS ZERO SELF-AWARENESS.
Is that supposed to be a pickup line?

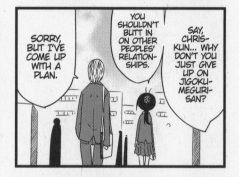

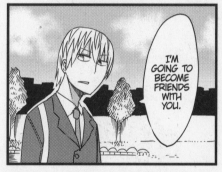

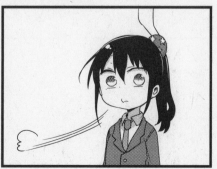

The Tables Have Turned

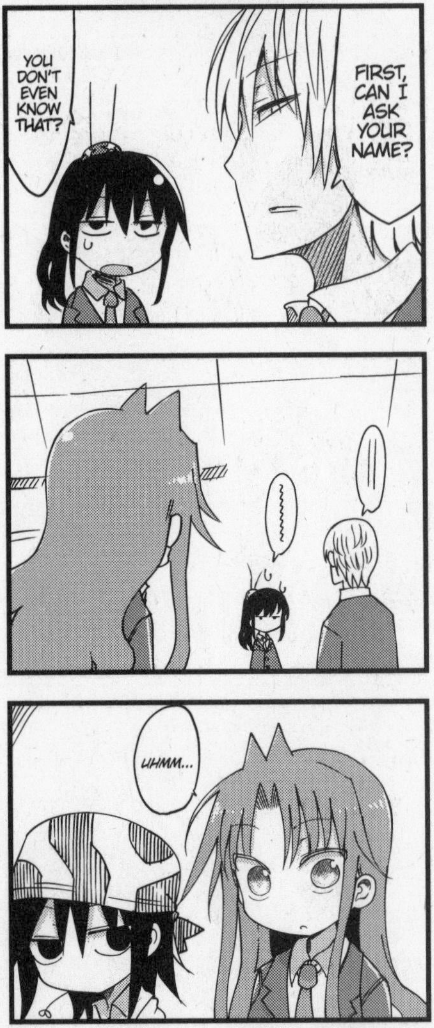
FIRST, CAN I ASK YOUR NAME?
YOU DON'T EVEN KNOW THAT?
!!
UHMM...

Good Points

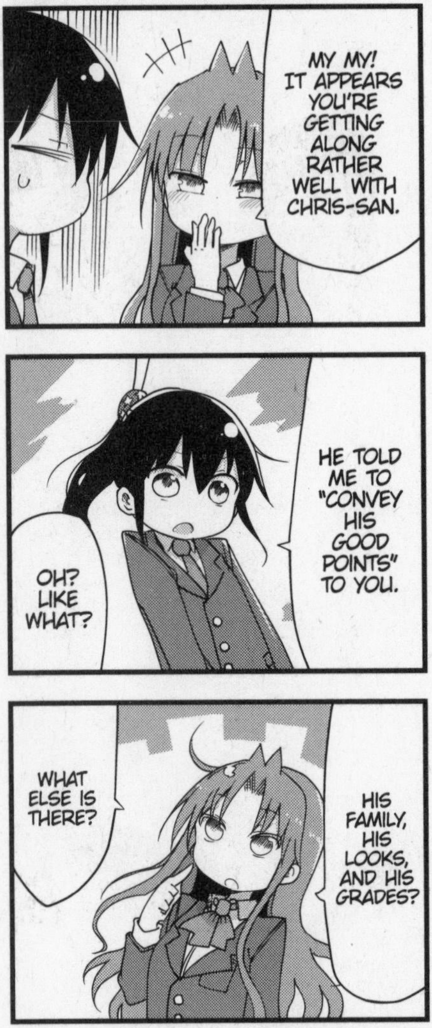
MY MY! IT APPEARS YOU'RE GETTING ALONG RATHER WELL WITH CHRIS-SAN.
HE TOLD ME TO "CONVEY HIS GOOD POINTS" TO YOU.
OH? LIKE WHAT?
HIS FAMILY, HIS LOOKS, AND HIS GRADES?
WHAT ELSE IS THERE?
THAT SEEMS TO BE IT.
I SEE.
YEP.
......

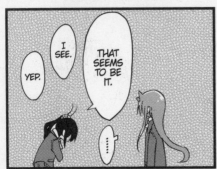

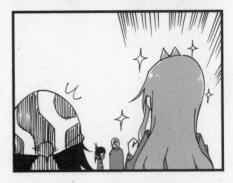

More Than Chris Himself

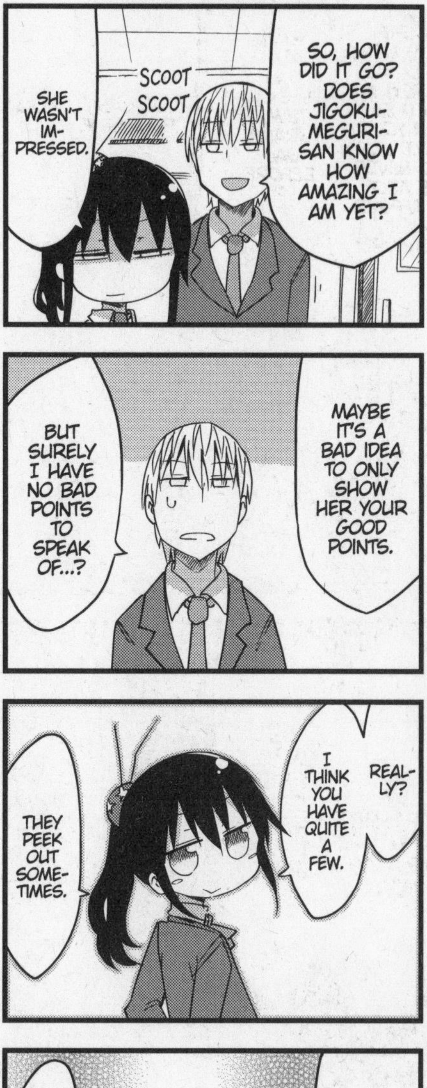
SO, HOW DID IT GO? DOES JIGOKU-MEGURI-SAN KNOW HOW AMAZING I AM YET?
SCOOT SCOOT
SHE WASN'T IMPRESSED.
MAYBE IT'S A BAD IDEA TO ONLY SHOW HER YOUR GOOD POINTS.
BUT SURELY I HAVE NO BAD POINTS TO SPEAK OF...?
REALLY?
I THINK YOU HAVE QUITE A FEW.
THEY PEEK OUT SOMETIMES.
AND NOW THAT I HAVE THE WHOLE PICTURE, I FEEL LIKE WE'RE A LITTLE CLOSER.
I SEE. SO THAT'S HOW THIS WORKS.

You're Not Wrong

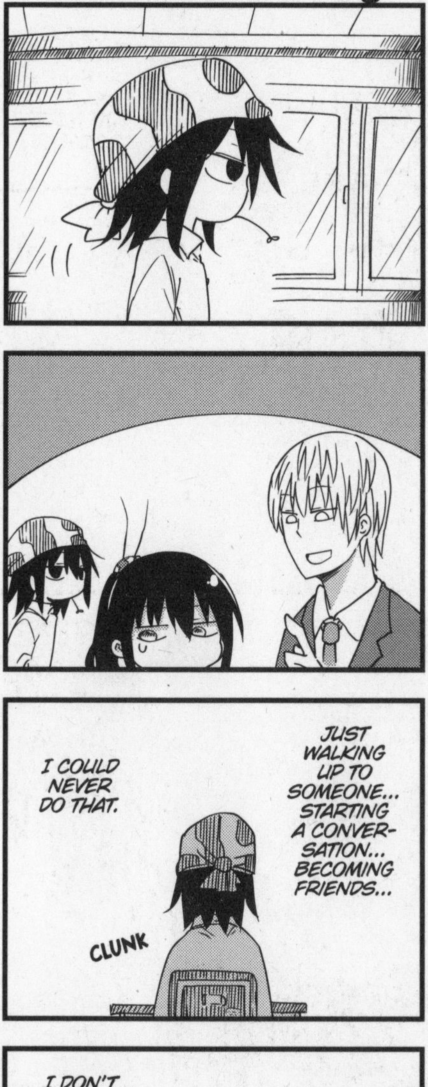
JUST WALKING UP TO SOMEONE... STARTING A CONVERSATION... BECOMING FRIENDS...
CLUNK
I COULD NEVER DO THAT.
I DON'T EVEN REMEMBER HOW I MADE FRIENDS WITH JIGOKU-MEGURI.

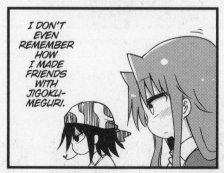

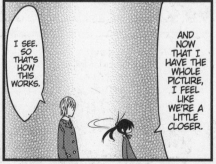

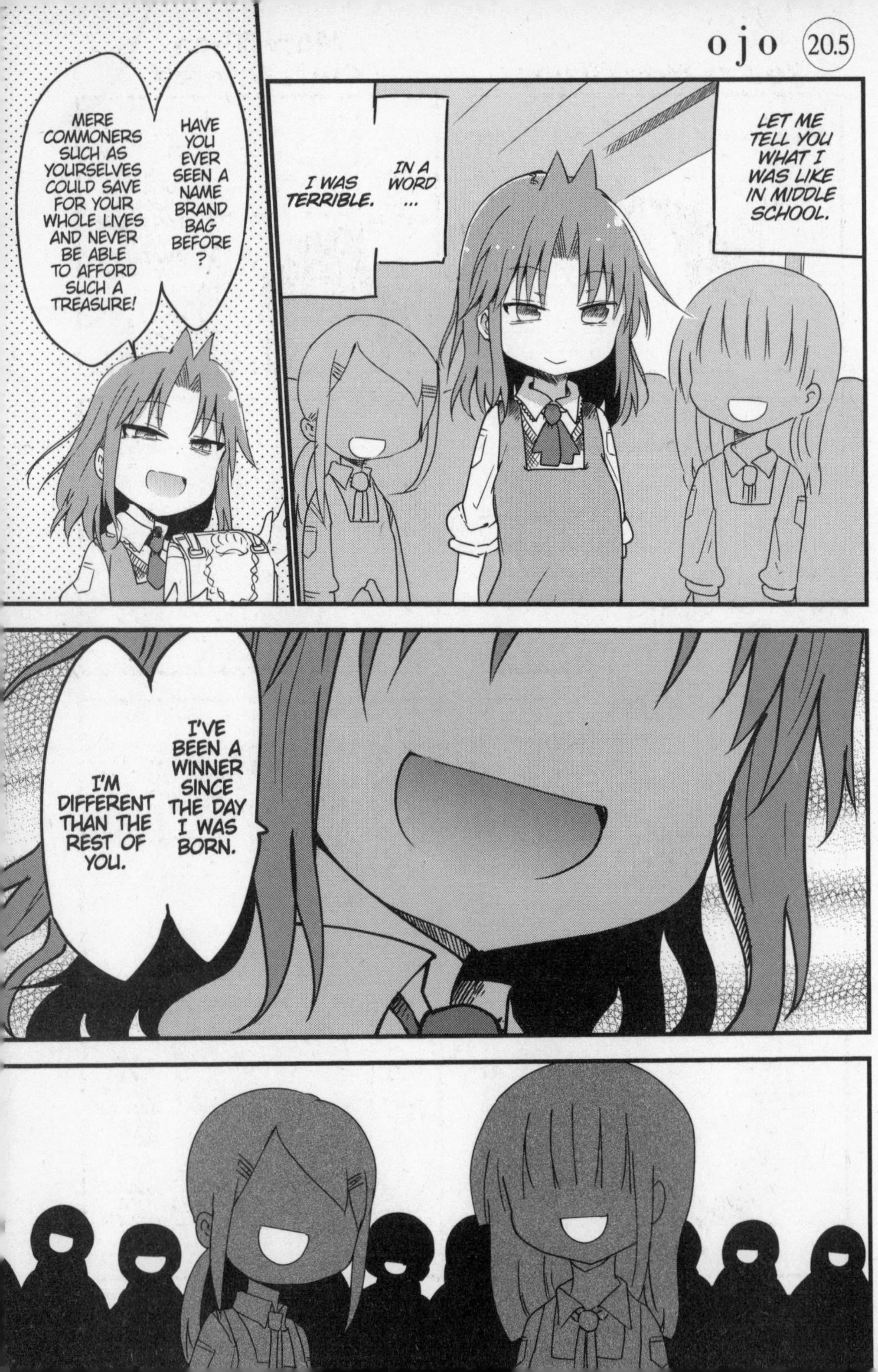
LET ME TELL YOU WHAT I WAS LIKE IN MIDDLE SCHOOL.
IN A WORD ...
I WAS TERRIBLE.
HAVE YOU EVER SEEN A NAME BRAND BAG BEFORE?
MERE COMMONERS SUCH AS YOURSELVES COULD SAVE FOR YOUR WHOLE LIVES AND NEVER BE ABLE TO AFFORD SUCH A TREASURE!
I'VE BEEN A WINNER SINCE THE DAY I WAS BORN.
I'M DIFFERENT THAN THE REST OF YOU.

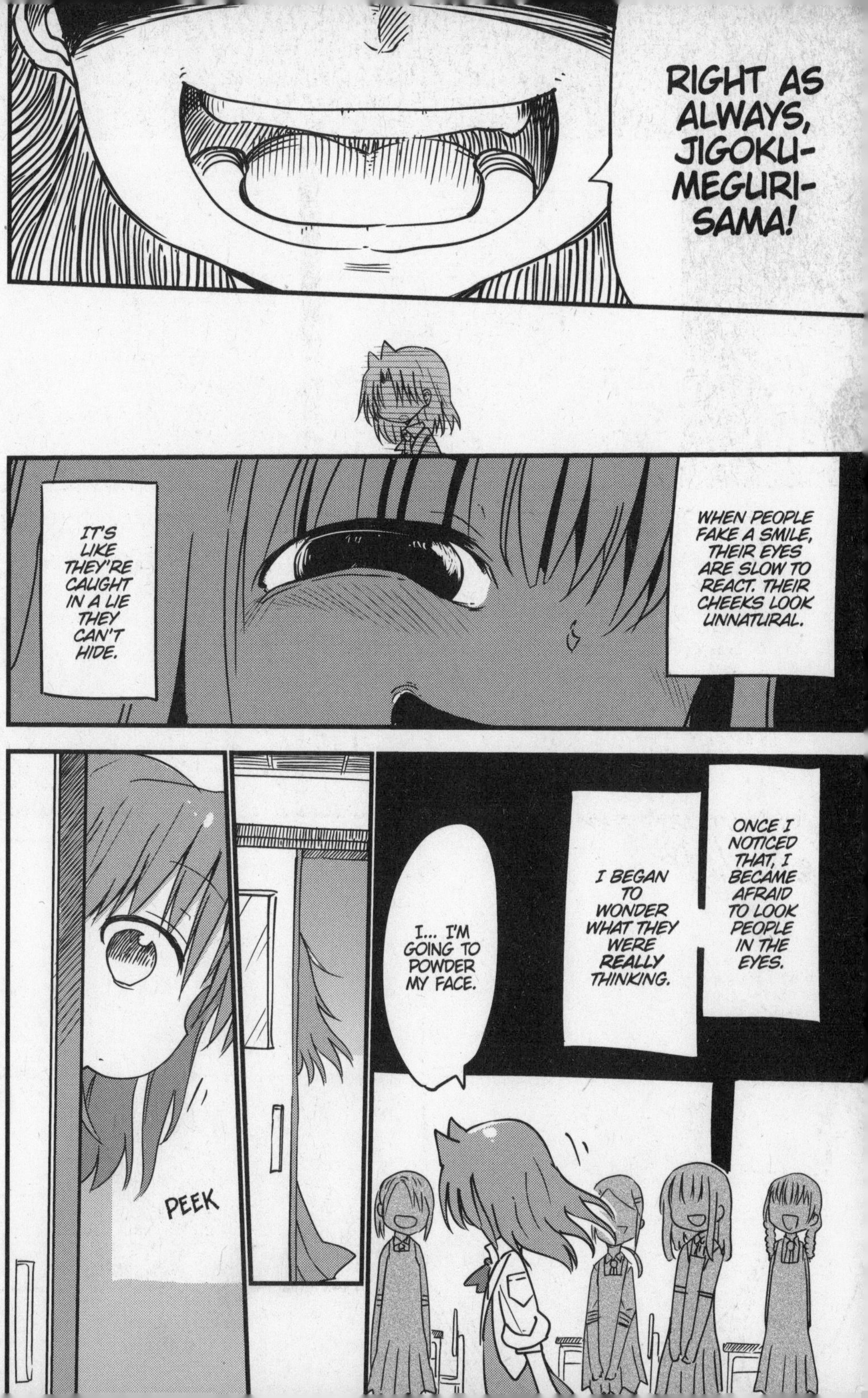
RIGHT AS ALWAYS, JIGOKU-MEGURI-SAMA!
WHEN PEOPLE FAKE A SMILE, THEIR EYES ARE SLOW TO REACT. THEIR CHEEKS LOOK UNNATURAL.
IT'S LIKE THEY'RE CAUGHT IN A LIE THEY CAN'T HIDE.
ONCE I NOTICED THAT, I BECAME AFRAID TO LOOK PEOPLE IN THE EYES.
I BEGAN TO WONDER WHAT THEY WERE REALLY THINKING.
I... I'M GOING TO POWDER MY FACE.
PEEK

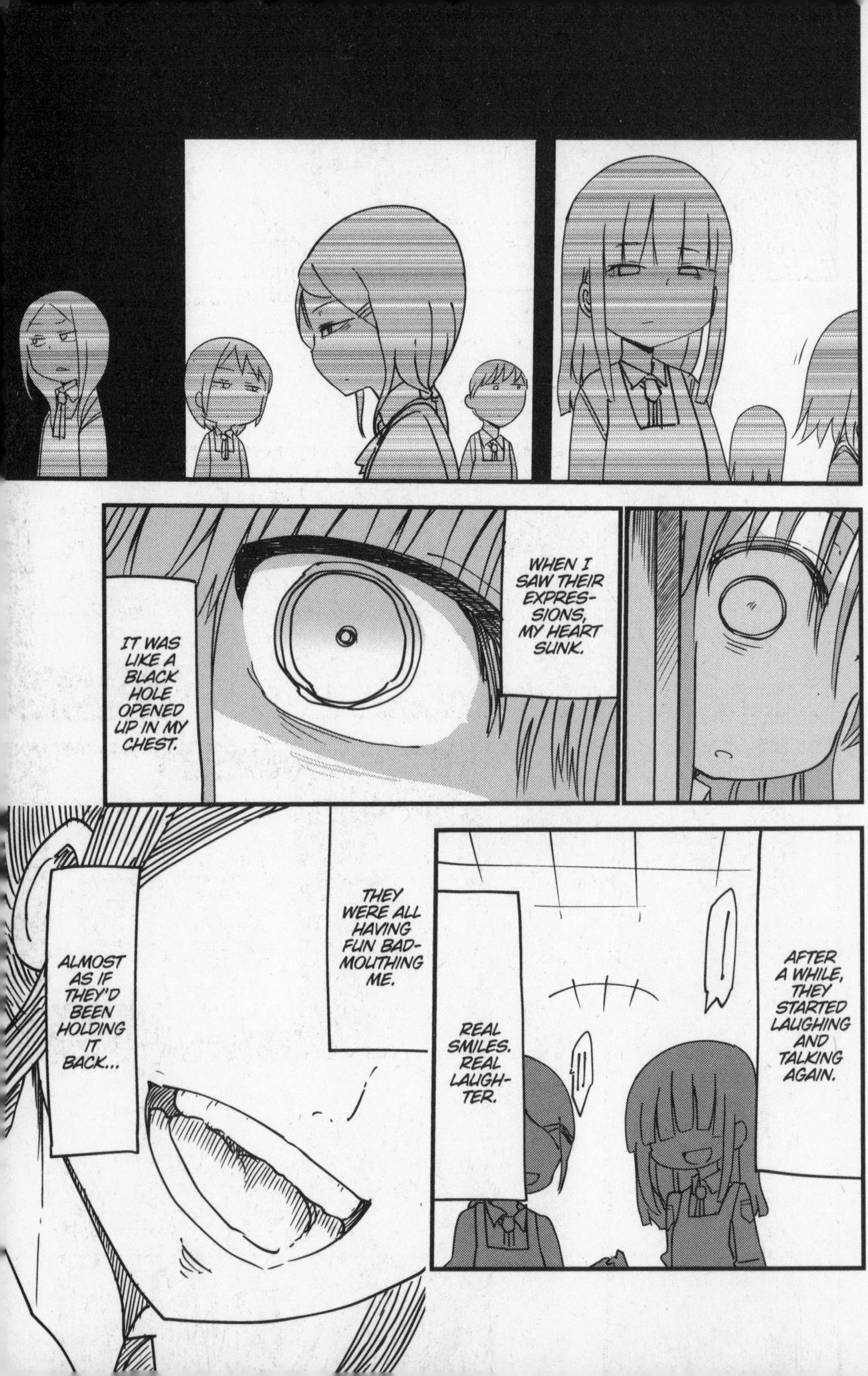

WHEN I SAW THEIR EXPRES- SIONS, MY HEART SUNK.
IT WAS LIKE A BLACK HOLE OPENED UP IN MY CHEST.
AFTER A WHILE, THEY STARTED LAUGHING AND TALKING AGAIN.
REAL SMILES. REAL LAUGH- TER.
THEY WERE ALL HAVING FUN BAD- MOUTHING ME.
ALMOST AS IF THEY'D BEEN HOLDING IT BACK...

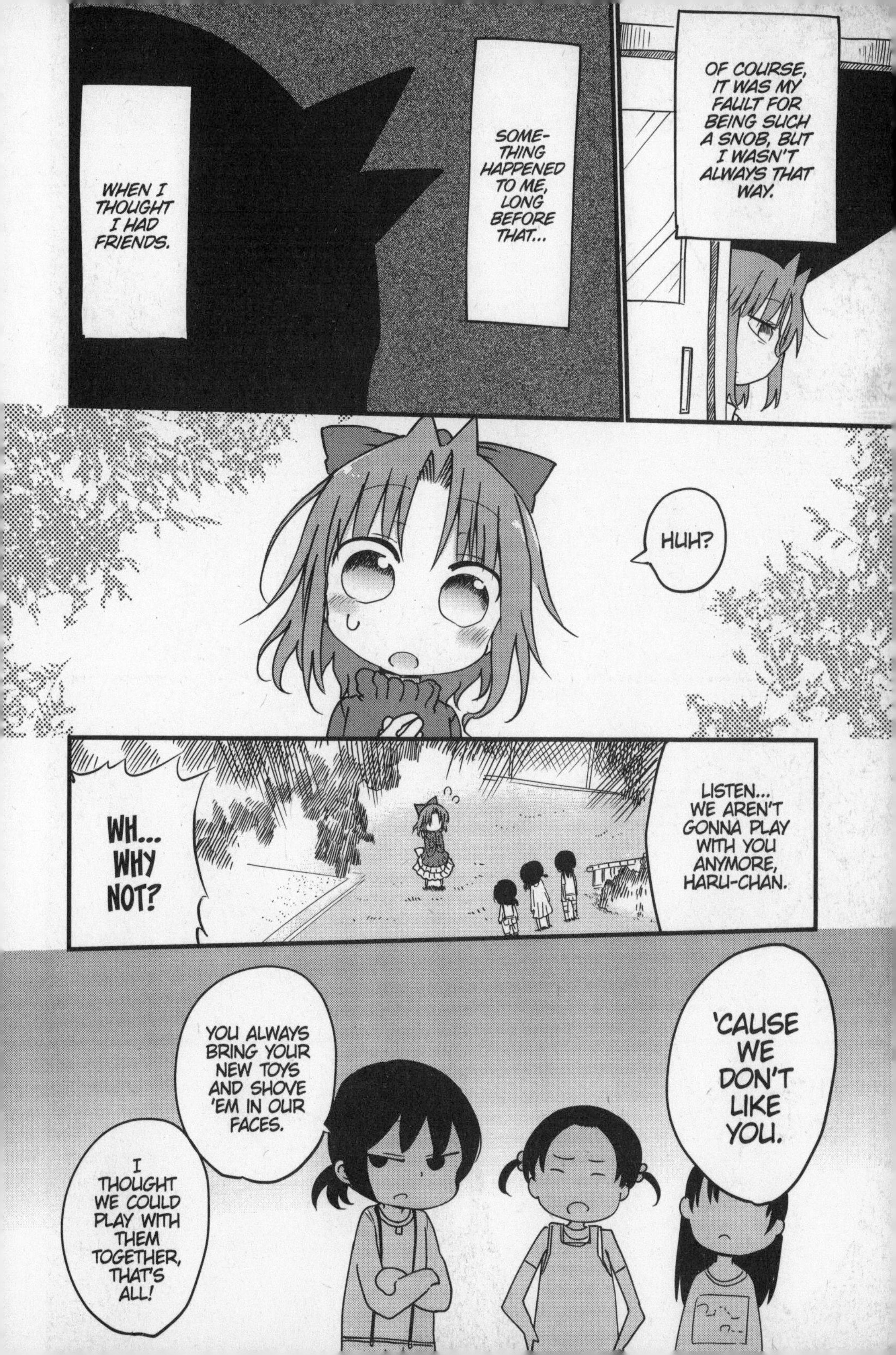
OF COURSE, IT WAS MY FAULT FOR BEING SUCH A SNOB, BUT I WASN'T ALWAYS THAT WAY.
SOME-THING HAPPENED TO ME, LONG BEFORE THAT...
WHEN I THOUGHT I HAD FRIENDS.
HUH?
LISTEN... WE AREN'T GONNA PLAY WITH YOU ANYMORE, HARU-CHAN.
WH... WHY NOT?
'CAUSE WE DON'T LIKE YOU.
YOU ALWAYS BRING YOUR NEW TOYS AND SHOVE 'EM IN OUR FACES.
I THOUGHT WE COULD PLAY WITH THEM TOGETHER, THAT'S ALL!

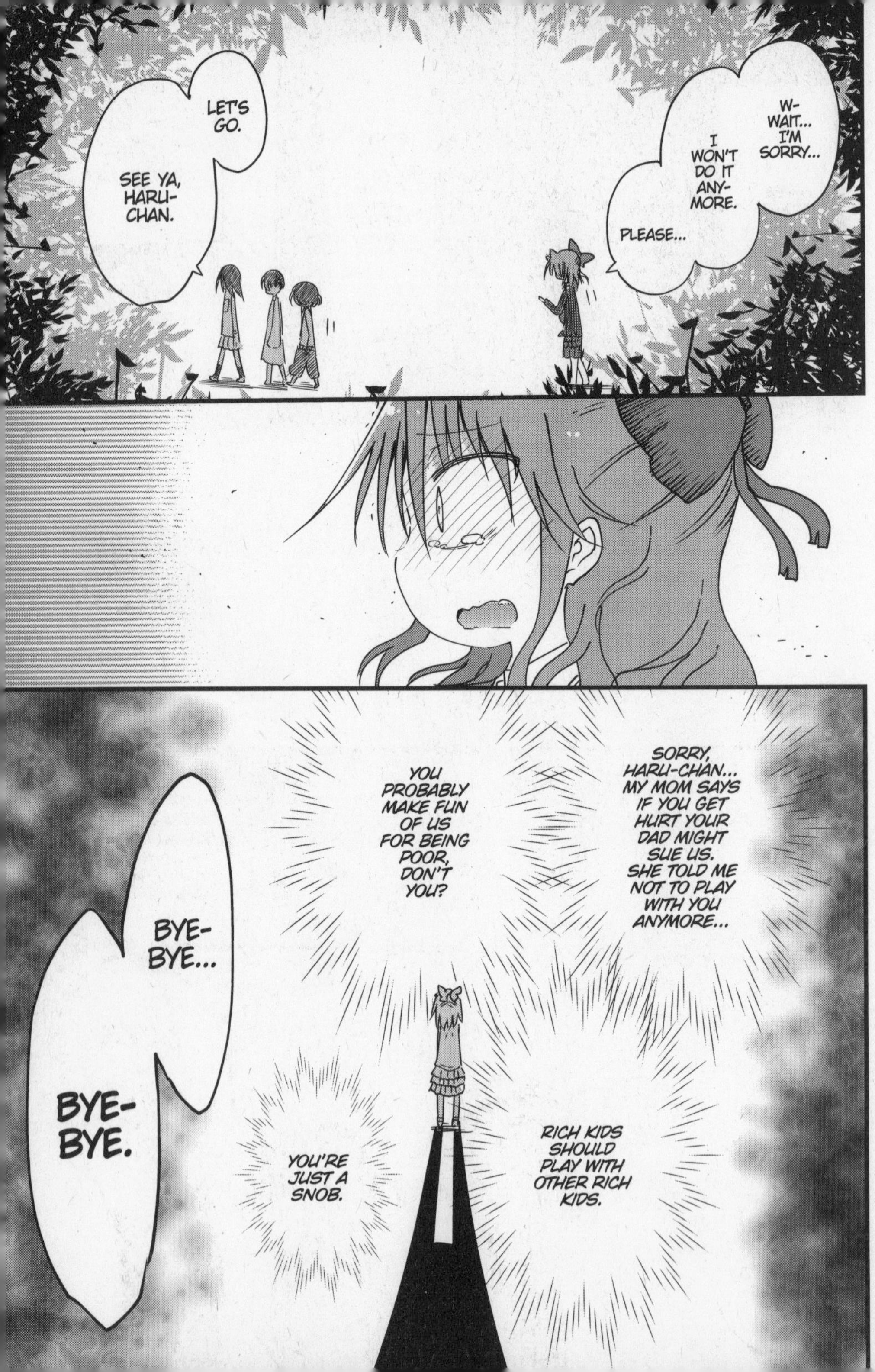
W-WAIT... I'M SORRY... I WON'T DO IT ANYMORE. PLEASE...
LET'S GO. SEE YA, HARU-CHAN.
SORRY, HARU-CHAN... MY MOM SAYS IF YOU GET HURT YOUR DAD MIGHT SUE US. SHE TOLD ME NOT TO PLAY WITH YOU ANYMORE...
YOU PROBABLY MAKE FUN OF US FOR BEING POOR, DON'T YOU?
BYE-BYE...
RICH KIDS SHOULD PLAY WITH OTHER RICH KIDS.
YOU'RE JUST A SNOB.
BYE-BYE.

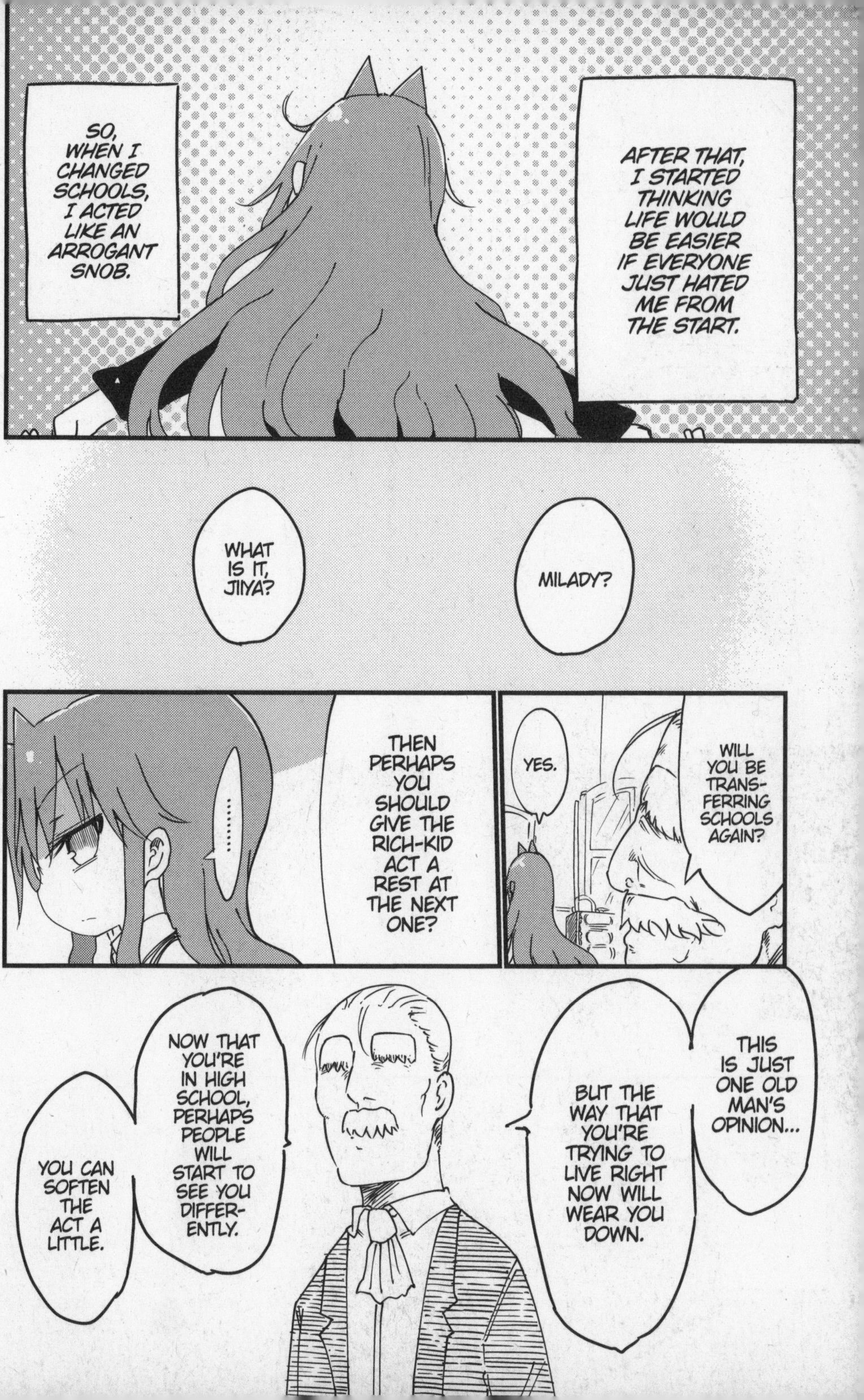
AFTER THAT, I STARTED THINKING LIFE WOULD BE EASIER IF EVERYONE JUST HATED ME FROM THE START.
SO, WHEN I CHANGED SCHOOLS, I ACTED LIKE AN ARROGANT SNOB.
MILADY?
WHAT IS IT, JIIYA?
WILL YOU BE TRANS-FERRING SCHOOLS AGAIN?
YES.
THEN PERHAPS YOU SHOULD GIVE THE RICH-KID ACT A REST AT THE NEXT ONE?
......
THIS IS JUST ONE OLD MAN'S OPINION...
BUT THE WAY THAT YOU'RE TRYING TO LIVE RIGHT NOW WILL WEAR YOU DOWN.
NOW THAT YOU'RE IN HIGH SCHOOL, PERHAPS PEOPLE WILL START TO SEE YOU DIFFER-ENTLY.
YOU CAN SOFTEN THE ACT A LITTLE.

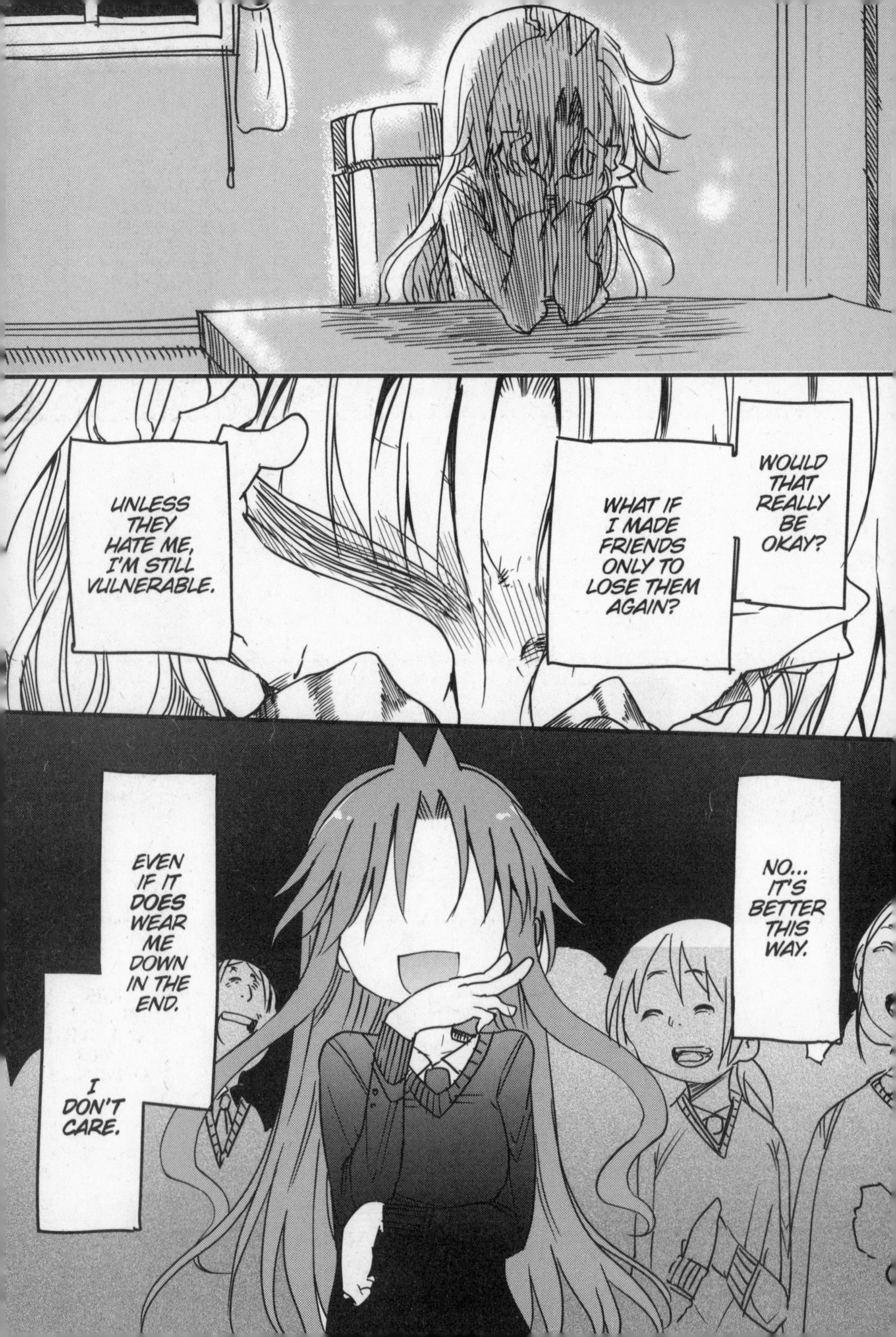
WOULD THAT REALLY BE OKAY?
WHAT IF I MADE FRIENDS ONLY TO LOSE THEM AGAIN?
UNLESS THEY HATE ME, I'M STILL VULNERABLE.
NO... IT'S BETTER THIS WAY.
EVEN IF IT DOES WEAR ME DOWN IN THE END.
I DON'T CARE.

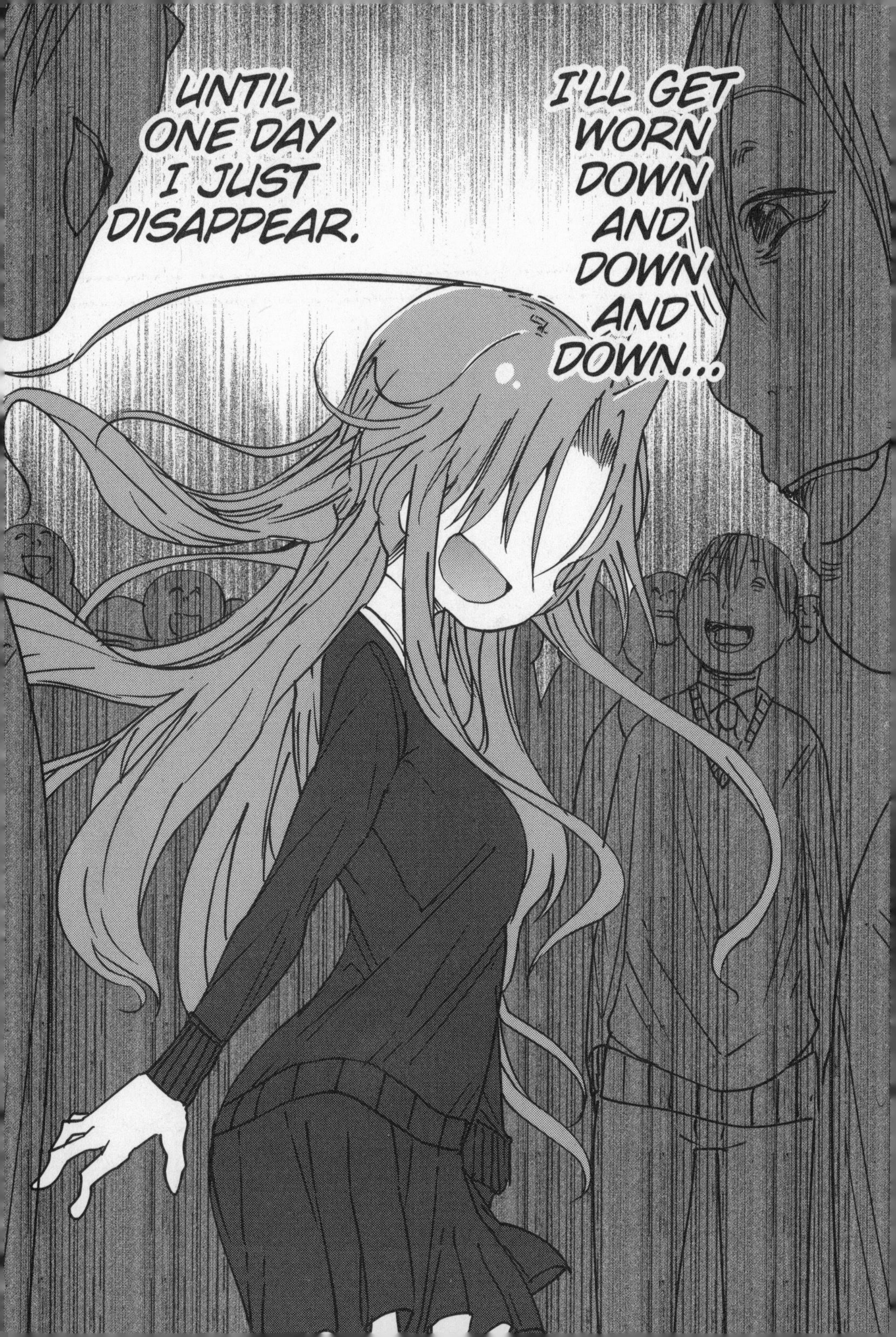
I'LL GET WORN DOWN AND DOWN AND DOWN...
UNTIL ONE DAY I JUST DISAPPEAR.

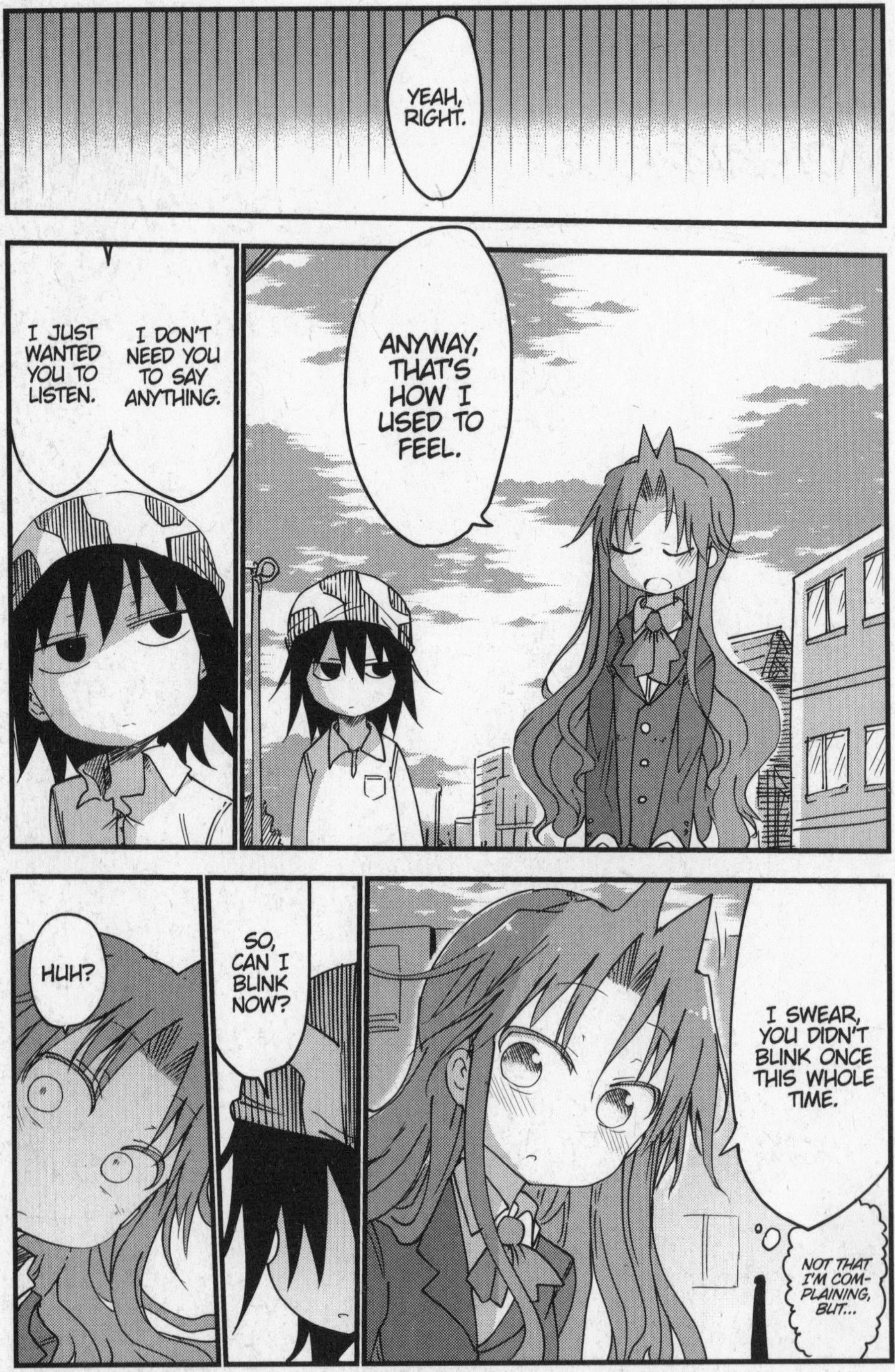
YEAH, RIGHT.
ANYWAY, THAT'S HOW I USED TO FEEL.
I DON'T NEED YOU TO SAY ANYTHING.
I JUST WANTED YOU TO LISTEN.
I SWEAR, YOU DIDN'T BLINK ONCE THIS WHOLE TIME.
NOT THAT I'M COM-PLAINING, BUT...
SO, CAN I BLINK NOW?
HUH?

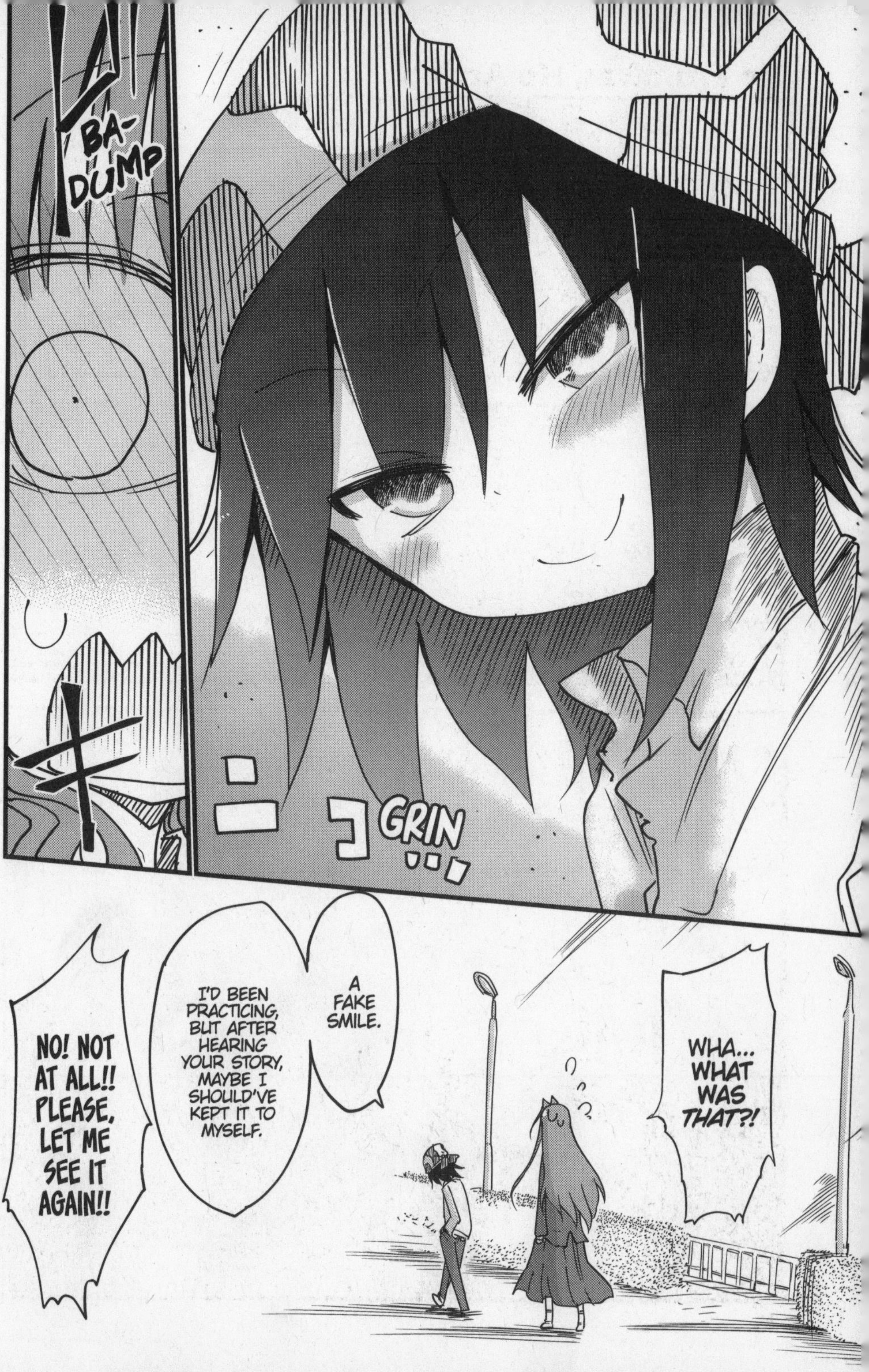
GRIN
BA-DUMP
WHA... WHAT WAS THAT?!
A FAKE SMILE.
I'D BEEN PRACTICING, BUT AFTER HEARING YOUR STORY, MAYBE I SHOULD'VE KEPT IT TO MYSELF.
NO! NOT AT ALL!! PLEASE, LET ME SEE IT AGAIN!!

No Promises, No Action

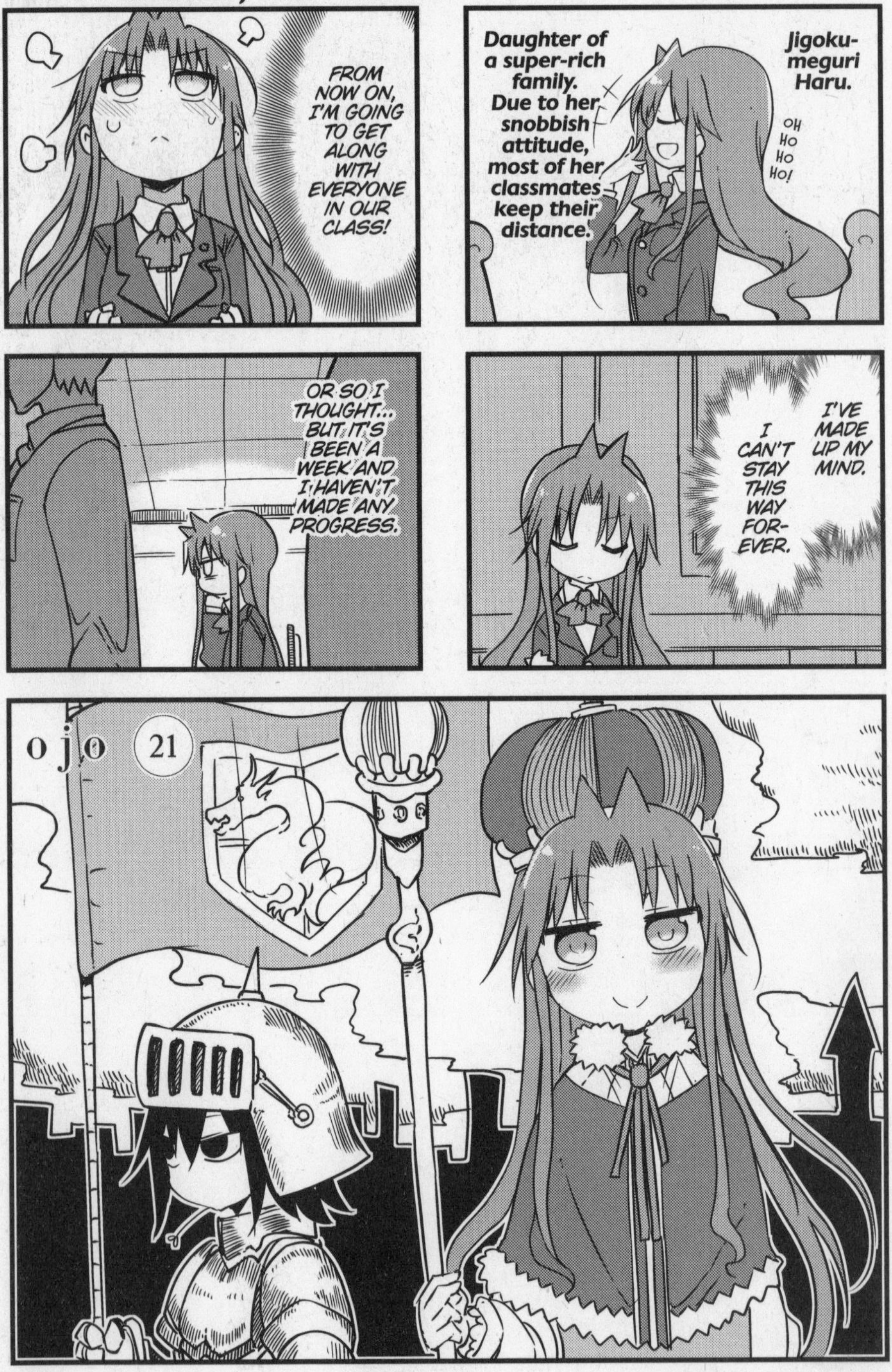
Jigoku-meguri Haru.
OH HO HO HO!
Daughter of a super-rich family. Due to her snobbish attitude, most of her classmates keep their distance.
FROM NOW ON, I'M GOING TO GET ALONG WITH EVERYONE IN OUR CLASS!
I'VE MADE UP MY MIND.
I CAN'T STAY THIS WAY FOREVER.
OR SO I THOUGHT... BUT IT'S BEEN A WEEK AND I HAVEN'T MADE ANY PROGRESS.
ojo 21

Brain on Auto-Correct

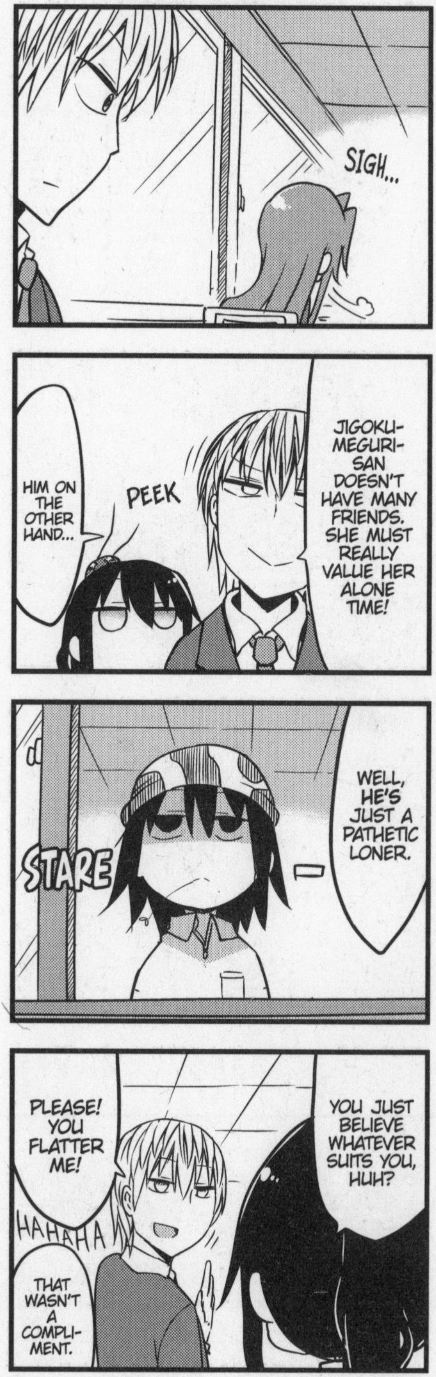
SIGH...
JIGOKU-MEGURI-SAN DOESN'T HAVE MANY FRIENDS. SHE MUST REALLY VALUE HER ALONE TIME!
PEEK
HIM ON THE OTHER HAND...
WELL, HE'S JUST A PATHETIC LONER.
STARE
YOU JUST BELIEVE WHATEVER SUITS YOU, HUH?
PLEASE! YOU FLATTER ME!
HAHAHA
THAT WASN'T A COMPLIMENT.

Operation Hell Climb

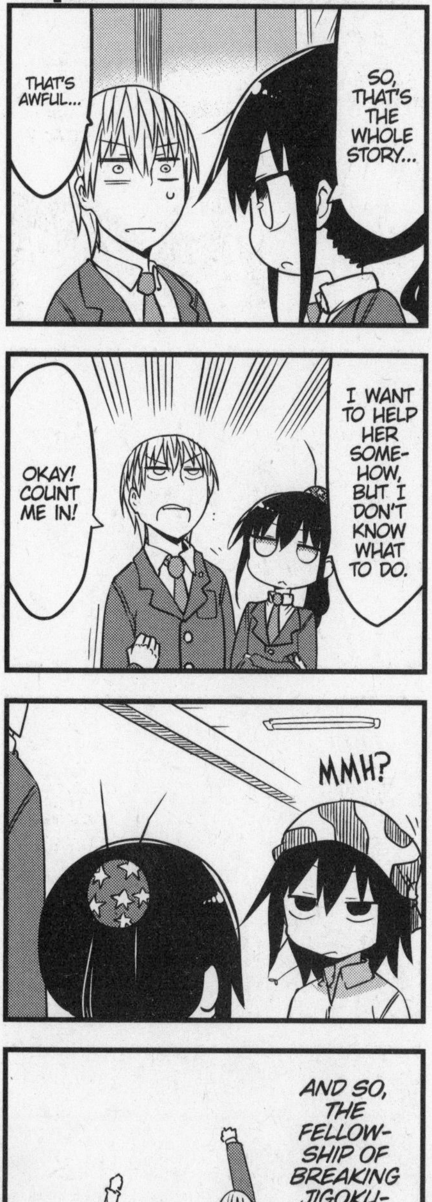
SO, THAT'S THE WHOLE STORY...
THAT'S AWFUL...
I WANT TO HELP HER SOMEHOW, BUT I DON'T KNOW WHAT TO DO.
OKAY! COUNT ME IN!
MMH?
AND SO, THE FELLOWSHIP OF BREAKING JIGOKU-MEGURI HARU OUT OF HER SOLITUDE SETS FORTH.
?

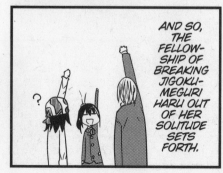

The Things He Can See

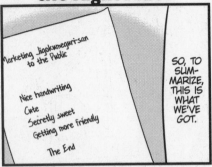

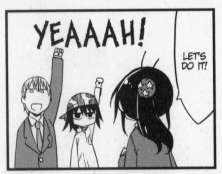

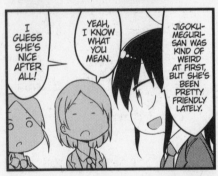

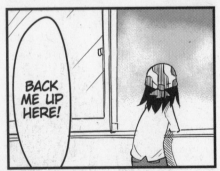

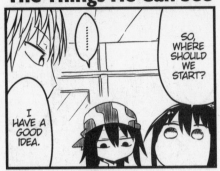

SO, WHERE SHOULD WE START?
......
I HAVE A GOOD IDEA.
WHEN WE TALK TO OUR OTHER CLASSMATES, WE SHOULD CASUALLY MENTION JIGOKU-MEGURI-SAN.
WHAT SHOULD WE TELL THEM?
SOME OF HER GOOD POINTS, RIGHT?
YES. FOR EXAMPLE, SHE HAS A WORLD-LEADING ORGANIZATION WITH INCREDIBLE CAPITAL, THAT EXERCISES A HUGE IMPACT ON ALL AREAS OF ECONOMIC DEVELOPMENT AND BOASTS AN OVER-WHELMING SHARE IN ALL ASPECTS OF...
YOU'RE JUST TALKING ABOUT HER DAD!
SHE HAS NICE HAND-WRITING.
THAT'S ALL YOU'VE GOT? YOU'RE HER BOY-FRIEND!

Right Person in the Right Place

SO, TO SUM-MARIZE, THIS IS WHAT WE'VE GOT.
Marketing Jigokumeguri-san to the Public
Nice handwriting
Cute
Secretly sweet
Getting more friendly
The End
LET'S DO IT!
YEAAAH!
JIGOKU-MEGURI-SAN WAS KIND OF WEIRD AT FIRST, BUT SHE'S BEEN PRETTY FRIENDLY LATELY.
YEAH, I KNOW WHAT YOU MEAN.
I GUESS SHE'S NICE AFTER ALL!
BACK ME UP HERE!

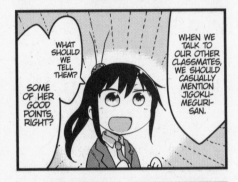

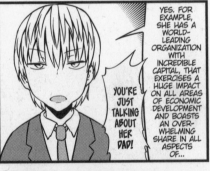

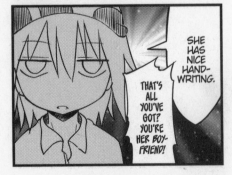

Understanding

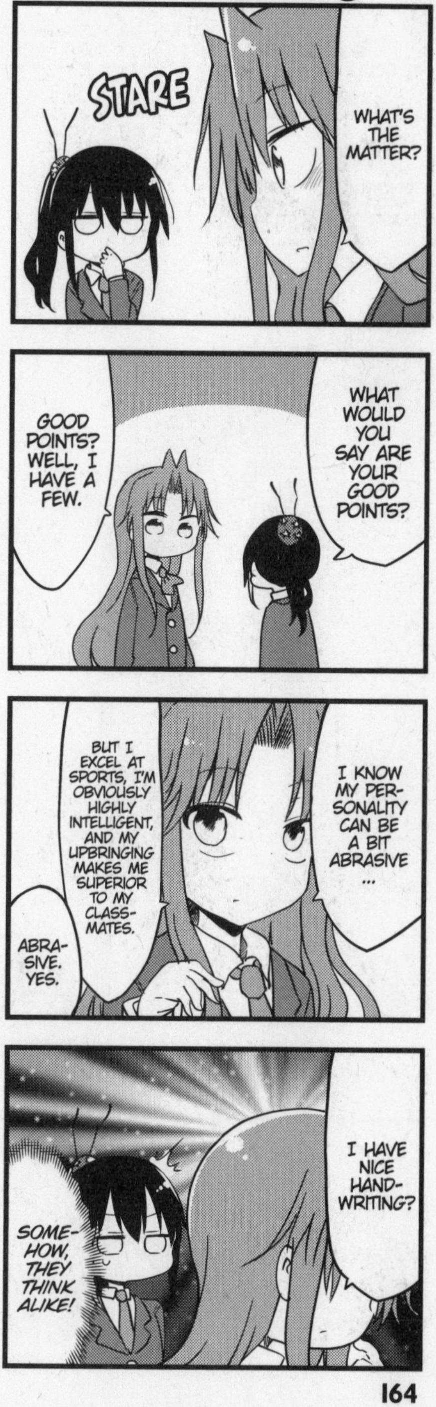

WHAT'S THE MATTER?
STARE
WHAT WOULD YOU SAY ARE YOUR GOOD POINTS?
GOOD POINTS? WELL, I HAVE A FEW.
I KNOW MY PER-SONALITY CAN BE A BIT ABRASIVE ...
BUT I EXCEL AT SPORTS, I'M OBVIOUSLY HIGHLY INTELLIGENT, AND MY UPBRINGING MAKES ME SUPERIOR TO MY CLASS-MATES.
ABRA-SIVE. YES.
I HAVE NICE HAND-WRITING?
SOME-HOW, THEY THINK ALIKE!

Sorry

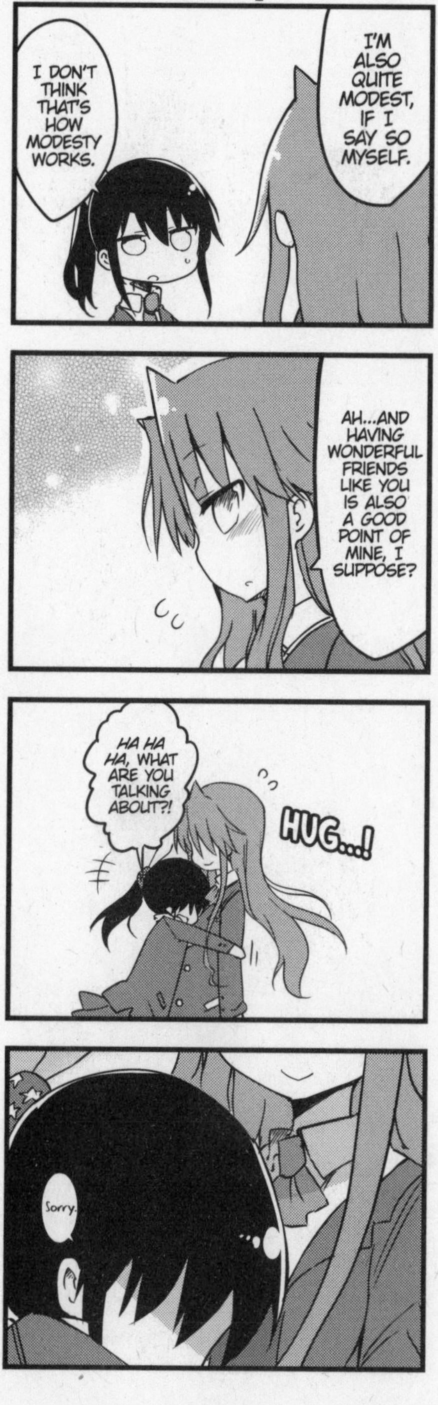

I'M ALSO QUITE MODEST, IF I SAY SO MYSELF.
I DON'T THINK THAT'S HOW MODESTY WORKS.
AH...AND HAVING WONDERFUL FRIENDS LIKE YOU IS ALSO A GOOD POINT OF MINE, I SUPPOSE?
HA HA HA, WHAT ARE YOU TALKING ABOUT?!
HUG...!
Sorry.

Feeling

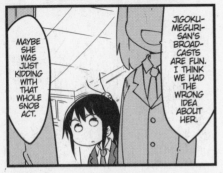

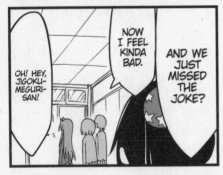

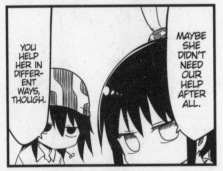

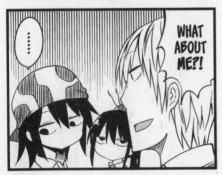

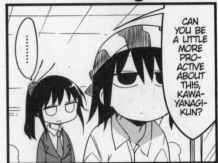

CAN YOU BE A LITTLE MORE PROACTIVE ABOUT THIS, KAWAYANAGI-KUN?
......
DO YOU THINK JIGOKUMEGURI-SAN'S HAPPY THE WAY THINGS ARE?
NO. PROBABLY NOT.
BUT I THINK SHE CAN DO THIS HERSELF.
HUH?
SHE MADE FRIENDS WITH SOMEONE LIKE ME, AFTER ALL.
I BELIEVE IN HER.

You...Uh...Yeah

JIGOKUMEGURI-SAN'S BROADCASTS ARE FUN. I THINK WE HAD THE WRONG IDEA ABOUT HER.
MAYBE SHE WAS JUST KIDDING WITH THAT WHOLE SNOB ACT.
AND WE JUST MISSED THE JOKE?
NOW I FEEL KINDA BAD.
OH! HEY, JIGOKUMEGURI-SAN!
MAYBE SHE DIDN'T NEED OUR HELP AFTER ALL.
YOU HELP HER IN DIFFERENT WAYS, THOUGH.
WHAT ABOUT ME?!
......

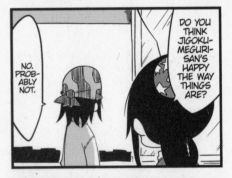

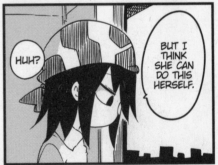

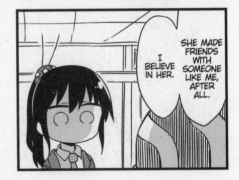

Part of the Crowd

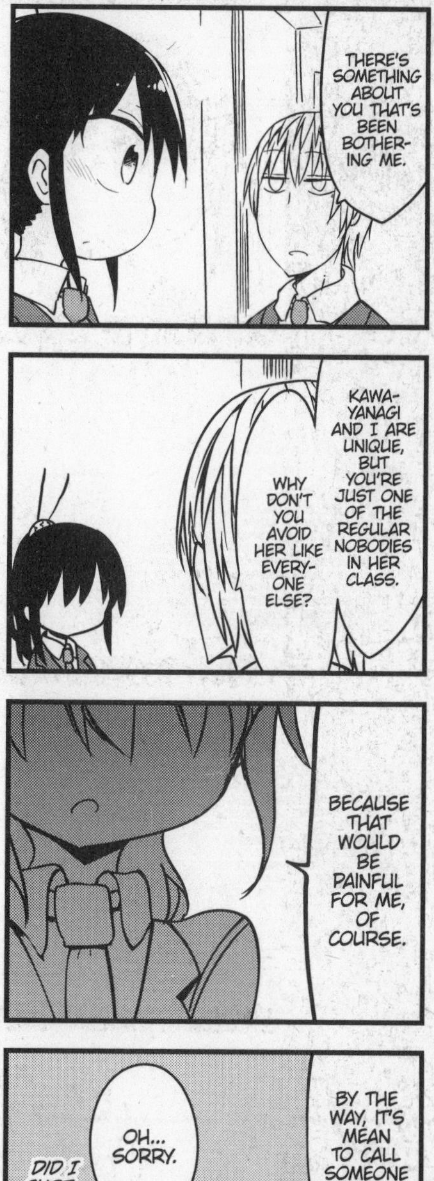
THERE'S SOMETHING ABOUT YOU THAT'S BEEN BOTHERING ME.
KAWAYANAGI AND I ARE UNIQUE, BUT YOU'RE JUST ONE OF THE REGULAR NOBODIES IN HER CLASS.
WHY DON'T YOU AVOID HER LIKE EVERYONE ELSE?
BECAUSE THAT WOULD BE PAINFUL FOR ME, OF COURSE.
BY THE WAY, IT'S MEAN TO CALL SOMEONE A "NOBODY"!
OH... SORRY.
DID I JUST... APOLOGIZE?

The Fellowship's Victory

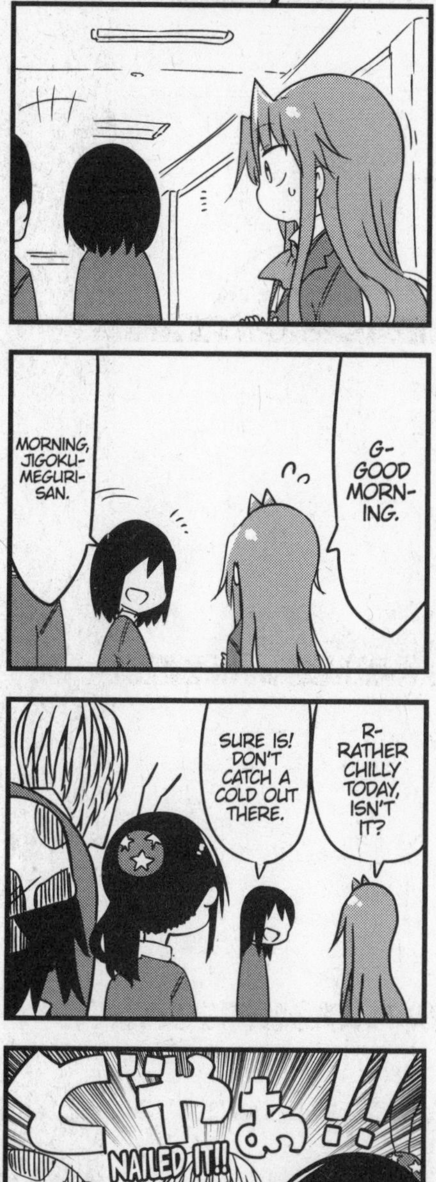
G-GOOD MORNING.
MORNING, JIGOKUMEGURI-SAN.
R-RATHER CHILLY TODAY, ISN'T IT?
SURE IS! DON'T CATCH A COLD OUT THERE.
どやぁ!!
NAILED IT!!

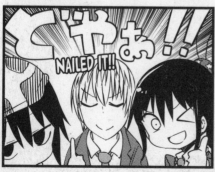

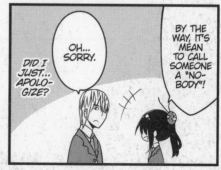

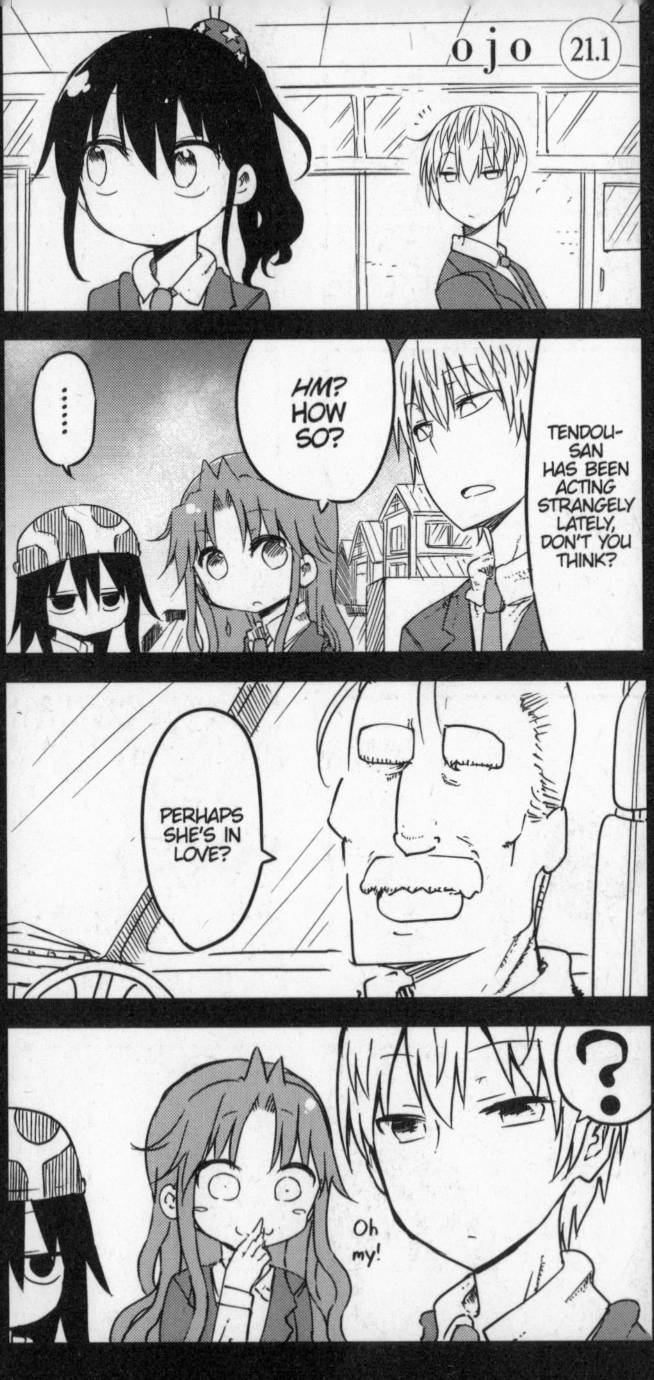
ojo 21.1
TENDOU-SAN HAS BEEN ACTING STRANGELY LATELY, DON'T YOU THINK?
HM? HOW SO?
......
PERHAPS SHE'S IN LOVE?
?
Oh my!

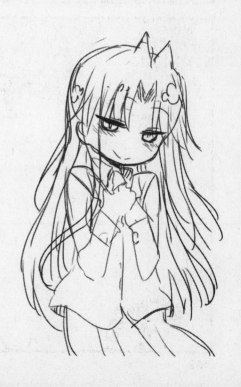

Too Excited

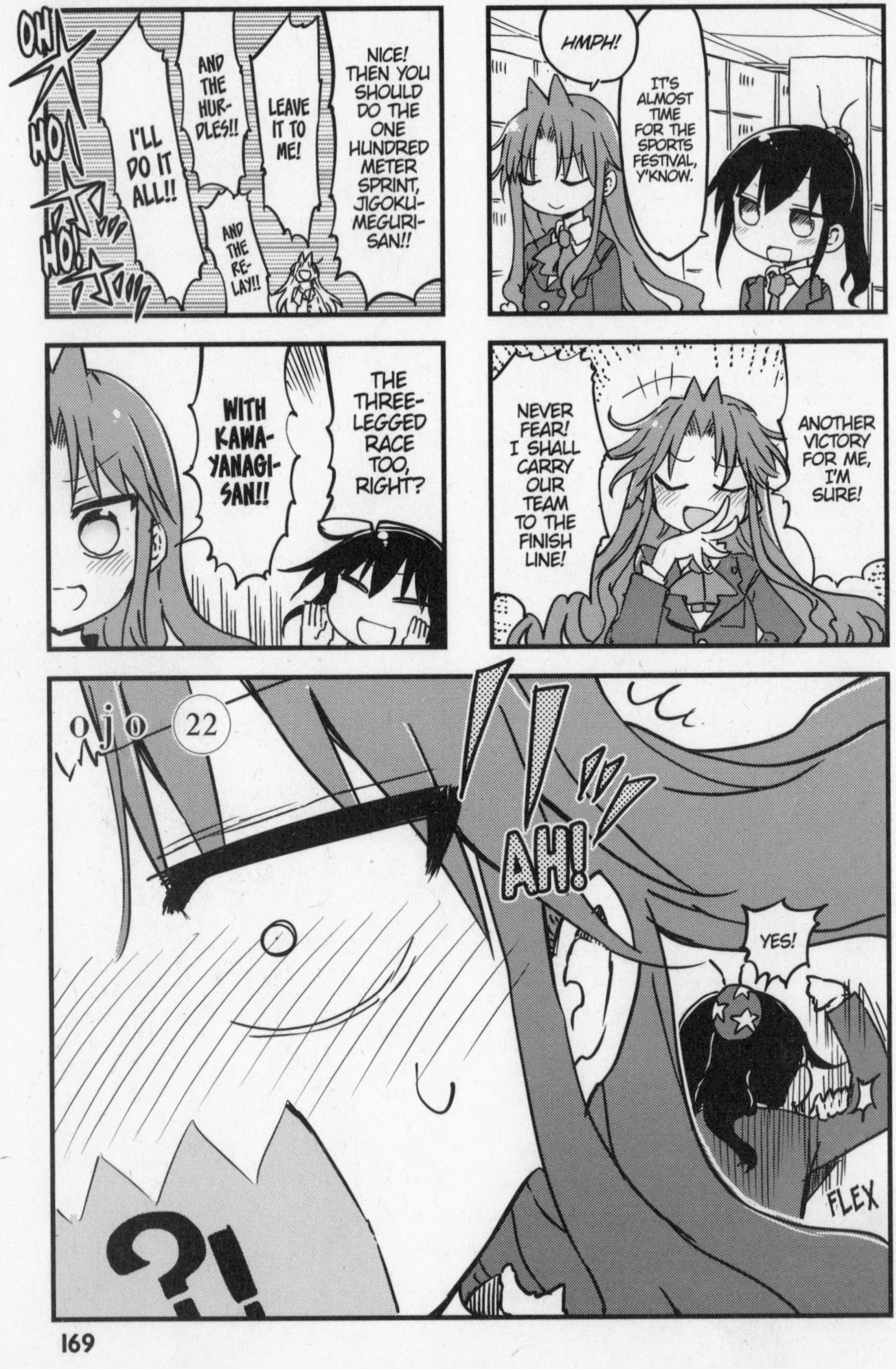

HMPH!
IT'S ALMOST TIME FOR THE SPORTS FESTIVAL, Y'KNOW.
NICE! THEN YOU SHOULD DO THE ONE HUNDRED METER SPRINT, JIGOKU-MEGURI-SAN!!
LEAVE IT TO ME!
AND THE HUR-DLES!!
AND THE RE-LAY!!
I'LL DO IT ALL!!
OH HO HO!
ANOTHER VICTORY FOR ME, I'M SURE!
NEVER FEAR! I SHALL CARRY OUR TEAM TO THE FINISH LINE!
THE THREE-LEGGED RACE TOO, RIGHT?
WITH KAWA-YANAGI-SAN!!
AH!
YES!
FLEX
?!
ojo 22

I Couldn't Possibly Do That

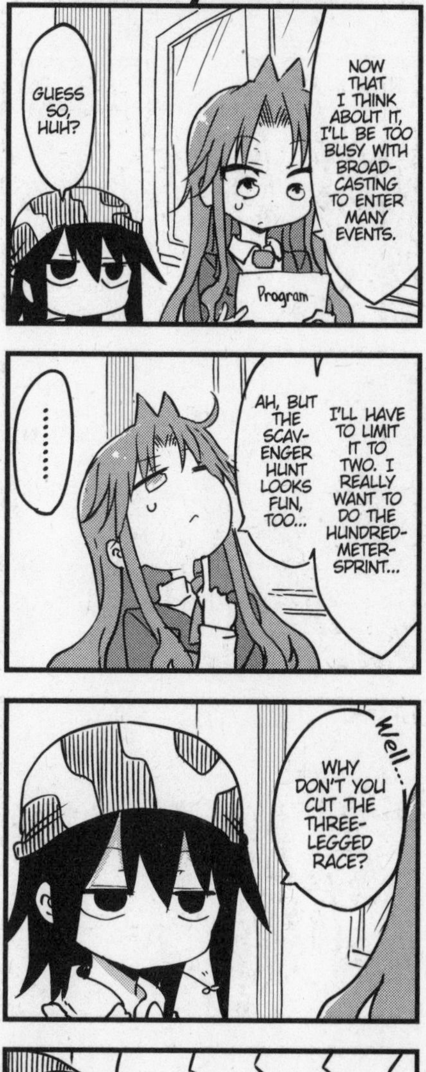
NOW THAT I THINK ABOUT IT, I'LL BE TOO BUSY WITH BROADCASTING TO ENTER MANY EVENTS.
GUESS SO, HUH?
Program
I'LL HAVE TO LIMIT IT TO TWO. I REALLY WANT TO DO THE HUNDRED-METER-SPRINT...
AH, BUT THE SCAVENGER HUNT LOOKS FUN, TOO...
....
Well...
WHY DON'T YOU CUT THE THREE-LEGGED RACE?
GLARE...
GRRRR...!
?

All Right

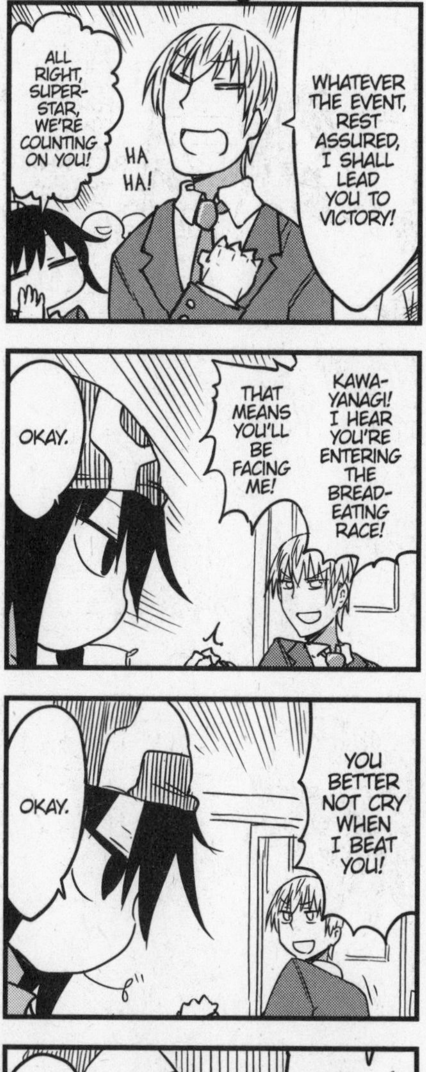
WHATEVER THE EVENT, REST ASSURED, I SHALL LEAD YOU TO VICTORY!
HA HA!
ALL RIGHT, SUPERSTAR, WE'RE COUNTING ON YOU!
KAWAYANAGI! I HEAR YOU'RE ENTERING THE BREAD-EATING RACE!
THAT MEANS YOU'LL BE FACING ME!
OKAY.
YOU BETTER NOT CRY WHEN I BEAT YOU!
OKAY.
....
ACTUALLY, COULD YOU CRY A LITTLE, PLEASE?
OKAY.

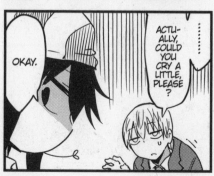

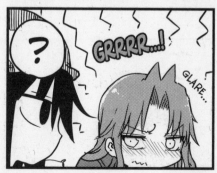

So Close!!

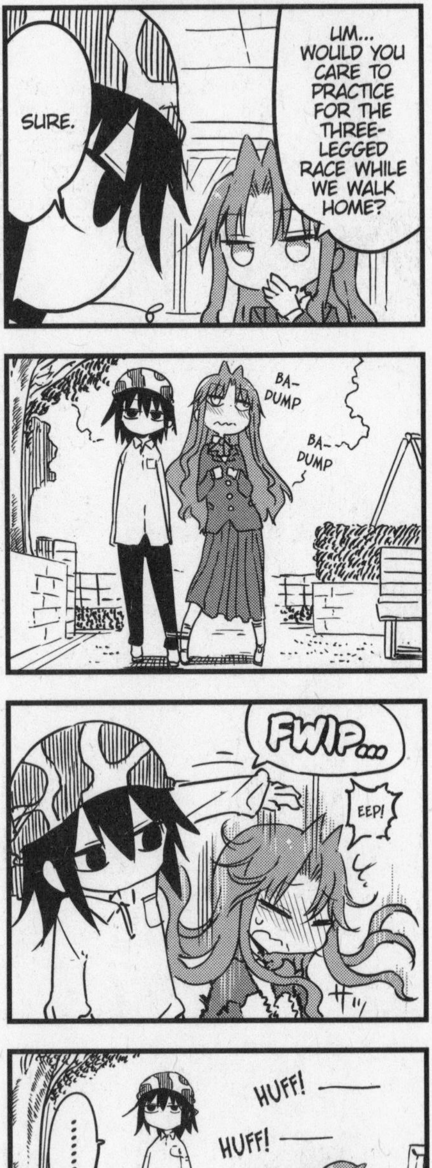
UM... WOULD YOU CARE TO PRACTICE FOR THE THREE-LEGGED RACE WHILE WE WALK HOME?
SURE.
BA-DUMP
BA-DUMP
FWIP...
EEP!
HUFF!
HUFF!
......

45cm, Slightly Broad Step

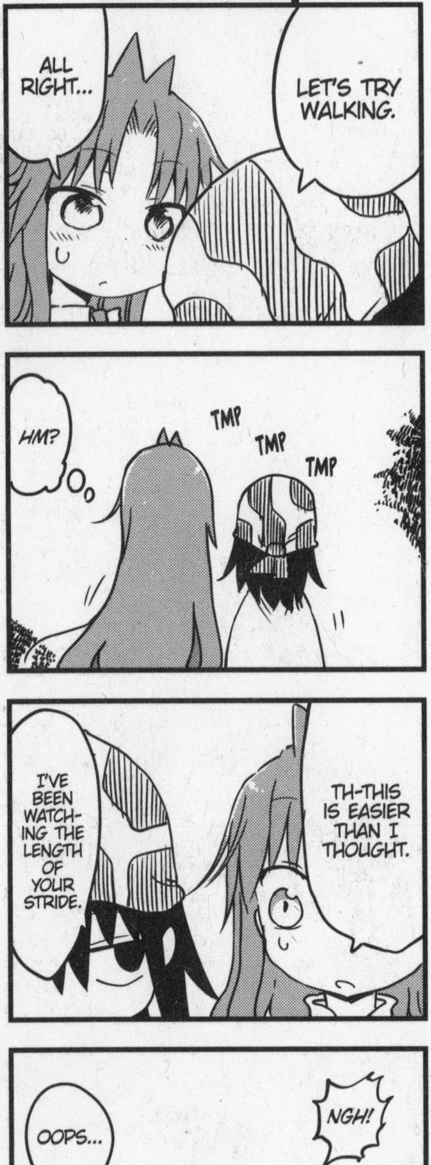
LET'S TRY WALKING.
ALL RIGHT...
TMP
TMP
TMP
HM?
TH-THIS IS EASIER THAN I THOUGHT.
I'VE BEEN WATCHING THE LENGTH OF YOUR STRIDE.
NGH!
TRIP
OOPS...

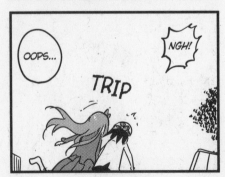

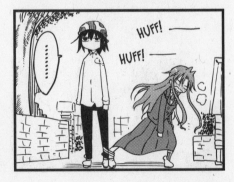

Giving It a Try

The Broadcasting Committee.
WE NEED AN ANNOUNCER FOR THE SPORTS FESTIVAL.
I'M IN THREE EVENTS. I WON'T HAVE TIME.
SAME HERE.
MURMUR...
IS THERE ANYONE WHO ISN'T DOING MUCH?
MURMUR
FWP
YOU'RE VOLUNTEERING?
IT'LL BE FINE.

Doing It

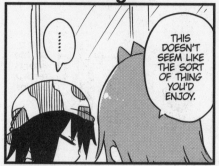

THIS DOESN'T SEEM LIKE THE SORT OF THING YOU'D ENJOY.
......
I'M NOT GOOD AT CONVERSATION, BUT I'LL BE FINE IF I HAVE A SCRIPT.
I WANT TO SHOW YOU THAT I CAN DO THIS.
I WANT TO SHOW YOU THAT I CAN...
I HEARD YOU! I HEARD YOU THE FIRST TIME!!

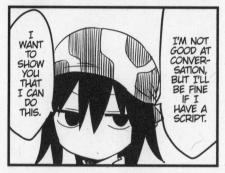

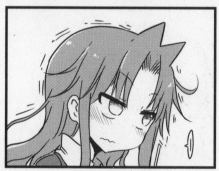

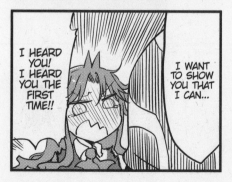

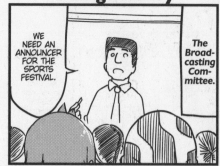

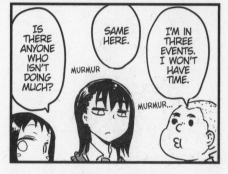

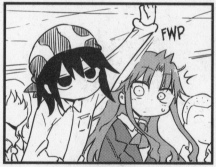

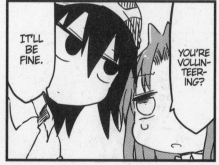

Hungry for Victory

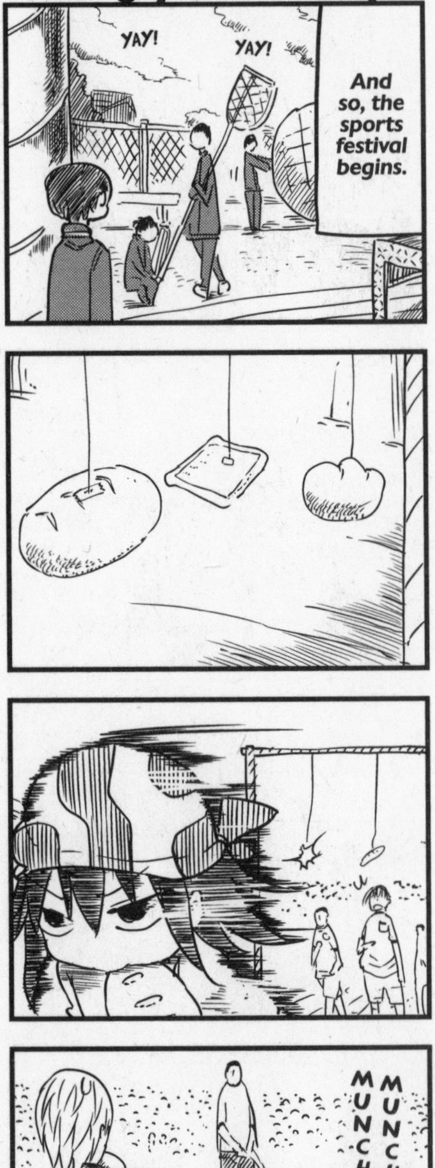

YAY!
YAY!
And so, the sports festival begins.
MUNCH MUNCH

He Can't Be Reading This

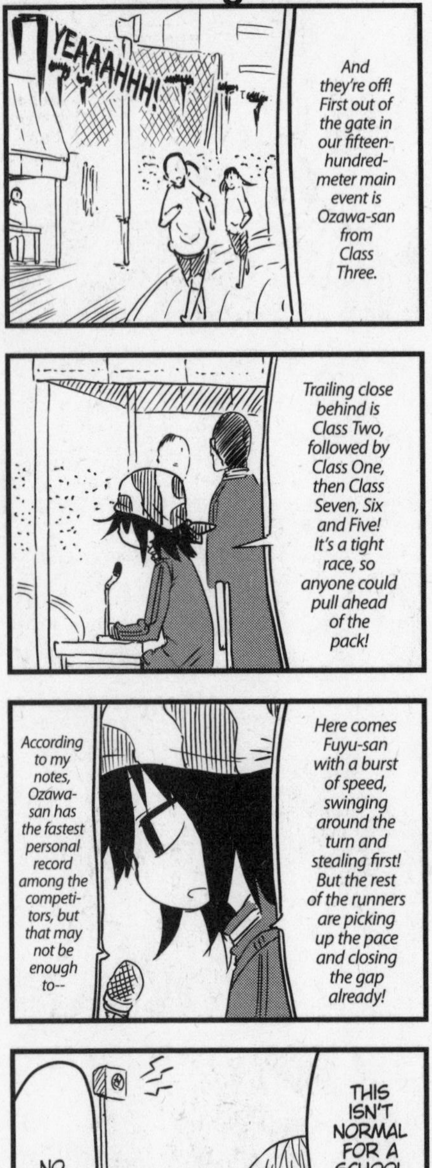

YEAAAHHH!
And they're off! First out of the gate in our fifteen-hundred-meter main event is Ozawa-san from Class Three.
Trailing close behind is Class Two, followed by Class One, then Class Seven, Six and Five! It's a tight race, so anyone could pull ahead of the pack!
Here comes Fuyu-san with a burst of speed, swinging around the turn and stealing first! But the rest of the runners are picking up the pace and closing the gap already!
According to my notes, Ozawa-san has the fastest personal record among the competitors, but that may not be enough to--
THIS ISN'T NORMAL FOR A SCHOOL EVENT, IS IT?
NO. NOT EVEN CLOSE.

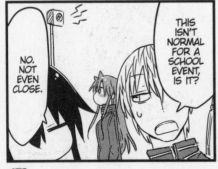

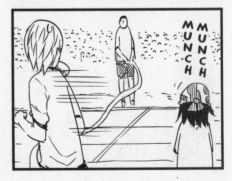

Tag Force

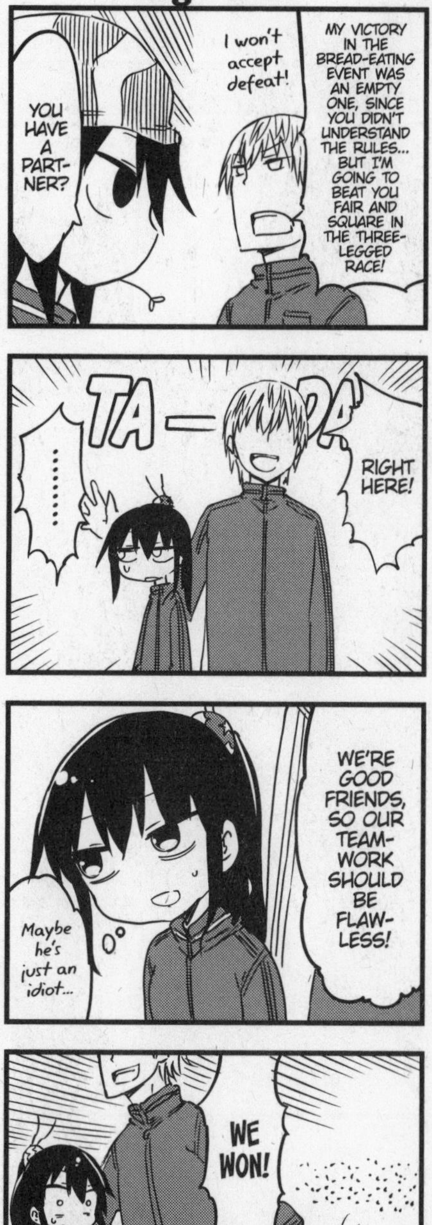
MY VICTORY IN THE BREAD-EATING EVENT WAS AN EMPTY ONE, SINCE YOU DIDN'T UNDERSTAND THE RULES... BUT I'M GOING TO BEAT YOU FAIR AND SQUARE IN THE THREE-LEGGED RACE!
I won't accept defeat!
YOU HAVE A PARTNER?
TA—DA
RIGHT HERE!
......
WE'RE GOOD FRIENDS, SO OUR TEAMWORK SHOULD BE FLAWLESS!
Maybe he's just an idiot...
WE WON!
HOW?!

As Fast as a 38cm Stride

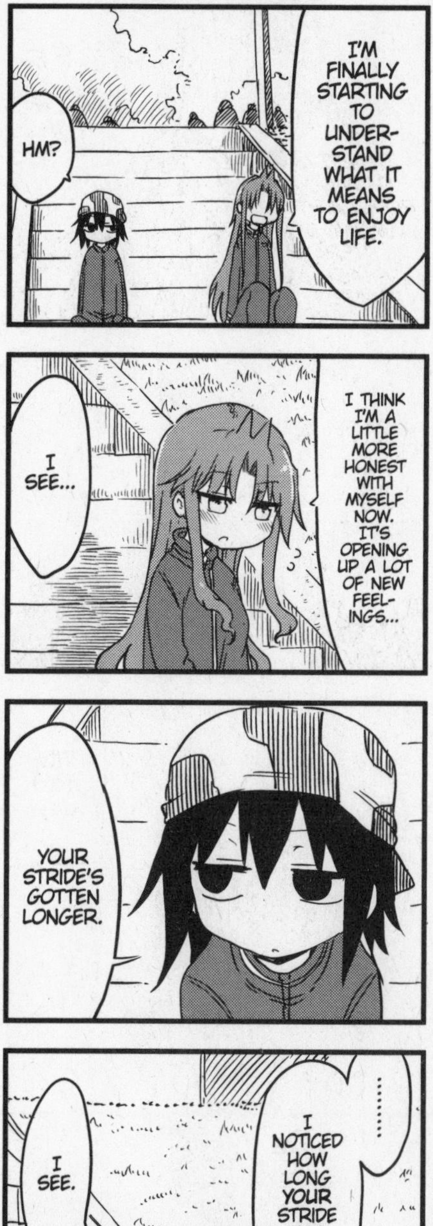
I'M FINALLY STARTING TO UNDERSTAND WHAT IT MEANS TO ENJOY LIFE.
HM?
I THINK I'M A LITTLE MORE HONEST WITH MYSELF NOW. IT'S OPENING UP A LOT OF NEW FEELINGS...
I SEE...
YOUR STRIDE'S GOTTEN LONGER.
......
I NOTICED HOW LONG YOUR STRIDE HAS GOTTEN, TOO.
I SEE.

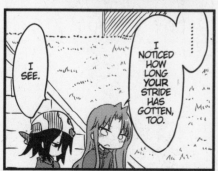

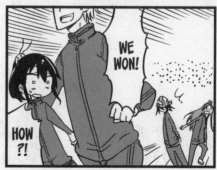

Wandering Kawayanagi

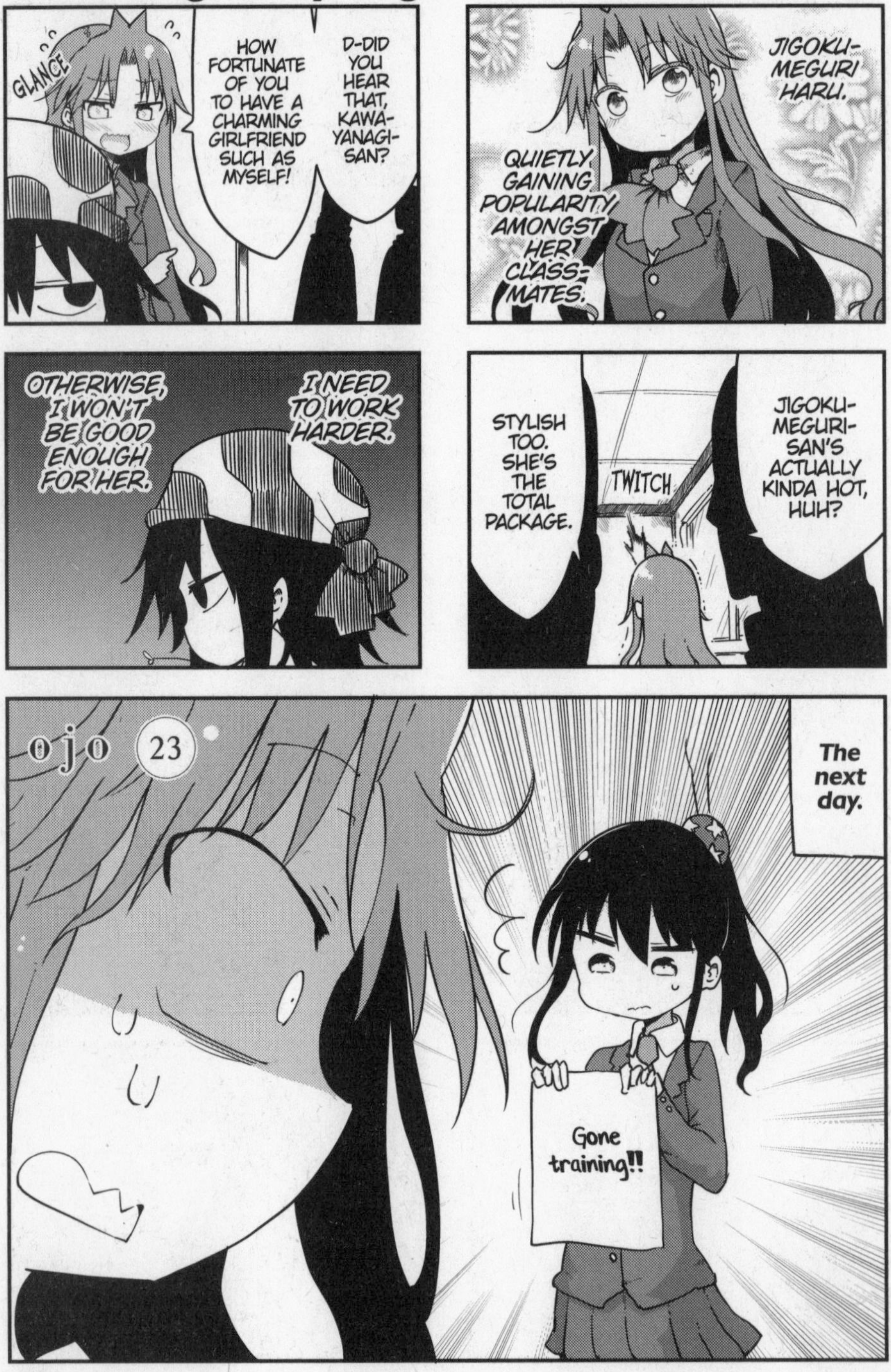

JIGOKU-MEGURI HARU.
QUIETLY GAINING POPULARITY AMONGST HER CLASS-MATES.
D-DID YOU HEAR THAT, KAWA-YANAGI-SAN?
HOW FORTUNATE OF YOU TO HAVE A CHARMING GIRLFRIEND SUCH AS MYSELF!
GLANCE
JIGOKU-MEGURI-SAN'S ACTUALLY KINDA HOT, HUH?
STYLISH TOO. SHE'S THE TOTAL PACKAGE.
TWITCH
I NEED TO WORK HARDER.
OTHERWISE, I WON'T BE GOOD ENOUGH FOR HER.
ojo 23
The next day.
Gone training!!

Find Him! No Matter What!

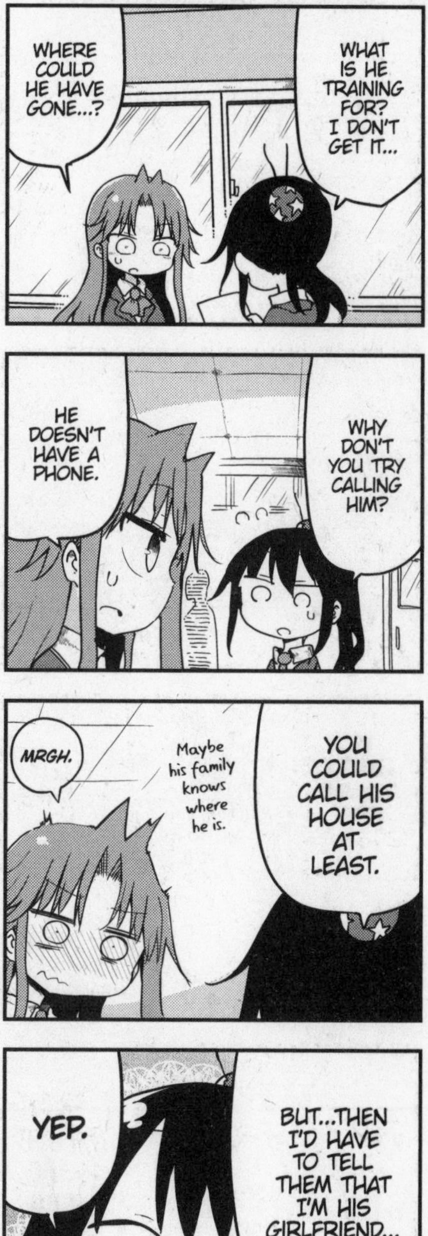
WHAT IS HE TRAINING FOR? I DON'T GET IT...
WHERE COULD HE HAVE GONE...?
WHY DON'T YOU TRY CALLING HIM?
HE DOESN'T HAVE A PHONE.
YOU COULD CALL HIS HOUSE AT LEAST.
Maybe his family knows where he is.
MRGH.
BUT...THEN I'D HAVE TO TELL THEM THAT I'M HIS GIRLFRIEND...
YEP.

That Doesn't Sound Like My Little Brother

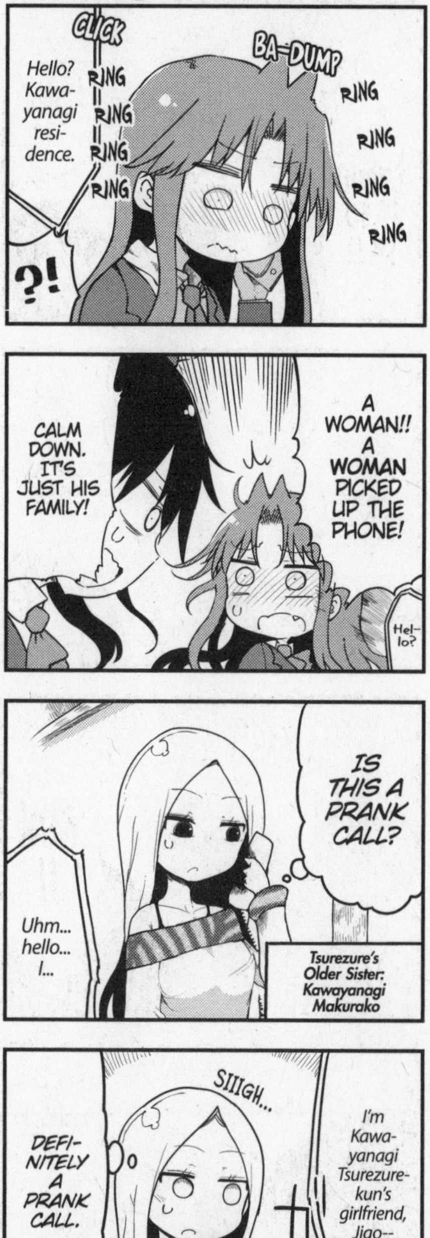
RING
RING
RING
RING
BA-DUMP
RING
RING
RING
RING
CLICK
Hello? Kawayanagi residence.
?!
A WOMAN!! A WOMAN PICKED UP THE PHONE!
Hel-lo?
CALM DOWN. IT'S JUST HIS FAMILY!
IS THIS A PRANK CALL?
Tsurezure's Older Sister: Kawayanagi Makurako
Uhm... hello... I...
I'm Kawayanagi Tsurezure-kun's girlfriend, Jigo--
CLICK
SIIIGH...
DEFINITELY A PRANK CALL.

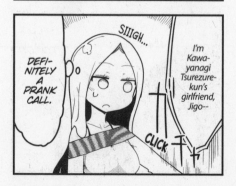

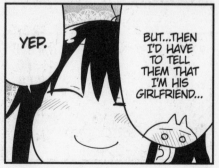

Chris: Max Power

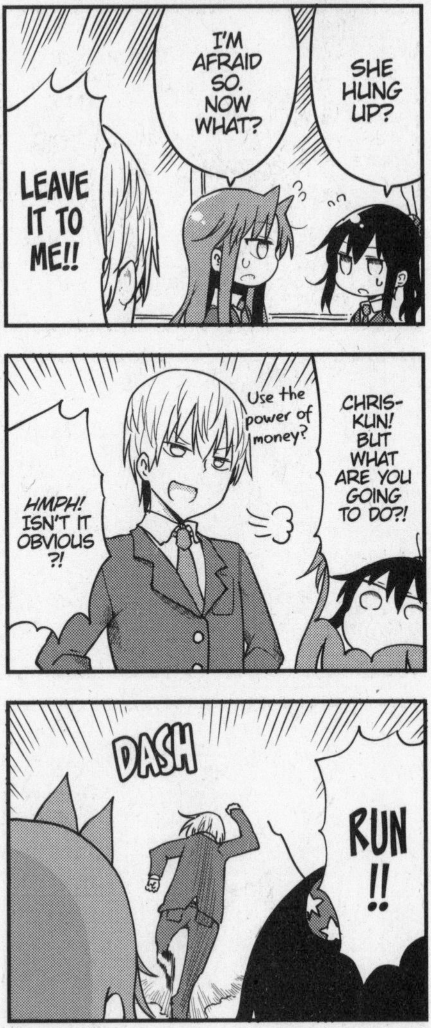
SHE HUNG UP?
I'M AFRAID SO. NOW WHAT?
LEAVE IT TO ME!!
CHRIS-KUN! BUT WHAT ARE YOU GOING TO DO?!
Use the power of money?
HMPH! ISN'T IT OBVIOUS?!
RUN!!
DASH
SHOULD WE FOLLOW HIM?
NAH.

Jiiya: Max Power

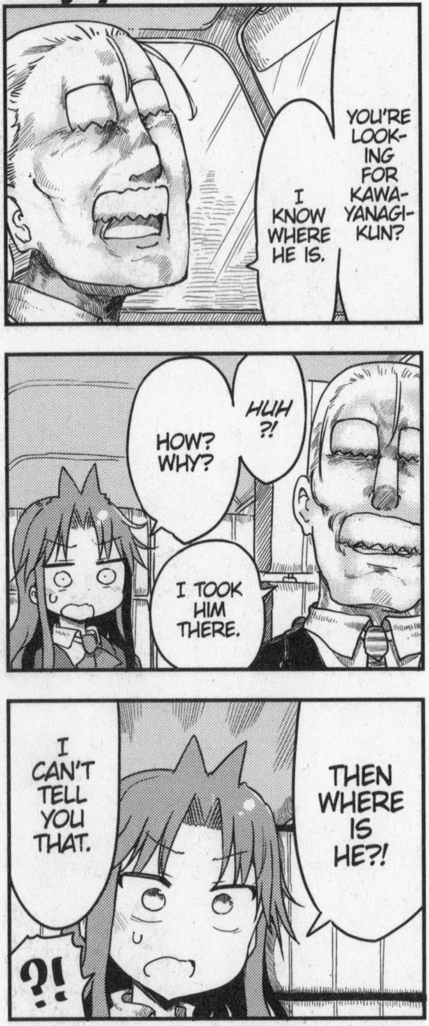
YOU'RE LOOKING FOR KAWAYANAGI-KUN?
I KNOW WHERE HE IS.
HUH?!
HOW? WHY?
I TOOK HIM THERE.
THEN WHERE IS HE?!
I CAN'T TELL YOU THAT.
?!
TORMENTING YOU IS TOO MUCH FUN, AFTER ALL!
JIIYA!!

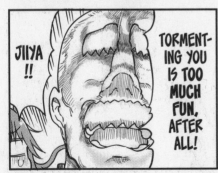

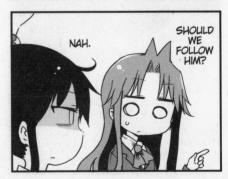

A Classic

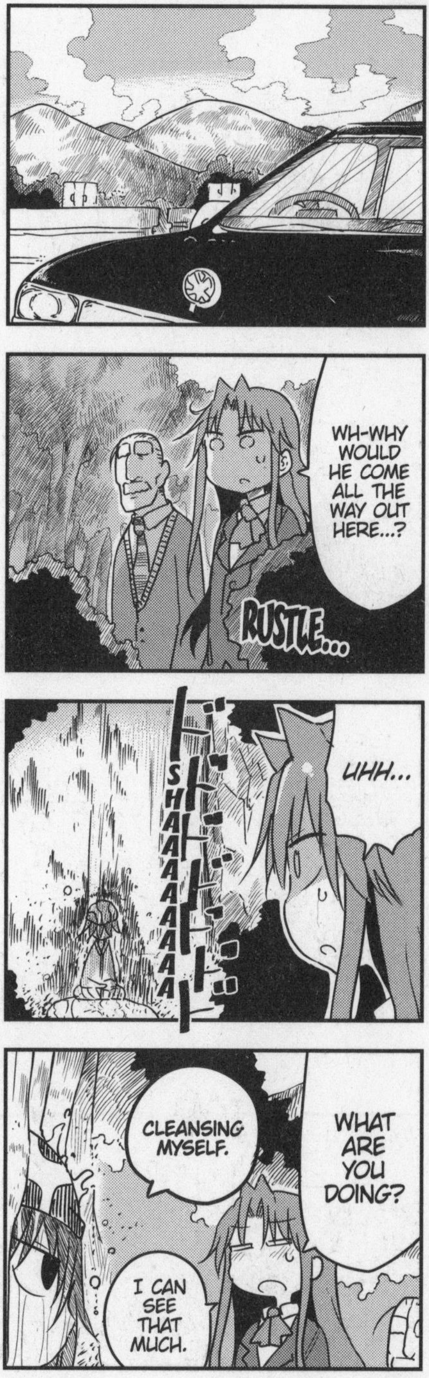
WH-WHY WOULD HE COME ALL THE WAY OUT HERE...?
RUSTLE...
UHH...
SHAAAAAAAAAA
WHAT ARE YOU DOING?
CLEANSING MYSELF.
I CAN SEE THAT MUCH.

In the End

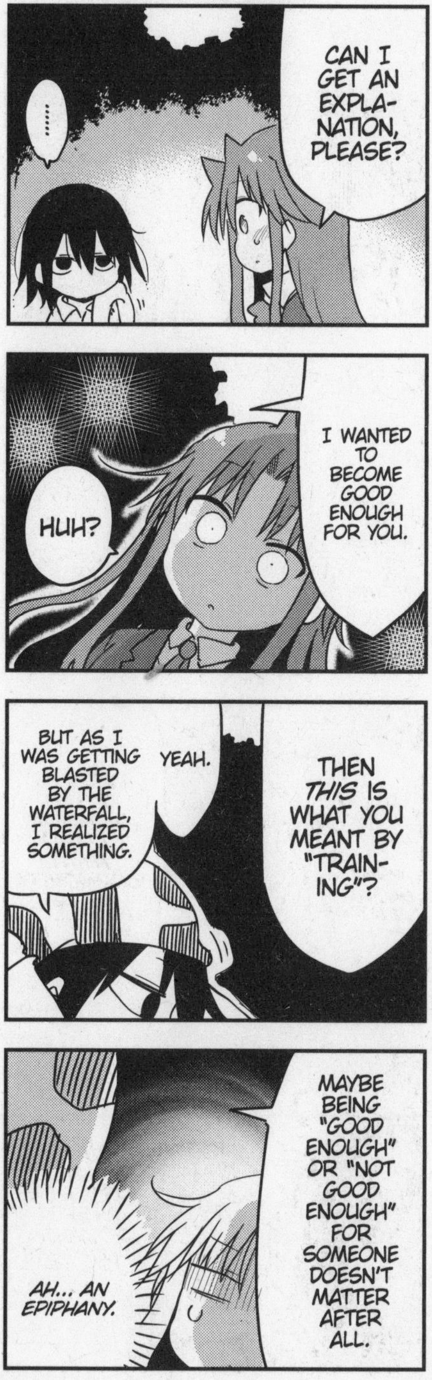
CAN I GET AN EXPLANATION, PLEASE?
……
I WANTED TO BECOME GOOD ENOUGH FOR YOU.
HUH?
THEN *THIS* IS WHAT YOU MEANT BY "TRAINING"?
YEAH.
BUT AS I WAS GETTING BLASTED BY THE WATERFALL, I REALIZED SOMETHING.
MAYBE BEING "GOOD ENOUGH" OR "NOT GOOD ENOUGH" FOR SOMEONE DOESN'T MATTER AFTER ALL.
AH... AN EPIPHANY.

Worst Move

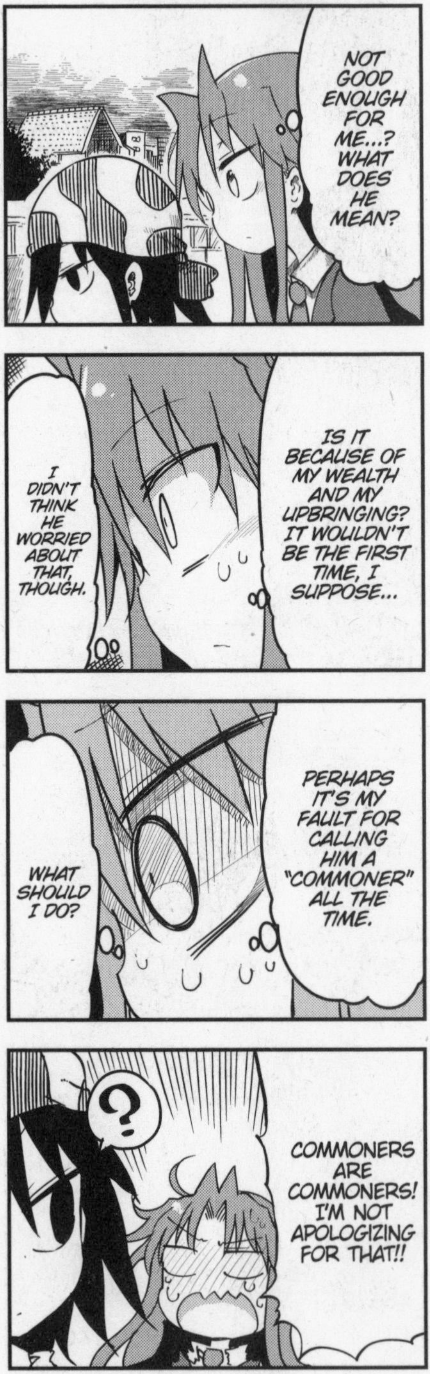
NOT GOOD ENOUGH FOR ME...? WHAT DOES HE MEAN?
IS IT BECAUSE OF MY WEALTH AND MY UPBRINGING? IT WOULDN'T BE THE FIRST TIME, I SUPPOSE...
I DIDN'T THINK HE WORRIED ABOUT THAT, THOUGH.
PERHAPS IT'S MY FAULT FOR CALLING HIM A "COMMONER" ALL THE TIME.
WHAT SHOULD I DO?
COMMONERS ARE COMMONERS! I'M NOT APOLOGIZING FOR THAT!!
?

Relief

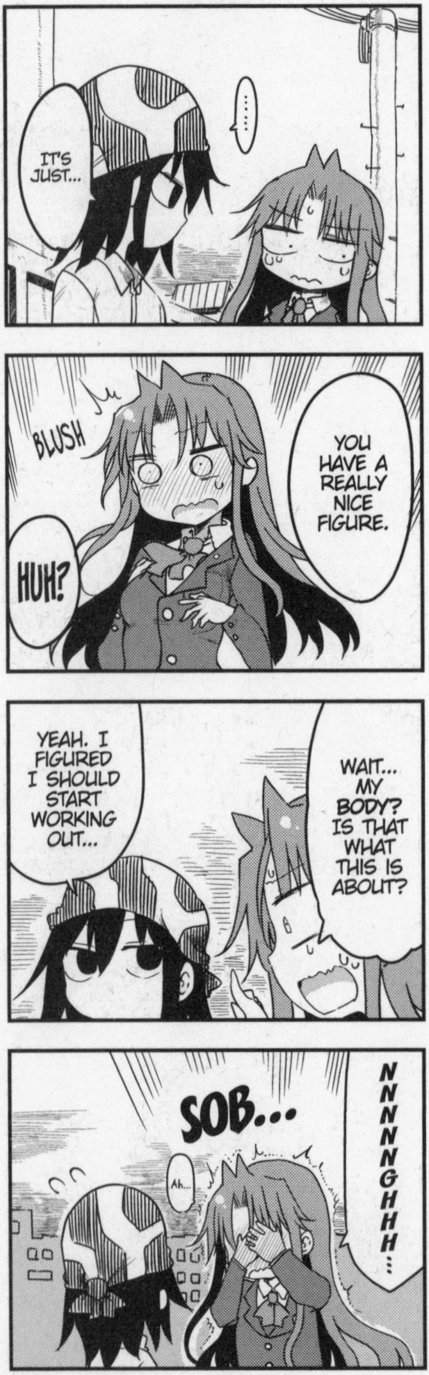
......
IT'S JUST...
YOU HAVE A REALLY NICE FIGURE.
BLUSH
HUH?
WAIT... MY BODY? IS THAT WHAT THIS IS ABOUT?
YEAH. I FIGURED I SHOULD START WORKING OUT...
NNNNNGHHH...
SOB...
Ah...

With Bigger Strides

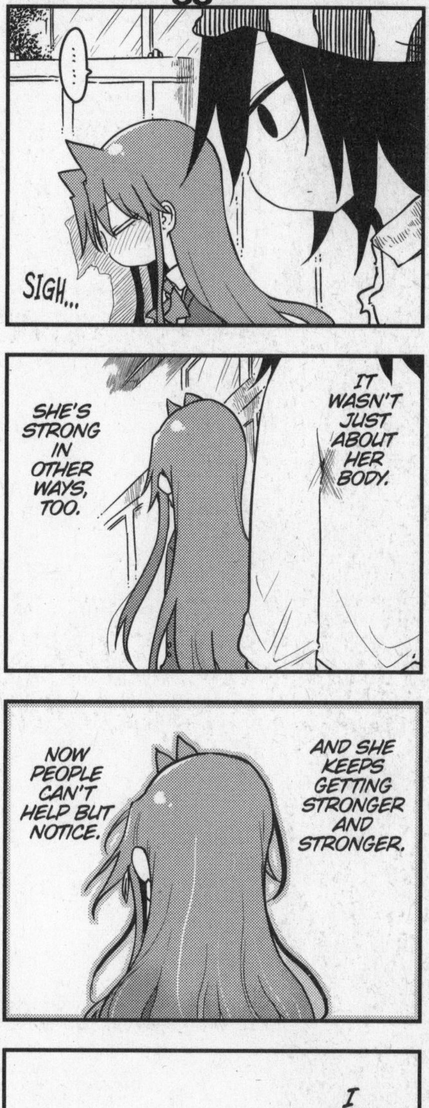
...
SIGH...
IT WASN'T JUST ABOUT HER BODY.
SHE'S STRONG IN OTHER WAYS, TOO.
AND SHE KEEPS GETTING STRONGER AND STRONGER.
NOW PEOPLE CAN'T HELP BUT NOTICE.
I WANT TO BE LIKE THAT, TOO.

Max Power Chris: To the Other Side

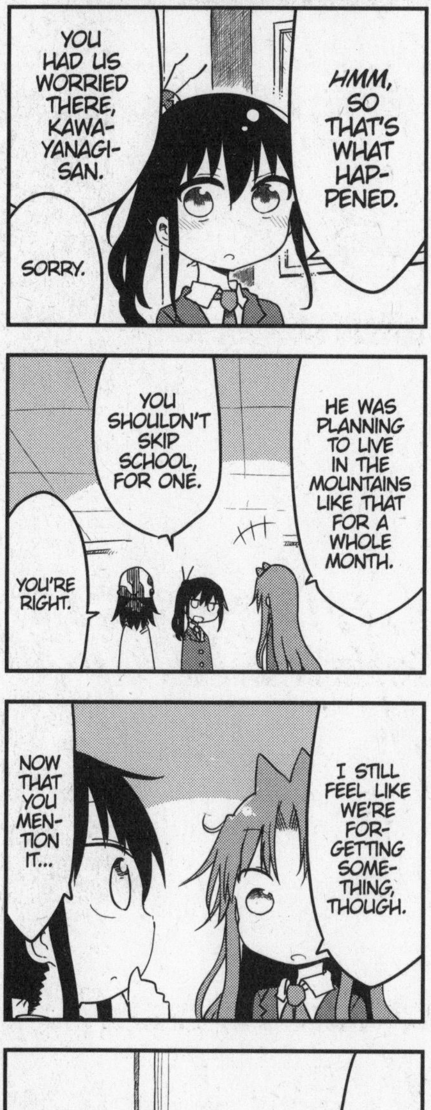
HMM, SO THAT'S WHAT HAP-PENED.
YOU HAD US WORRIED THERE, KAWA-YANAGI-SAN.
SORRY.
HE WAS PLANNING TO LIVE IN THE MOUNTAINS LIKE THAT FOR A WHOLE MONTH.
YOU SHOULDN'T SKIP SCHOOL, FOR ONE.
YOU'RE RIGHT.
I STILL FEEL LIKE WE'RE FOR-GETTING SOME-THING, THOUGH.
NOW THAT YOU MEN-TION IT...
WHERE'S CHRIS?
Kawa-yanagi!!
Where are you?! Kawa-yanagi!
UHM...

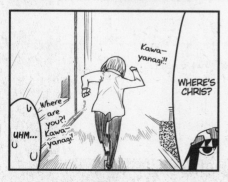

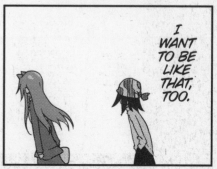

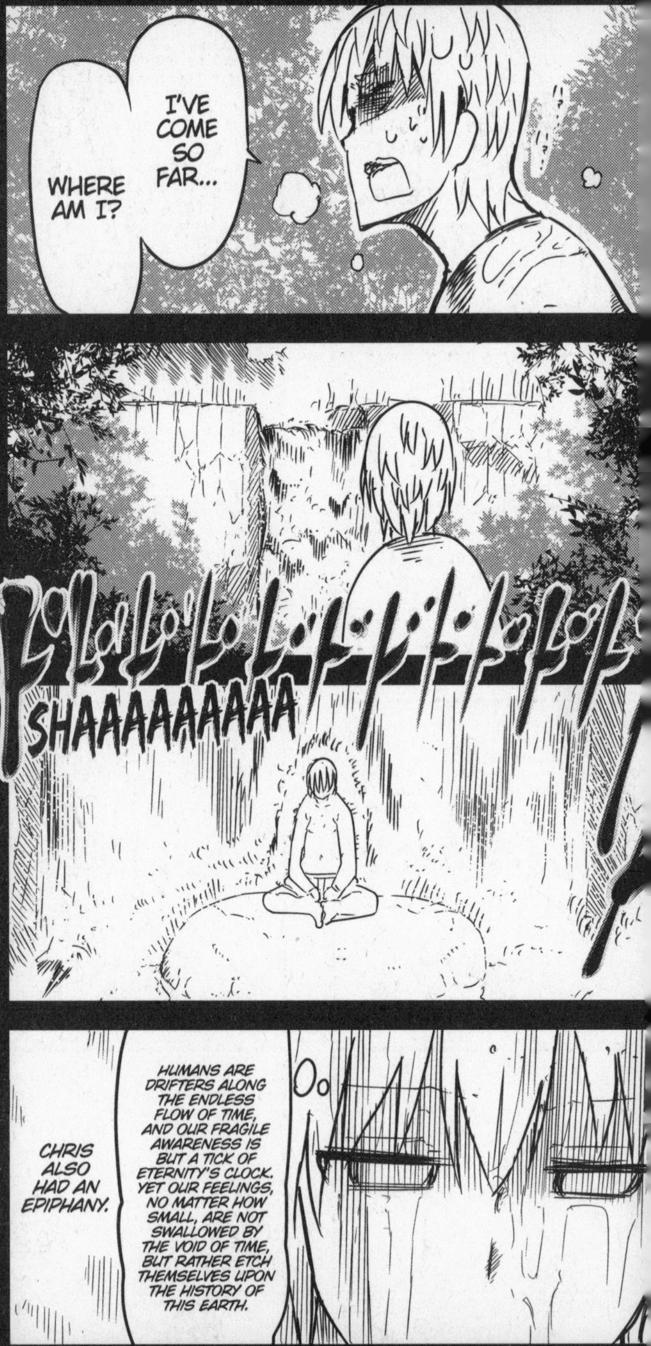
I'VE COME SO FAR...
WHERE AM I?
SHAAAAAAAAA
HUMANS ARE DRIFTERS ALONG THE ENDLESS FLOW OF TIME, AND OUR FRAGILE AWARENESS IS BUT A TICK OF ETERNITY'S CLOCK. YET OUR FEELINGS, NO MATTER HOW SMALL, ARE NOT SWALLOWED BY THE VOID OF TIME, BUT RATHER ETCH THEMSELVES UPON THE HISTORY OF THIS EARTH.
CHRIS ALSO HAD AN EPIPHANY.

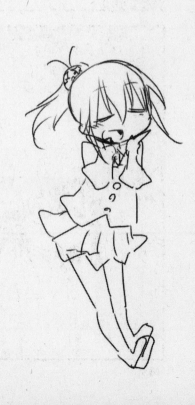

Mask Season

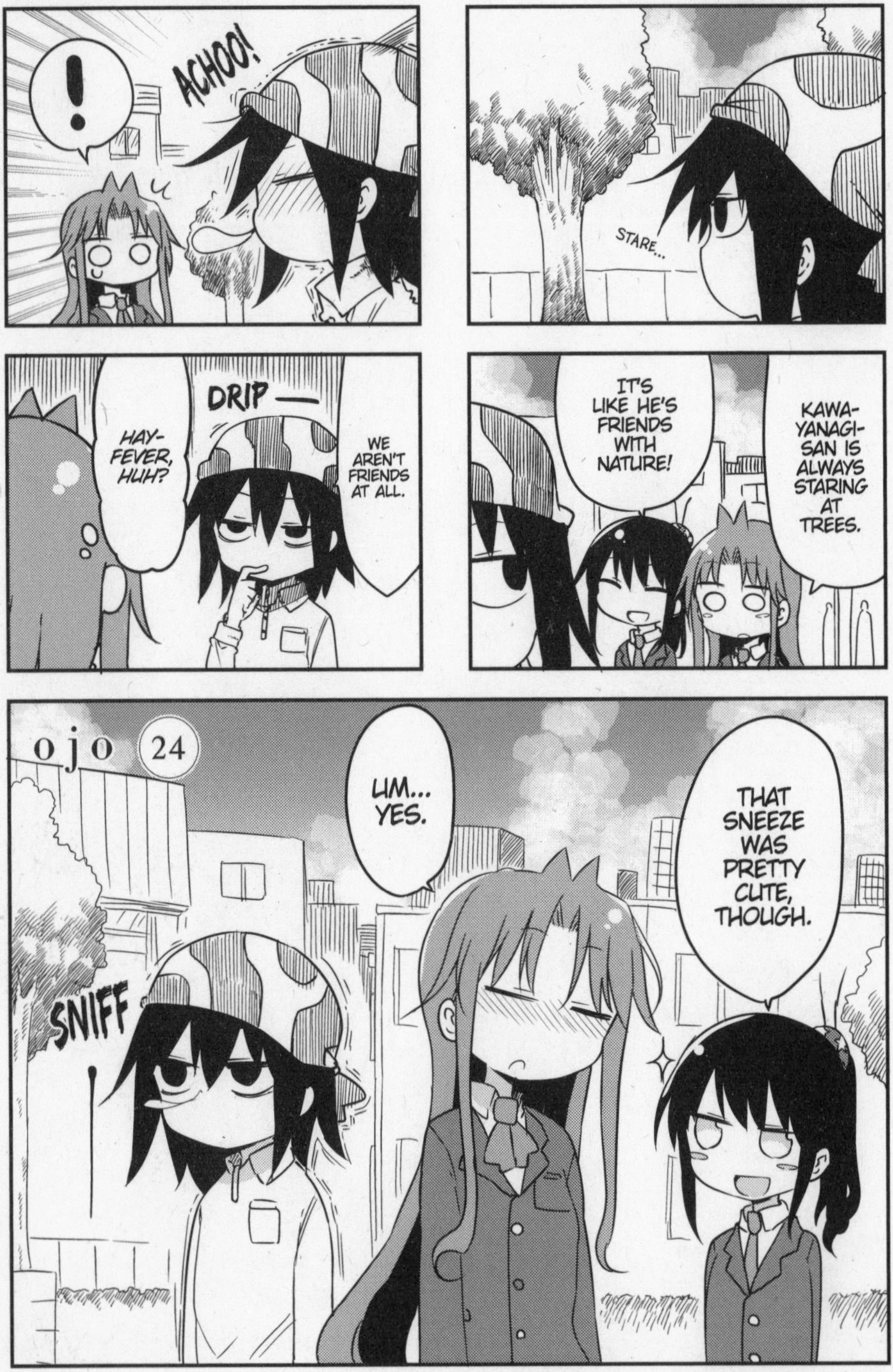
STARE...
ACHOO!
!
KAWA-YANAGI-SAN IS ALWAYS STARING AT TREES.
IT'S LIKE HE'S FRIENDS WITH NATURE!
WE AREN'T FRIENDS AT ALL.
DRIP —
HAY-FEVER, HUH?
THAT SNEEZE WAS PRETTY CUTE, THOUGH.
UM... YES.
ojo 24
SNIFF

Prevention Is Key

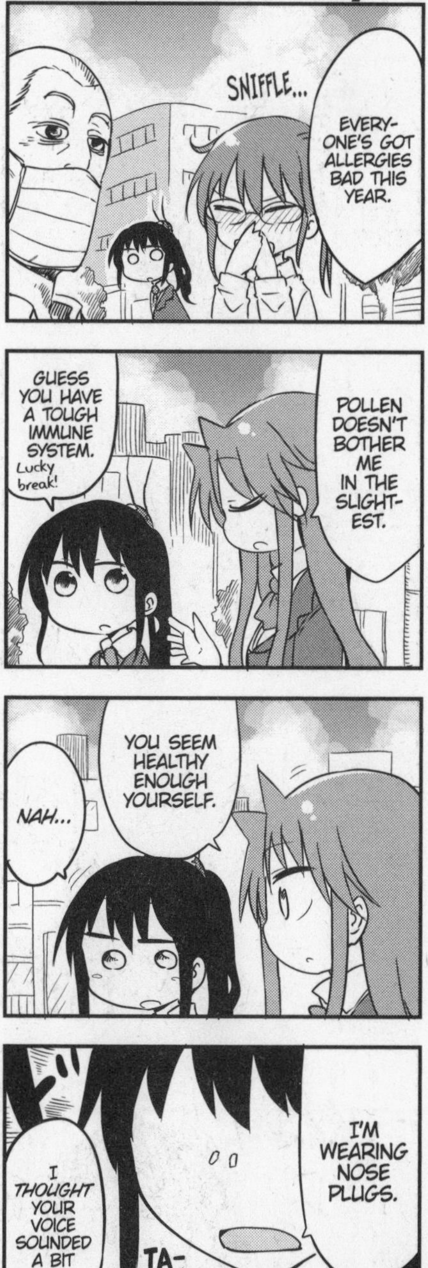
EVERY-ONE'S GOT ALLERGIES BAD THIS YEAR.
SNIFFLE...
POLLEN DOESN'T BOTHER ME IN THE SLIGHT-EST.
GUESS YOU HAVE A TOUGH IMMUNE SYSTEM. Lucky break!
YOU SEEM HEALTHY ENOUGH YOURSELF.
NAH...
I'M WEARING NOSE PLUGS.
TA-DA
I *THOUGHT* YOUR VOICE SOUNDED A BIT ODD.

Almost Tempting

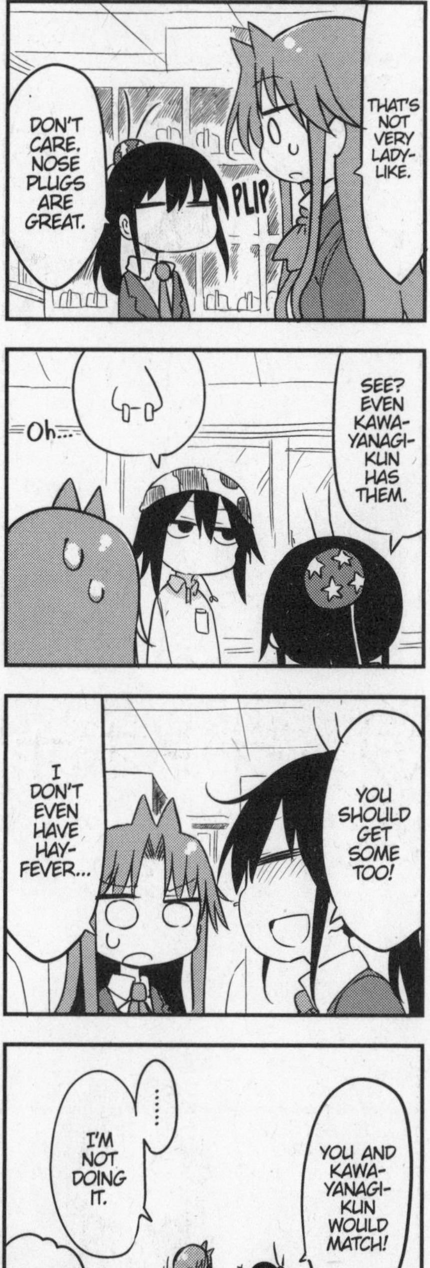
THAT'S NOT VERY LADY-LIKE.
PLIP
DON'T CARE. NOSE PLUGS ARE GREAT.
SEE? EVEN KAWA-YANAGI-KUN HAS THEM.
Oh...
YOU SHOULD GET SOME TOO!
I DON'T EVEN HAVE HAY-FEVER...
YOU AND KAWA-YANAGI-KUN WOULD MATCH!
......
I'M NOT DOING IT.
SHE THOUGHT ABOUT IT, THOUGH.

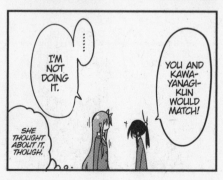

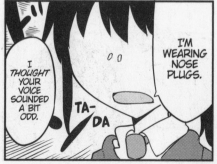

Brought It from Home

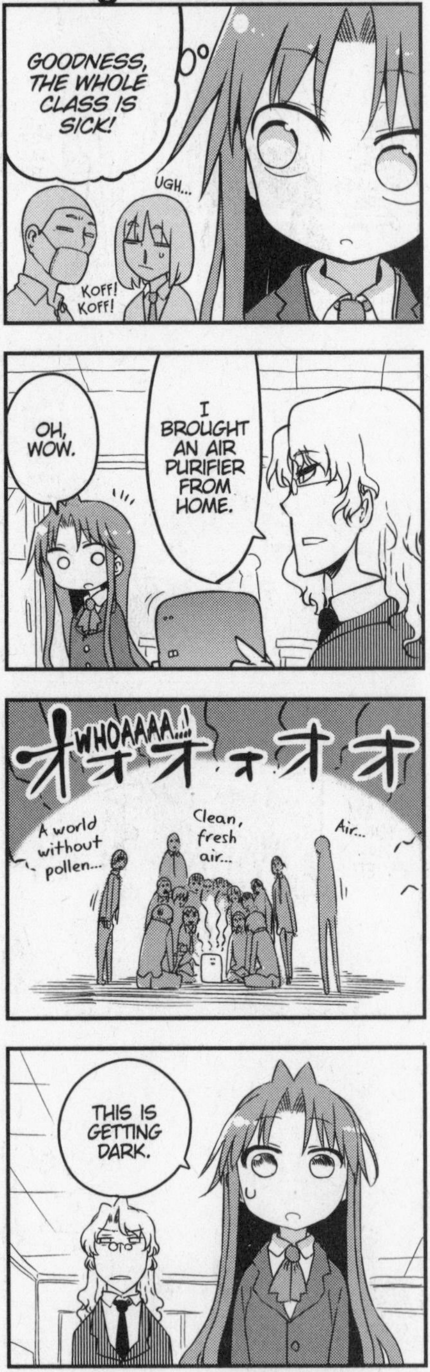
GOODNESS, THE WHOLE CLASS IS SICK!
UGH...
KOFF! KOFF!
I BROUGHT AN AIR PURIFIER FROM HOME.
OH, WOW.
WHOAAAA...!
オォオォォオオ
Air...
Clean, fresh air...
A world without pollen...
THIS IS GETTING DARK.

Now You've Said It

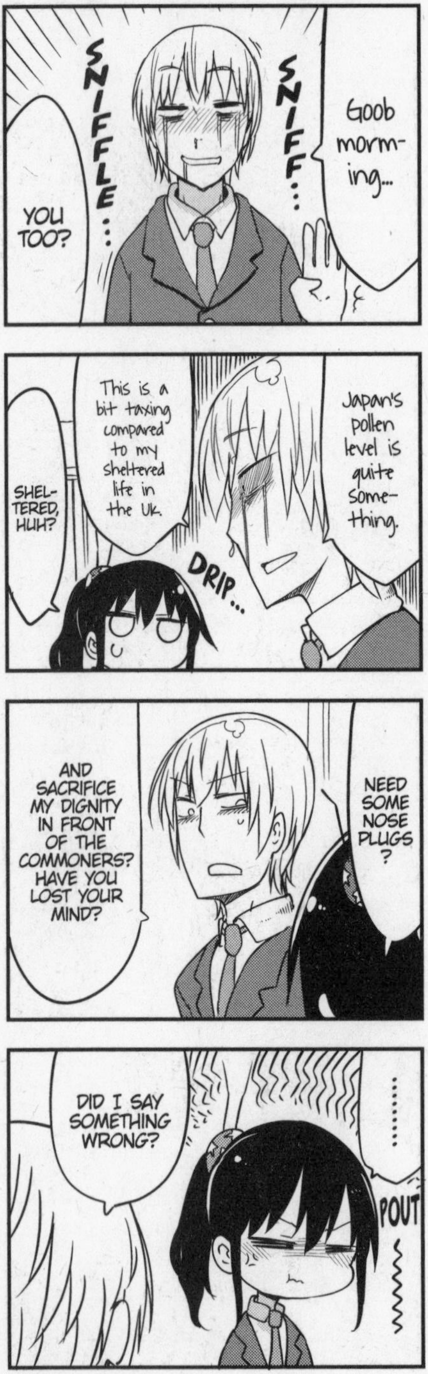
Goob morm-ing...
SNIFF...
SNIFFLE...
YOU TOO?
Japan's pollen level is quite some-thing.
This is a bit taxing compared to my sheltered life in the UK.
DRIP...
SHEL-TERED, HUH?
NEED SOME NOSE PLUGS?
AND SACRIFICE MY DIGNITY IN FRONT OF THE COMMONERS? HAVE YOU LOST YOUR MIND?
......
POUT
DID I SAY SOMETHING WRONG?

Persistent Tissue Shortage

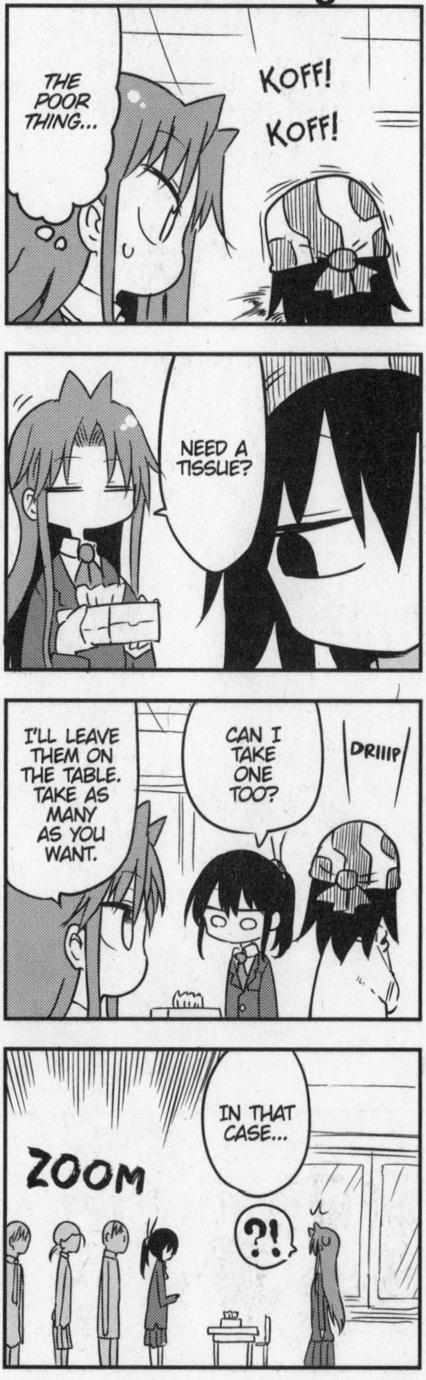
KOFF!
KOFF!
THE POOR THING...
NEED A TISSUE?
DRIIIP
CAN I TAKE ONE TOO?
I'LL LEAVE THEM ON THE TABLE. TAKE AS MANY AS YOU WANT.
IN THAT CASE...
ZOOM
?!

Forbidden Power

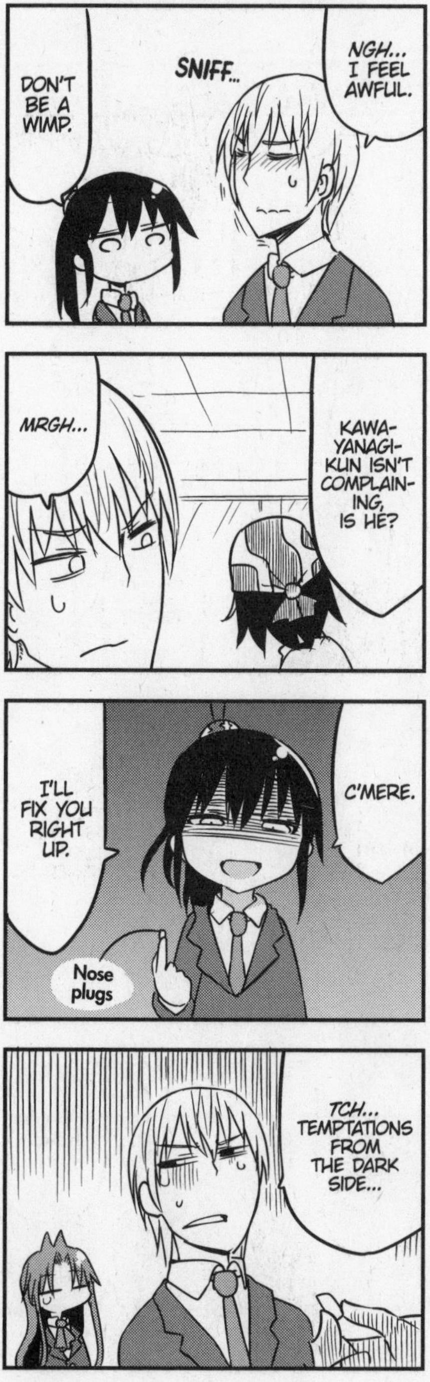
NGH... I FEEL AWFUL.
SNIFF...
DON'T BE A WIMP.
KAWAYANAGI-KUN ISN'T COMPLAINING, IS HE?
MRGH...
C'MERE.
I'LL FIX YOU RIGHT UP.
Nose plugs
TCH... TEMPTATIONS FROM THE DARK SIDE...

Recollection

WELCOME HOME, HARU.
OH! HELLO, FATHER!
THE POLLEN IS TRULY DREADFUL THIS YEAR.
ARE YOU FEELING ALL RIGHT?
QUITE.
I SEE... YOU'RE STRONG, JUST LIKE YOUR MOTHER.
FATHER ...
HERE.
BUT YOU GET YOUR KINDNESS FROM ME.
FWP
Thank you.

I Tried to Ignore You

HUFF...
HUFF...
YOU SAW NOTHING.
HUFF...
HUFF...

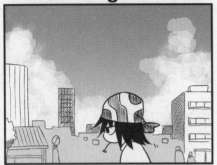

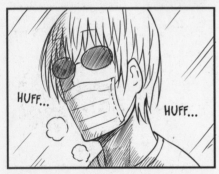

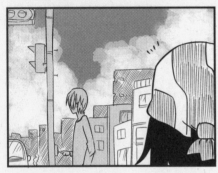

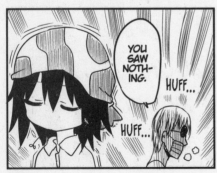

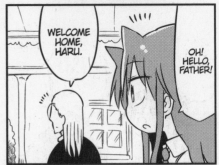

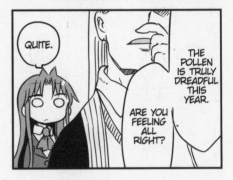

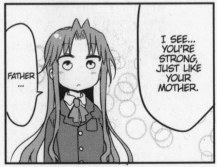

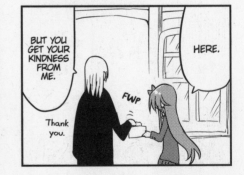

Go ahead!!

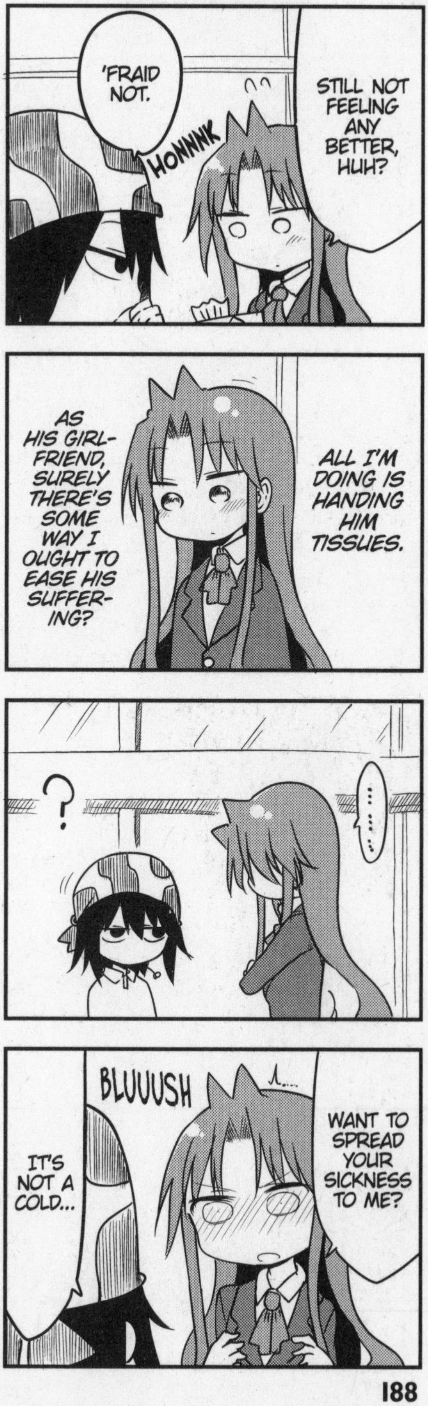
STILL NOT FEELING ANY BETTER, HUH?
'FRAID NOT.
HONNNK
ALL I'M DOING IS HANDING HIM TISSUES.
AS HIS GIRL-FRIEND, SURELY THERE'S SOME WAY I OUGHT TO EASE HIS SUFFER-ING?
......
?
WANT TO SPREAD YOUR SICKNESS TO ME?
BLUUUSH
IT'S NOT A COLD...

Moved to Tears

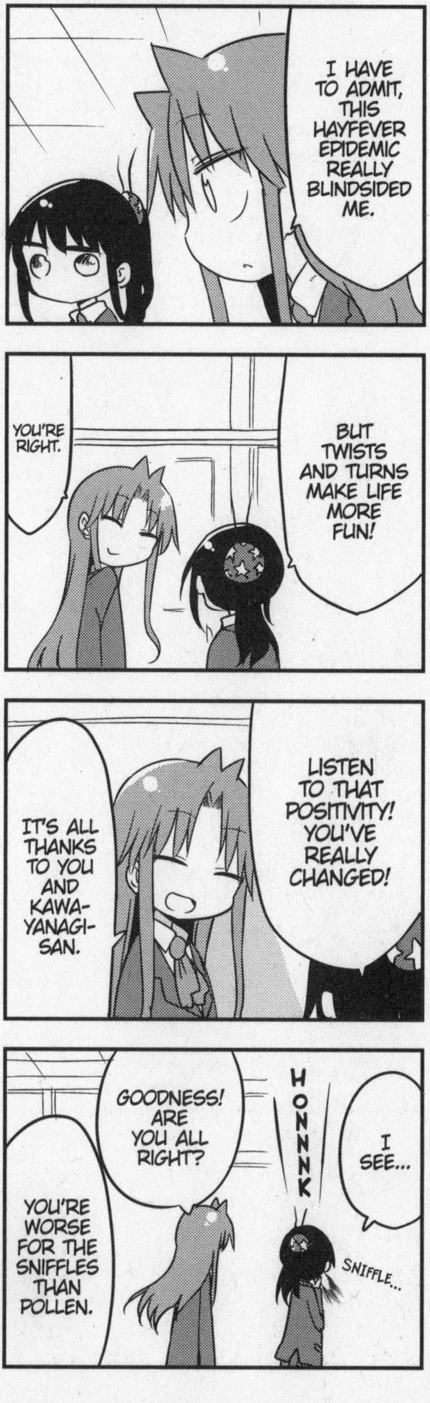
I HAVE TO ADMIT, THIS HAYFEVER EPIDEMIC REALLY BLINDSIDED ME.
BUT TWISTS AND TURNS MAKE LIFE MORE FUN!
YOU'RE RIGHT.
LISTEN TO THAT POSITIVITY! YOU'VE REALLY CHANGED!
IT'S ALL THANKS TO YOU AND KAWA-YANAGI-SAN.
I SEE...
HONNNK
SNIFFLE...
GOODNESS! ARE YOU ALL RIGHT?
YOU'RE WORSE FOR THE SNIFFLES THAN POLLEN.

The Missing Photograph

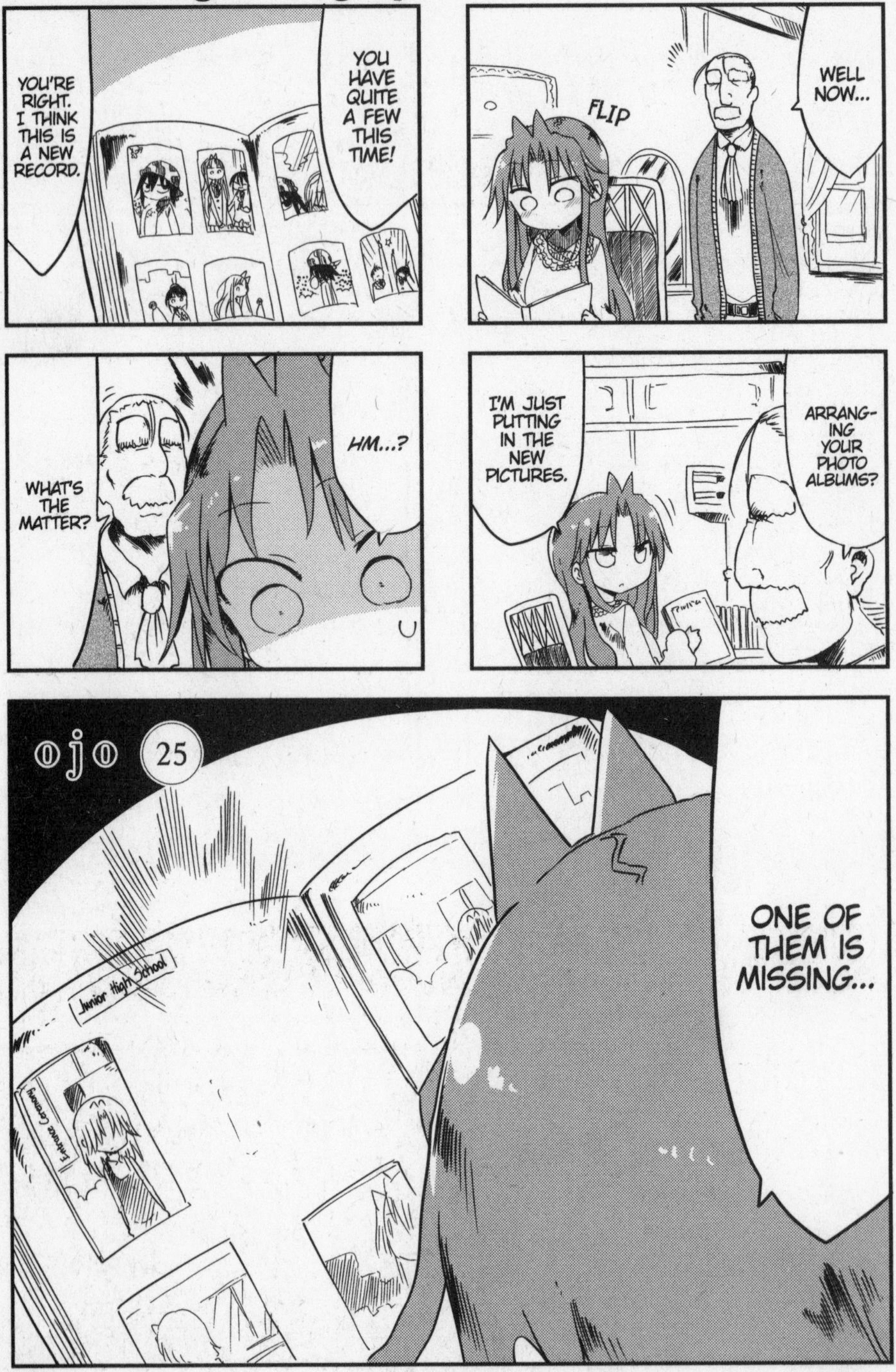

WELL NOW...
FLIP
YOU HAVE QUITE A FEW THIS TIME!
YOU'RE RIGHT. I THINK THIS IS A NEW RECORD.
ARRANGING YOUR PHOTO ALBUMS?
I'M JUST PUTTING IN THE NEW PICTURES.
HM...?
WHAT'S THE MATTER?
ojo 25
ONE OF THEM IS MISSING...
Junior High School
Entrance Ceremony

How Many Millions?

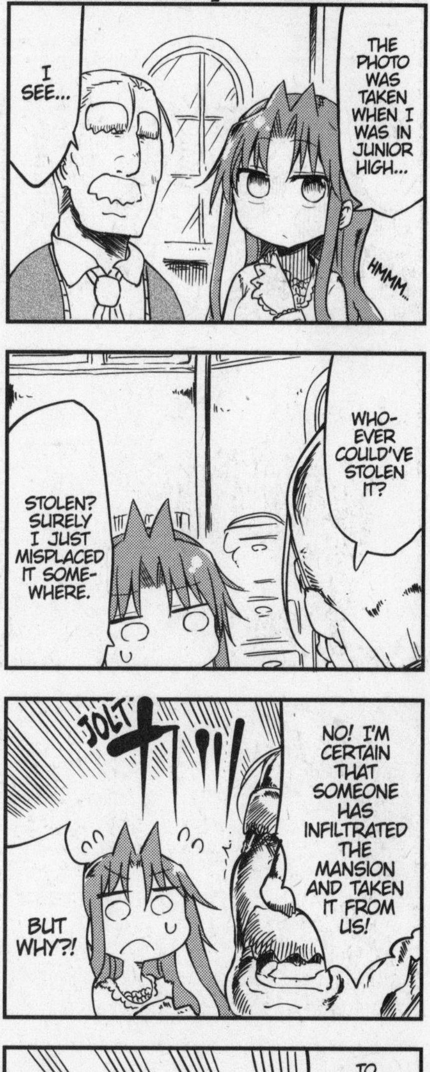
THE PHOTO WAS TAKEN WHEN I WAS IN JUNIOR HIGH...
HMMM...
I SEE...
WHOEVER COULD'VE STOLEN IT?
STOLEN? SURELY I JUST MISPLACED IT SOMEWHERE.
NO! I'M CERTAIN THAT SOMEONE HAS INFILTRATED THE MANSION AND TAKEN IT FROM US!
JOLT
BUT WHY?!
TO SELL IT! PICTURES OF JUNIOR HIGH GIRLS FETCH A HIGH PRICE!!
STOP THIS INSTANT! YOU'RE CREEPING ME OUT!!

Straightforward

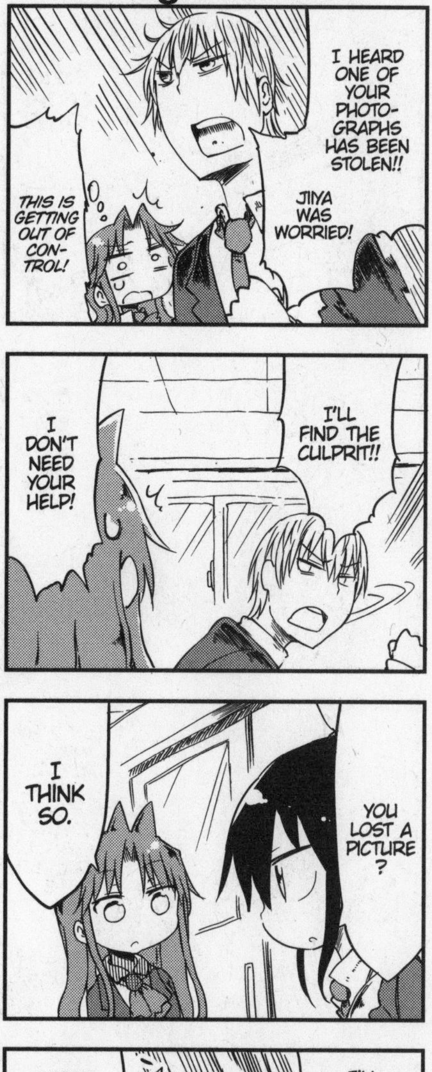
I HEARD ONE OF YOUR PHOTOGRAPHS HAS BEEN STOLEN!!
JIIYA WAS WORRIED!
THIS IS GETTING OUT OF CONTROL!
I'LL FIND THE CULPRIT!!
I DON'T NEED YOUR HELP!
YOU LOST A PICTURE?
I THINK SO.
I'LL SEARCH EVERY CORNER OF THIS EARTH!
HYAAAH!
YOU HAVE A LOT OF ENERGY TO BURN, DON'T YOU?

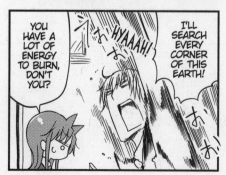

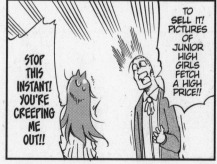

Having a Little Too Much Fun

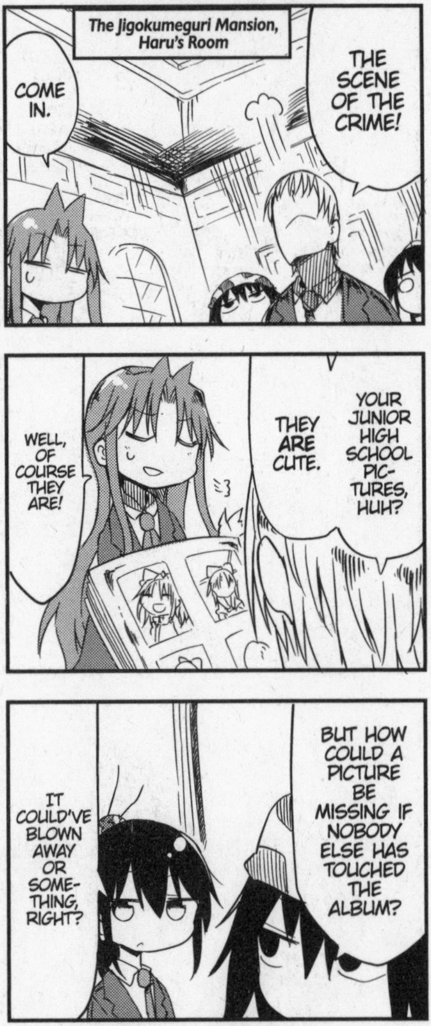
THE SCENE OF THE CRIME!
The Jigokumeguri Mansion, Haru's Room
COME IN.
YOUR JUNIOR HIGH SCHOOL PICTURES, HUH?
THEY ARE CUTE.
WELL, OF COURSE THEY ARE!
BUT HOW COULD A PICTURE BE MISSING IF NOBODY ELSE HAS TOUCHED THE ALBUM?
IT COULD'VE BLOWN AWAY OR SOMETHING, RIGHT?
WHICH MEANS OUR SUSPECT CAN CONTROL THE WIND!
GULP...
ARE YOU WRITING A MYSTERY OR A FANTASY NOVEL HERE?

For Both Their Sakes

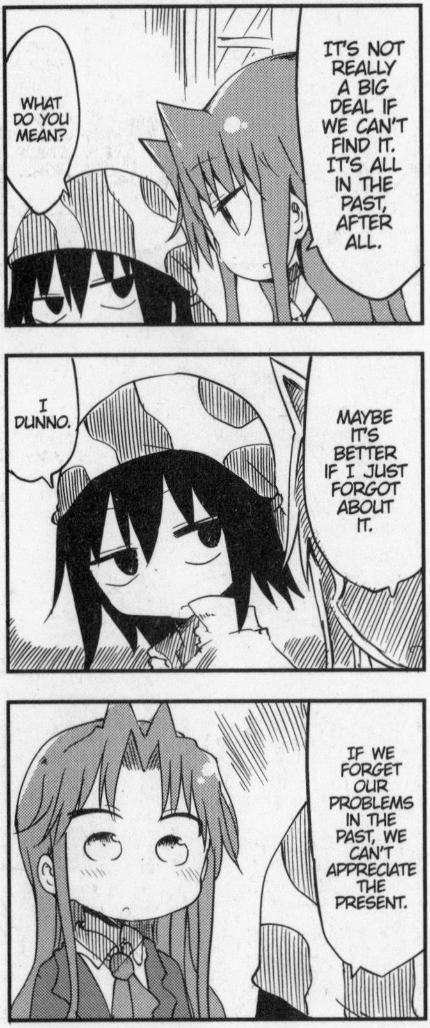
IT'S NOT REALLY A BIG DEAL IF WE CAN'T FIND IT. IT'S ALL IN THE PAST, AFTER ALL.
WHAT DO YOU MEAN?
MAYBE IT'S BETTER IF I JUST FORGOT ABOUT IT.
I DUNNO.
IF WE FORGET OUR PROBLEMS IN THE PAST, WE CAN'T APPRECIATE THE PRESENT.
I SUPPOSE MEMORIES CAN SERVE AS A VALUABLE MEASURING STICK...
NOW YOU GET IT.

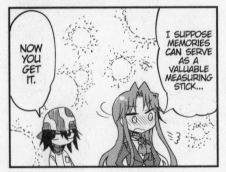

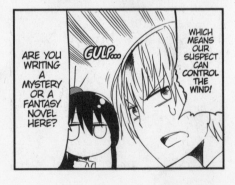

Having a Little Too Much Fun 2

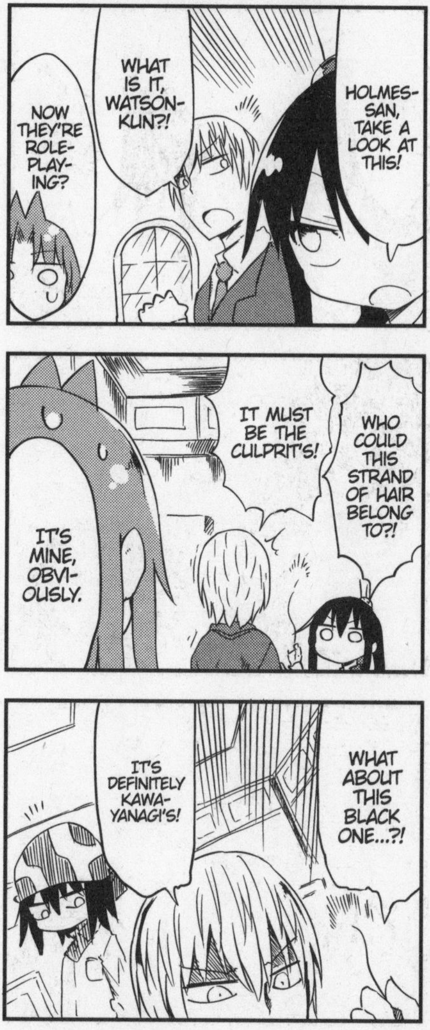
HOLMES-SAN, TAKE A LOOK AT THIS!
WHAT IS IT, WATSON-KUN?!
NOW THEY'RE ROLE-PLAYING?
WHO COULD THIS STRAND OF HAIR BELONG TO?!
IT MUST BE THE CULPRIT'S!
IT'S MINE, OBVIOUSLY.
WHAT ABOUT THIS BLACK ONE...?!
IT'S DEFINITELY KAWAYANAGI'S!
THAT MEANS THEY'RE MEETING UP TOGETHER! ALONE!!
HOW SCANDALOUS!

With Precise Timing

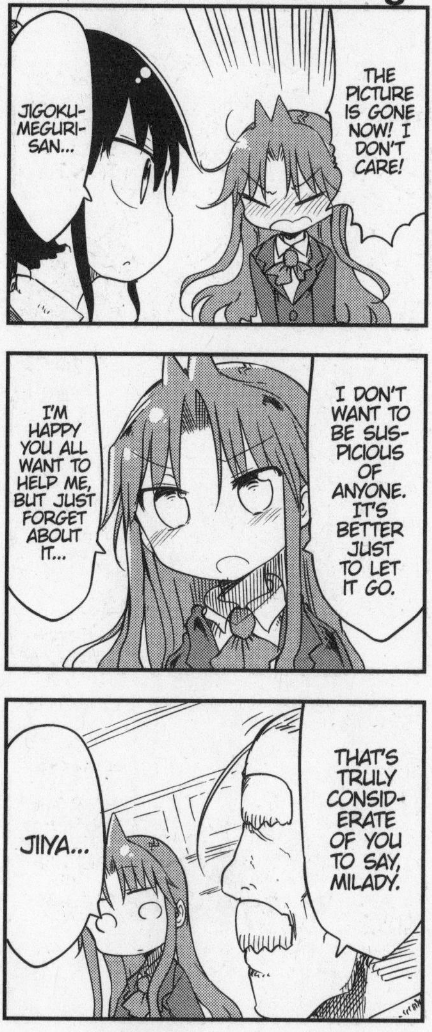
THE PICTURE IS GONE NOW! I DON'T CARE!
JIGOKUMEGURI-SAN...
I DON'T WANT TO BE SUSPICIOUS OF ANYONE. IT'S BETTER JUST TO LET IT GO.
I'M HAPPY YOU ALL WANT TO HELP ME, BUT JUST FORGET ABOUT IT...
THAT'S TRULY CONSIDERATE OF YOU TO SAY, MILADY.
JIIYA...
AND BY THE WAY, I AM THE CULPRIT.

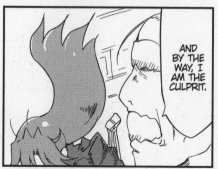

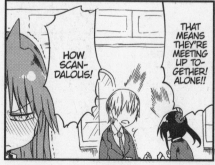

Maybe It's My Imagination

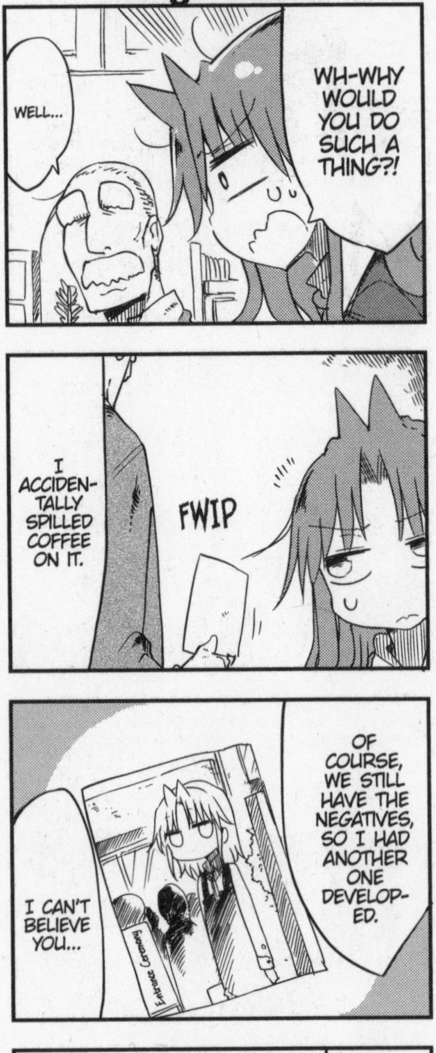
WH-WHY WOULD YOU DO SUCH A THING?!
WELL...
FWIP
I ACCIDENTALLY SPILLED COFFEE ON IT.
OF COURSE, WE STILL HAVE THE NEGATIVES, SO I HAD ANOTHER ONE DEVELOPED.
Entrance Ceremony
I CAN'T BELIEVE YOU...
HM? THERE'S SOMETHING STRANGE ABOUT THIS PICTURE.

Truth

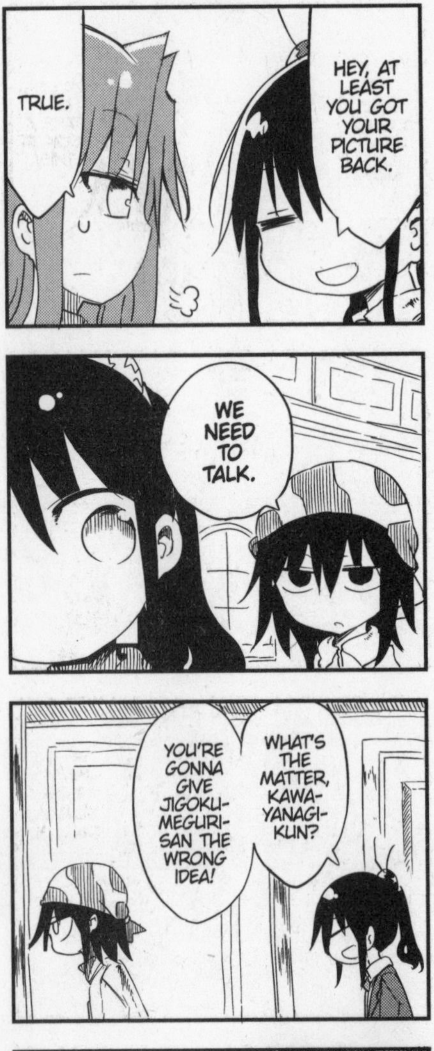
HEY, AT LEAST YOU GOT YOUR PICTURE BACK.
TRUE.
WE NEED TO TALK.
WHAT'S THE MATTER, KAWAYANAGI-KUN?
YOU'RE GONNA GIVE JIGOKUMEGURI-SAN THE WRONG IDEA!
I THINK YOU NEED TO GIVE THAT PICTURE BACK.

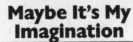

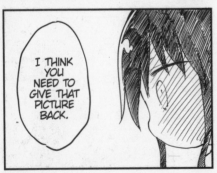

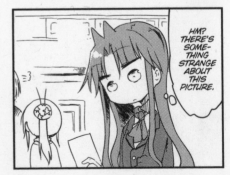

What Kawayanagi Saw

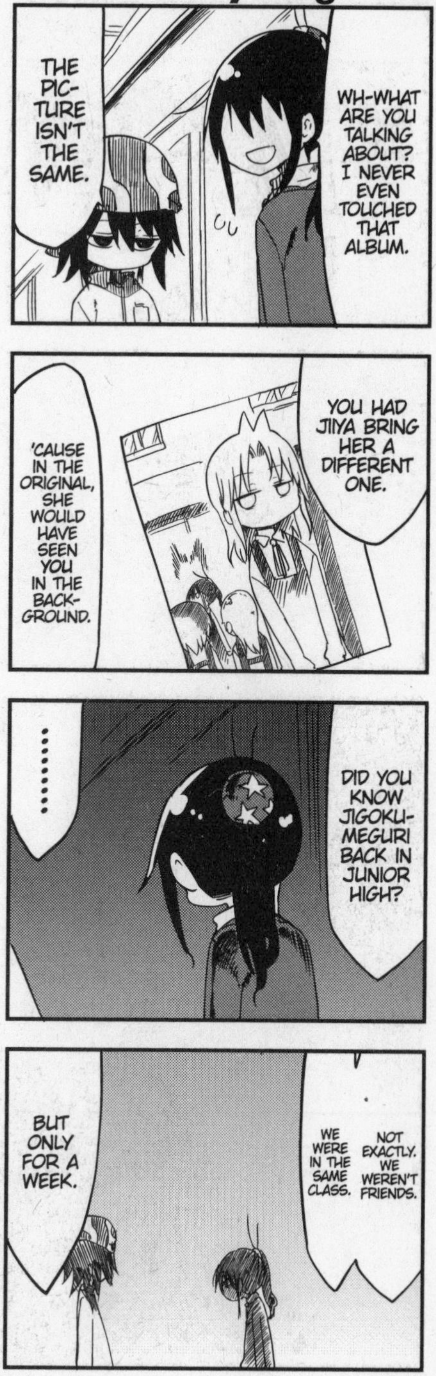
WH-WHAT ARE YOU TALKING ABOUT? I NEVER EVEN TOUCHED THAT ALBUM.
THE PICTURE ISN'T THE SAME.
YOU HAD JIIYA BRING HER A DIFFERENT ONE.
'CAUSE IN THE ORIGINAL, SHE WOULD HAVE SEEN YOU IN THE BACKGROUND.
DID YOU KNOW JIGOKU-MEGURI BACK IN JUNIOR HIGH?
......
NOT EXACTLY. WE WEREN'T FRIENDS.
WE WERE IN THE SAME CLASS.
BUT ONLY FOR A WEEK.

What Kawayanagi Didn't See

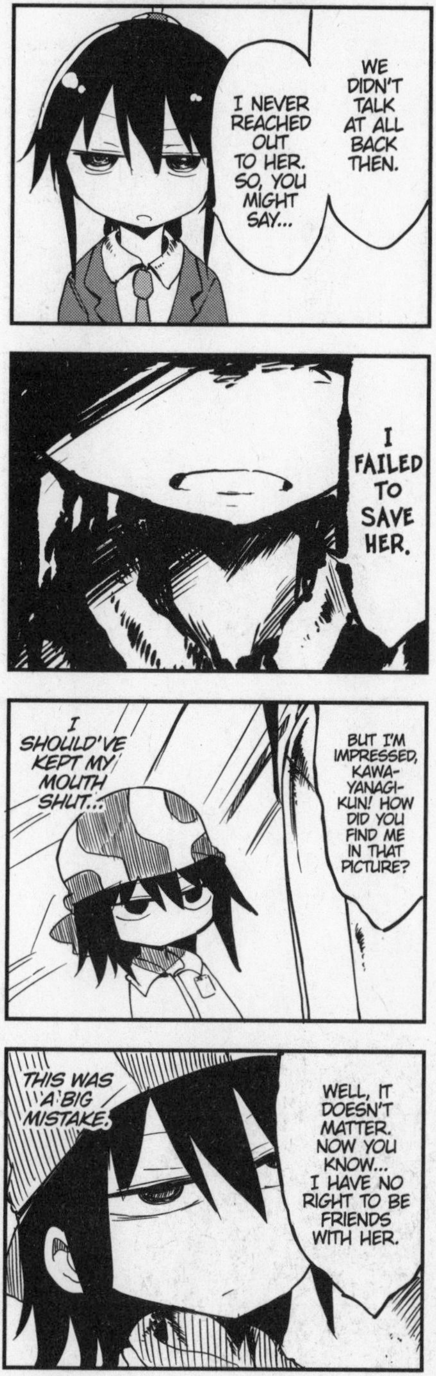
WE DIDN'T TALK AT ALL BACK THEN.
I NEVER REACHED OUT TO HER. SO, YOU MIGHT SAY...
I FAILED TO SAVE HER.
BUT I'M IMPRESSED, KAWAYANAGI-KUN! HOW DID YOU FIND ME IN THAT PICTURE?
I SHOULD'VE KEPT MY MOUTH SHUT...
WELL, IT DOESN'T MATTER. NOW YOU KNOW... I HAVE NO RIGHT TO BE FRIENDS WITH HER.
THIS WAS A BIG MISTAKE.

Not like Herself at All

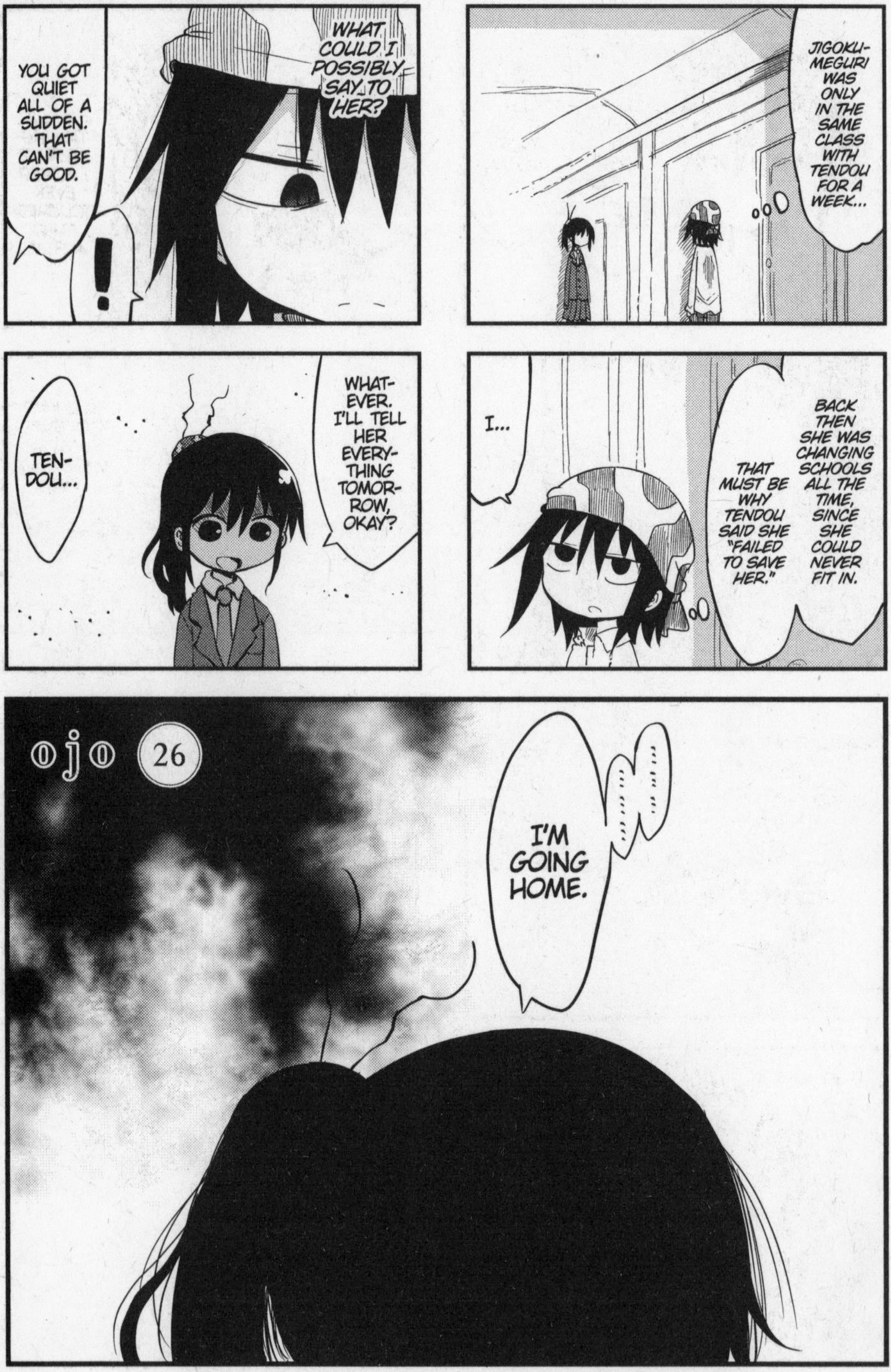
JIGOKU-MEGURI WAS ONLY IN THE SAME CLASS WITH TENDOU FOR A WEEK...
WHAT COULD I POSSIBLY SAY TO HER?
YOU GOT QUIET ALL OF A SUDDEN. THAT CAN'T BE GOOD.
!
BACK THEN SHE WAS CHANGING SCHOOLS ALL THE TIME, SINCE SHE COULD NEVER FIT IN.
THAT MUST BE WHY TENDOU SAID SHE "FAILED TO SAVE HER."
I...
WHAT-EVER. I'LL TELL HER EVERY-THING TOMOR-ROW, OKAY?
TEN-DOU...
ojo 26
......
I'M GOING HOME.

Unseeing, Unspeaking

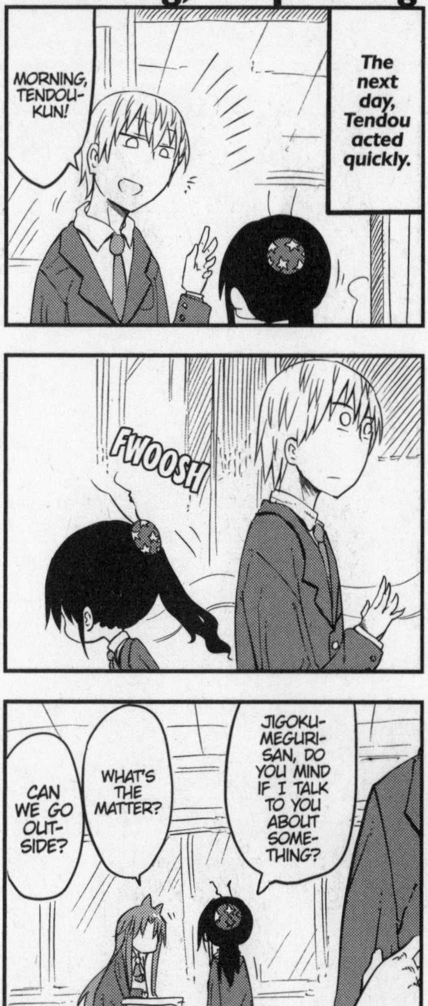
The next day, Tendou acted quickly.
MORNING, TENDOU-KUN!
FWOOSH
JIGOKU-MEGURI-SAN, DO YOU MIND IF I TALK TO YOU ABOUT SOME-THING?
WHAT'S THE MATTER?
CAN WE GO OUT-SIDE?
DID I DO SOMETHING WRONG?
I don't get it.
IT'S MY FAULT.

Almost the Opposite

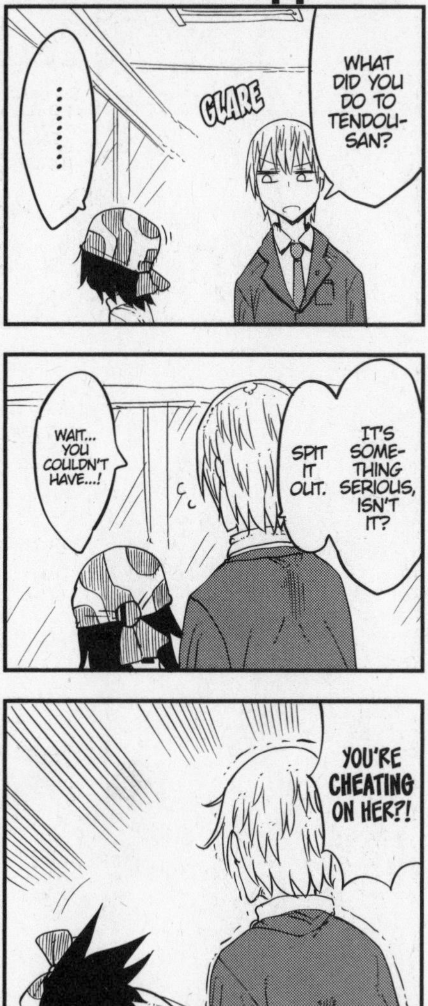
WHAT DID YOU DO TO TENDOU-SAN?
GLARE
......
IT'S SOME-THING SERIOUS, ISN'T IT?
SPIT IT OUT.
WAIT... YOU COULDN'T HAVE...!
YOU'RE CHEATING ON HER?!
I WON'T FORGIVE YOU FOR THIS, KAWA-YANAGI!!
GET BACK HERE! I'M NOT DONE WITH YOU!

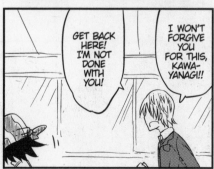

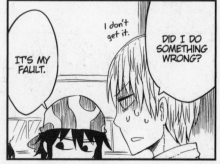

Cold

YOU WENT TO MY OLD SCHOOL, AND YOU NEVER SAID A THING?
YEAH...
I NEVER TALKED TO YOU OR ANY-THING, SO IT'S NO SURPRISE YOU DIDN'T NOTICE.
I JUST... WATCHED YOU FROM A DISTANCE.
I ALWAYS FELT GUILTY ABOUT IT. I SHOULD HAVE DONE SOME-THING TO HELP YOU.
SO WHEN I MET YOU HERE AGAIN...
I THOUGHT I COULD MAKE THINGS RIGHT.
THAT'S WHY I BECAME FRIENDS WITH YOU.
I'M SORRY.

Endless Enduring

......
AH!
GOOD-BYE.
HEY, TENDOU-KUN?
BUMP
...?

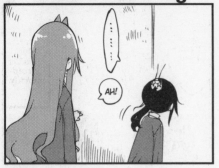

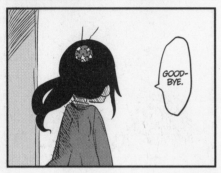

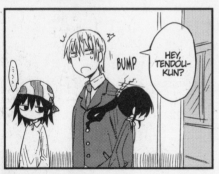

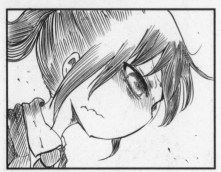

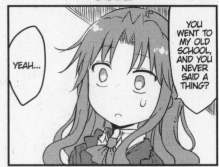

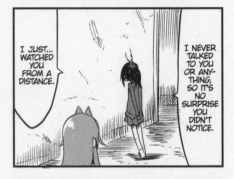

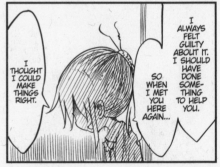

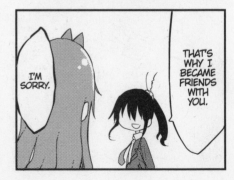

Tearing at My Heart

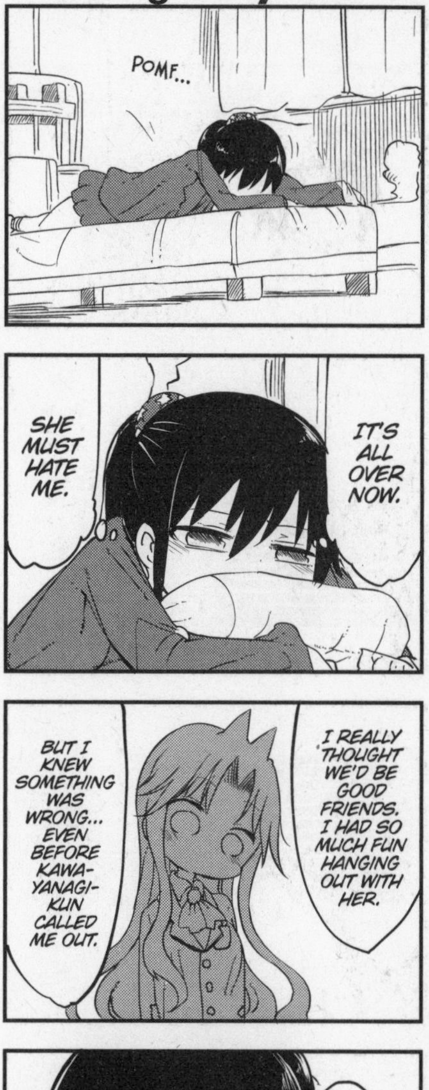
POMF...
IT'S ALL OVER NOW.
SHE MUST HATE ME.
I REALLY THOUGHT WE'D BE GOOD FRIENDS. I HAD SO MUCH FUN HANGING OUT WITH HER.
BUT I KNEW SOMETHING WAS WRONG... EVEN BEFORE KAWA-YANAGI-KUN CALLED ME OUT.
MAYBE I WANTED HER TO HATE ME...

No Way Back

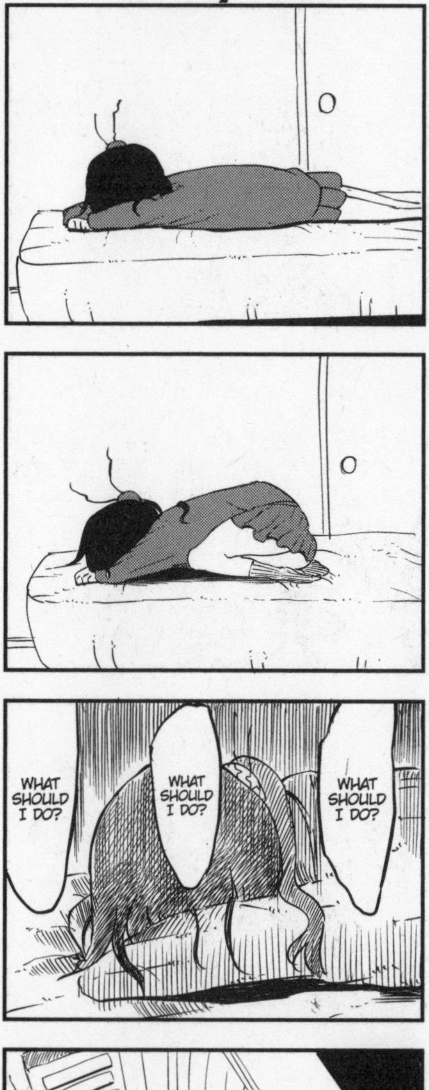
WHAT SHOULD I DO?
WHAT SHOULD I DO?
WHAT SHOULD I DO?
MMGH...
AHH...

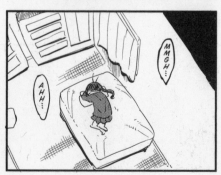

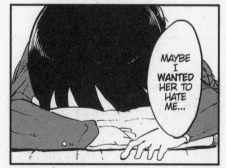

At Least He Hasn't Changed

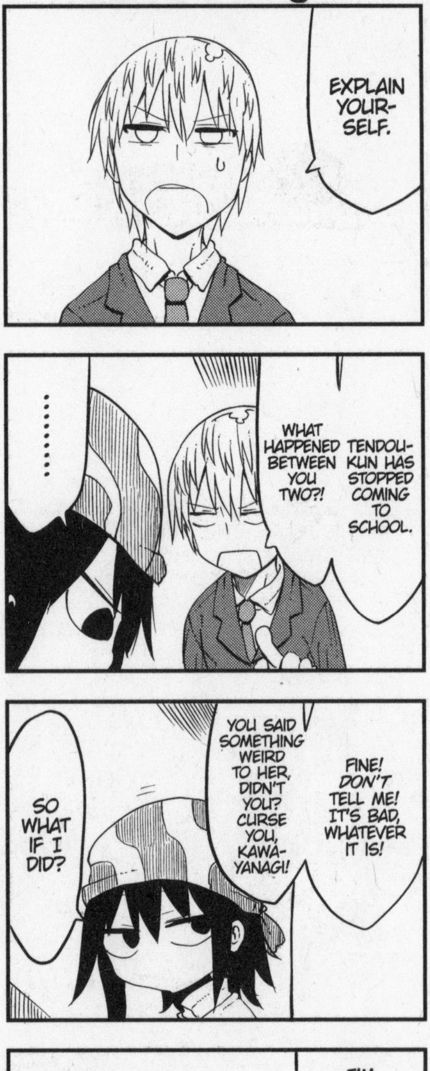
EXPLAIN YOURSELF.
TENDOU-KUN HAS STOPPED COMING TO SCHOOL.
WHAT HAPPENED BETWEEN YOU TWO?!
......
YOU SAID SOMETHING WEIRD TO HER, DIDN'T YOU? CURSE YOU, KAWAYANAGI!
SO WHAT IF I DID?
FINE! *DON'T* TELL ME! IT'S BAD, WHATEVER IT IS!
I'M GOING TO GO CHEER HER UP. AS HER FRIEND, IT'S THE LEAST I CAN DO!
......

Here She Goes Again

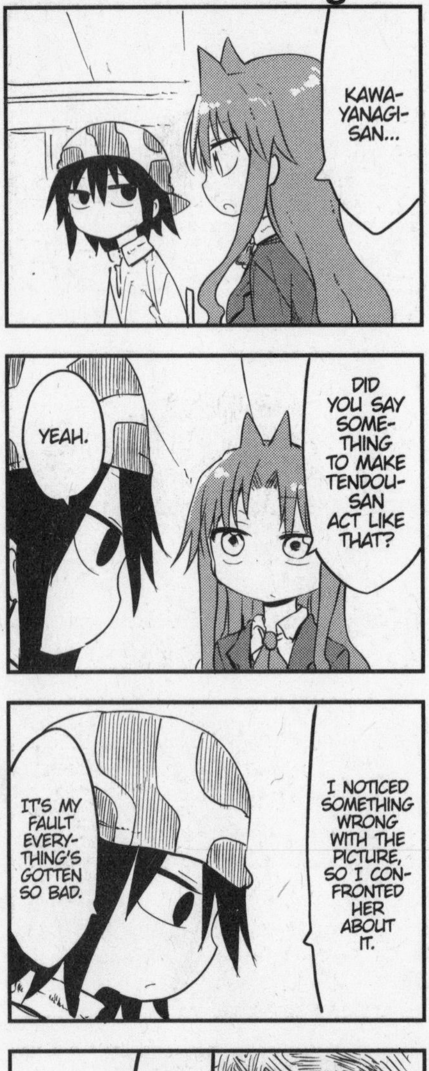
KAWAYANAGI-SAN...
DID YOU SAY SOMETHING TO MAKE TENDOU-SAN ACT LIKE THAT?
YEAH.
I NOTICED SOMETHING WRONG WITH THE PICTURE, SO I CONFRONTED HER ABOUT IT.
IT'S MY FAULT EVERYTHING'S GOTTEN SO BAD.
HEH...
HEH HEH HEH HEH HEH...

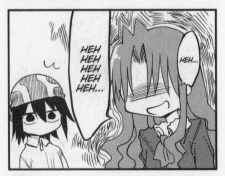

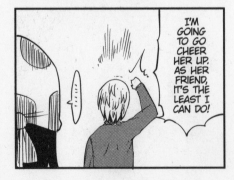

Down to the Depths of Hell

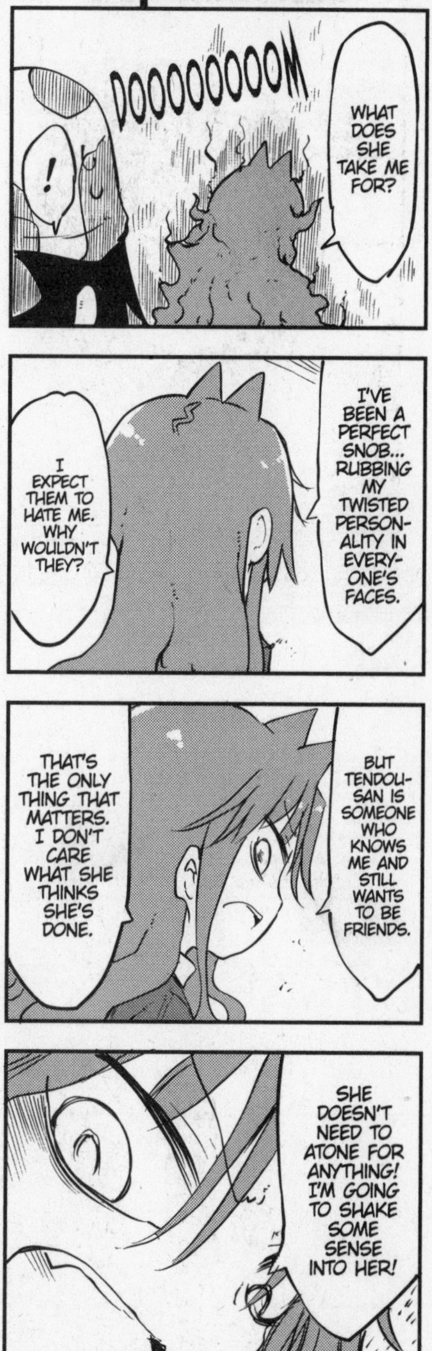
WHAT DOES SHE TAKE ME FOR?
DOOOOOOOOM
!
I'VE BEEN A PERFECT SNOB... RUBBING MY TWISTED PERSONALITY IN EVERYONE'S FACES.
I EXPECT THEM TO HATE ME. WHY WOULDN'T THEY?
BUT TENDOU-SAN IS SOMEONE WHO KNOWS ME AND STILL WANTS TO BE FRIENDS.
THAT'S THE ONLY THING THAT MATTERS. I DON'T CARE WHAT SHE THINKS SHE'S DONE.
SHE DOESN'T NEED TO ATONE FOR ANYTHING! I'M GOING TO SHAKE SOME SENSE INTO HER!

Kawayanagi!

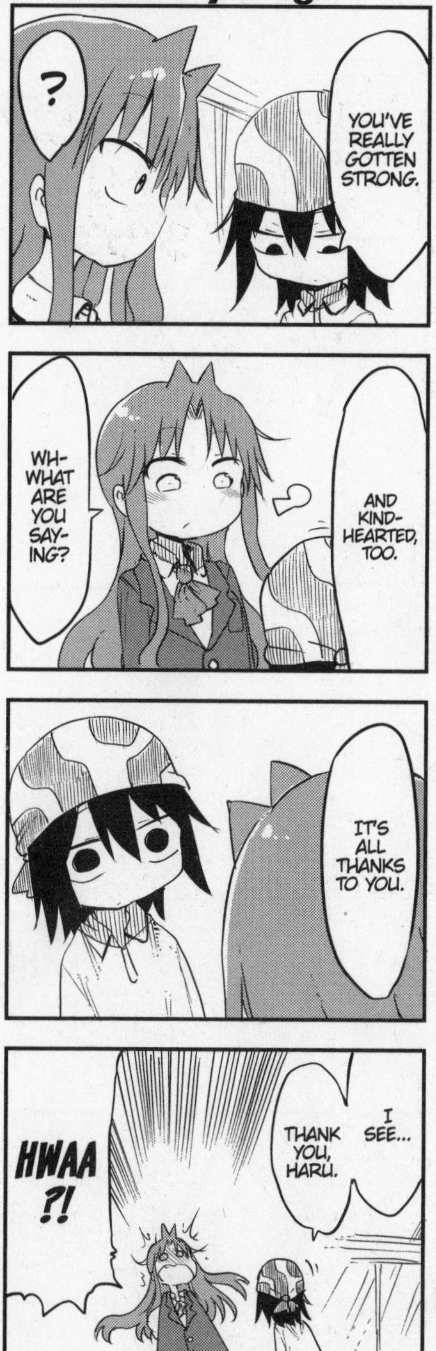
YOU'VE REALLY GOTTEN STRONG.
?
AND KIND-HEARTED, TOO.
WH-WHAT ARE YOU SAYING?
IT'S ALL THANKS TO YOU.
I SEE...
THANK YOU, HARU.
HWAA ?!

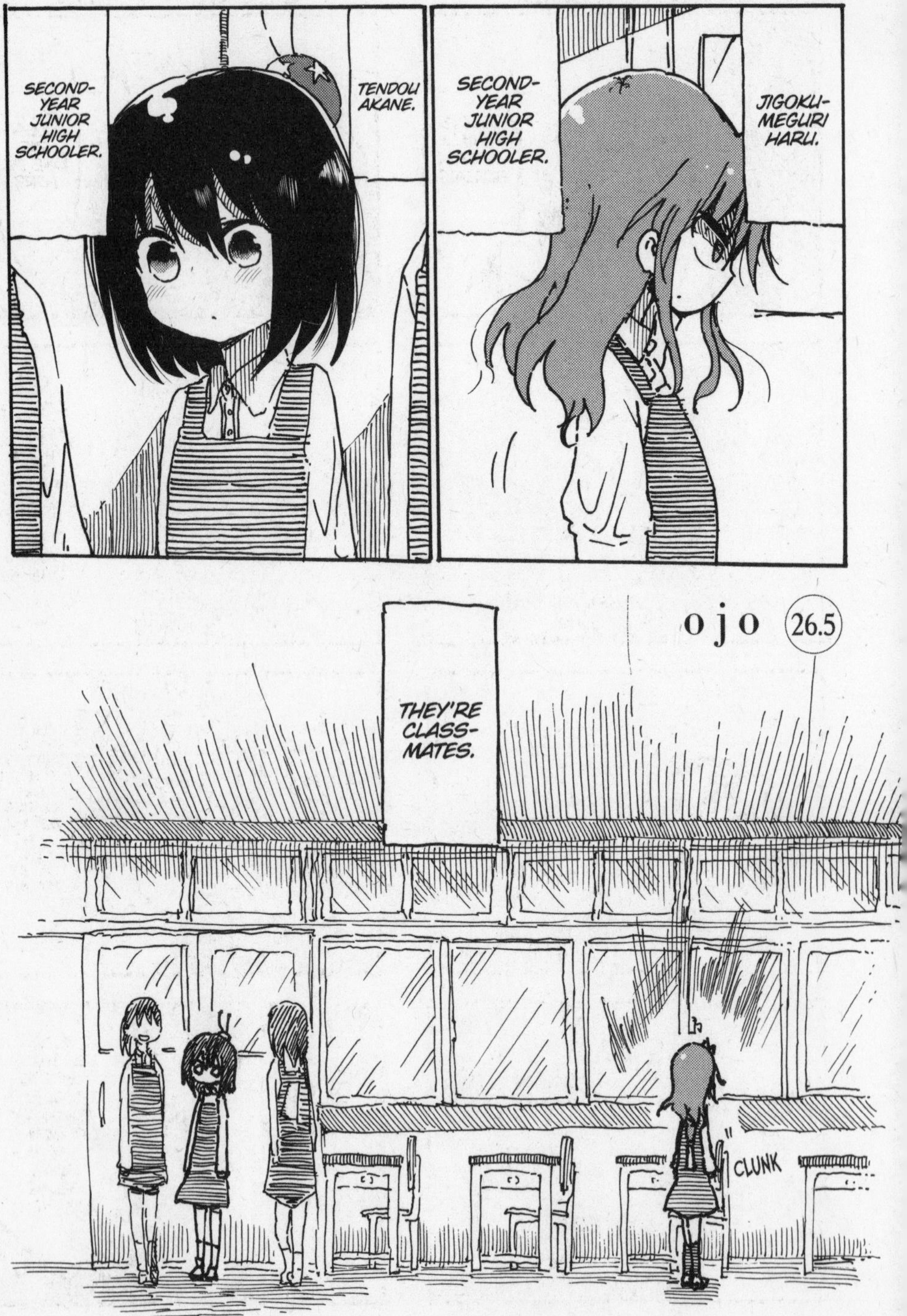
JIGOKU-MEGURI HARU.
SECOND-YEAR JUNIOR HIGH SCHOOLER.
TENDOU AKANE.
SECOND-YEAR JUNIOR HIGH SCHOOLER.
ojo 26.5
THEY'RE CLASS-MATES.
CLUNK

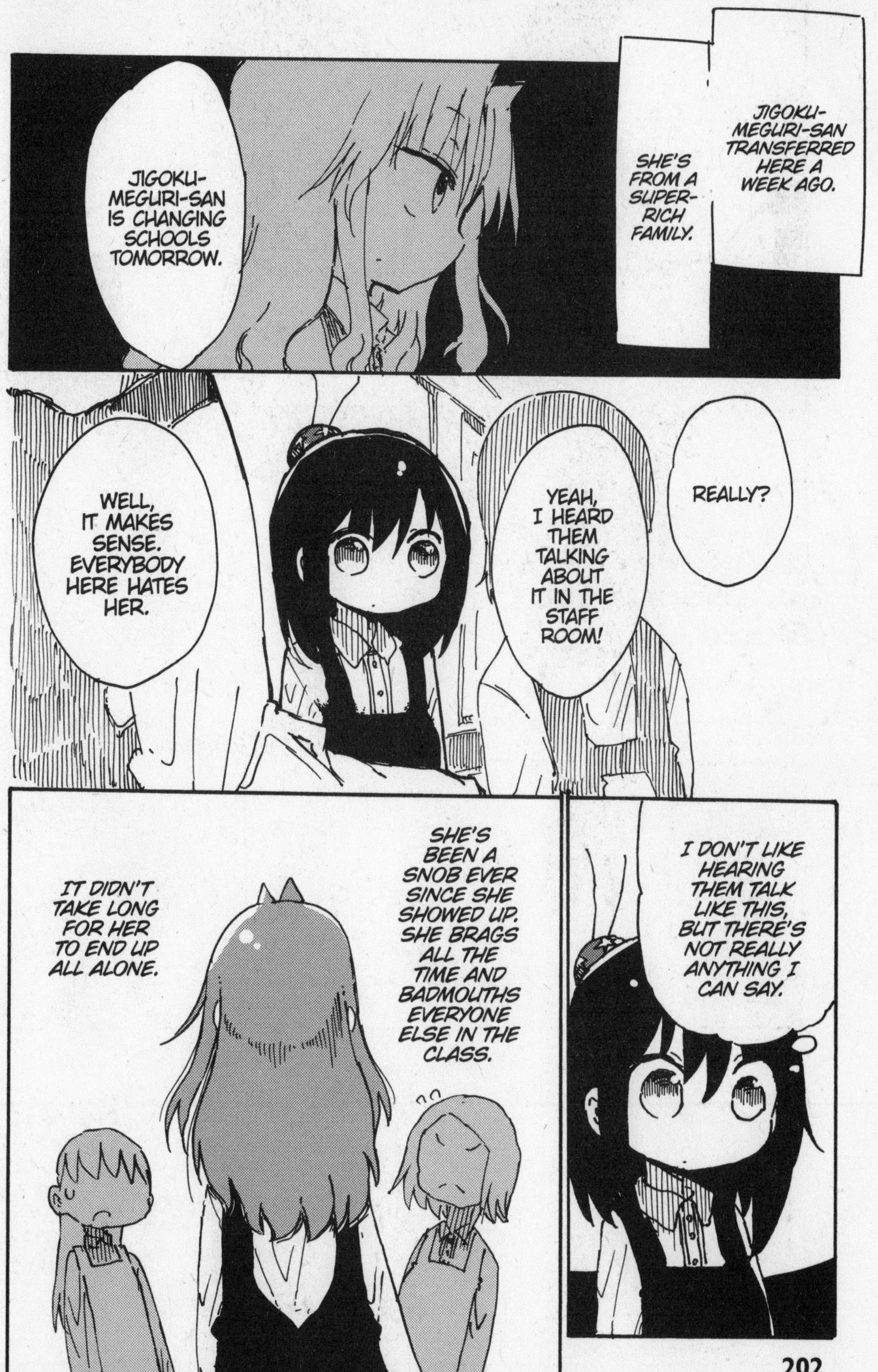
JIGOKU-MEGURI-SAN TRANSFERRED HERE A WEEK AGO.
SHE'S FROM A SUPER-RICH FAMILY.
JIGOKU-MEGURI-SAN IS CHANGING SCHOOLS TOMORROW.
REALLY?
YEAH, I HEARD THEM TALKING ABOUT IT IN THE STAFF ROOM!
WELL, IT MAKES SENSE. EVERYBODY HERE HATES HER.
I DON'T LIKE HEARING THEM TALK LIKE THIS, BUT THERE'S NOT REALLY ANYTHING I CAN SAY.
SHE'S BEEN A SNOB EVER SINCE SHE SHOWED UP. SHE BRAGS ALL THE TIME AND BADMOUTHS EVERYONE ELSE IN THE CLASS.
IT DIDN'T TAKE LONG FOR HER TO END UP ALL ALONE.

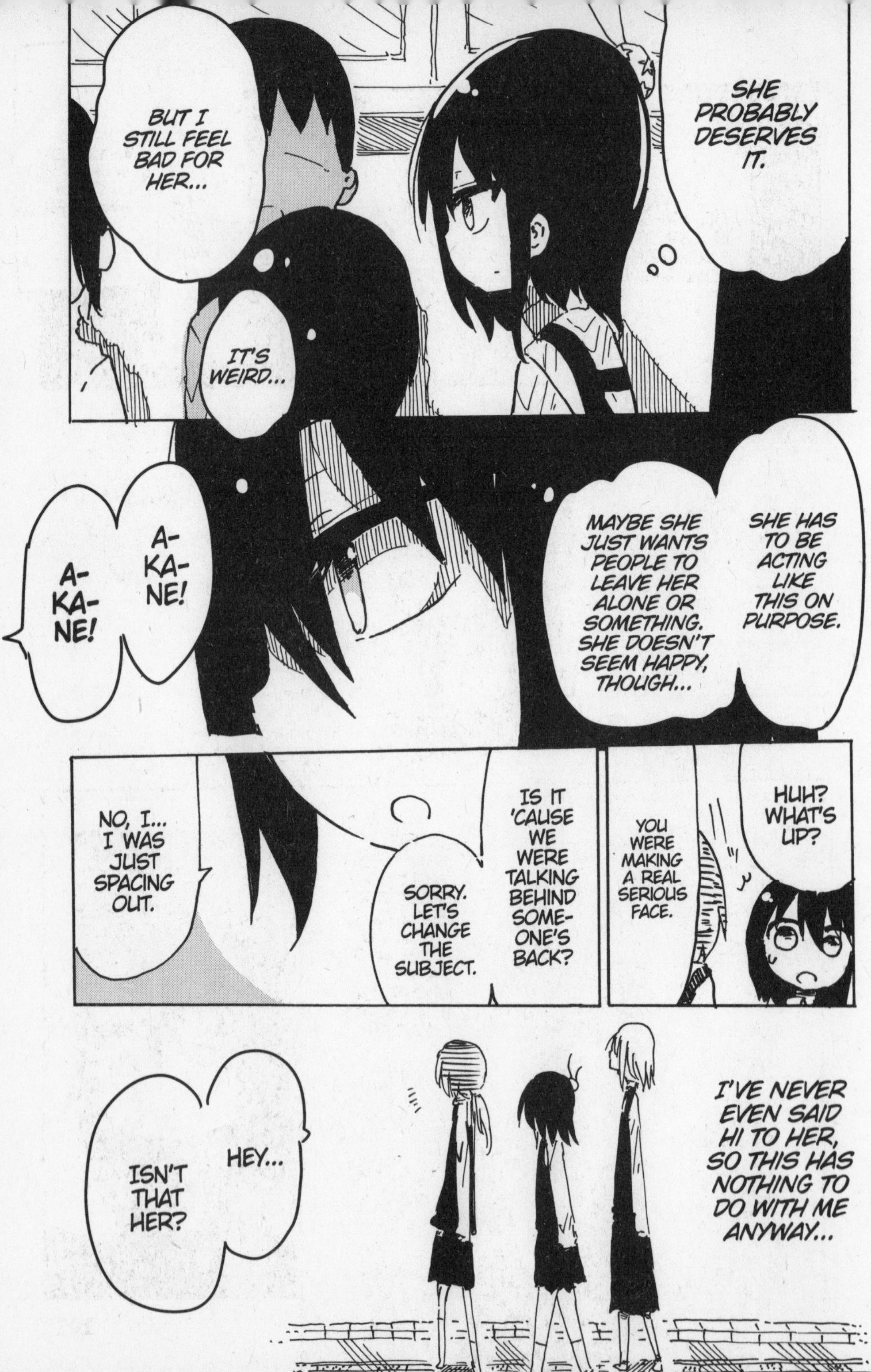
SHE PROBABLY DESERVES IT.
BUT I STILL FEEL BAD FOR HER...
IT'S WEIRD...
SHE HAS TO BE ACTING LIKE THIS ON PURPOSE.
MAYBE SHE JUST WANTS PEOPLE TO LEAVE HER ALONE OR SOMETHING. SHE DOESN'T SEEM HAPPY, THOUGH...
A-KANE!
A-KA-NE!
HUH? WHAT'S UP?
YOU WERE MAKING A REAL SERIOUS FACE.
IS IT 'CAUSE WE WERE TALKING BEHIND SOME-ONE'S BACK?
SORRY. LET'S CHANGE THE SUBJECT.
NO, I... I WAS JUST SPACING OUT.
I'VE NEVER EVEN SAID HI TO HER, SO THIS HAS NOTHING TO DO WITH ME ANYWAY...
HEY...
ISN'T THAT HER?

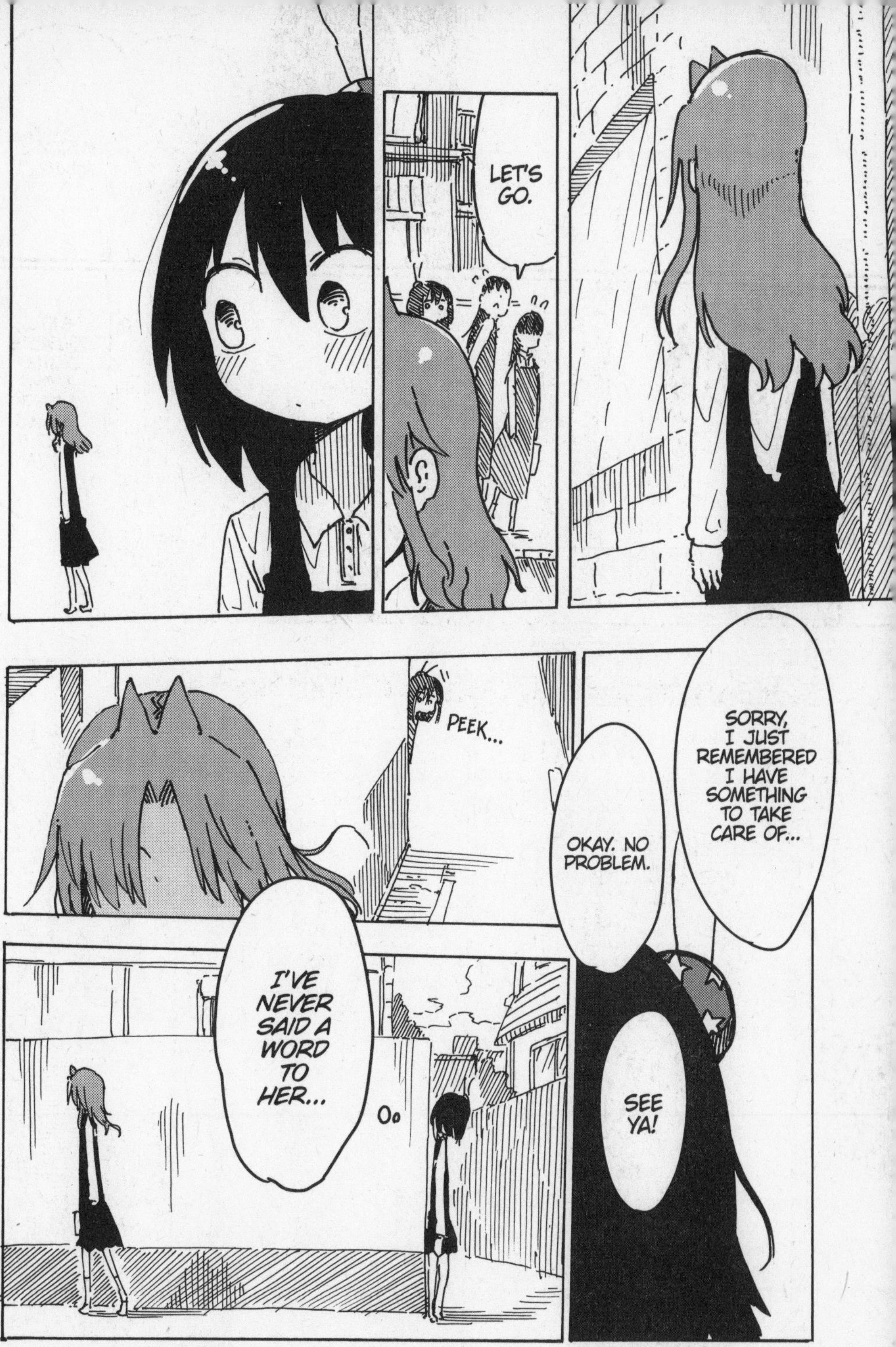
LET'S GO.
SORRY, I JUST REMEMBERED I HAVE SOMETHING TO TAKE CARE OF...
OKAY. NO PROBLEM.
SEE YA!
PEEK...
I'VE NEVER SAID A WORD TO HER...
Oo

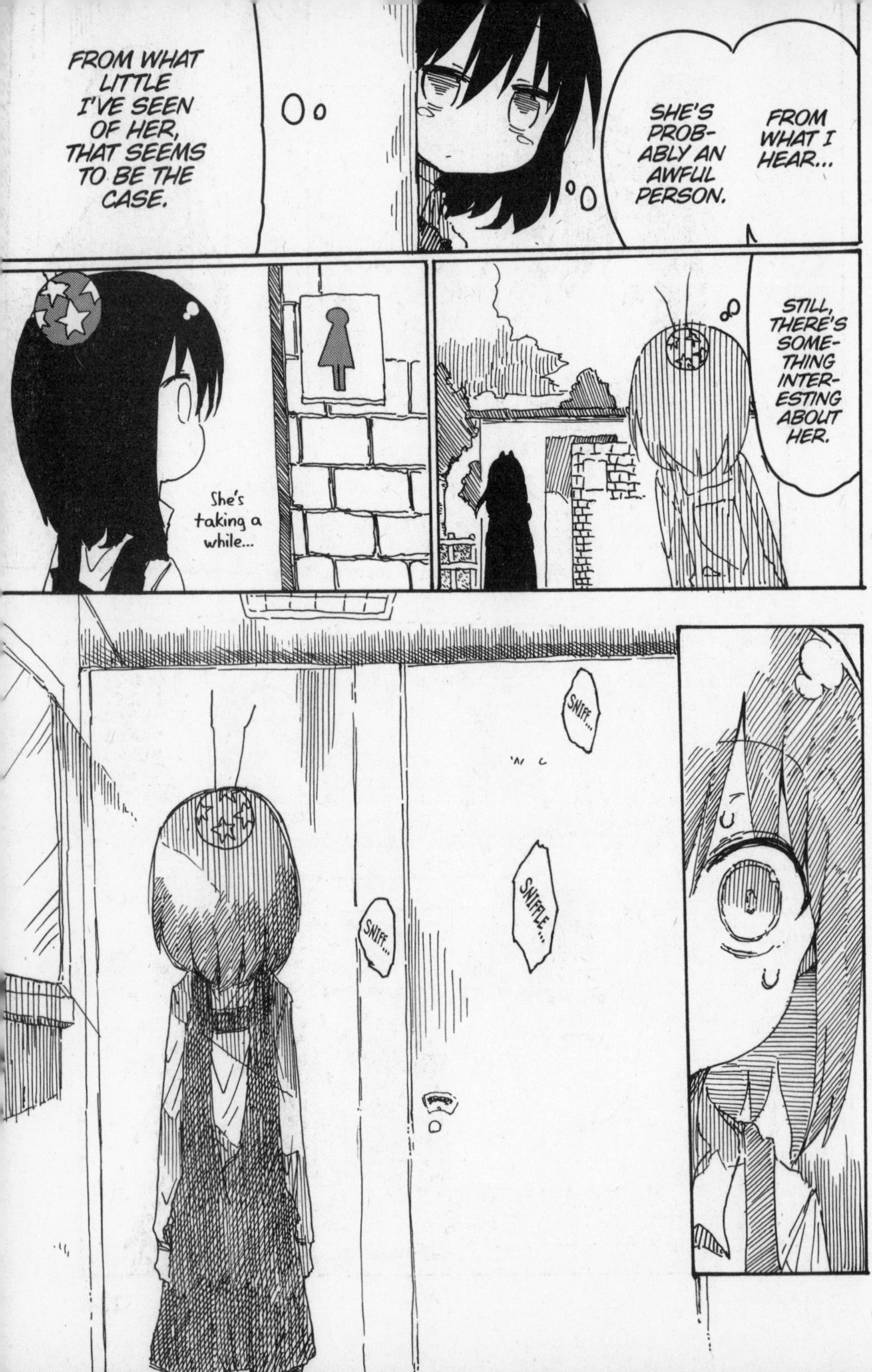
FROM WHAT I HEAR...
SHE'S PROB-ABLY AN AWFUL PERSON.
FROM WHAT LITTLE I'VE SEEN OF HER, THAT SEEMS TO BE THE CASE.
STILL, THERE'S SOME-THING INTER-ESTING ABOUT HER.
She's taking a while...
SNIFF...
SNIFFLE...
SNIFF...

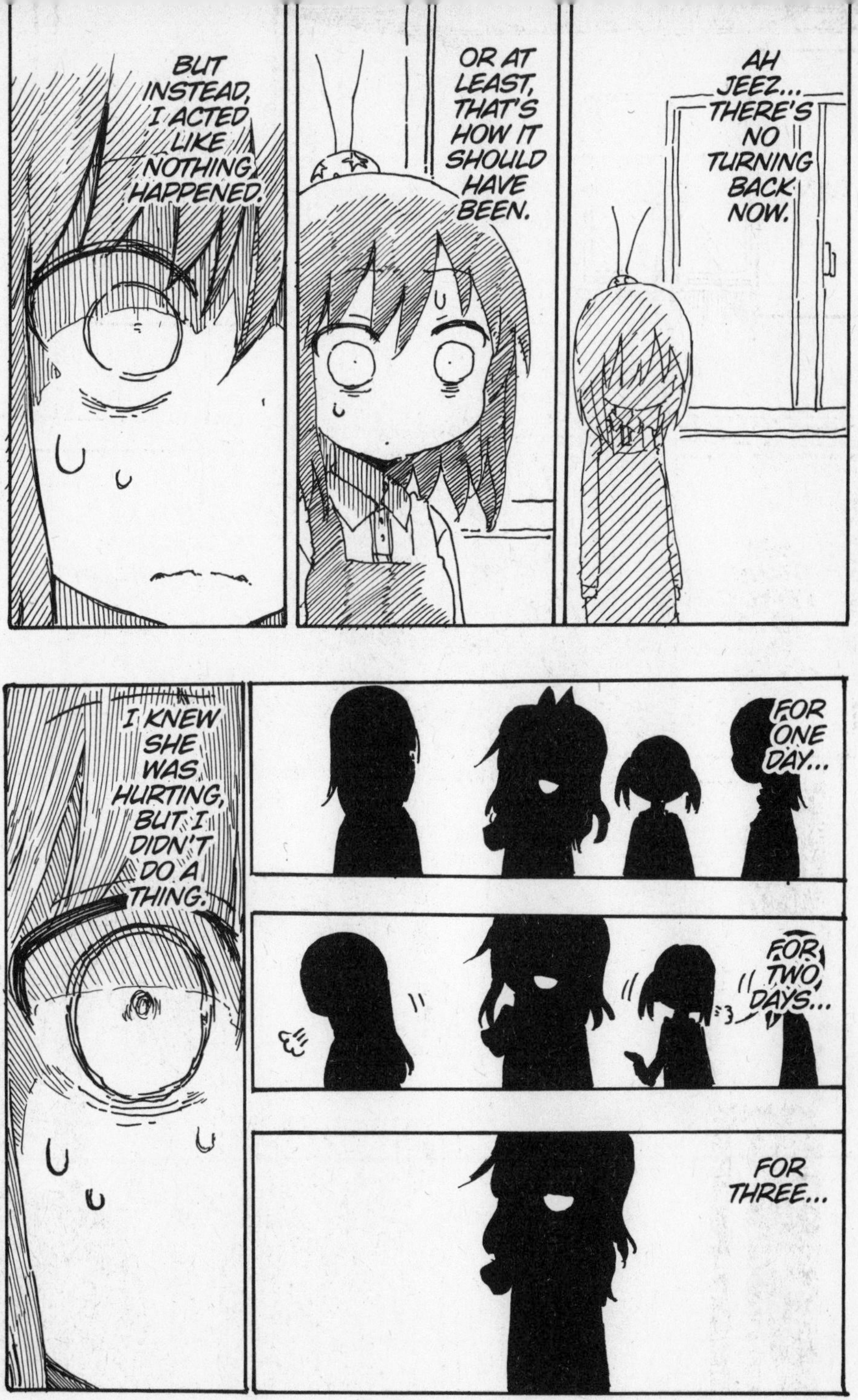
AH JEEZ... THERE'S NO TURNING BACK NOW.
OR AT LEAST, THAT'S HOW IT SHOULD HAVE BEEN.
BUT INSTEAD, I ACTED LIKE NOTHING HAPPENED.
FOR ONE DAY...
FOR TWO DAYS...
FOR THREE...
I KNEW SHE WAS HURTING, BUT I DIDN'T DO A THING.

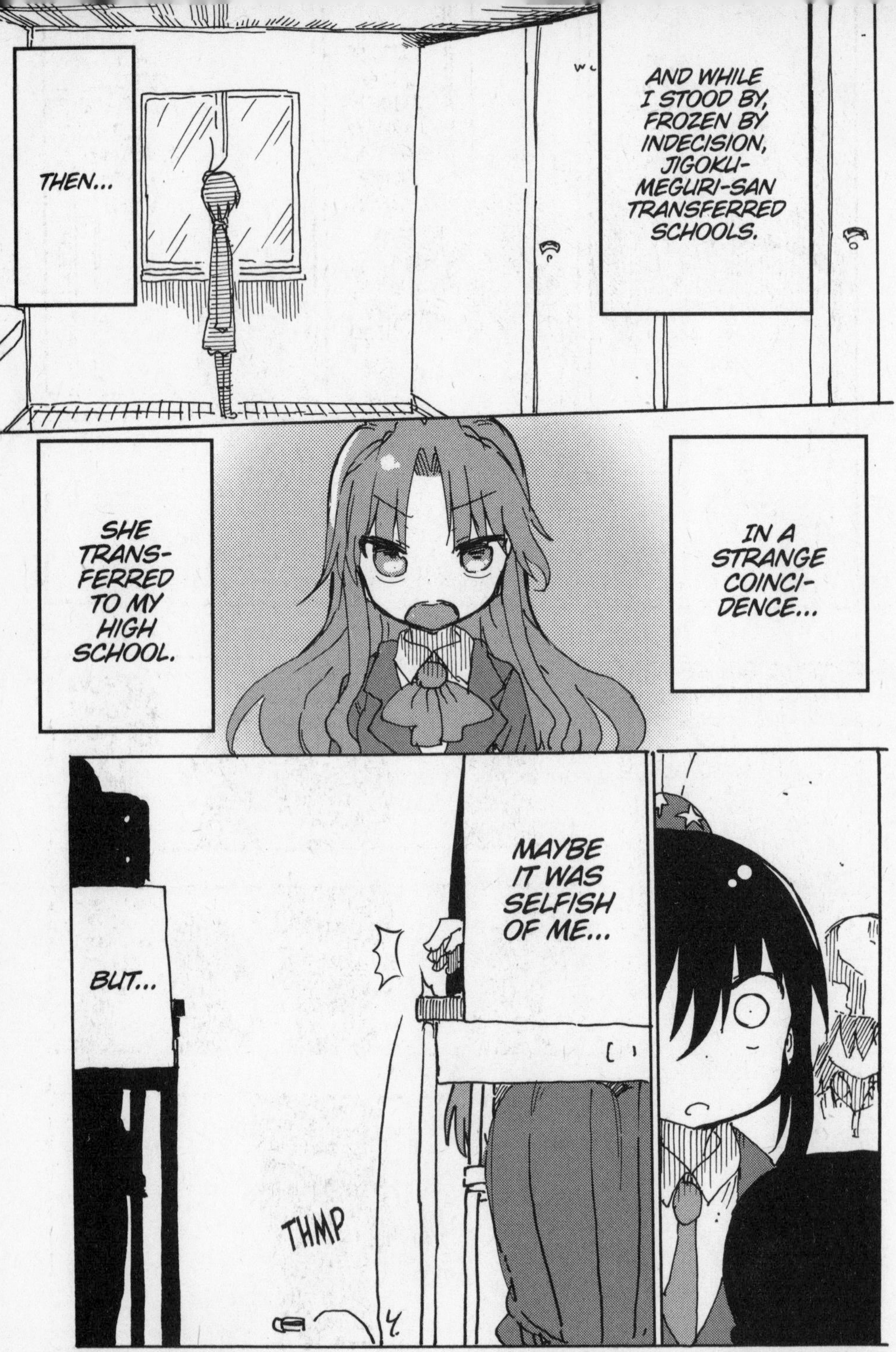
AND WHILE I STOOD BY, FROZEN BY INDECISION, JIGOKU-MEGURI-SAN TRANSFERRED SCHOOLS.
THEN...
IN A STRANGE COINCIDENCE...
SHE TRANSFERRED TO MY HIGH SCHOOL.
MAYBE IT WAS SELFISH OF ME...
BUT...
THMP

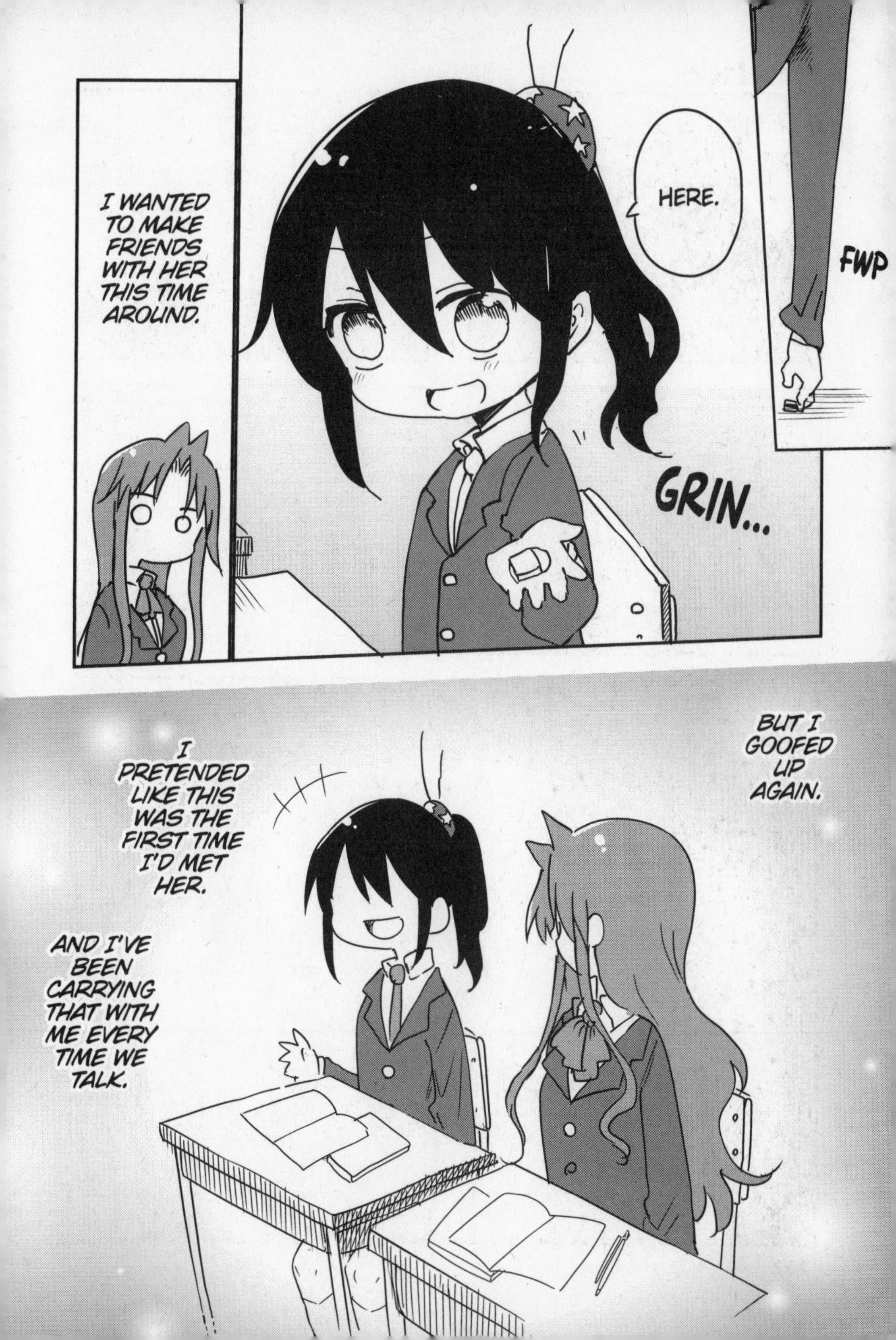
FWP
HERE.
GRIN...
I WANTED TO MAKE FRIENDS WITH HER THIS TIME AROUND.
BUT I GOOFED UP AGAIN.
I PRETENDED LIKE THIS WAS THE FIRST TIME I'D MET HER.
AND I'VE BEEN CARRYING THAT WITH ME EVERY TIME WE TALK.

He's Here

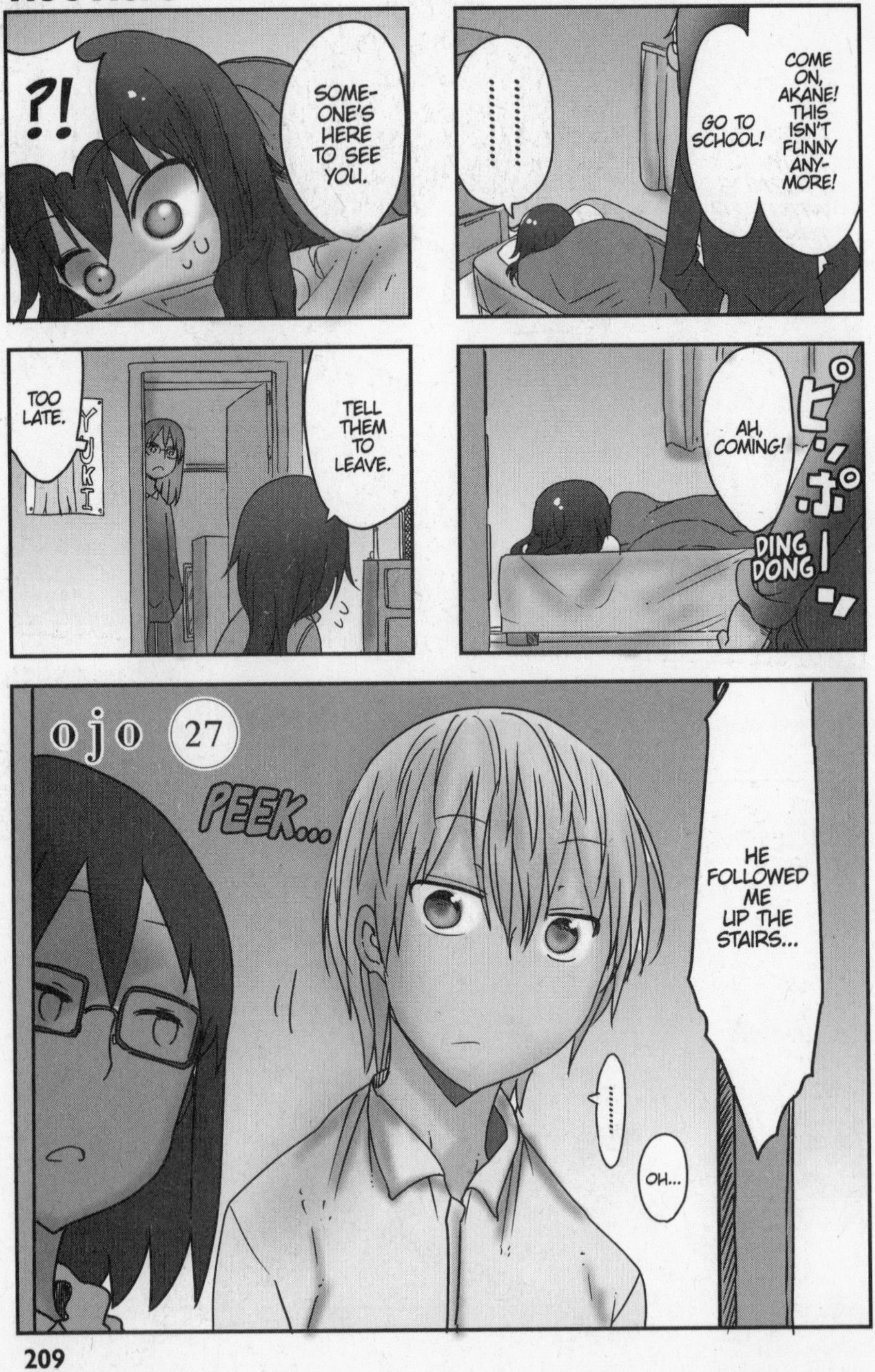
COME ON, AKANE! THIS ISN'T FUNNY ANYMORE!
GO TO SCHOOL!
......
?!
SOME-ONE'S HERE TO SEE YOU.
DING DONG!
AH, COMING!
TELL THEM TO LEAVE.
TOO LATE.
YUKI
ojo 27
HE FOLLOWED ME UP THE STAIRS...
PEEK...
......
OH...

Same as Always

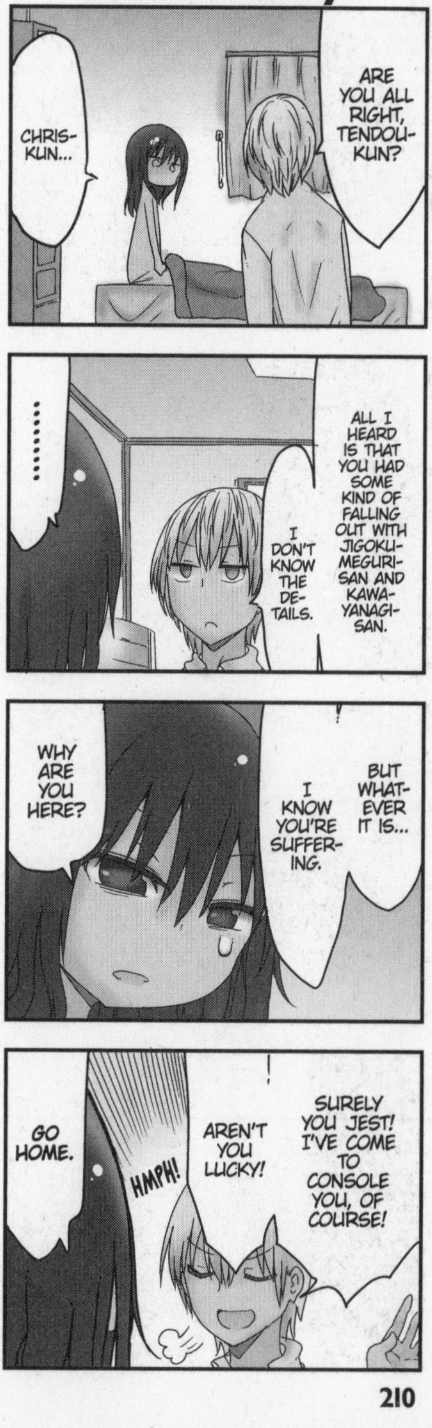

ARE YOU ALL RIGHT, TENDOU-KUN?
CHRIS-KUN...
ALL I HEARD IS THAT YOU HAD SOME KIND OF FALLING OUT WITH JIGOKU-MEGURI-SAN AND KAWA-YANAGI-SAN.
I DON'T KNOW THE DE-TAILS.
......
BUT WHAT-EVER IT IS...
I KNOW YOU'RE SUFFER-ING.
WHY ARE YOU HERE?
SURELY YOU JEST! I'VE COME TO CONSOLE YOU, OF COURSE!
AREN'T YOU LUCKY!
HMPH!
GO HOME.

Something Important

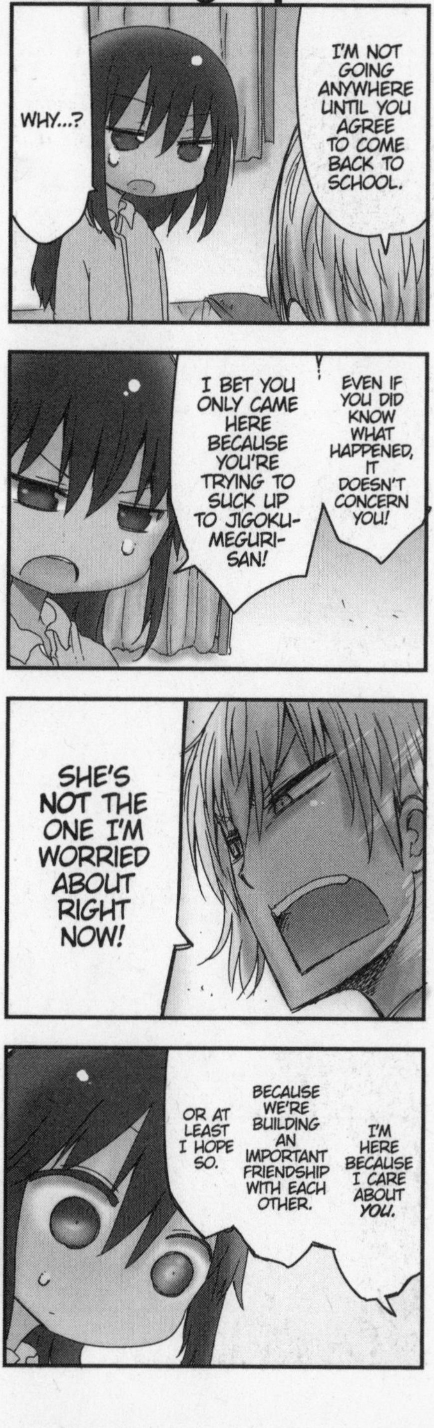

I'M NOT GOING ANYWHERE UNTIL YOU AGREE TO COME BACK TO SCHOOL.
WHY...?
EVEN IF YOU DID KNOW WHAT HAPPENED, IT DOESN'T CONCERN YOU!
I BET YOU ONLY CAME HERE BECAUSE YOU'RE TRYING TO SUCK UP TO JIGOKU-MEGURI-SAN!
SHE'S NOT THE ONE I'M WORRIED ABOUT RIGHT NOW!
I'M HERE BECAUSE I CARE ABOUT *YOU*.
BECAUSE WE'RE BUILDING AN IMPORTANT FRIENDSHIP WITH EACH OTHER.
OR AT LEAST I HOPE SO.

The Things You Should See

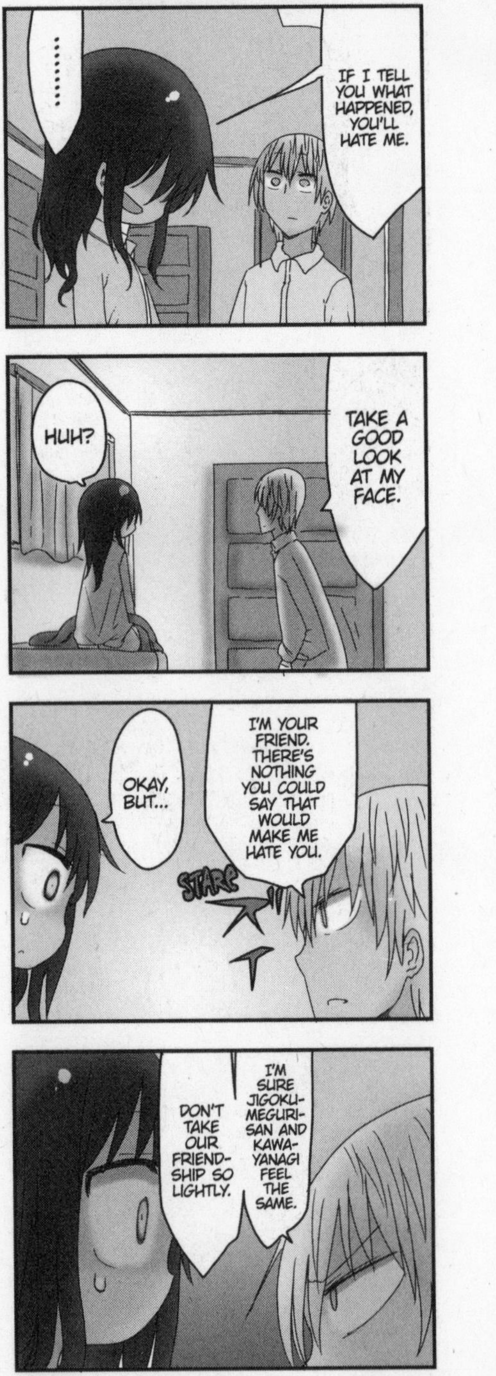
IF I TELL YOU WHAT HAPPENED, YOU'LL HATE ME.
......
TAKE A GOOD LOOK AT MY FACE.
HUH?
I'M YOUR FRIEND. THERE'S NOTHING YOU COULD SAY THAT WOULD MAKE ME HATE YOU.
OKAY, BUT...
STARE
I'M SURE JIGOKUMEGURI-SAN AND KAWAYANAGI FEEL THE SAME.
DON'T TAKE OUR FRIENDSHIP SO LIGHTLY.

Accept Their Kindness or Else

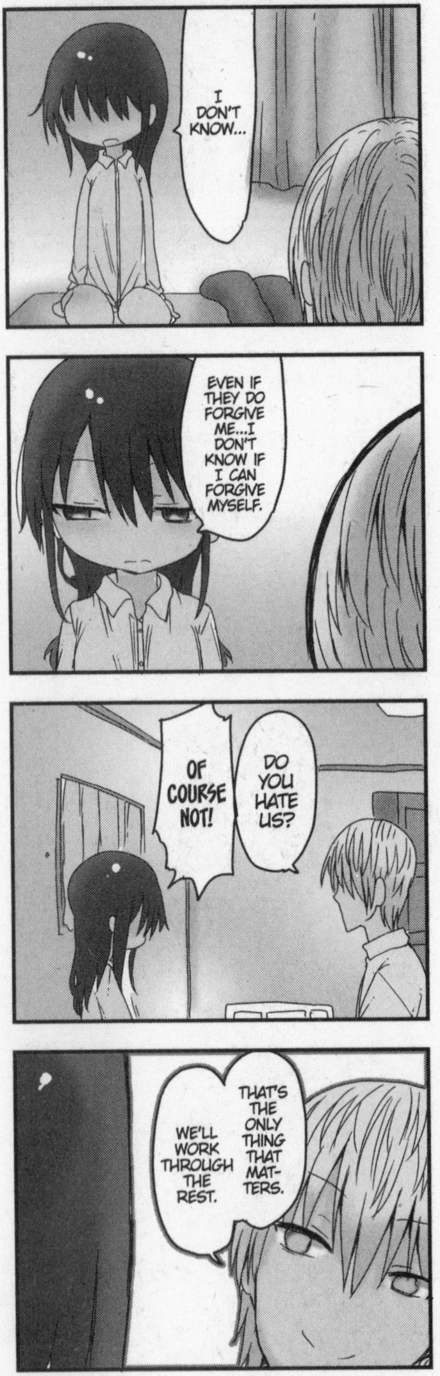
I DON'T KNOW...
EVEN IF THEY DO FORGIVE ME...I DON'T KNOW IF I CAN FORGIVE MYSELF.
DO YOU HATE US?
OF COURSE NOT!
THAT'S THE ONLY THING THAT MATTERS.
WE'LL WORK THROUGH THE REST.

Monologue

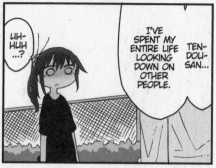

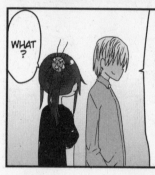

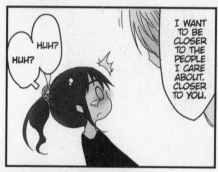

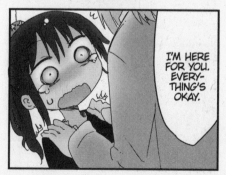

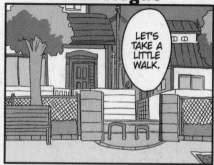

LET'S TAKE A LITTLE WALK.
I...
I DON'T KNOW IF I CAN FACE JIGOKU-MEGURI-SAN AGAIN.
I TURNED MY BACK ON HER, JUST LIKE BEFORE...

Huh?

TEN-DOU-SAN...
I'VE SPENT MY ENTIRE LIFE LOOKING DOWN ON OTHER PEOPLE.
UH-HUH...?
BUT EVER SINCE I MOVED TO JAPAN, I'VE STARTED MAKING FRIENDS. I'M TIRED OF PUSHING PEOPLE AWAY.
WHAT?
I WANT TO BE CLOSER TO THE PEOPLE I CARE ABOUT. CLOSER TO YOU.
HUH?
HUH?
I'M HERE FOR YOU. EVERY-THING'S OKAY.

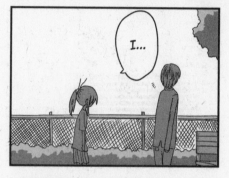

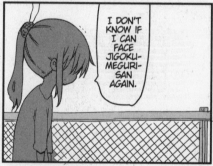

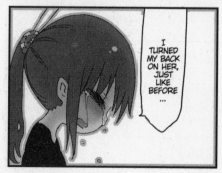

Obviously

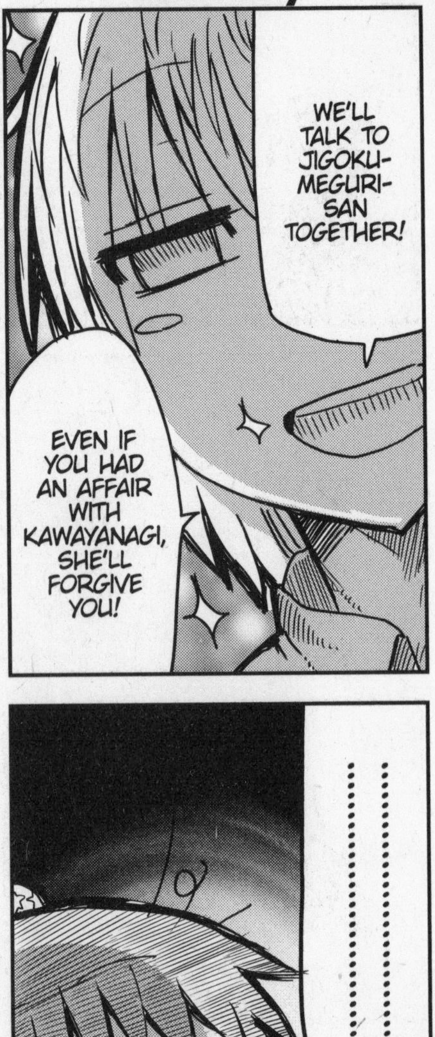
WE'LL TALK TO JIGOKU-MEGURI-SAN TOGETHER!
EVEN IF YOU HAD AN AFFAIR WITH KAWAYANAGI, SHE'LL FORGIVE YOU!
......
WHAT?

Just like Always

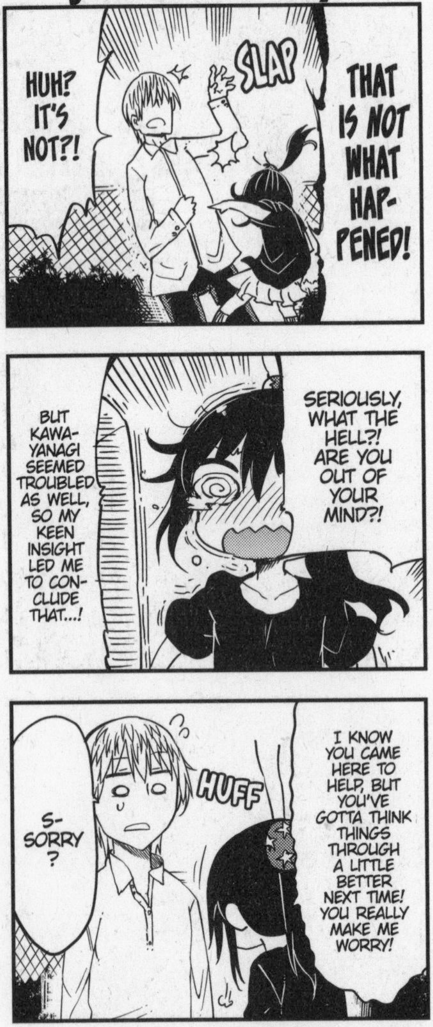
THAT IS NOT WHAT HAP-PENED!
SLAP
HUH? IT'S NOT?!
SERIOUSLY, WHAT THE HELL?! ARE YOU OUT OF YOUR MIND?!
BUT KAWA-YANAGI SEEMED TROUBLED AS WELL, SO MY KEEN INSIGHT LED ME TO CON-CLUDE THAT...!
I KNOW YOU CAME HERE TO HELP, BUT YOU'VE GOTTA THINK THINGS THROUGH A LITTLE BETTER NEXT TIME! YOU REALLY MAKE ME WORRY!
HUFF
S-SORRY?
NO... THANK YOU...

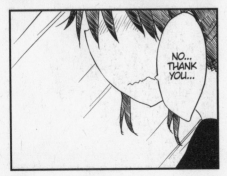

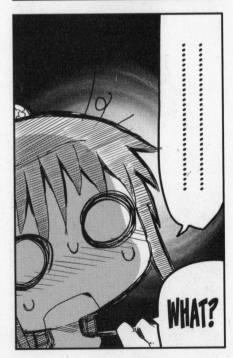

What Are Your True Feelings?

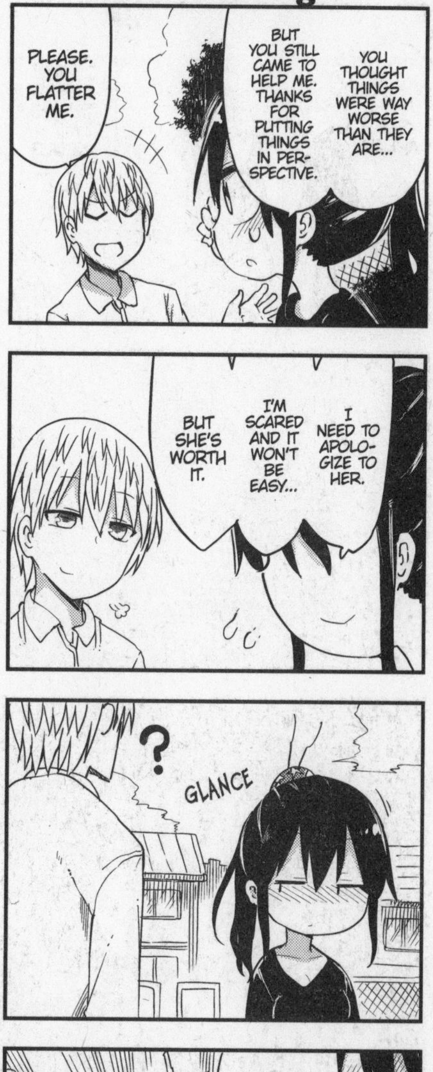

YOU THOUGHT THINGS WERE WAY WORSE THAN THEY ARE...
BUT YOU STILL CAME TO HELP ME. THANKS FOR PUTTING THINGS IN PERSPECTIVE.
PLEASE. YOU FLATTER ME.
I NEED TO APOLOGIZE TO HER.
I'M SCARED AND IT WON'T BE EASY...
BUT SHE'S WORTH IT.
GLANCE
I GUESS IT WAS A COMPLIMENT THIS TIME...
SCREEECH

The Real Thing

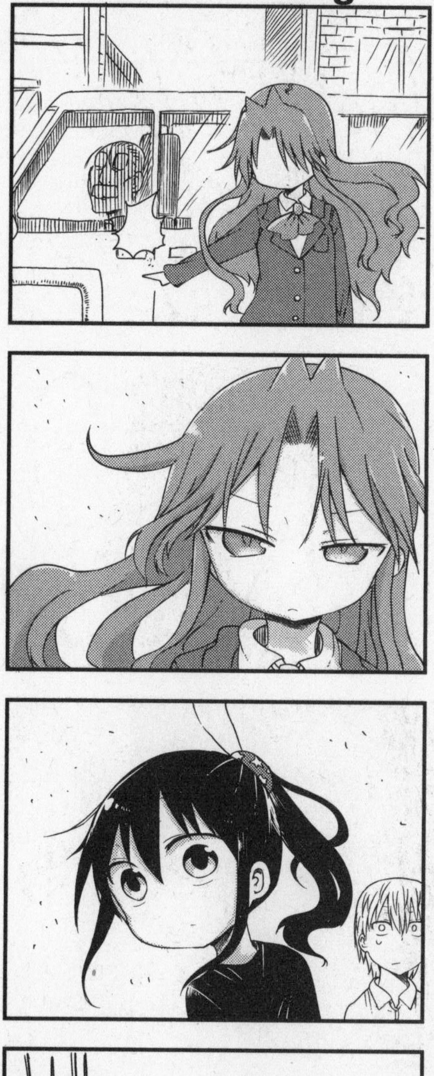

HWOOOO

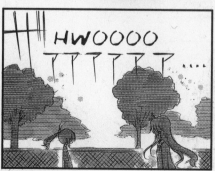

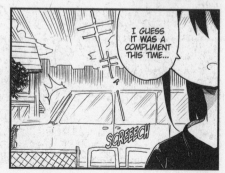

Conflicting Emotions

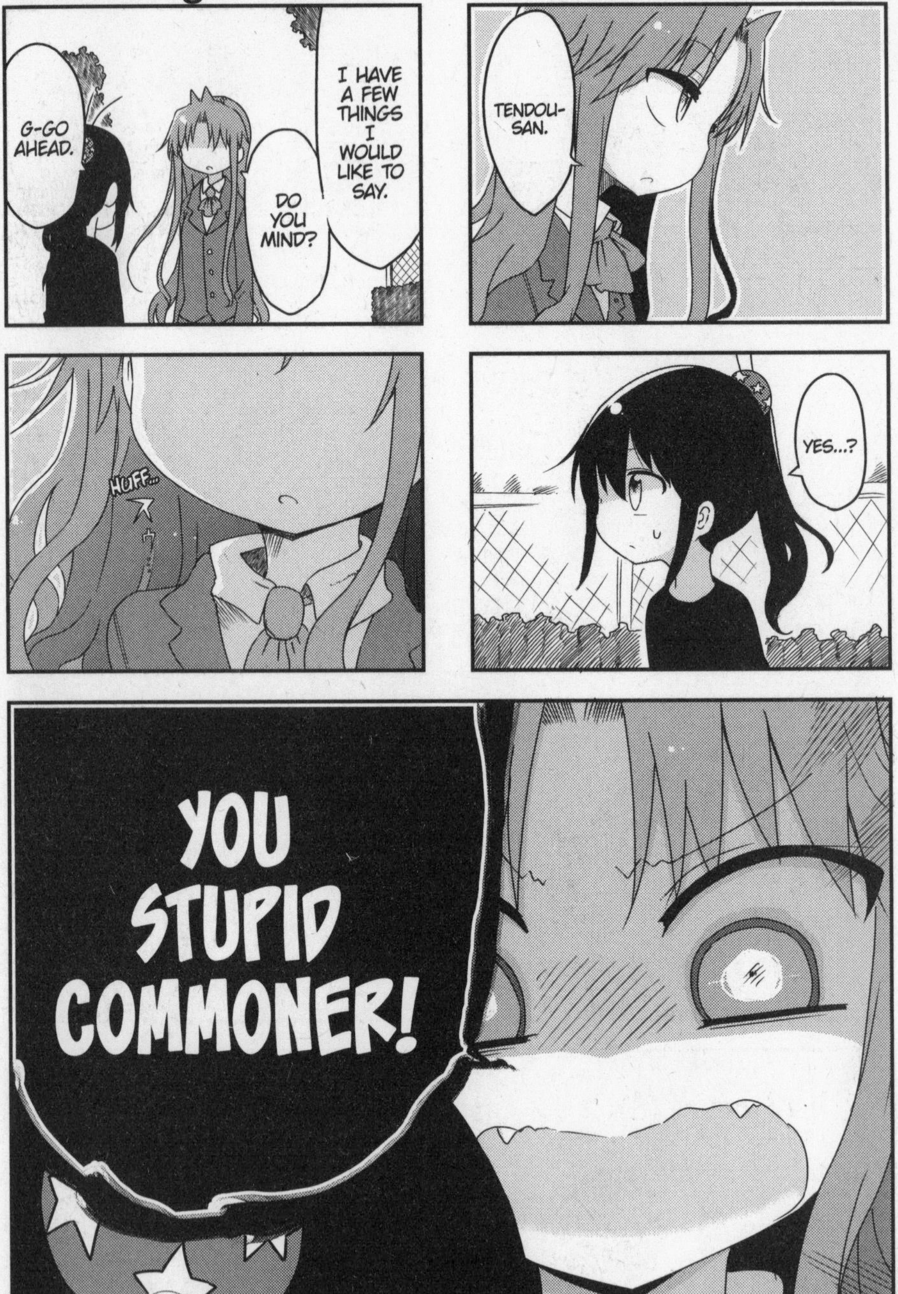
TENDOU-SAN.
I HAVE A FEW THINGS I WOULD LIKE TO SAY.
DO YOU MIND?
G-GO AHEAD.
YES...?
HUFF...
YOU STUPID COMMONER!
ojo 28

My Feelings

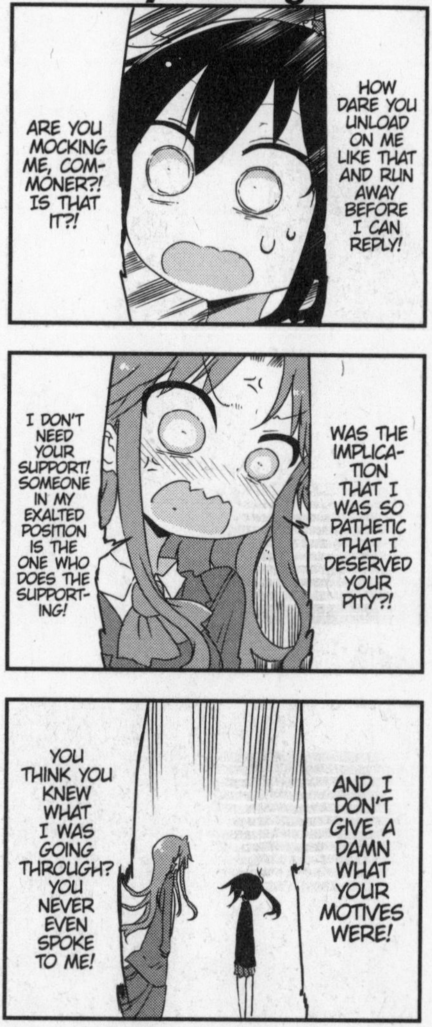
HOW DARE YOU UNLOAD ON ME LIKE THAT AND RUN AWAY BEFORE I CAN REPLY!
ARE YOU MOCKING ME, COM-MONER?! IS THAT IT?!
WAS THE IMPLICA-TION THAT I WAS SO PATHETIC THAT I DESERVED YOUR PITY?!
I DON'T NEED YOUR SUPPORT! SOMEONE IN MY EXALTED POSITION IS THE ONE WHO DOES THE SUPPORT-ING!
AND I DON'T GIVE A DAMN WHAT YOUR MOTIVES WERE!
YOU THINK YOU KNEW WHAT I WAS GOING THROUGH? YOU NEVER EVEN SPOKE TO ME!
I USED TO BE COM-PLETELY ALONE, TRUE...
BUT I WAS ALONE BECAUSE I WANTED TO BE! I DON'T NEED YOU FEELING GUILTY OVER SOMETHING THAT NEVER CONCERNED YOU IN THE FIRST PLACE!!
AH, ACTU-ALLY I...
?!
THMP

My Feelings 2

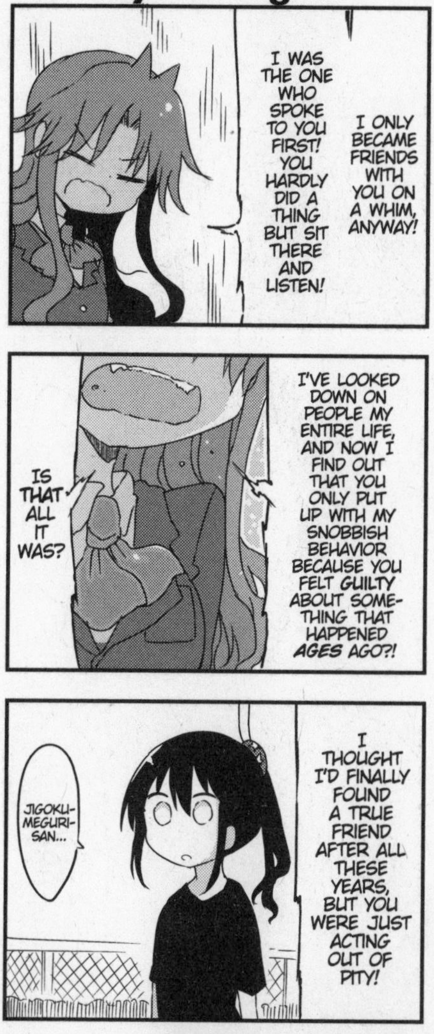
I ONLY BECAME FRIENDS WITH YOU ON A WHIM, ANYWAY!
I WAS THE ONE WHO SPOKE TO YOU FIRST! YOU HARDLY DID A THING BUT SIT THERE AND LISTEN!
I'VE LOOKED DOWN ON PEOPLE MY ENTIRE LIFE, AND NOW I FIND OUT THAT YOU ONLY PUT UP WITH MY SNOBBISH BEHAVIOR BECAUSE YOU FELT GUILTY ABOUT SOME-THING THAT HAPPENED AGES AGO?!
IS THAT ALL IT WAS?
I THOUGHT I'D FINALLY FOUND A TRUE FRIEND AFTER ALL THESE YEARS, BUT YOU WERE JUST ACTING OUT OF PITY!
JIGOKU-MEGURI-SAN...
I WASN'T "PUTTING UP" WITH YOU AT ALL...

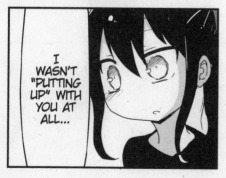

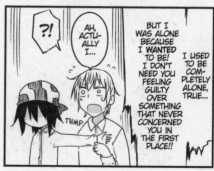

Their Feelings

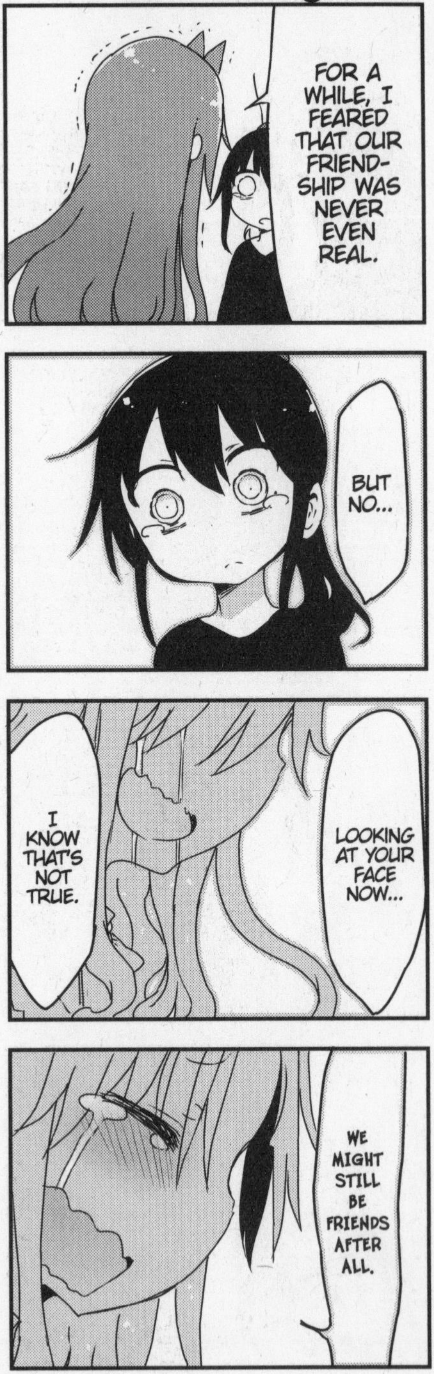
FOR A WHILE, I FEARED THAT OUR FRIEND-SHIP WAS NEVER EVEN REAL.
BUT NO...
LOOKING AT YOUR FACE NOW...
I KNOW THAT'S NOT TRUE.
WE MIGHT STILL BE FRIENDS AFTER ALL.

Soaked in Tears

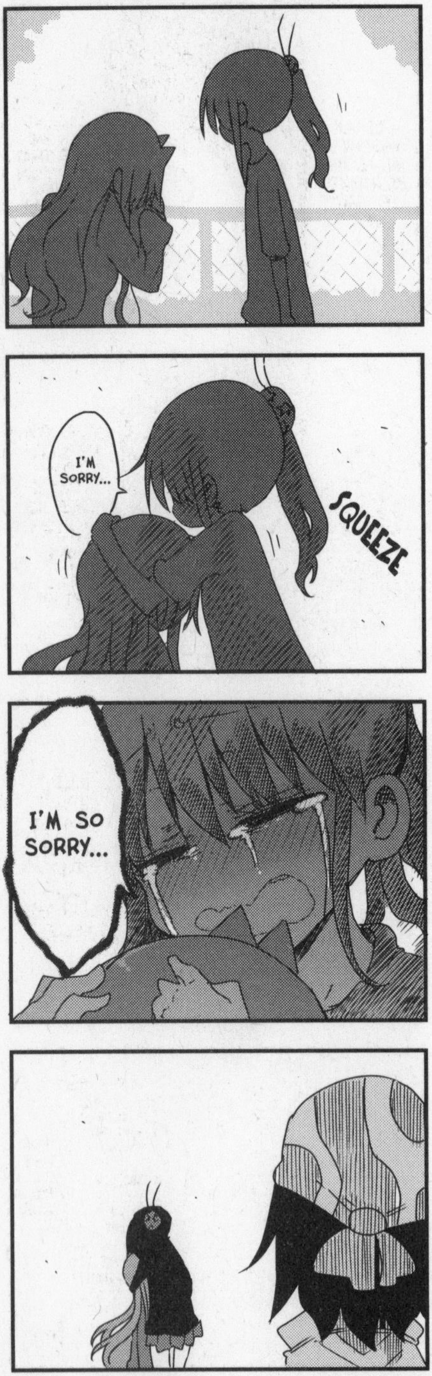
I'M SORRY...
SQUEEZE
I'M SO SORRY...

The Real MVP

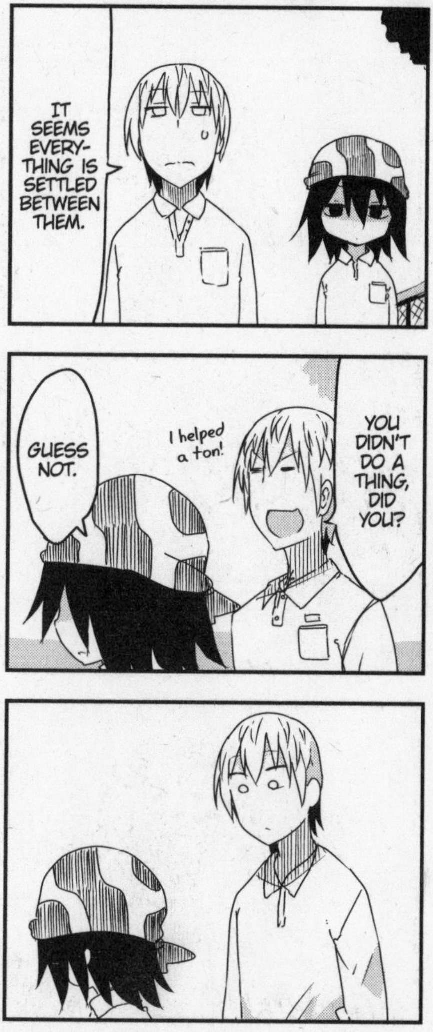
IT SEEMS EVERYTHING IS SETTLED BETWEEN THEM.
YOU DIDN'T DO A THING, DID YOU?
I helped a ton!
GUESS NOT.
BUT I FEEL LIKE THINGS WOULDN'T HAVE WORKED OUT THIS WAY WITHOUT YOU.
Let's make sure this doesn't happen again.
OKAY.

Sorry, but Not with You

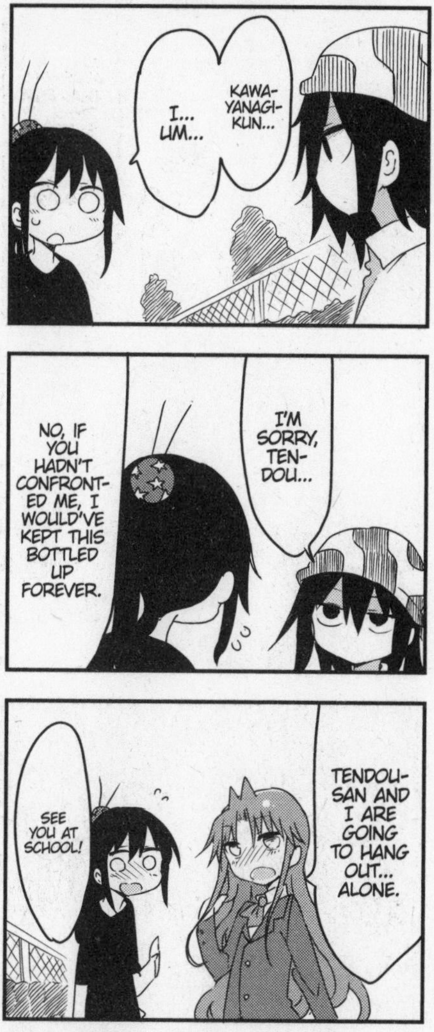
KAWA-YANAGI-KUN...
I... UM...
I'M SORRY, TEN-DOU...
NO, IF YOU HADN'T CONFRONTED ME, I WOULD'VE KEPT THIS BOTTLED UP FOREVER.
TENDOU-SAN AND I ARE GOING TO HANG OUT... ALONE.
SEE YOU AT SCHOOL!
YOU WANT TO HANG OUT?
I'M GOING HOME.

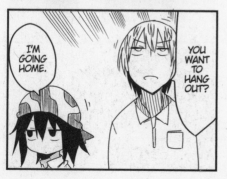

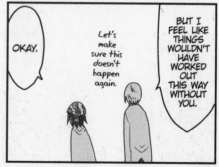

Time to Think

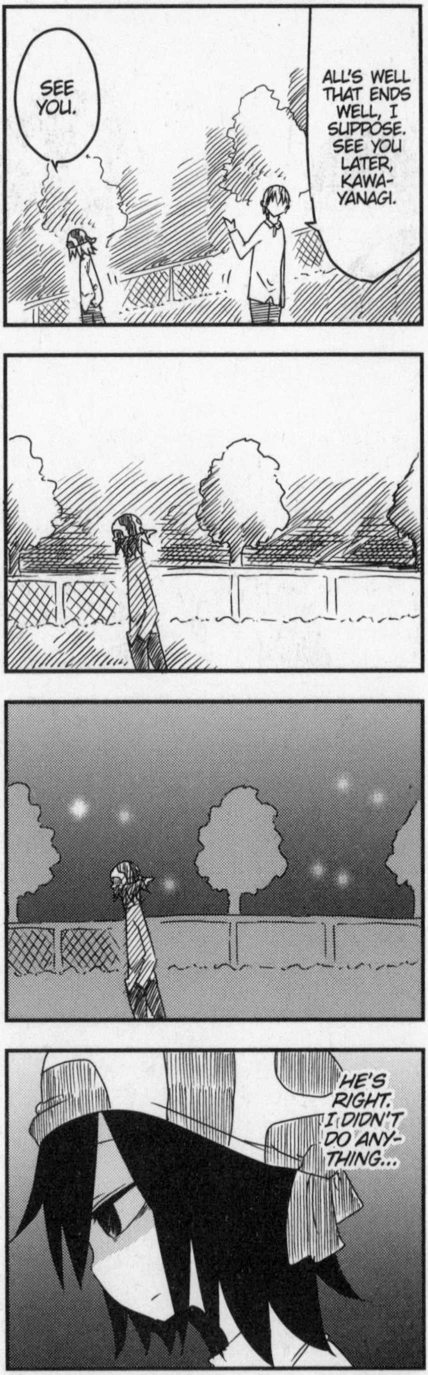
ALL'S WELL THAT ENDS WELL, I SUPPOSE. SEE YOU LATER, KAWA-YANAGI.
SEE YOU.
HE'S RIGHT. I DIDN'T DO ANY-THING...

Boyfriend and Girlfriend

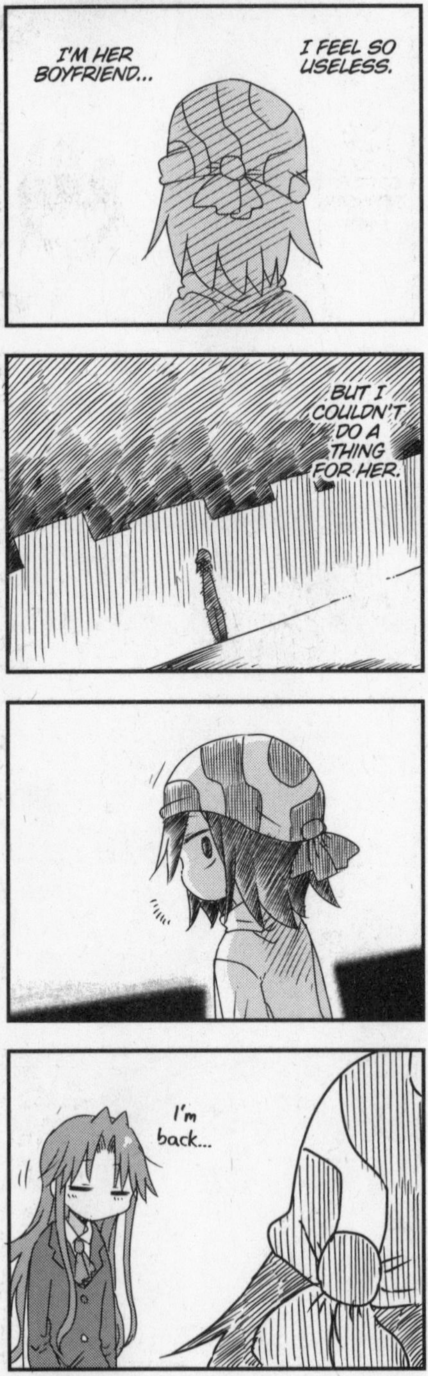
I FEEL SO USELESS.
I'M HER BOYFRIEND...
BUT I COULDN'T DO A THING FOR HER.
I'm back...

The Thing You're Always Giving Me

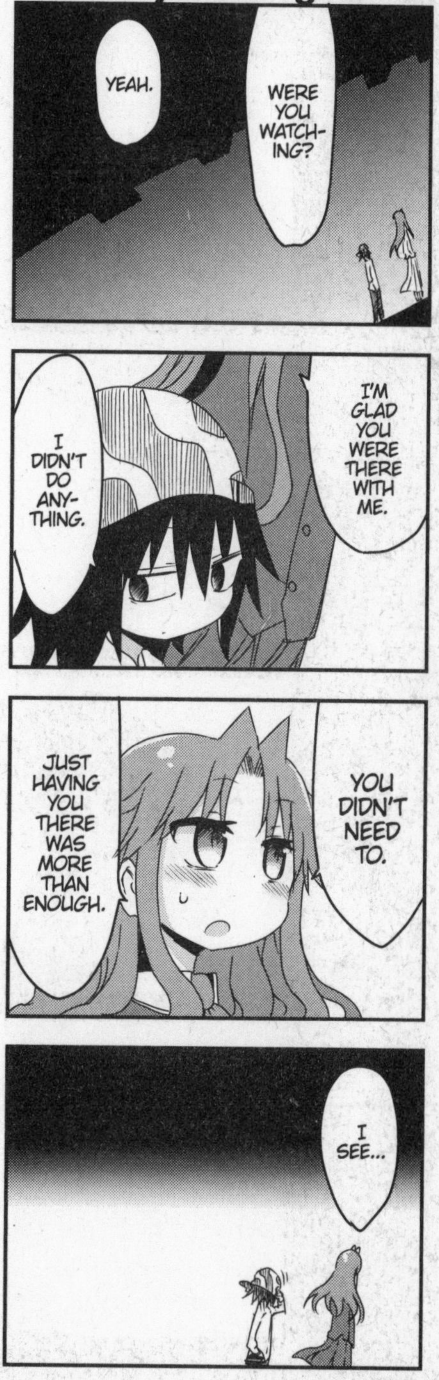
WERE YOU WATCHING?
YEAH.
I'M GLAD YOU WERE THERE WITH ME.
I DIDN'T DO ANYTHING.
YOU DIDN'T NEED TO.
JUST HAVING YOU THERE WAS MORE THAN ENOUGH.
I SEE...

Between the Two of Them

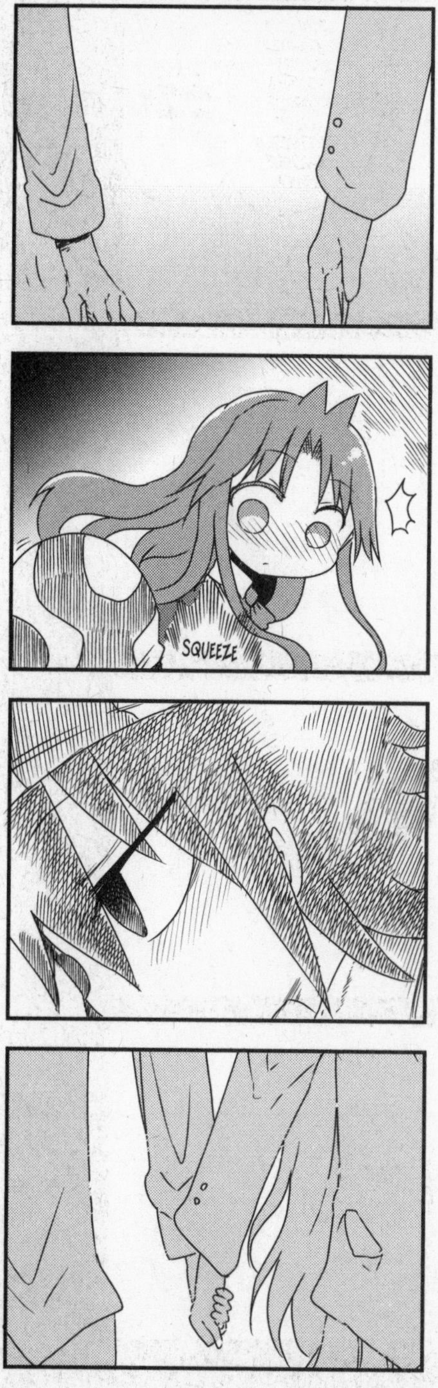
SQUEEZE

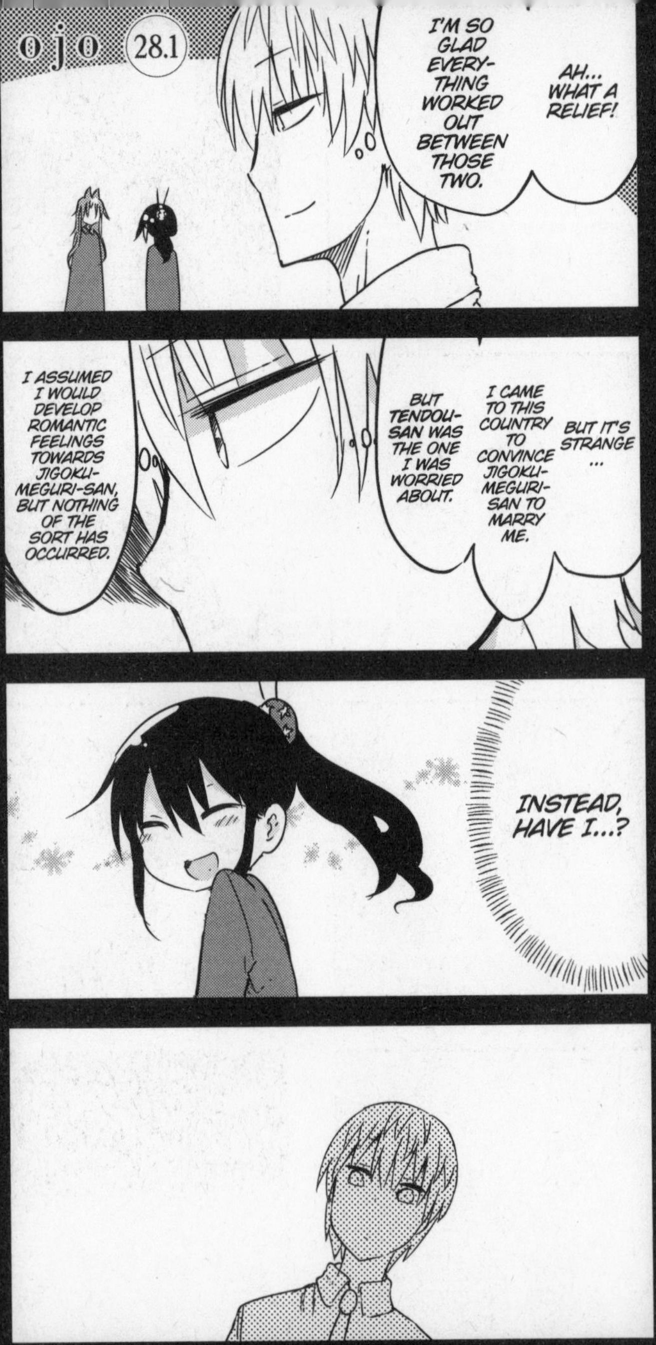
ojo 28.1
AH... WHAT A RELIEF!
I'M SO GLAD EVERYTHING WORKED OUT BETWEEN THOSE TWO.
BUT IT'S STRANGE...
I CAME TO THIS COUNTRY TO CONVINCE JIGOKU-MEGURI-SAN TO MARRY ME.
BUT TENDOU-SAN WAS THE ONE I WAS WORRIED ABOUT.
I ASSUMED I WOULD DEVELOP ROMANTIC FEELINGS TOWARDS JIGOKU-MEGURI-SAN, BUT NOTHING OF THE SORT HAS OCCURRED.
INSTEAD, HAVE I...?

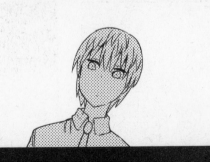

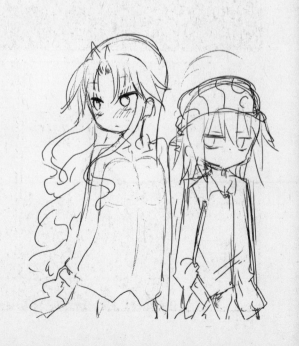

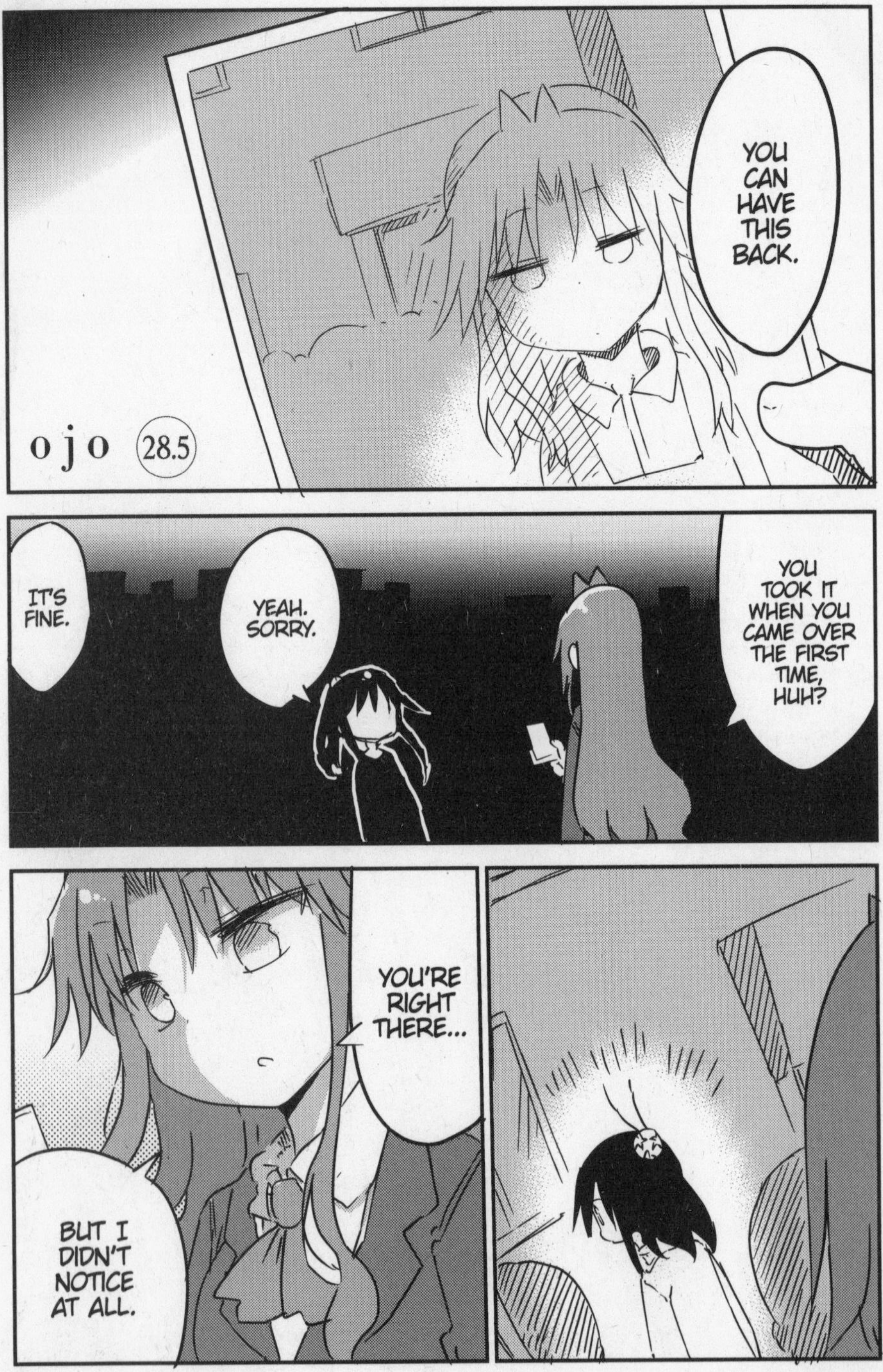
YOU CAN HAVE THIS BACK.
ojo 28.5
YOU TOOK IT WHEN YOU CAME OVER THE FIRST TIME, HUH?
YEAH. SORRY.
IT'S FINE.
YOU'RE RIGHT THERE...
BUT I DIDN'T NOTICE AT ALL.

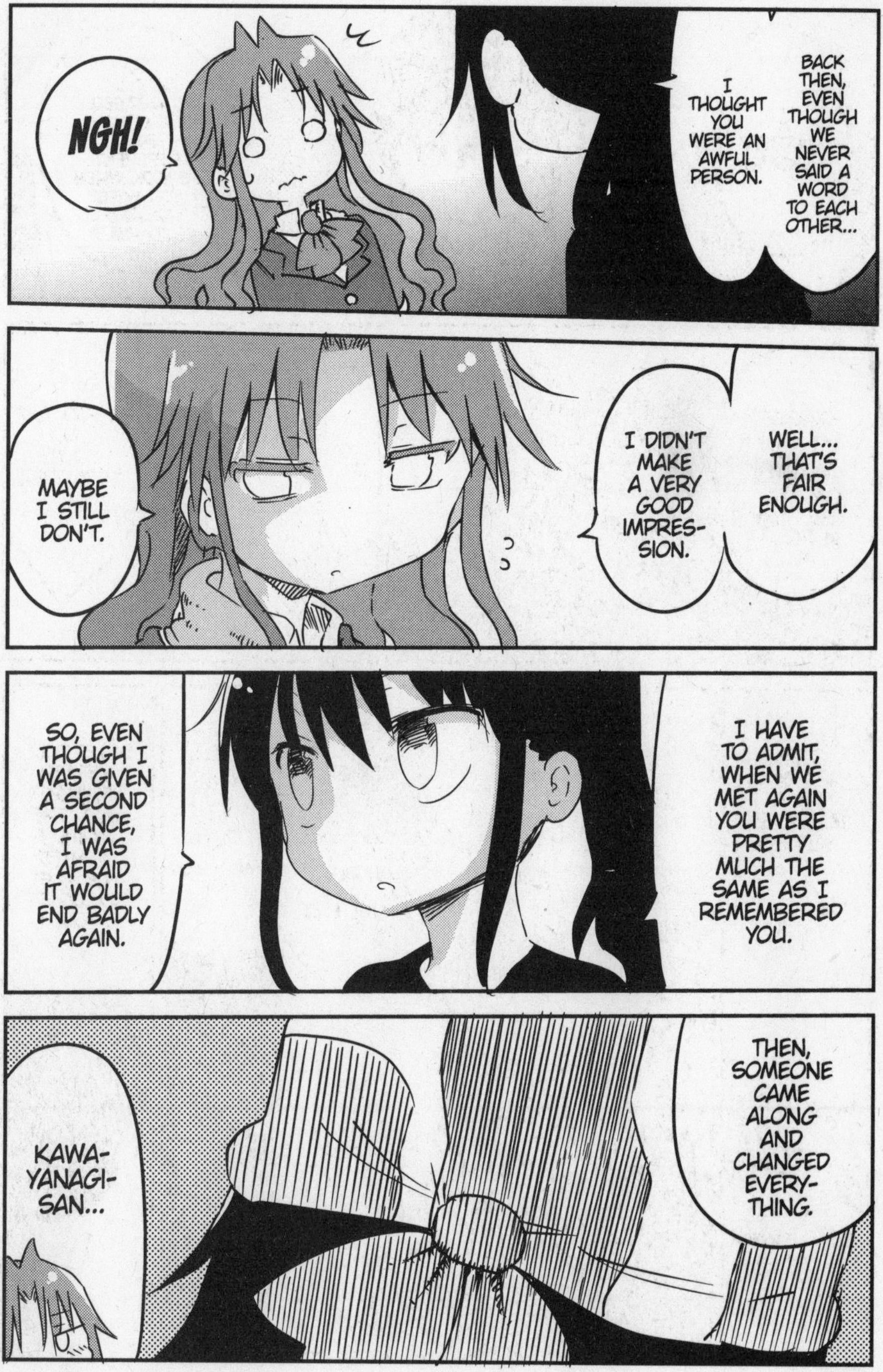
BACK THEN, EVEN THOUGH WE NEVER SAID A WORD TO EACH OTHER...
I THOUGHT YOU WERE AN AWFUL PERSON.
NGH!
WELL... THAT'S FAIR ENOUGH.
I DIDN'T MAKE A VERY GOOD IMPRES-SION.
MAYBE I STILL DON'T.
I HAVE TO ADMIT, WHEN WE MET AGAIN YOU WERE PRETTY MUCH THE SAME AS I REMEMBERED YOU.
SO, EVEN THOUGH I WAS GIVEN A SECOND CHANCE, I WAS AFRAID IT WOULD END BADLY AGAIN.
THEN, SOMEONE CAME ALONG AND CHANGED EVERY-THING.
KAWA-YANAGI-SAN...

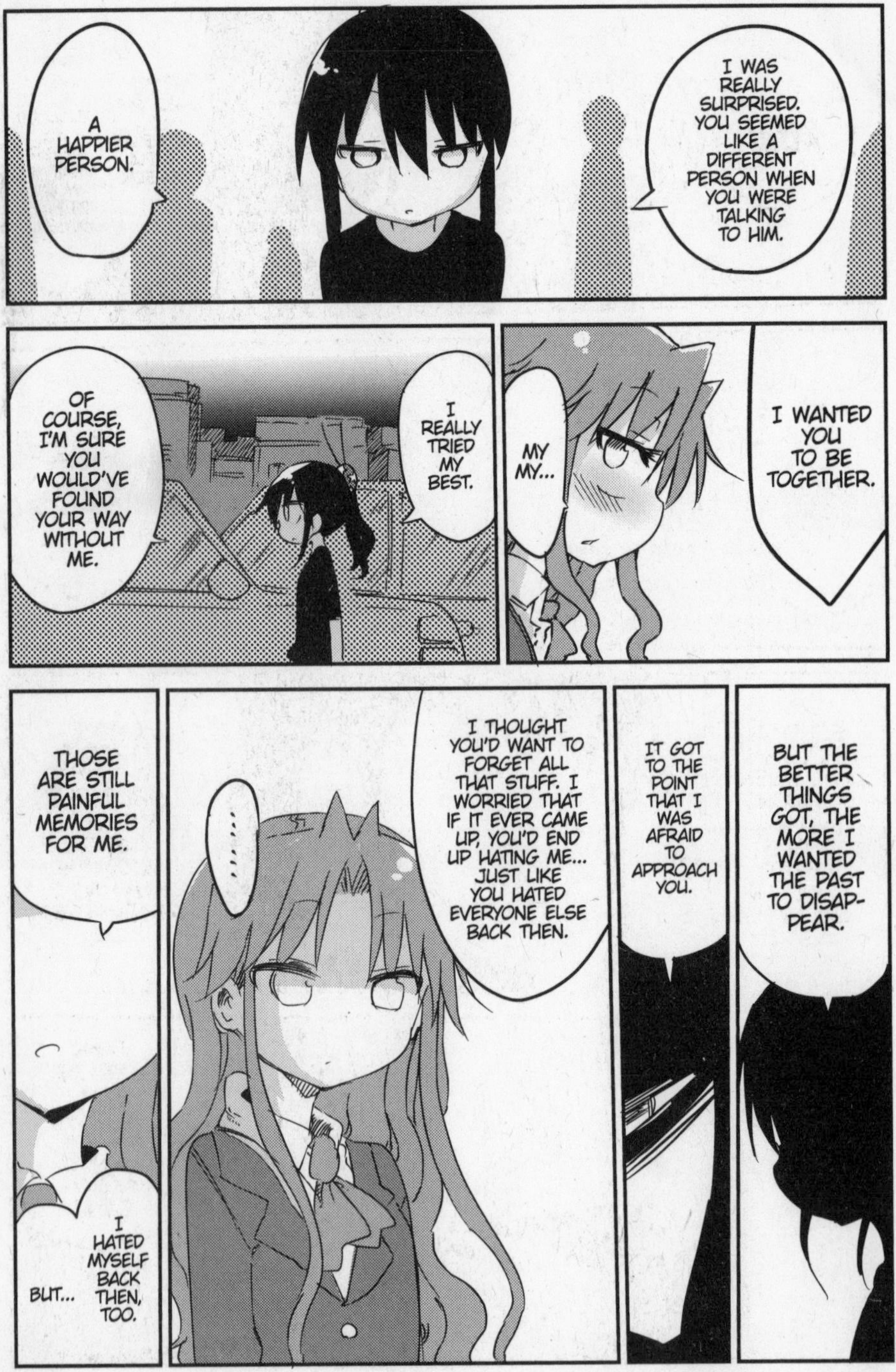
I WAS REALLY SURPRISED. YOU SEEMED LIKE A DIFFERENT PERSON WHEN YOU WERE TALKING TO HIM.
A HAPPIER PERSON.
I WANTED YOU TO BE TOGETHER.
MY MY...
I REALLY TRIED MY BEST.
OF COURSE, I'M SURE YOU WOULD'VE FOUND YOUR WAY WITHOUT ME.
BUT THE BETTER THINGS GOT, THE MORE I WANTED THE PAST TO DISAP-PEAR.
IT GOT TO THE POINT THAT I WAS AFRAID TO APPROACH YOU.
I THOUGHT YOU'D WANT TO FORGET ALL THAT STUFF. I WORRIED THAT IF IT EVER CAME UP, YOU'D END UP HATING ME... JUST LIKE YOU HATED EVERYONE ELSE BACK THEN.
......
THOSE ARE STILL PAINFUL MEMORIES FOR ME.
I HATED MYSELF BACK THEN, TOO.
BUT...

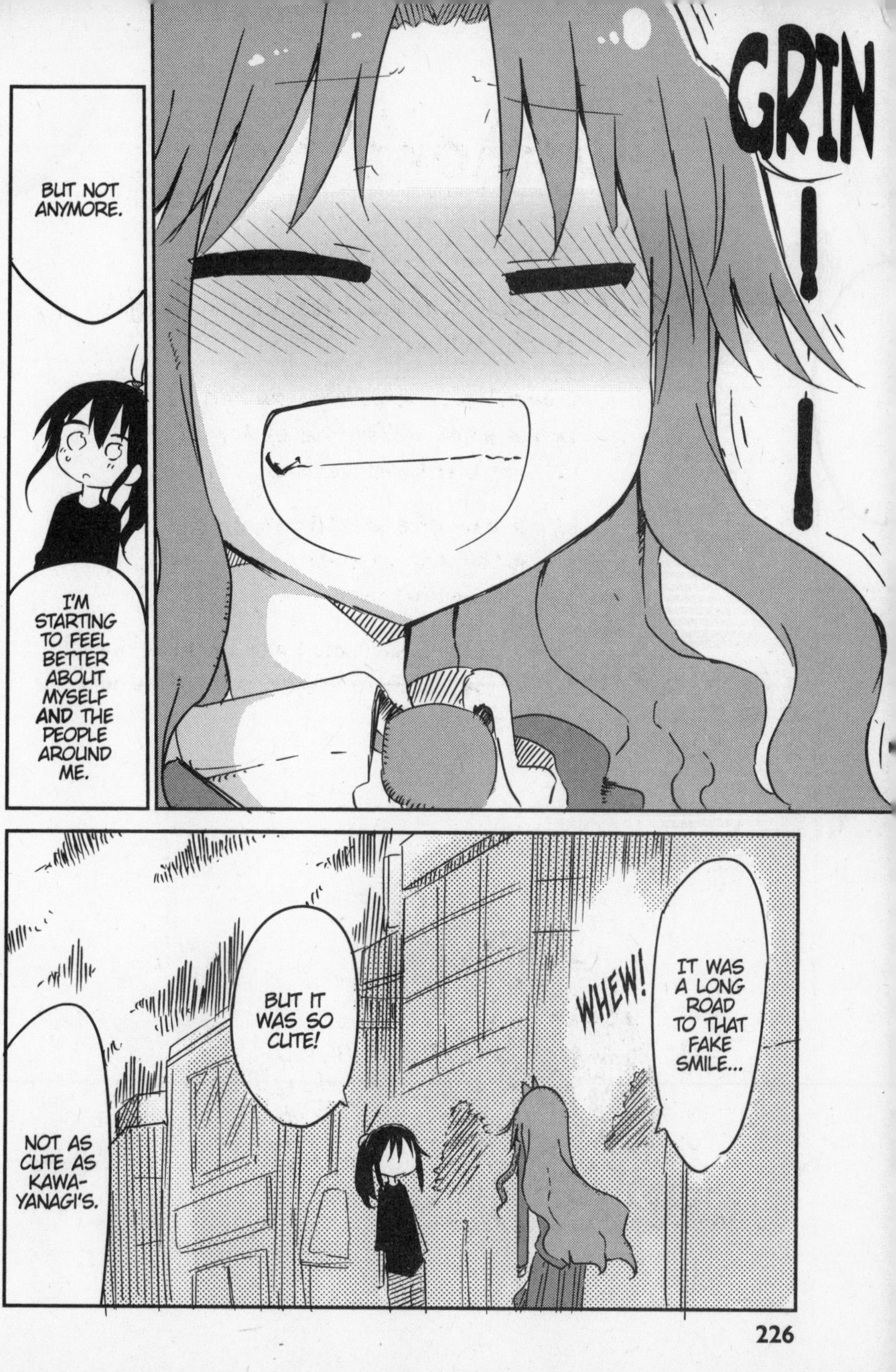
GRIN!!
BUT NOT ANYMORE.
I'M STARTING TO FEEL BETTER ABOUT MYSELF AND THE PEOPLE AROUND ME.
IT WAS A LONG ROAD TO THAT FAKE SMILE...
WHEW!
BUT IT WAS SO CUTE!
NOT AS CUTE AS KAWA-YANAGI'S.

Author's Note

This is coolkyousinnjya.

Thank you so much for buying Ojojojo's second volume.

I wasn't sure exactly how the manga would go on after the ending in the last volume, but here we are!

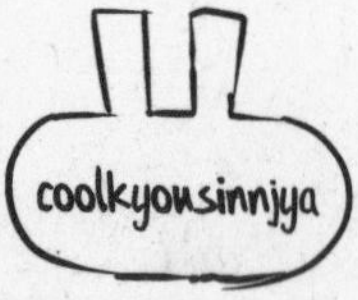
coolkyousinnjya

I had only intended to make one book, so I tried to wrap up everything cleanly at the end of volume one.

That being said, now I get the feeling I'll be at this a little longer...so see you next volume!

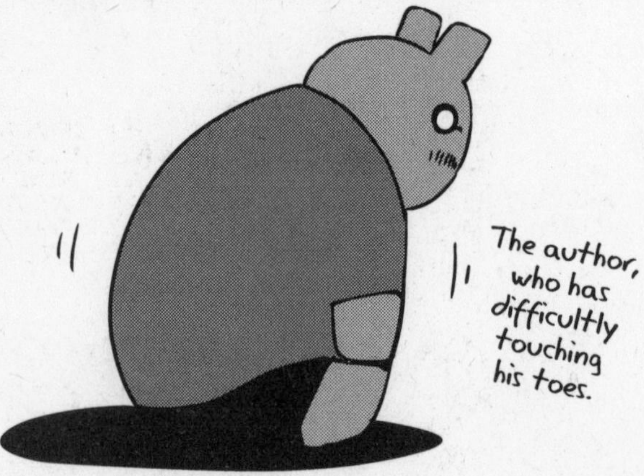
The author, who has difficultly touching his toes.

ojojojo

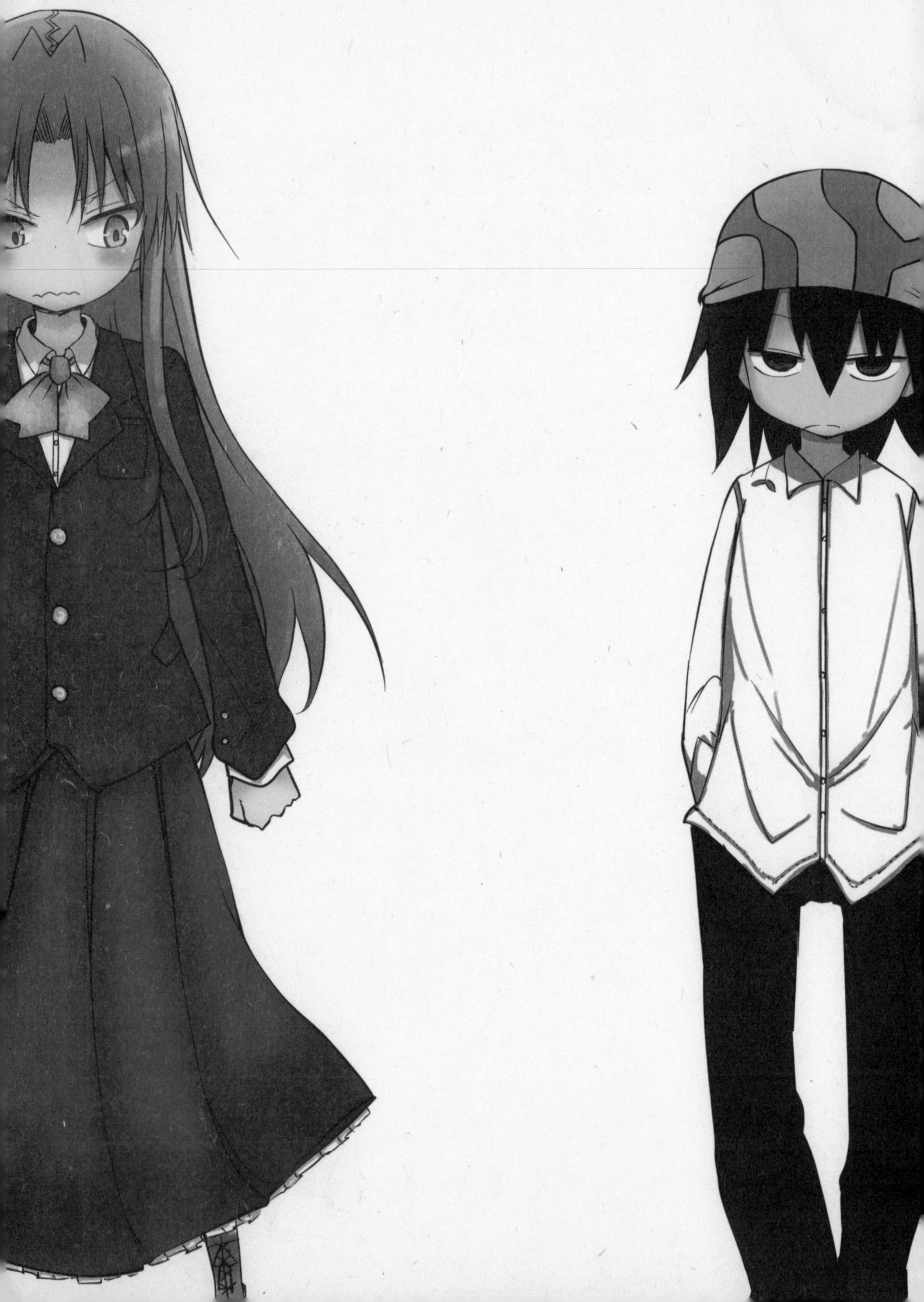

Bonus Corner

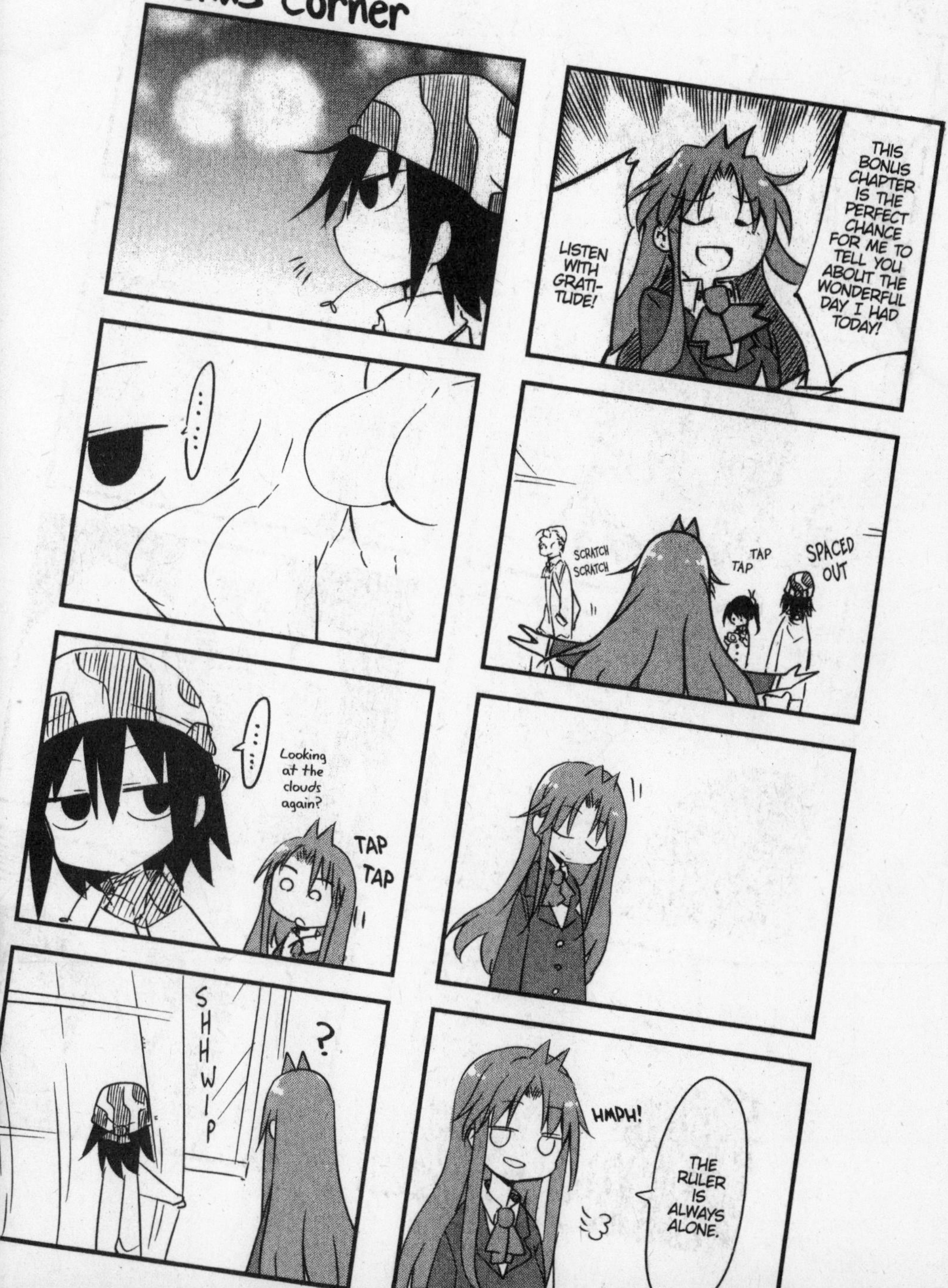
THIS BONUS CHAPTER IS THE PERFECT CHANCE FOR ME TO TELL YOU ABOUT THE WONDERFUL DAY I HAD TODAY!
LISTEN WITH GRATI-TUDE!
SPACED OUT
TAP TAP
SCRATCH SCRATCH
THE RULER IS ALWAYS ALONE.
HMPH!
...
TAP TAP
Looking at the clouds again?
...
?
SHHWIP

Bonus Corner 2

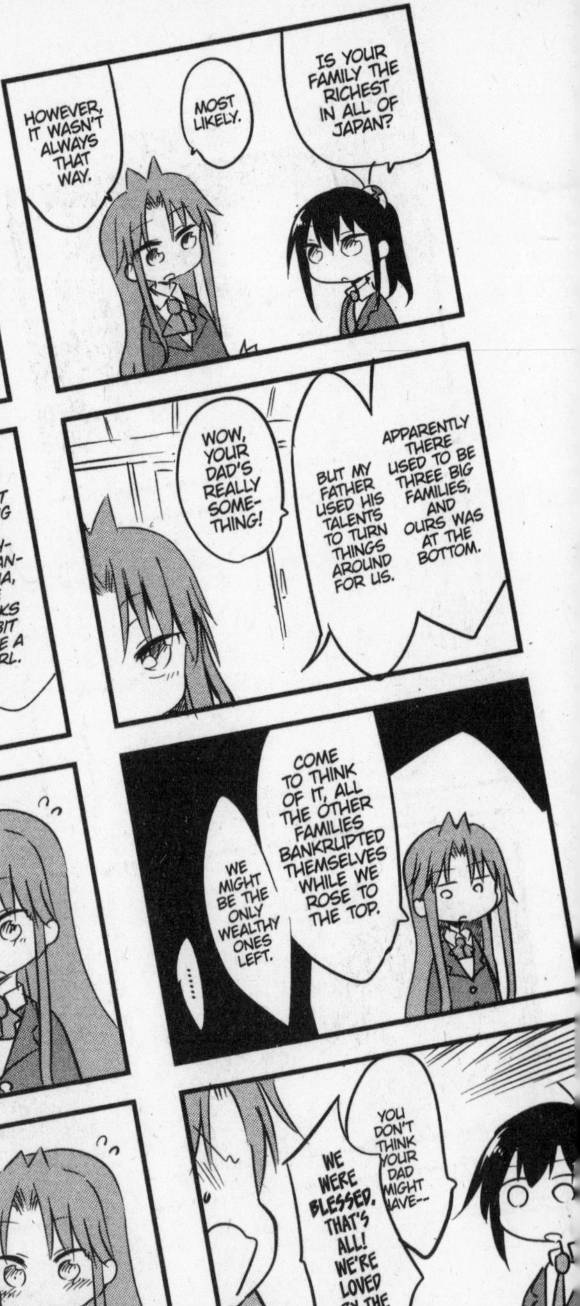
IS YOUR FAMILY THE RICHEST IN ALL OF JAPAN?
MOST LIKELY.
HOWEVER, IT WASN'T ALWAYS THAT WAY.
APPARENTLY THERE USED TO BE THREE BIG FAMILIES, AND OURS WAS AT THE BOTTOM.
BUT MY FATHER USED HIS TALENTS TO TURN THINGS AROUND FOR US.
WOW, YOUR DAD'S REALLY SOME-THING!
COME TO THINK OF IT, ALL THE OTHER FAMILIES BANKRUPTED THEMSELVES WHILE WE ROSE TO THE TOP.
WE MIGHT BE THE ONLY WEALTHY ONES LEFT.
......
YOU DON'T THINK YOUR DAD MIGHT HAVE--
WE WERE BLESSED. THAT'S ALL! WE'RE LOVED BY THE GODS!

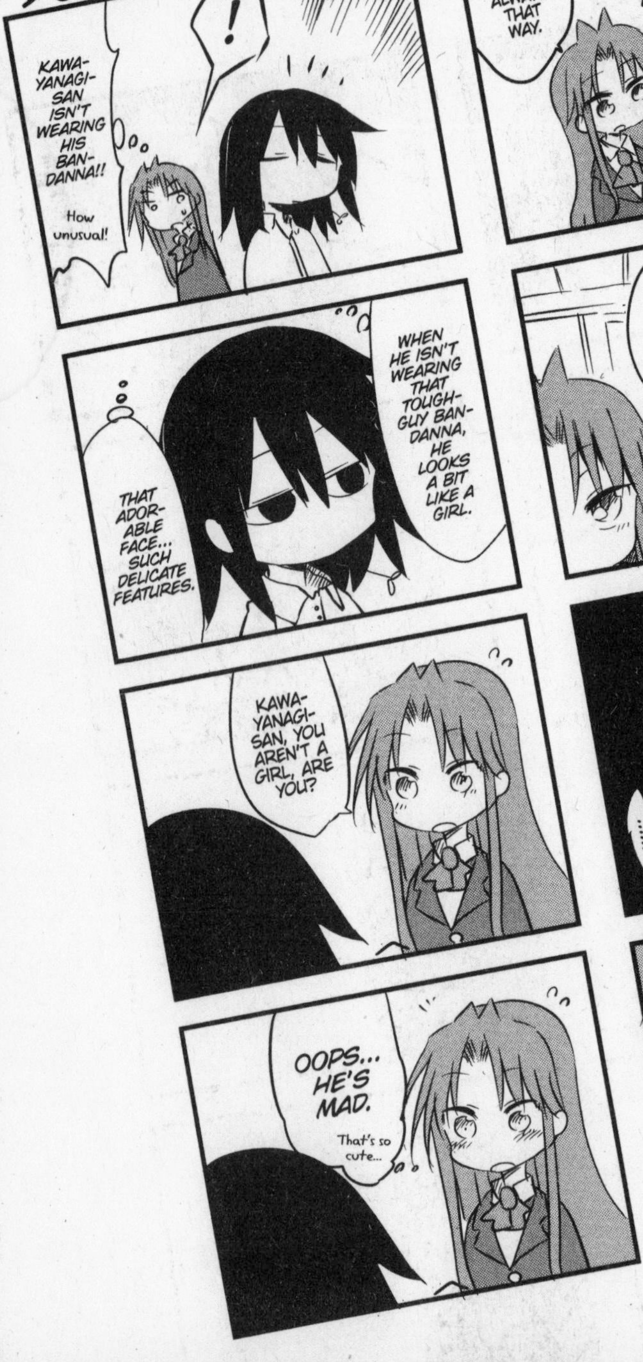
!
KAWA-YANAGI-SAN ISN'T WEARING HIS BAN-DANNA!!
How unusual!
WHEN HE ISN'T WEARING THAT TOUGH-GUY BAN-DANNA, HE LOOKS A BIT LIKE A GIRL.
THAT ADORABLE FACE... SUCH DELICATE FEATURES.
KAWA-YANAGI-SAN, YOU AREN'T A GIRL, ARE YOU?
OOPS... HE'S MAD.
That's so cute...

ojojojo

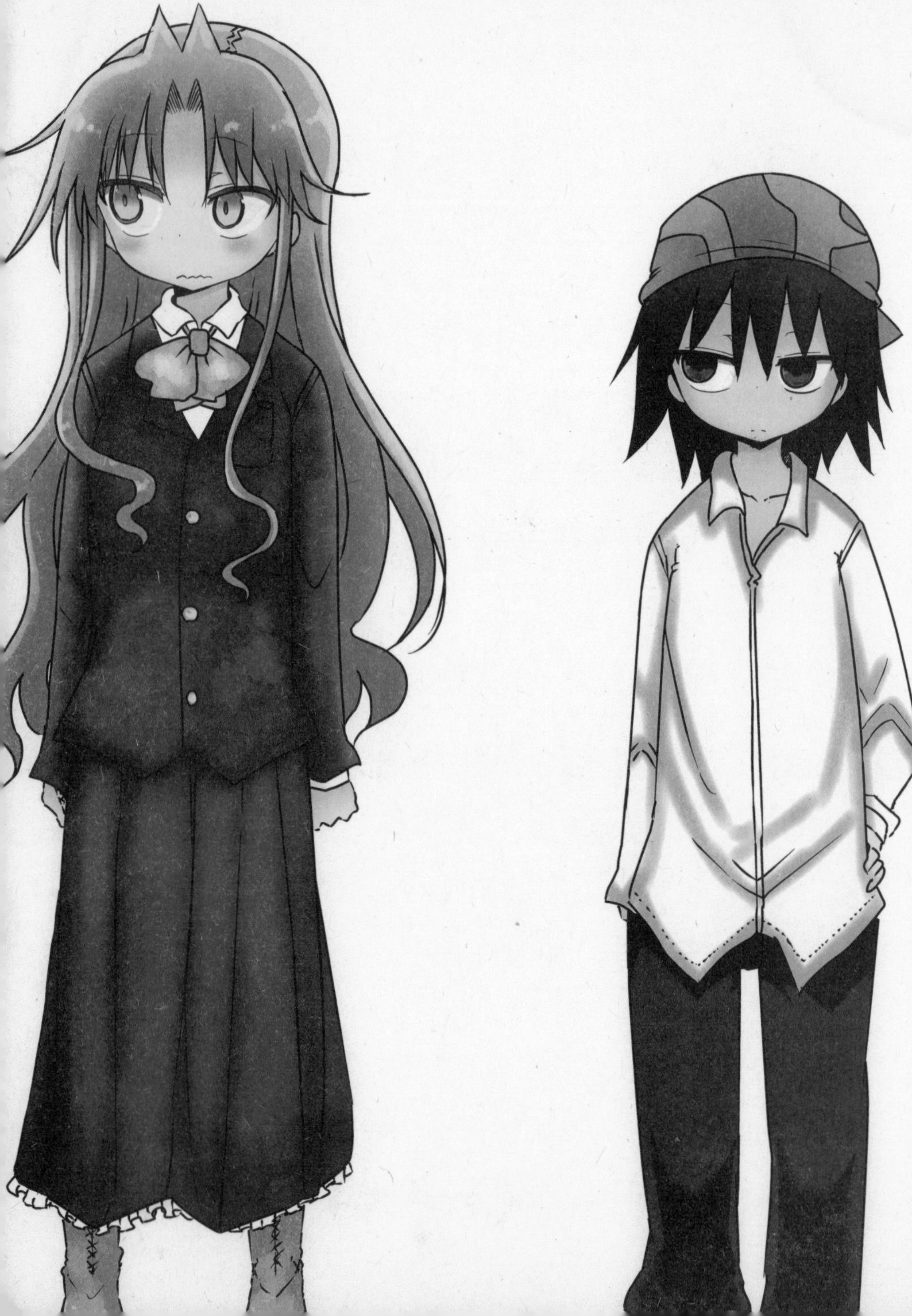

Bonus Corner

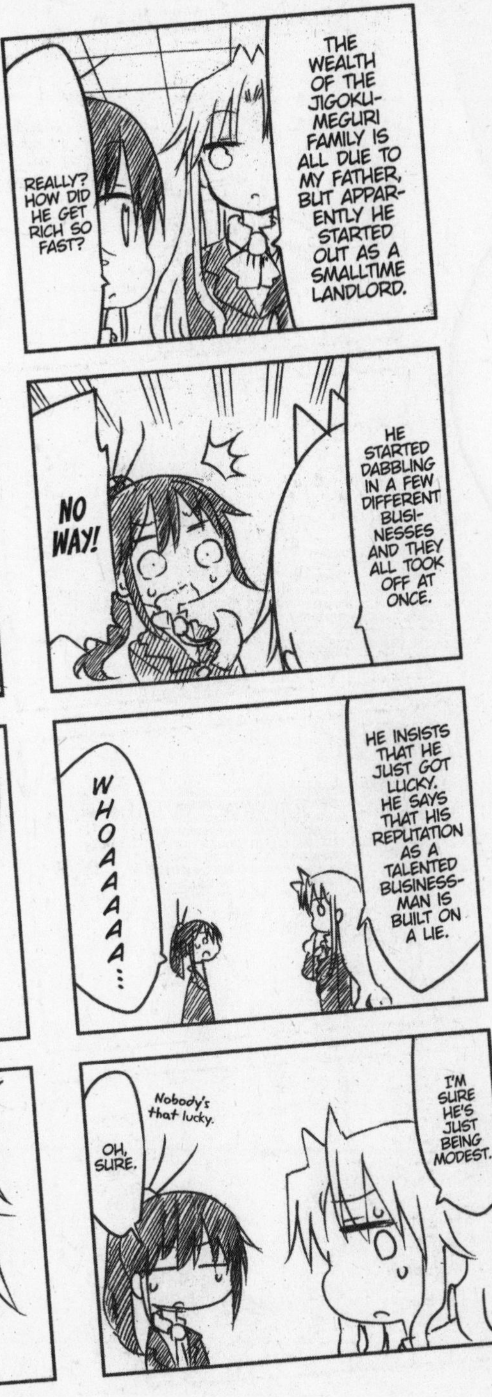

THE WEALTH OF THE JIGOKU-MEGURI FAMILY IS ALL DUE TO MY FATHER, BUT APPAR-ENTLY HE STARTED OUT AS A SMALLTIME LANDLORD.
REALLY? HOW DID HE GET RICH SO FAST?
HE STARTED DABBLING IN A FEW DIFFERENT BUSI-NESSES AND THEY ALL TOOK OFF AT ONCE.
NO WAY!
HE INSISTS THAT HE JUST GOT LUCKY. HE SAYS THAT HIS REPUTATION AS A TALENTED BUSINESS-MAN IS BUILT ON A LIE.
WHOAAAAA...
I'M SURE HE'S JUST BEING MODEST.
Nobody's that lucky.
OH, SURE.

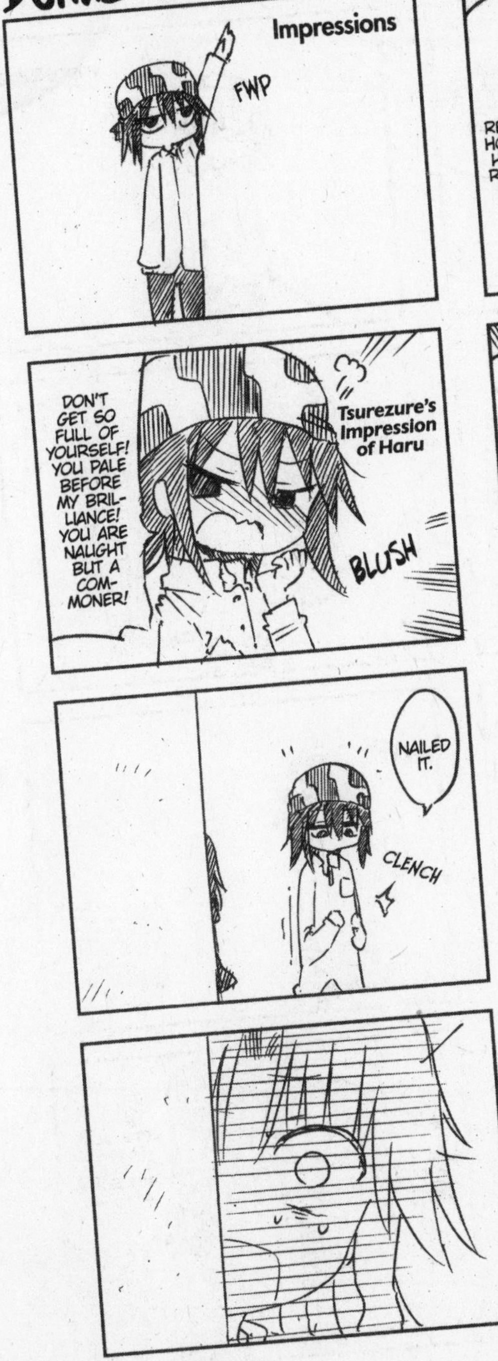

Impressions
FWP
Tsurezure's Impression of Haru
DON'T GET SO FULL OF YOURSELF! YOU PALE BEFORE MY BRIL-LIANCE! YOU ARE NAUGHT BUT A COM-MONER!
BLUSH
NAILED IT.
CLENCH

Ojojojo 1 – CHARACTERS

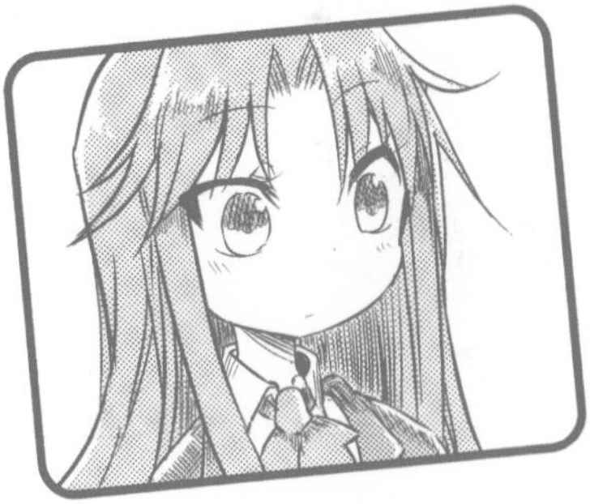

Jigokumeguri Haru

The teenage daughter of a ridiculously wealthy family, she is an arrogant and incredibly selfish high school student. Thanks to her privileged upbringing and overbearing attitude, she has almost no friends.

Kawayanagi Tsurezure

A high school boy with a flair for the antique. His interests include grossly outdated fashion and rakugo stage performances. Tons of people think he's a weirdo.

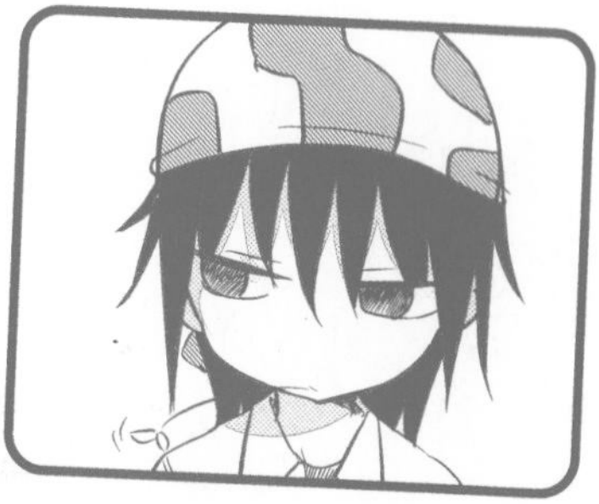

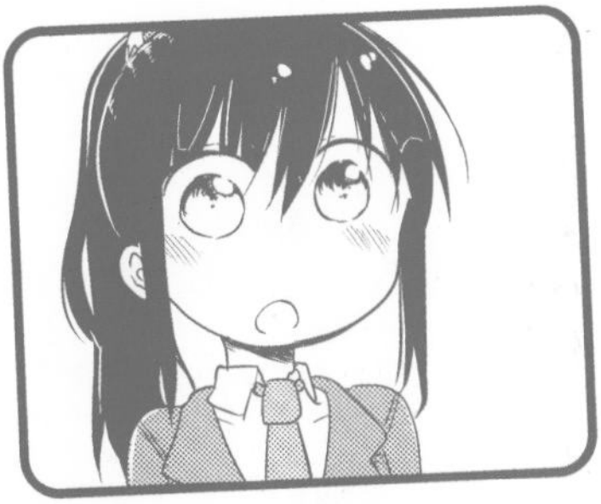

Tendou Akane

One of Haru's classmates. She's taken a special interest in the relationship forming between Haru and Tsurezure.

Jiiya

Haru's butler.
His blunt remarks cut Haru to the bone.

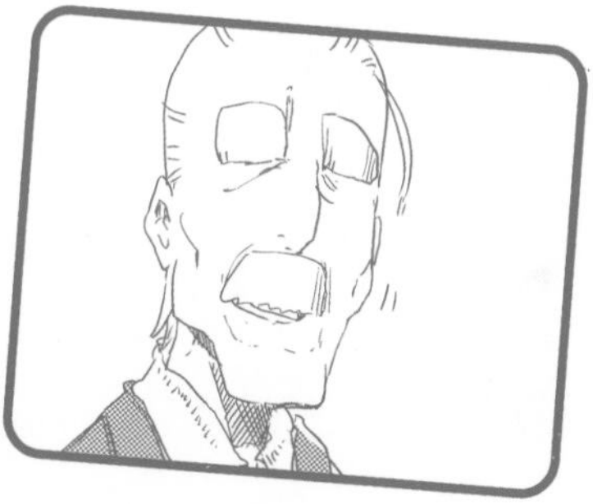

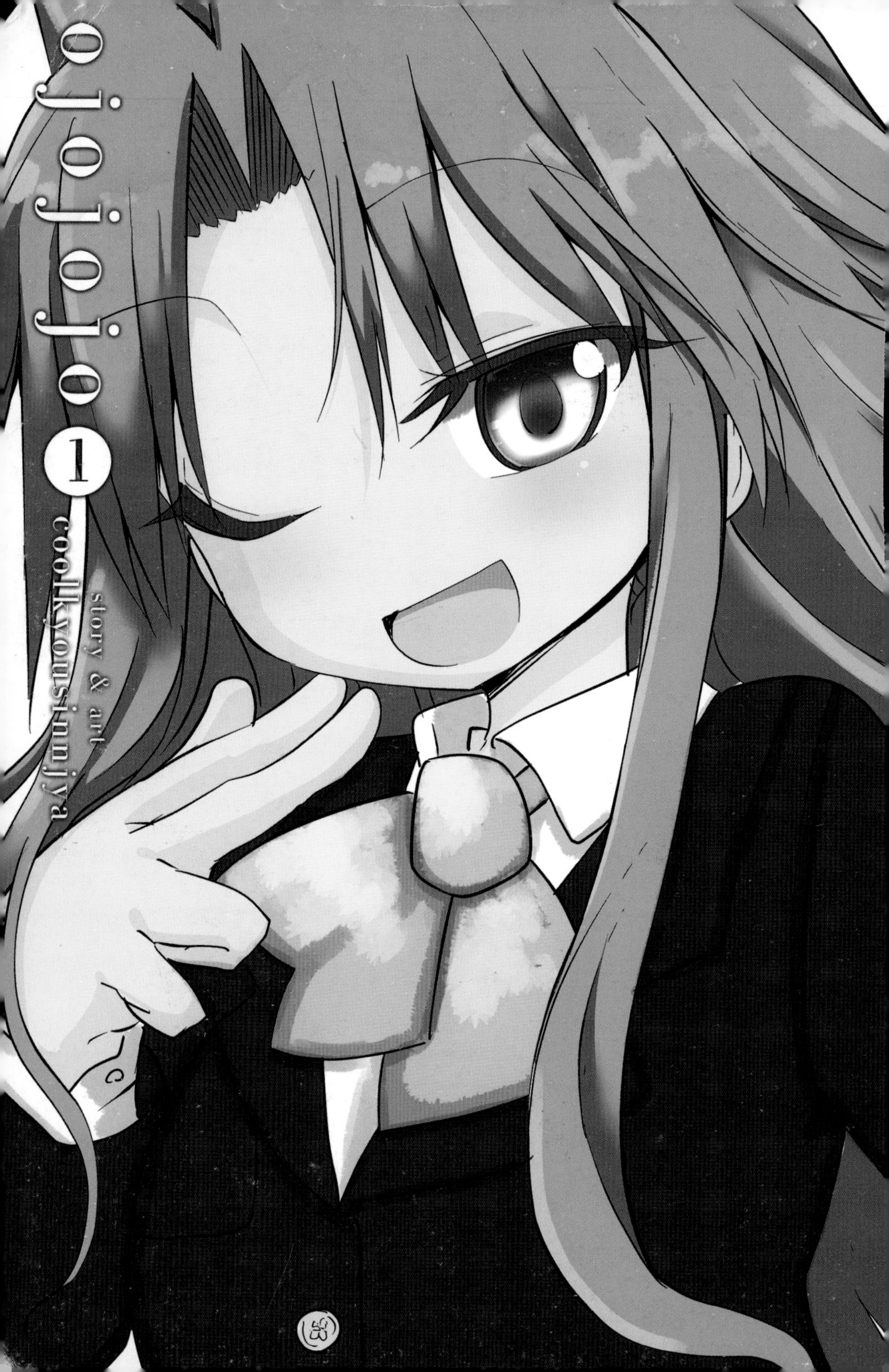
ojojojo
1
story & art
coolkyousinnjya

Bonus Corner 2

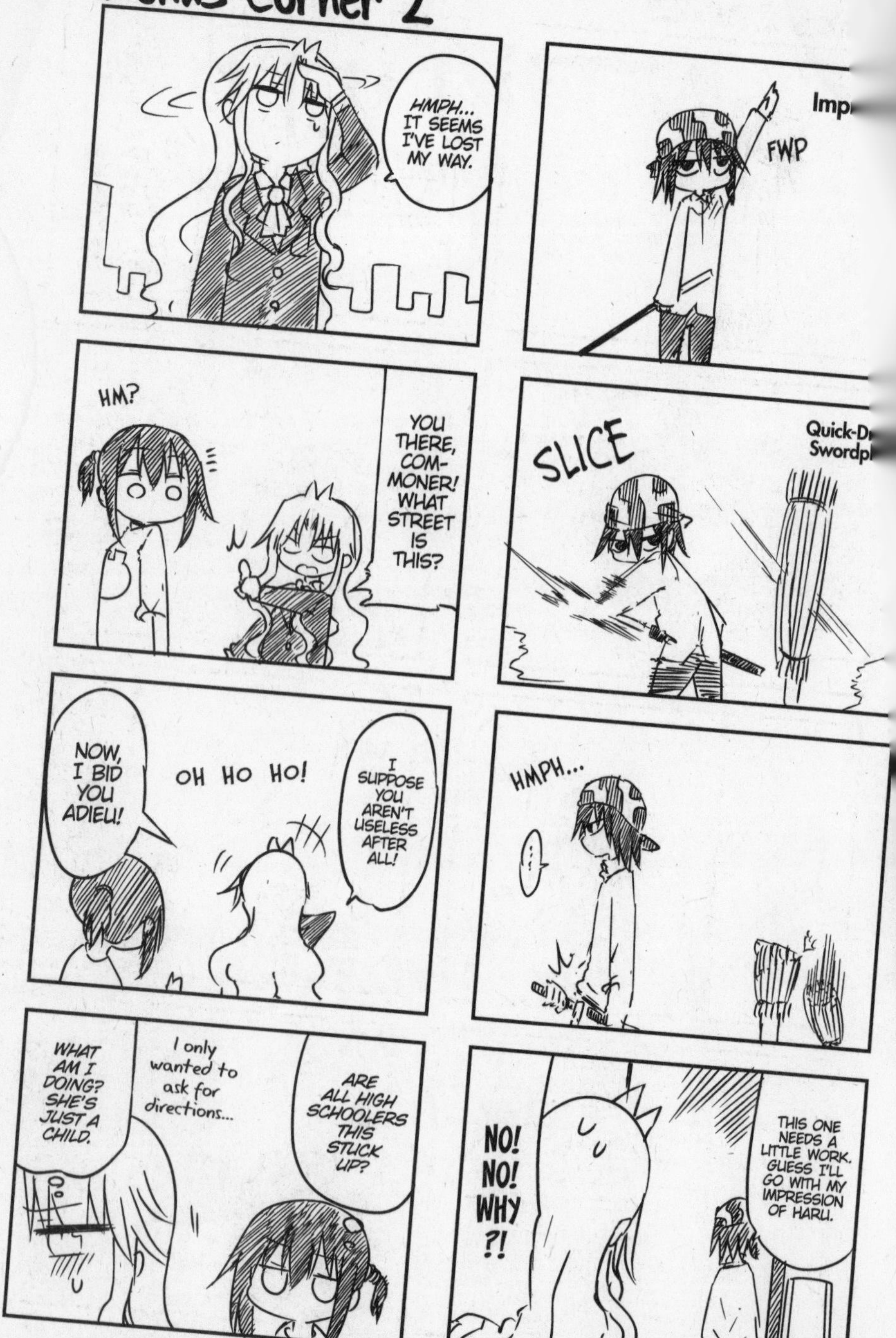
FWP
SLICE
HMPH...
...
THIS ONE NEEDS A LITTLE WORK. GUESS I'LL GO WITH MY IMPRESSION OF HARU.
NO! NO! WHY?!
HMPH... IT SEEMS I'VE LOST MY WAY.
YOU THERE, COMMONER! WHAT STREET IS THIS?
HM?
I SUPPOSE YOU AREN'T USELESS AFTER ALL!
OH HO HO!
NOW, I BID YOU ADIEU!
ARE ALL HIGH SCHOOLERS THIS STUCK UP?
I only wanted to ask for directions...
WHAT AM I DOING? SHE'S JUST A CHILD.

SEVEN SEAS ENTERTAINMENT PRESENTS

MRtW
10-19

ojojojo

story and art by COOLKYOUSINN[...]

W9-BTZ-442

TRANSLATION
Ben Robert Trethewey

ADAPTATION
Clint Bickham

LETTERING AND RETOUCH
Kaitlyn Wiley

COVER DESIGN
KC Fabellon

PROOFREADER
Cae Hawksmoor
Christina Lynn

EDITOR
J.P. Sullivan

PRODUCTION MANAGER
Lissa Pattillo

EDITOR-IN-CHIEF
Adam Arnold

PUBLISHER
Jason DeAngelis

OJYOJYOJYO Volumes 1-2
© 2013, 2014 COOLKYOUSINNJYA
Originally published in Japan in 2013 and 2014 by TAKESHOBO Co.LTD., Tokyo.
English translation rights arranged with TAKESHOBO Co.LTD., Tokyo,
through TOHAN CORPORATION, Tokyo.

Seven Seas books may be purchased in bulk for promotional, educational, or
business use. Please contact your local bookseller or the Macmillan Corporate
and Premium Sales Department at 1-800-221-7945, extension 5442, or by
e-mail at MacmillanSpecialMarkets@macmillan.com.

Seven Seas and the Seven Seas logo are trademarks of
Seven Seas Entertainment, LLC. All rights reserved.

ISBN: 978-1-626929-68-5

Printed in Canada

First Printing: December 2018

10 9 8 7 6 5 4 3 2 1

FOLLOW US ONLINE: **www.sevenseasentertainment.com**

READING DIRECTIONS

This book reads from *right to left*, Japanese style.
If this is your first time reading manga, you start
reading from the top right panel on each page and
take it from there. If you get lost, just follow the
numbered diagram here. It may seem backwards at
first, but you'll get the hang of it! Have fun!!

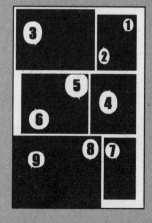